Nicos Poulantzas

NLB

Classes in
Contemporary Capitalism

Translated from the French by David Fernbach

First published as *Les Classes Sociales dans le Capitalisme Aujourd'hui* by Editions du Seuil, 1974

© Editions du Seuil, 1974

English language copyright NLB, 1975

Third impression, 1979

NLB, 7 Carlisle Street, London W1

Printed in Great Britain by
Lowe & Brydone Printers Ltd., Thetford, Norfolk

ISBN 902308 06 8 (cloth)
ISBN 86091 702 9 (paper)

Classes in
Contemporary Capitalism

Foreword

Presenting this work to my readers requires some preliminary information.

1. It comprises a series of essays which bear principally on social classes, and secondarily on the state apparatuses, in the present phase of imperialist/monopoly capitalism. Essentially, these essays concern the imperialist metropolises, and Europe in particular.

(a) The essays do not provide a systematic theory of these social formations in their present phase. Their limits are imposed by objective factors: no individual theoretical worker or militant, nor even a group of theorists or militants, is in a position to elaborate such a theory. This could only be the product of the working class's own organizations of class struggle.

(b) If these essays have as their principal object the imperialist metropolises, and Europe in particular, this is because these countries constitute a specific field, as I shall attempt to prove in the first essay.

2. The partial character of the essays will be clear from the more specific objects with which they are concerned:

(a) The first essay is an attempt to discern the general characteristics of the present phase and the effects of these on the social formations in question, while the second essay seeks to give a more precise analysis of the bourgeoisie and the third essay an analysis of the petty bourgeoisie, both traditional and new—the so-called 'new middle strata'. The analyses are thus particularly concerned with the working class's enemy, and with its potential allies.

The essays do not deal directly with the working class, the class that is situated beneath the exploitation which the bourgeoisie imposes on the popular masses, and the class to which the leadership of the revolutionary process falls. Those classes with which the present work is especially concerned have been relatively neglected by Marxist theory. Yet I think that today it is more than ever the case that an essential component of revolutionary strategy consists in knowing the enemy well, and in being able to establish correct alliances.

If I say that these essays do not deal directly with the working class, this class is nevertheless constantly present, in two ways: (1) through the fact that the analysis of the bourgeoisie, its internal contradictions and its present relationship to the state, constantly refers back to the principal contradiction, i.e. to the relation of the bourgeoisie to the working class; (2) through the fact that the analysis of the petty bourgeoisie, and of the new petty bourgeoisie in particular, concentrates on' those traits which simultaneously assimilate it to the working class and distinguish it from the latter; it thus also refers to the characteristic features of the working class.

(b) While these essays are based on the concrete forms of the class struggle that are being waged today, they do not provide an inventory or a systematic classification of this struggle. I have preferred to deal with the objective determinations of these struggles, which are often neglected.

3. Certain other peculiarities of this work follow from the fact that is a compilation of essays:

Even though they are linked together, each of these essays has its own characteristic theme, and this gives rise to certain inevitable repetitions. Certain theoretical concepts and analyses present in one of the essays are sometimes recalled, sometimes taken up again and gone into in more detail in the others. This is particularly the case with the relationship between the first and the second essays; for example, concepts and analysis concerning the periodization of capitalism and the modifications in the relations of production that mark its stages and phases, which are already present in the first essay, are repeated and strengthened in the second.

Only a part of the Introduction ('Social Classes and their Extended Reproduction') and the first essay ('The Internationalization of Capitalist Relations and the Nation-State') have previously been published. This part of the Introduction had originally been commissioned by the CFDT, and published by the latter's Bureau de Recherches et d'Études Économiques (BRAEC) as a cyclostyled paper; it was then reprinted in *L'Homme et la Société* (no. 24–5, April–September 1972) and in *New Left Review*, 78, March–April 1973. The first essay appeared in *Les Temps Modernes* (February 1973) and appeared in an English translation in *Economy and Society*, vol. 3 no. 2, May 1974. But these texts have both been considerably modified, in the light of comment and criticism made to me on their appearance, as well as of the requirements of this volume as a whole.

4. The essays include both theoretical and concrete analyses. The plan for which I opted, which seemed to me the only correct one, was to link these two levels closely together in the presentation. Instead of first presenting a series of theoretical propositions for which the concrete analysis would simply be illustration, I have rather introduced the theoretical propositions *pari passu* with the concrete analysis.

5. An analysis of the present phase of imperialism, which also deals with more general problems, also necessarily concerns the dominated and dependent countries. However, since the main object of the present work is the imperialist formations, and the European formations in particular, the empirical material presented here also relates primarily to these countries. Furthermore, particular attention is paid here to France, despite its marked differences from the other social formations in question. This is not because it is, at least not in all aspects, an exemplary case, but is quite simply because my own personal experience is situated here. However, it should be equally obvious that my arguments bear on all these formations, with certain particularities, and that in certain aspects they relate to the imperialist chain as a whole.

6. Given both the contemporary nature and the complexity of the problems I am dealing with, as well as the reasons for the unsystematic and partial character of this work, the arguments presented here are, in the end, but propositions put forward for discussion and rectification. There is nothing definitive about them, among other things because this is not a finished text, but one which presents arguments for criticism.

This also explains the critical and sometimes even polemical character with which my own arguments are put forward. Instead of suppressing differences and thus inevitably choosing to brush fundamental problems under the carpet, I have preferred to dwell on them, in so far as criticism alone can advance Marxist theory. Thus the criticism that I have on certain points levelled at some authors in no way detracts, in my view, from the value of their analyses on other points, analyses which have been of great help to me personally.

Finally, so as not to overburden the text, and since the Marxist literature on the subjects dealt is very great, I have chosen to restrict my references to those strictly necessary.

7. Several of the concepts and theoretical analyses presented here in a relatively simple fashion and directly oriented to contemporary problems, refer to my two previous works: *Political Power and Social Classes* (NLB/Sheed and Ward, 1973) and *Fascism and Dictatorship* (NLB, 1974), where they are established theoretically and explained. Since it is possible to refer the reader to these works, I do not think it is necessary to repeat the whole of these expositions. I have instead referred the reader to the relevant passages. However, certain analyses and formulations that figure there, particularly in the first work, have been rectified and adjusted in the present text: the reader will find all the relevant developments of theory embodied in the following concrete analyses.

Introduction:
Social Classes and their
Extended Reproduction

The purpose of these introductory remarks is not to present a systematic Marxist theory of social classes, as a preliminary to the concrete analysis undertaken in the essays that follow; the line of development followed in the present work is to link theoretical analysis very closely with concrete analysis, introducing the former at the rhythm required by the latter. These introductory remarks aim simply to present some very general landmarks to facilitate the reading of the essays that follow, where they will be taken up and gone into in more detail.[1]

1. The arguments put forward in this section are based on those of *Political Power and Social Classes*; here they are made somewhat more detailed and are in some respects rectified, a process already begun in *Fascism and Dictatorship*. However, both the theoretical framework and the essence of the earlier arguments are maintained. I should mention here that although my own writings and those of a number of my colleagues have been received, and have even to a great extent functioned, as if they shared a common problematic, fundamental differences have always existed between some of these texts. In the domain of historical materialism, for instance, fundamental differences already existed between, on the one hand, my *Political Power and Social Classes* (and also Bettelheim's texts, though I am speaking here only for myself), and on the other hand Balibar's text in *Reading Capital*, 'The Basic Concepts of Historical Materialism' (1966), which is marked by both economism and structuralism. These differences are still more clear today, now that Balibar has made a self-criticism, which is correct on a certain number of points ('Sur la dialectique historique', in *La Pensée*, August 1973). The reader, who looks this up, will find that a large number of the points on which this self-criticism bears (the question of class struggle, the concept of mode of production, its connection to that of social formation, the concept of conjuncture, the question of instances, etc.) involve precisely the questions on which essential differences existed between our respective texts. I myself, while making certain rectifications, maintain the basic analyses contained in my previous works.

I

What are social classes in Marxist theory?

1. They are groupings of social agents, defined principally but not exclusively by their place in the production process, i.e. in the economic sphere. The economic place of the social agents has a principal role in determining social classes. But from that we cannot conclude that this economic place is sufficient to determine social classes. Marxism states that the economic does indeed have the determinant role in a mode of production or a social formation; but the political and the ideological (the superstructure) also have a very important role. In fact, whenever Marx, Engels, Lenin and Mao analyse social classes, far from limiting themselves to economic criteria alone, they make explicit reference to political and ideological criteria.

2. For Marxism, social classes involve in one and the same process both class contradictions and class struggle; social classes do not firstly exist as such, and only then enter into a class struggle. Social classes coincide with class practices, i.e. the class struggle, and are only defined in their mutual opposition.

3. The class determination, while it coincides with the practices (struggle) of classes and includes political and ideological relations, designates certain objective places occupied by the social agents in the social division of labour: places which are independent of the will of these agents.

It may thus be said that a social class is defined by its place in the ensemble of social practices, i.e. by its place in the social division of labour as a whole. This includes political and ideological relations. Social class, in this sense, is a concept which denotes the effects of the structure within the social division of labour (social relations and social practices). This place thus corresponds to what I shall refer to as the structural determination of class, i.e. to the existence within class practices of determination by the structure – by the relations of production, and by the places of political and ideological domination/subordination. Classes exist only in the class struggle.

4. This structural determination of classes, which thus exists only as the class struggle, must however be distinguished from class position in each specific conjuncture – the focal point of the always unique historic individuality of a social formation, in other words the concrete situation of the class struggle. In stressing the importance of political and ideological relations in determining social classes, and the fact that social classes only exist in the form of class struggle and practices, class determination must not be reduced, in

a voluntarist fashion, to class position. The importance of this lies in those cases in which a distance arises between the structural determination of classes and the class positions in the conjuncture. In order to make this more clear, I have appended the following diagram, which I shall go on to explain:

PRACTICES/CLASS STRUGGLE		
STRUCTURAL DETERMINATION/ CLASS PLACES		CONJUNCTURE/ CLASS POSITIONS

<table>
<tr>
<td rowspan="3">social classes, fractions, strata, categories</td>
<td rowspan="3">SOCIAL DIVISION OF LABOUR</td>
<td>

IDEOLOGY
relations of ideological
domination/subordination
      ideological struggle

</td>
<td rowspan="3">concepts of strategy: social forces, power bloc, 'people'</td>
</tr>
<tr>
<td>

POLITICS
relations of political
domination/subordination
      political struggle

</td>
</tr>
<tr>
<td>

ECONOMICS
relations of production/
relations of exploitation
      economic struggle

</td>
</tr>
</table>

(a) A social class, or a fraction or stratum of a class, may take up a class position that does not correspond to its interests, which are defined by the class determination that fixes the horizon of the class's struggle. The typical example of this is the labour aristocracy, which in certain conjunctures takes up class positions that are in fact bourgeois. This does not mean, however, that it becomes, in such cases, a part of the bourgeoisie; it remains, from the fact of its structural class determination, part of the working class, and constitutes, as Lenin put it, a 'stratum' of the latter. In other words, its class determination is not reducible to its class position.

If we now take the inverse case, certain classes or fractions and strata of classes other than the working class, and the petty bourgeoisie in particular, may in specific conjunctures take up proletarian class positions, or positions aligned with that of the working class. This does not then mean that they become part of the working class. To give a simple example: production technicians often have proletarian class positions, frequently taking the side of the working class in strikes, for instance. But this does not mean that they have then become part of the working class, since their structural class determination is not reducible to their class position.

Moreover, it is precisely by virtue of its class determination that this grouping sometimes takes the side of the working class, and sometimes the side of the bourgeoisie (bourgeois class positions). Technicians no more form part of the bourgeoisie each time that they take up bourgeois class positions, than they form part of the proletariat when they take up the positions of the latter. To reduce the structural determination of class to class position would be tantamount to abandoning the objective determination of the places of social classes for a 'relational' ideology of 'social movements'.

(b) It must be emphasized that ideological and political relations, i.e. the places of political and ideological domination and subordination, are themselves part of the structural determination of class: there is no question of objective place being the result only of economic place within the relations of production, while political and ideological elements belong simply to class positions. We are not faced, as an old error would have it, on the one hand with an economic 'structure' that alone defines class places, and on the other hand with a class struggle extending to the political and ideological domain. This error today often takes the form of a distinction between '(economic) class situation' on the one hand, and politico-ideological class position on the other. From the start structural class determination involves economic, political and ideological class struggle, and these struggles are all expressed in the form of class positions in the conjuncture.

This also means that the analyses presented here have nothing in common with the Hegelian schema with its class-in-itself (economic class situation, uniquely objective determination of class by the process of production) and class-for-itself (class endowed with its own 'class consciousness' and an autonomous political organization = class struggle), which in the Marxist tradition is associated with Lukács. This in turn implies:

(a) That every objective class place in the productive process is necessarily characterized by effects on the structural determination of this class in all aspects, i.e. also by a specific place of this class in the political and ideological relations of the social division of labour. For example, to say that there is a working class in economic relations necessarily implies a specific place for this class in ideological and political relations, even if in certain countries and certain historical periods this class does not have its own 'class consciousness' or an autonomous political organization. This means that in such cases, even if it is heavily contaminated by bourgeois ideology, its economic existence is still expressed in certain specific material politico-ideological practices which burst through its bourgeois 'discourse': this is what Lenin designated, if very descriptively, as class instinct. To understand this, of course, it is necessary to break with a whole conception of ideology as a 'system of ideas' or a coherent 'discourse', and to understand it as an ensemble of material practices. This gives the lie to all those ideologies arguing the 'integration' of the working class, and ultimately it means only one thing: there is no need for there to be 'class consciousness' or autonomous political organizations for the class struggle to take place, and to take place in every domain of social reality.

(b) 'Class consciousness' and autonomous political organization, i.e. as far as the working class is concerned, a revolutionary proletarian ideology and an autonomous party of class struggle, refer to the terrain of class positions and the conjuncture, and constitute the conditions for the intervention of classes as social forces.

5. The principal aspect of an analysis of social classes is that of their places in the class struggle; it is not that of the agents that compose them. Social classes are not empirical groups of individuals, social groups, that are 'composed' by simple addition; the relations of these agents among themselves are thus not inter-personal relations. The class membership of the various agents depends on the class places that they occupy: it is moreover distinct from the class origin, the social origin, of the agents. The importance of these questions will become clear when we discuss the problem of the reproduction of social classes and their agents. Let us just signal here:

(a) in the relation between social classes and their agents, the pertinent question that needs to be posed is not that of the class to which this or that particular individual belongs (since what really matters are social groupings), nor that of the statistical and rigidly empirical boundaries of 'social groups' (since what really matters are the classes in the class struggle);

(b) the major factor in this respect is not that of 'social inequalities' between groups or individuals: these social inequalities are only the effect, on the agents, of the social classes, i.e. of the objective places they occupy, which can only disappear with the abolition of the division of society into classes. In a word, class society is not a matter of some inequality of 'opportunity' between 'individuals', a notion which implies that there is opportunity and that this depends wholly (or almost so) on the individuals, in the sense that the most capable and best individuals can always rise above their 'social milieu'.

6. In the determination of social classes, the principal role is played by place in the economic relations. What then does Marxist theory mean by 'economic'?

The economic sphere (or space) is determined by the *process* of production, and the place of the agents, their distribution into social classes, is determined by the *relations* of production.

Of course, the economic includes not only production, but also the whole cycle of production-consumption-distribution, the 'moments' of this appearing, in their unity, as those of the production process. In the capitalist mode of production, what is involved is the overall reproduction cycle of social capital: productive capital, commodity capital, money capital. In this unity, however, it is production which plays the determinant role. The distinction between the classes at this level is not, for example, a distinction based on relative sizes of income (a distinction between 'rich' and 'poor'), as was believed by a long pre-Marxist tradition and as is still believed today by a whole series of sociologists. The undoubted distinction between relative levels of income is itself only a consequence of the relations of production.

What then is the production process, and what are the relations of production which constitute it? In the production process, we find first of all the labour process: this refers to man's relation to nature in general. But the labour process always appears in a historically determined social form. It exists only in its unity with certain relations of production.

In a society divided into classes, the relations of production consist of a double relationship which encompasses men's relations to nature in material production. The two relationships are, first, the relationship between the agents of production and the object and means of labour (the productive forces); second, and through this, relations between men and other men, class relations.

These two relationships thus involve:

(a) the relationship between the non-worker (the owner) and the object and means of labour;

(b) the relationship between the immediate producer (the direct worker) and the object and means of labour.

The relationships have two aspects to them:

(a) economic ownership: by this is meant real economic control of the means of production, i.e. the power to assign the means of production to given uses and so to dispose of the products obtained;

(b) possession; by this is meant the capacity to put the means of production into operation.

In every society divided into classes, the first relationship (owners/ means of production) always goes together with the first aspect: it is the owners who have real control of the means of production and thus exploit the direct producers by extorting surplus labour from them in various forms.

But this ownership is to be understood as real economic ownership, control of the means of production, to be distinguished from legal ownership, which is sanctioned by law and belongs to the superstructure. The law, of course, generally ratifies economic ownership, but it is possible for the forms of legal ownership not to coincide with real economic ownership. In this case, it is the latter which is determinant in defining the places of social classes, that is to say, the place of the dominant and exploiting class.

The second relationship – that between the direct producers (the workers) and the means and object of labour, defines the exploited class in the relations of production. It can take various forms, according to the various modes of production in which it occurs.

In pre-capitalist modes of production, the direct producers (the workers) were not entirely 'separated' from the object and means of labour. In the case of the feudal mode of production, for instance, even though the lord had both legal and economic ownership of the land, the serf had possession of his parcel of land, which was protected by custom. He could not be purely and simply dispossessed by the lord; this was only achieved, as in England for example, by way of the whole bloody process of enclosures in the transition from feudalism to capitalism, what Marx referred to as the primitive accumulation of capital. In such modes of production, exploitation is predominantly by direct extraction of surplus labour, in the form of corvée payable in labour or in kind. In other words, economic ownership and possession are distinct in that they do not both depend on the same relationship between owners and means of production.

In the capitalist mode of production, by contrast, the direct producers (the working class) are completely dispossessed of their means of labour, of which the capitalists have the actual possession; Marx called this the phenomenon of the 'naked worker'. The worker possesses nothing but his labour-power, which he sells. It is this decisive modification of the place of the direct producers in the relations of production which makes labour itself into a commodity, and this determines the generalization of the commodity form, rather than the other way round: the fact that labour is a commodity is not the effect of a prior generalization of the celebrated 'commodity relations'. The extraction of surplus-value is thus achieved in this case not directly, but by way of the labour incorporated into commodities, in other words by the creation and monopolization of surplus-value.

7. This entails the following:

The relations of production must be understood both as an articulation of the various relationships which constitute them, and in their union with the labour process: it is this which defines the dominant relation of exploitation characterizing a mode of production, and which determines the class that is exploited within this dominant relation. The property relationship should not be used alone, to denote negatively all those who do not dispose of economic ownership, i.e. all non-owners, as the class exploited within this dominant relation. The class exploited within this dominant relation (the basic exploited class: the working class in the capitalist mode of production) is that which performs the productive labour of that mode of production. Therefore in the capitalist mode of production, all non-owners are not thereby workers.

The production process, on the other hand, is defined not by technological factors, but by the relationships between agents and the means of labour, and hence between the agents themselves, in other words by the unity of the labour process, the productive forces and the relations of production. The labour process and the productive forces, including technology, do not exist in themselves, but always in their constitutive connection with the relations of production. Hence one cannot speak, in societies divided into classes, of 'productive labour' as such, in a neutral sense. In a society divided into classes, that labour is productive which corresponds to the relations of production of the mode in question, i.e. that which gives rise to the specific and dominant form of exploitation. Production, in these societies, means at the same time, and as one and the same process, class division, exploitation, and class struggle.

8. It follows that it is not wages that define the working class economically: wages are a form of distribution of the social product, corresponding to market relations and the forms of 'contract' governing the purchase and sale of labour-power. Although every worker is a wage-earner, every wage-earner is certainly not a worker, for not every wage-earner is engaged in productive labour. If social classes are not defined at the economic level by a gradation of incomes (rich/poor), they are still less defined by the location of their agents in the hierarchy of wages and salaries. This location certainly has its value as an important index of class determination, but it is only the effect of the latter, just as are all those things that are generally referred to as social inequalities: the distribution of income, taxation, etc. No more than other social inequalities is the wage differential a unilinear scale, a continuous and homogenous staircase, with or without landings, on which individuals or groups are located, certain groups at a 'higher' level, others at a 'lower' one: wage differentials are, rather, the *effect* of class barriers.

This being said, it is still necessary to emphasize that these class barriers and their extended reproduction have the effect of imposing specific and concentrated social inequalities on certain groupings of agents, according to the various classes in which they are distributed: in particular, on young people and on old people, not to enter here into the case of women, which is of a different order and besides, more complex. This is because, in the case of women, what is involved is not simply certain over-determined effects on them of the division of society into classes, but, more precisely, a specific articulation, within the social division of labour, of the class division and the sexual division.

9. The production process is thus composed of the unity of the labour process and the relations of production. But within this unity, it is not the labour process, including technology and the technical process, that plays the dominant role; the relations of production always dominate the labour process and the productive forces, stamping them with their own pattern and appearance. It is precisely this domination of the forces of production by the relations of production which gives their articulation the form of a *process* of production and reproduction.

This dominant role of the relations of production over the productive forces and the labour process is what gives rise to the constitutive role of political and ideological relations in the structural determination of social classes. The relations of production and the relationships which comprise them (economic ownership/possession) are expressed in the form of powers which derive from them, in other words class powers; these powers are constitutively tied to the political and ideological relations which sanction and legitimize them. These relations are not simply added on to relations of production that are 'already there', but are themselves present, in the form specific to each mode of production, in the constitution of the relations of production. The process of production and exploitation is at the same time a process of reproduction of the relations of political and ideological domination and subordination.

This implies, finally, that in the places of the social classes within the relations of production themselves, it is the social division of labour, in the form that this is given by the specific presence of political and ideological relations actually within the production process, which dominates the technical division of labour; we shall see the full consequences of this particularly in the question of the 'management and supervision' of the labour process, but also in that of the class determination of engineers and production technicians. Let us simply note here that it is by taking account of these basic Marxist propositions that we shall be able to grasp the decisive role of the division between manual labour and mental labour in the determination of social classes.

10. This is the right point to recall the basic distinction between mode of production and social formation: I shall restrict myself

here to a few summary remarks, for this distinction has a theoretical importance which I shall have ample occasion to return to in the following essays.

In speaking of a mode of production, an abstract and formal object, one is still keeping to a general and abstract level, even though the concept mode of production itself already embraces relations of production, political relations and ideological relations: for example, the slave, feudal, capitalist modes of production, etc. These modes of production, however, only exist and reproduce themselves within social formations that are historically determinate: France, German, Britain, etc. at such and such a moment of the historic process. These social formations are always unique, because they are concrete and singular real objects.

Now a social formation comprises several modes – and also forms – of production, in a specific articulation. For example, European capitalist societies at the start of the twentieth century were composed of (i) elements of the feudal mode of production, (ii) the form of simple commodity production and manufacture (the form of the transition from feudalism to capitalism) and (iii) the capitalist mode of production in its competitive and monopoly forms. Yet these societies were certainly capitalist societies, in so far as the capitalist mode of production was dominant in them. In fact, in every social formation, we find the dominance of one mode of production, which produces complex effects of dissolution and conservation on the other modes of production and which gives these societies their overall character (feudal, capitalist, etc.). The one exception is the case of societies in transition, which are, on the contrary, characterized by an equilibrium between the various modes and forms of production.

To return to social classes. If we confine ourselves to modes of production alone, we find that each of them involves two classes present in their full economic, political and ideological determination – the exploiting class, which is politically and ideologically dominant, and the exploited class, which is politically and ideologically dominated: masters and slaves in the slave mode of production, lords and serfs in the feudal mode of production, bourgeois and workers in the capitalist mode of production. But a concrete society (a social formation) involves more than two classes, in so far as it is composed of various modes and forms of production. No social formation involves only two classes, but the two fundamental classes of any social formation are those of the dominant mode of production in that formation.

Social formations, however, are not the simple concretization or extension of modes and forms of production existing in their 'pure' form; they are not produced by the latter being simply 'stacked together' in space. The social formations in which the class struggle is enacted are the actual sites of the existence and reproduction of the modes and forms of production. A mode of production does not reproduce itself, or even exist, in the pure state, and still less can it be historically periodized as such. It is the class struggle in the social formations which is the motor of history; the process of history has these formations as its locus of existence.

This has considerable implications for the analysis of social classes. The classes of a social formation cannot be 'deduced', in their concrete struggle, from an abstract analysis of the modes and forms of production which are present in it, for this is not how they are found in the social formation. On the one hand, their very existence is affected by the concrete struggle that takes place within the social formation, and it is here in particular that we find the phenomenon of the polarization of other classes and class fractions around the two basic classes. In capitalist societies these are the bourgeoisie and the proletariat, which has decisive and very complex effects on these other classes, as well as on the two basic classes themselves. On the other hand, the classes of one social formation only exist in the context of the relations of this formation with other social formations, hence of the class relations of this formation with those of other formations. Here we have touched on the problem of imperialism and the imperialist chain; imperialism, which precisely is the extended reproduction of capitalism, has its locus of existence in social formations, and not in the capitalist mode of production as such.

11. The Marxist theory of social classes further distinguishes *fractions* and *strata* of a class, according to the various classes, on the basis of differentiations in the economic sphere, and of the role, a quite particular one in these cases, of political and ideological relations. The theory also distinguishes social *categories*, defined principally by their place in the political and ideological relations: these include the state bureaucracy, defined by its relation to the state apparatuses, and the intellectuals, defined by their role in elaborating and deploying ideology. These differentiations, for which reference to political and ideological relations is always indispensable, are of great importance; these fractions, strata and categories may often, in suitable concrete conjunctures, assume the rule of relatively autonomous social forces.

It is none the less the case that we are not confronted here with 'social groups' external to, alongside, or above classes. The fractions are class fractions: the commercial bourgeoisie for example is a fraction of the bourgeoisie; similarly, the labour aristocracy is a fraction of the working class. Even social categories have a class membership, their agents generally belonging to several different social classes.

This is one of the particular and basic points of difference between the Marxist theory and the various ideologies of social stratification that dominate present-day sociology. According to these, social classes – whose existence all contemporary sociologists admit – would only be one form of classification, a partial and regional one (bearing in particular on the economic level alone) within a more general stratification. This stratification would give rise, in political and ideological relations, to social groups parallel and external to classes, to which they were superimposed. Max Weber already showed the way in this, and the various currents of political 'elite theory' need only be mentioned here.

12. The articulation of the structural determination of classes and of class positions within a social formation, the locus of existence of conjunctures, requires particular concepts. I shall call these *concepts of strategy*, embracing in particular such phenomena as class polarization and class alliance. Among these, on the side of the dominant classes, is the concept of the 'power bloc', designating a specific alliance of dominant classes and fractions; also, on the side of the dominated classes, the concept of the 'people', designating a specific alliance of these classes and fractions. These concepts are not of the same status as those with which we have dealt up till now: whether a class, fraction or stratum forms part of the power bloc, or part of the people, will depend on the social formation, its stages, phases and conjunctures. But this also indicates that the classes, fractions and strata that form part of these alliances, do not for all that lose their class determination and dissolve into an undifferentiated type of merger or alliance. Just to take one example: when the national bourgeoisie forms part of the people, it still remains a bourgeoisie (leading to contradictions among the people); these classes and fractions do not dissolve into one another, as a certain idealist usage of the term 'popular masses', or even the term 'wage-earning class', might suggest.

II

13. We can now pose the question of the apparatuses, in particular the branches and apparatuses of the state, and the question of their relation to social classes. Here I shall confine myself to indicating certain of the roles played by the state apparatuses in the existence and reproduction of social classes.

The principal role of the state apparatuses is to maintain the unity and cohesion of a social formation by concentrating and sanctioning class domination, and in this way reproducing social relations, i.e. class relations. Political and ideological relations are materialized and embodied, as material practices, in the state apparatuses. These apparatuses include, on the one hand, the repressive state apparatus in the strict sense and its branches: army, police, prisons, judiciary, civil service; on the other hand, the ideological state apparatuses: the educational apparatus, the religious apparatus (the churches), the information apparatus (radio, television, press), the cultural apparatus (cinema, theatre, publishing), the trade-union apparatus of class collaboration and the bourgeois and petty-bourgeois political parties, etc., as well as in a certain respect, at least in the capitalist mode of production, the family. But as well as the state apparatuses, there is also the economic apparatus in the most strict sense of the term, the 'business' or the 'factory' which, as the centre of appropriation of nature, materializes and embodies the economic relations in their articulation with politico-ideological relations.

Given that the determination of classes involves political and ideological relations, and that the latter only exist in so far as they are materialized in the apparatuses, the analysis of social classes (class struggle) can only be undertaken in terms of their relationship with the apparatuses, and with the state apparatuses in particular. Social classes and their reproduction only exist by way of the relationship linking them to the state and economic apparatuses; these apparatuses are not simply 'added on' to the class struggle as appendices, but play a constitutive role in it. In particular, whenever we go on to analyse politico-ideological relations, from the division between manual and mental labour to the bureaucratization of certain work processes and the despotism of the factory, we shall be concretely examining the apparatuses.

It remains none the less true that it is the class struggle that plays the primary and basic role in the complex relationship between class struggles and apparatuses, and this is a decisive point to note, given the errors of numerous present-day arguments on these questions. The apparatuses are never anything other than the materialization and condensation of class relations; in a sense, they 'presuppose' them, so long as it is understood that what is involved here is not a relation of chronological causality (the chicken or the egg). Now according to a constant of bourgeois ideology in the 'social sciences', which might be loosely referred to as the 'institutionalist-functionalist' current, it is apparatuses and institutions that determine social groups (classes), with class relations arising from the situation of agents in institutional relationships. This current exhibits in specific forms the couple idealism/empiricism, in the

specific form of humanism/economism, both of which are characteristic of bourgeois ideology. This was already notably so with Max
Weber; for him it was relations of 'power' which resulted in class
relations, these 'power' relations having as their specific field and
original locus of constitution relations within institutions or associa-
tions of the 'authoritarian' type (*Herrschaftsverbände*). This ideological lineage (and rooting a bit further back, one always comes
across Hegel) has considerable repercussions, even in the most concrete questions, and permeates the whole of academic sociology in
the currently dominant form of 'organization theory'. It is not
restricted to the state apparatuses, but takes in the economic
apparatus itself (the problem of the 'enterprise').

We can thus define both the relationship and the distinction
between state power and state apparatuses. State apparatuses do not
possess a 'power' of their own, but materialize and concentrate class
relations, relations which are precisely what is embraced by the
concept 'power'. The state is not an 'entity' which an intrinsic
instrumental essence, but it is itself a relation, more precisely the
condensation of a class relation. This implies that:

(a) the various functions (economic, political, ideological) that the
state apparatuses fulfil in the reproduction of social relations are not
'neutral' functions *sui generis*, initially existing as such and later
being simply 'diverted' or 'misappropriated' by the ruling classes;
these functions depend on the state power inscribed in the very
structure of its apparatuses, in other words on the classes and class
fractions which occupy the terrain of political domination;

(b) this political domination is itself bound up with the existence
and functioning of the state apparatuses.

It follows that a radical transformation of social relations cannot
be limited to a change in state power, but has to 'revolutionize' the
state apparatuses themselves. In the process of socialist revolution,
the working class cannot confine itself to taking the place of the
bourgeoisie at the level of state power, but it has also radically to
transform (to 'smash') the apparatuses of the bourgeois state and
replace them by proletarian state apparatuses.

Here again, however, it is state power, directly articulated with
the class struggle, that determines the role and the functioning of
the state apparatuses.

(a) This is expressed, from the point of view of the revolutionization of the state apparatuses, by the fact that the working class and
the popular masses cannot 'smash' the state apparatuses except by
seizing state power.

(b) It is also expressed in the overall concrete functioning of the
state apparatuses in every social formation. If the state apparatuses

are not reducible to state power, it is none the less true that it is the particular configuration of the terrain of class domination, of state power (power bloc, hegemonic and governing classes or fractions, etc., as well as class alliances and supporting classes) which determines, in the last instance, both the role of this or that apparatus or branch of the state in the reproduction of social relations, the articulation of economic, political and ideological functions within this apparatus or branch, and the concrete arrangement of the various apparatuses and branches. In other words, the role that this or that apparatus or branch of the state (education, army, parties, etc.) plays in the cohesion of the social formation, the representation of class interests and the reproduction of social relations, is not a function of its intrinsic nature, but depends on the state power.

More generally, any analysis of a social formation must take into direct consideration both the relations of class struggle, the power relations, and the state apparatuses which materialize, concentrate and reflect these relations. Nevertheless, in the relationship between the class struggle and the apparatuses, it is the class struggle which is fundamental. It is not the 'institutional' forms and their modification which result in 'social movements', as for example current ideology about a 'blocked society' would have it, but rather the class struggle which determines the forms and modifications of the apparatuses.

14. These last points will stand out more clearly if one considers things from the point of view of the extended reproduction of social classes. In fact, social classes only exist in the context of the class struggle, with its historical and dynamic dimension. Classes, fractions, strata and categories can only be discerned, or even defined, by taking into consideration the historic perspective of the class struggle, and this directly raises the question of their reproduction.

A mode of production can only exist in social formations if it reproduces itself. In the last analysis, this reproduction is nothing other than the extended reproduction of its social relations: it is the class struggle that is the motor of history. Thus Marx says that in the end, what capitalism produces is simply the bourgeoisie and the proletariat; capitalism simply produces its own reproduction.

Thus the site of the reproduction process is not, as a superficial reading of the second volume of *Capital* might suggest, the 'economic space' alone, and the process does not consist of a self-regulating automatism by which social capital is accumulated. Reproduction, being understood as the extended reproduction of social classes, immediately means reproduction of the political and ideological relations of class determination.

This is why the state apparatuses, and the ideological state apparatuses in particular, have a decisive role in the reproduction of social classes: this role of the ideological apparatuses has recently attracted the attention of Marxist analysis. I do not intend here to go into this problem as a whole, as I shall return to it in the following essays; I shall merely attempt to clarify a few preliminary problems by choosing as a special example the role of the educational apparatus. These remarks will enable me to illustrate the propositions put forward above, and to advance a few supplementary reference points concerning the role of the apparatuses in the reproduction of social classes.

III

15. The state apparatuses, including the school as an ideological apparatus, do not create class divisions, but they contribute to them and so contribute also to their extended reproduction. It is necessary to bring out all the implications of this proposition; not only are the state apparatuses determined by the relations of production, but they also do not govern the class struggle, as the whole institutionalist tradition maintains: it is rather the class struggle at all its levels which governs the apparatuses.

The particular role of the ideological apparatuses in the reproduction of social relations (including relations of production) is in fact of the utmost importance, for it is their reproduction which dominates the process of reproduction as a whole, particularly the reproduction of labour-power and the means of labour. This is a consequence of the fact that it is the relations of production, themselves constitutively linked to the relations of political and ideological domination and subordination, which dominate the labour process within the production process.

The extended reproduction of social classes (of social relations) involves two aspects which cannot exist in isolation from one another. First, there is the extended reproduction of the places occupied by the agents. These places mark out the structural determination of classes, i.e. the manner in which determination by the structure (relations of production, political and ideological domination and subordination) operates in class practices. Secondly, there is the reproduction and distribution of the agents themselves to these places.

This second aspect of reproduction, which raises the question of who it is that occupies a given place, i.e. who is or becomes a bourgeois, proletarian, petty bourgeois, poor peasant, etc., and how and when he does so, is subordinate to the first aspect – the reproduction of the actual places occupied by the social classes; e.g. it is subordinate to the fact that in its extended reproduction, monopoly capitalism is reproducing the bourgeoisie, proletariat and petty bourgeoisie in a new form in its present phase, or to the fact that it is tending to eliminate certain classes and class fractions within the social formations in which its extended reproduction is taking place (e.g. the small-holding peasantry, traditional petty bourgeoisie, etc.). In other words, while it is true that the agents themselves must be reproduced – 'trained' and 'subjected' – in order to occupy certain places, it is equally true that the distribution of agents does not depend on their own choices or aspirations but on the reproduction of these places themselves. This is because the principal aspect of class determination is that of their places, and not that of the agents that occupy these places. The state apparatuses, including the school as an ideological apparatus, have different roles relative to these two aspects of reproduction.

The structural determination of classes is of course not restricted to places in the production process alone (to an economic situation of 'classes-in-themselves'), but extends to all levels of the social division of labour, so that the state apparatuses enter into the process of determining classes as the embodiment and materialization of ideological and political relations. It is in this way, through their role of reproducing ideological and political relations, that these apparatuses, and particularly the ideological state apparatuses, enter into the reproduction of the places which define social classes.

But if we are not to fall into an idealist and institutionalist view of social relations, according to which social classes and the class struggle are the product of the apparatuses, we must recognize that this aspect of reproduction goes beyond the apparatuses, generally escapes their control, and in fact assigns them their limits. We can say that there is a primary and fundamental reproduction of social classes in and by the class struggle, in which the extended reproduction of the structure (including the production relations) operates and which governs the functioning and the role of the apparatuses. To take a deliberately schematic example: it is not the existence of an educational system forming proletarians and new petty bourgeois which determines the existence and reproduction (increase, decrease, certain forms of categorization, etc.) of the working class and the new petty bourgeoisie; on the contrary, it is the production process in its articulation with the political and ideological relations, and thus the economic, political and ideological class struggle, which has the existing educational system as its effect. This explains why the process of reproduction by means of the apparatuses is marked by internal struggles, contradictions and frictions. It is in this way that we can understand the other side of the question: just as the extended reproduction of social relations depends on the class struggle, so also does their revolutionary transformation.

Thus the fundamental reproduction of social classes does not just involve places in the relations of production. There is no economic self-reproduction of classes over and against an ideological and political reproduction by means of the apparatuses. There is, rather, precisely a process of primary reproduction in and by the class struggle at all stages of the social division of labour. This reproduction of social classes (like their structural determination) also involves the political and ideological relations of the social division of labour; these latter have a decisive role in their relationship to the relations of production. The reason is that the social division of labour itself not only involves political and ideological relations but also the social relations of production within which it has dominance over the 'technical division' of labour. This is a consequence of the fact that within the production process, the production relations are dominant over the labour process.

To say that the primary reproduction of social classes depends on the class struggle also means that its concrete forms depend on the history of the social formation. Any given reproduction of the bourgeoisie, of the working class, of the peasant classes, of the old and new petty bourgeoisie, depends on the class struggle in that formation. For example, the specific form and tempo of the reproduction of the traditional petty-bourgeoisie and small-holding peasantry under capitalism in France depends on the specific forms of their long-standing alliance with the bourgeoisie. It is therefore only possible to locate the apparatuses in this reproduction by referring to this struggle: the particular role of the school in France can only be situated in relation to that alliance between bourgeoisie and petty bourgeoisie which has for so long been a mark of the French social formation.

16. Moreover, while extended reproduction of the places occupied by social classes involves the ideological state apparatuses (especially in the ideologico-political field), it is not confined to these.

Let us return to the case of the division between manual and mental labour mentioned above. This division, which has a role in determining places in the social division of labour, is by no means limited to the economic domain. In that domain, it should be noted, it has no role of its own to play in class division, since productive workers who produce surplus-value cannot simply be identified with manual workers. The division between manual and mental labour can be grasped only when it is seen in its extension to the political and ideological relations of (a) the social division of labour within the production process itself, where, in an economic apparatus or enterprise, authority and the direction of labour are linked to mental work and the secrecy of knowledge, and (b) the social division of labour as a whole – political and ideological relations which contribute to defining the places occupied by the social classes. But clearly it is neither the educational system nor any other ideological apparatus which creates this division; nor are these the sole or primary factors in reproducing it, even though they do enter into its reproduction while appearing (in their capitalist form) as the effect of this division and of its reproduction in and by the class struggle. In other words, the reason why the school reproduces within itself the mental/manual labour division is that because of its capitalist nature, it is already situated in an overall context characterized by a division between mental and manual labour; the reproduction of the educational system as an apparatus is also functionally determined by that division. It is a division which goes beyond education and assigns it its role: the separation of the school from production is linked with the direct producer's separation from and dispossession of the means of production.

In referring to ideological apparatuses, we must recognize that these apparatuses neither create ideology, nor are they even the sole or primary factors in reproducing relations of ideological domination and subordination. Ideological apparatuses only serve to fashion and inculcate (materialize) the dominant ideology. Thus Max Weber was wrong in claiming that the Church creates and perpetuates religion: rather it is religion which creates and perpetuates the Church. In the case of capitalist ideological relations, when Marx analyses the fetishism of commodities as relating directly to the process of valorization of capital, he offers us an excellent example of the reproduction of a dominant ideology which goes beyond the apparatuses; this was noted by Marx himself in his frequent references to a 'correspondence' between 'institutions' and 'forms of social consciousness', in which he implied a distinction. So the role of ideology and of the political in the extended reproduction of the places occupied by social classes directly coincides here with the class struggle which governs the apparatuses. It is here in particular that we come across, in the case of the working class, the phenomenon of class instinct referred to above. Just as the ideological state apparatuses do not create the dominant ideology, so the revolutionary apparatuses of the working class (the party) do not create proletarian ideology; they rather elaborate and systematize it, by producing revolutionary theory.

The reproduction of places in the relations of ideological and political domination does indeed involve the apparatuses, and it even involves apparatuses other than the ideological state apparatuses, and most importantly the economic apparatus itself. As the unit of production in its capitalist form, an enterprise is also an apparatus, in the sense that, by means of the social division of labour within it (the despotic organization of labour), the enterprise itself reproduces political and ideological relations affecting the places of the social classes. In other words, the reproduction of the all-important ideological relations is not the concern of the ideological apparatuses alone: just as not everything that goes on in 'production' involves only the 'economic', so the ideological apparatuses have no monopoly over reproducing the relations of ideological domination.

Finally, this reproduction of the places of social classes does not just involve the ideological state apparatuses and the economic apparatus; it also involves the branches of the repressive state apparatus in the strict sense. This is not principally via their direct function of repression, understood in the rigorous sense of organized physical force. This repression, although it is of course absolutely necessary for class relations of exploitation and domination, is not, in capitalist society, generally present directly and as such within the relations of production, but generally intervenes only in the form of maintaining the 'conditions' of exploitation. (The army is not directly present in the factories.) This is precisely one of the differences between the capitalist mode of production and pre-capitalist modes; in the latter, as Marx explains very succinctly, the direct producer is not totally separated from his means of labour – of which he in fact has possession – and the direct intervention of an extra-economic force is therefore necessary to compel him to produce surplus labour for the profit of the owner (the feudal lord for example). If the branches of the capitalist state's repressive apparatus intervene in the reproduction of the places of social classes, this is because, while their principal role is that of repression, which is what distinguishes them from the ideological apparatuses, they are not limited to this; they have also an ideological role, generally secondary, just as the ideological apparatuses themselves also have a repressive role, which is generally secondary. In this way, the army, the judiciary and the prisons (bourgeois 'justice'), etc., have, by virtue of their role in the materialization and the reproduction of ideological relations (bourgeois ideology), a key role in the reproduction of the places of social classes.

17. Let us now turn to the second aspect of reproduction, the reproduction of agents. This encompasses, as two moments of one and the same process, both the training and subjection of agents to enable them to occupy the places, and the distribution of agents to the places. It is especially necessary to grasp exactly how the two

aspects of reproduction (of places and agents) are articulated, if we are to understand the stupidity of the bourgeois problematic of social mobility, which we shall be discussing in detail in the following essays. In essence, this bourgeois problematic of the social mobility of groups and individuals presumes:

(a) that the principal question about 'social stratification', or even about its origin, is that of the 'circulation' or 'mobility' of individuals between strata. However, it is clear that, even on the absurd assumption that from one day to the next, or even from one generation to the next, the bourgeoisie would all take the places of workers and vice versa, nothing fundamental about capitalism would be changed, since the places of bourgeoisie and proletariat would still be there, and this is the principal aspect of the reproduction of capitalist relations;

(b) that the much deplored 'social rigidity' is simply due to the supposed social inequality of 'individuals' and 'environments', which would essentially be dissolved, like all other inequalities, in a capitalist society that had 'equality of opportunity'.

The ideological state apparatuses, and the educational apparatus in particular, play a decisive and quite special role in the reproduction of agents, in their training and subjection and their distribution. On this certain remarks are in order. The reproduction of agents, in particular the notorious 'training' of the agents of actual production, is no simple technical division of labour (technical education), but rather a real training and subjection which extends into political and ideological relations. The extended reproduction of agents in fact corresponds here to an aspect of the reproduction of social relations which stamps its pattern on the reproduction of labour-power.

While this does entail a particular role for the school, we must remember that it is not just on-the-job technical education, but the very process of training and subjection as such, which goes on even within the economic apparatus itself, since the enterprise is more than a simple production unit. And this entails a particular role for the enterprise as precisely that apparatus which distributes agents within itself. In the case of immigrant workers, the economic apparatus actually has the dominant role, though it is not limited to these. If we were to forget the role of the economic apparatus and consider that agents have already been completely distributed in school, prior to the economic apparatus, we would fall into the same type of one-way regressive explanation which considers that this complete distribution has already occurred in the family, prior to the school. Capitalist classes are not educational castes any more than they are hereditary castes. This regressive explanation does not hold for the relationship between family and school because the family remains an active force during schooling; and similarly it does not hold for the relationship between school and the economic apparatus because education remains an active force in the agents' economic activity, in the form of 'retraining'. I want finally to note, on top of what has already been said on the subject of the repressive state apparatus, the role of certain branches of the latter in the reproduction of agents: this is particularly the case with the army, whose role in the distribution of agents has for a very long while been important in France.

However, in order to break with the misunderstandings of the 'functionalist-institutionalist' tradition, which has always spoken of the role of 'institutions' in the training and distribution of 'individuals', particularly under the heading of the 'socialization process', it is necessary to go further. On the one hand, we must realize that this aspect of reproduction is indissolubly tied to the former, and in fact subordinated to it – it is because there is extended reproduction of places, and to the extent that there is so, that there is this or that reproduction and distribution of agents between places. On the other hand, we should not forget that the determining role, as far as the distribution of agents in the social formation as a whole is concerned, falls to the labour market, as the expression of the extended reproduction of the relations of production. This is the case even when there is not, strictly speaking, a unified labour market, i.e. when the labour market's demands are directed to a sphere which is already compartmentalized – due partly to the specific action of the ideological state apparatuses (an unemployed graduate will not fill a vacancy for a semi-skilled worker). The reason is that, underlying the distribution aspect as well, there is a constitutive relationship between the distributive apparatuses and work relations. Among other things, this constitutive relationship imposes limits on the action of the ideological state apparatuses in compartmentalizing the labour market. For example, it is not the school which makes peasants the principal occupants of spare places within the working class. On the contrary, it is the exodus from the countryside, i.e. the elimination of places in the countryside, in combination with the extended reproduction of the working class, which governs the school's role in this respect.

Finally, in the case of extended reproduction, and in so far as the second aspect of reproduction is subordinate to the first, we must define the direct effects which the places themselves have on the agents, and here we meet again the primacy of the class struggle over the apparatuses. Strictly speaking, we do not find agents who are in origin (in a world 'before' or 'outside' school) 'free' and 'mobile', who circulate among the places following the orders of the ideological apparatuses, the ideological inculcation and the education which they receive. It is true that in the capitalist mode of production and in a capitalist social formation, social classes are not castes, that agents are not tied by their origin to determinate places and that the school and the other apparatuses have an important role of their own in distributing agents to the places. But the effects of distribution show themselves in the fact that by means of the ideological apparatuses, the vast majority of bourgeois remain bourgeois, and their children do too, while the vast majority of proletarians (and their children after them) remain proletarians. This shows that the school is not the sole or principal reason for distribution taking this form. It is caused rather by the effects which the places themselves have on the agents, effects which go beyond the school and even beyond the family itself. We are not, as some current debates suggest, trying to decide which is primary in a causal sequence, family or school. We are not even considering the family/school couple as the basis of these effects of distribution. We are faced rather with a series of relationships between apparatuses, whose roots are deep in the class struggle. In other words, the primary distribution of agents is tied to the primary reproduction of the social classes. According to the stages and phases of the social formation, primary distribution assigns to a given apparatus or series of apparatuses the specific role which it is to play in the distribution of agents.

Part One

The Internationalization of Capitalist Relations and the Nation State

The latest phase of imperialism, and the upsurge of class struggle in the imperialist metropolises, have raised a series of key questions for revolutionary strategy: what exactly are the new relationships between the imperialist social formations (United States, Europe, Japan), and what are the effects of these on the state apparatuses? Is it still possible today to speak of a *national state* in the imperialist metropolises? What connections are there between these states and the internationalization of capital or the multinational firms? Are new super-state institutional forms tending to replace the national states, or alternatively, what modifications are these states undergoing to enable them to fulfil the new functions required by the extended reproduction of capital on the international level?

It is no secret that these questions have become particularly acute with the problem of the E.E.C. and the 'political future' of Europe. Their importance is decisive, for it is clear that the contemporary state, the nub of any revolutionary strategy, can only be studied in its relation to the present phase of imperialism and to the effects of this within the metropolitan zone. It is equally plain that these questions have held the attention of Marxist scholarship less than those concerning the relations between metropolises and dependent social formations, and the latter formations themselves. The political positions and the ideology of 'third-worldism' are certainly one of the reasons for this. The result is that, while we are beginning to understand clearly the effects of contemporary imperialist domination on the dominated and dependent social formations, its effects within the imperialist metropolises themselves have received much less study.

It is possible, however, at least schematically, to locate two major tendencies in the positions taken on this question:

1. The first tendency, represented in different ways by such writers as Paul Sweezy, Harry Magdoff, Martin Nicolaus, Pierre Jalée, etc., puts forward what could be called a contemporary left-

wing version of the Kautskyite theory of 'ultra-imperialism'.[1] These writers, while they have contributed greatly towards illustrating and exposing the dominant role of the U.S.A. in the capitalist world as a whole, underestimate the inter-imperialist contradictions resulting from uneven development, and see the sole line of division within the imperialist chain as that between metropolises and dominated formations. The relations of the imperialist metropolises among themselves are seen as characterized by a pacification and integration under the uncontested dominance and exploitation of American capital. This domination is even conceived, by analogy, as essentially similar to the relation between imperialist metropolises and dominated and dependent countries: it is seen as belonging to the same type of 'neo-colonialism', the limiting, but exemplary instance being the relationship between the U.S.A. and Canada. Within this perspective, we are faced with the rapid decline, if not the virtual disappearance of national state power within the imperialist metropolises, either under the domination of the American super-state, or under the domination of American or 'international' monopoly capital freed from its state 'fetters'.[2]

2. At the other extreme there are two positions put forward, which although they often diverge in their arguments, at least on this question display a common basis. We can thus treat them together here, without any intention of amalgamating them. On the one hand, there are writers such as Ernest Mandel, Michael Kidron, Bill Warren, Bob Rowthorn, and in France, J. Valier.[3] It would not be doing them an injustice to say that, for them, the present phase of imperialism is not characterized by any structural change in the mutual relations of the imperialist metropolises. Here also, the only structural cleavage in the imperialist chain is seen as that between the metropolises and the dominated formations, this cleavage being taken as an unchanging fact throughout the development of

1. Paul Baran and Paul Sweezy, *Monopoly Capital*, Harmondsworth, 1966; and various articles by Sweezy in *Monthly Review*; Harry Magdoff, *The Age of Imperialism*, New York, 1969; Martin Nicolaus, 'U.S.A.: The Universal Contradiction', in *New Left Review* 59, 1970; Pierre Jalée, *The Pillage of the Third World*, New York, 1970; and *Imperialism in the Seventies*, New York, 1968.

2. Robin Murray, 'The Internationalization of Capital and the Nation State', in *New Left Review* 67, 1971.

3. For Ernest Mandel, principally *Europe versus America*, NLB, 1970; Michael Kidron, *Western Capitalism since the War*, Harmondsworth, 1968; Bill Warren, 'How International is Capital?', in *New Left Review* 68, 1971; Bob Rowthorn, 'Imperialism in the Seventies: Unity or Rivalry', *New Left Review* 69, 1971; J. Valier, 'Impérialisme et révolution permanente' in *Critiques de l'économie politique*, nos. 4–5, 1971.

imperialism. Inter-imperialist contradictions within the metropolitan zone would thus have the same significance today as in the past: these contradictions are seen as located in a context of 'autonomous' and 'independent' states and bourgeoisies, struggling against each other for hegemony. These 'national bourgeoisies' and 'national states' would thus be related only externally, the tendency towards internationalization affecting, in the extreme case, market relationships alone. These theorists see the dominance of the United States over the imperialist metropolises as essentially similar to that of Great Britain in the past. The present period would be one in which this hegemony was once again threatened by the emergence of equivalent 'counter-imperialisms', those of Common Market Europe and Japan. The enlarged E.E.C., in particular, is considered as a form of 'cooperation' and 'internationalization' of European capital into a European supra-national state, with the aim of eliminating the supremacy of American capital. This thesis is, however, rather contradictory to that of the 'autonomous national states'.

On the other hand, there are the arguments of the western Communist Parties, and particularly those of the P.C.F.[4] Here the present relations between the metropolises are considered as based, not on modifications in the imperialist chain, but on the modification of the capitalist mode of production into national 'state monopoly capitalisms', seen as juxtaposed and simply added together. The furthest that the process of internationalization is considered to reach is the sphere of the so-called 'productive forces'. Intra-metropolitan relations are thus again basically seen in terms of external mutual pressure between autonomous and independent bourgeoisies and national states. The E.E.C. and 'European unification' are admittedly seen as the expression of an increased domination of American capital, but this domination is considered as rather like the grafting of a cosmopolitan foreign body onto the national European state monopoly capitalisms, in the interest of American or cosmopolitan capital, simply adding on new supernumerary functions to the 'national' functions of these states.

I shall return later and in more detail to the positions of these tendencies, and their political implications. It is my belief, however, that they have not managed to grasp the contemporary modifications

4. cf. *Traité* . . . , *le capitalisme monopoliste d'État*; Ph. Herzog, *Politique économique et planification* . . . , Paris, 1971, and his article: 'Nouveaux developpementes de l'internationalisaton du capital', in *Économie et Politique*, no. 198, 1971; J.-P. Delilez, *Les Monopoles*, Paris, 1970, and his article: 'Internationalisation de la production', in *Économie et Politique*, no. 212, 1972. It should be noted that there are certain differences between the positions of the different western CPs on the E.E.C.

in the imperialist chain and their effects on relations between the metropolises, and on the national states in particular. I am confining myself here to the case of the European metropolises, both because of its political importance for us here and now, and because of certain significant peculiarities of the Japanese case – even though these peculiarities in no way amount, in the long run, to an exception to the rule.

To carry out such an analysis of the present phase of imperialism, it will be necessary, given the present state of research, to tackle the problem at its root.

I

The Present Phase of Imperialism and the Domination of the U.S.A.

1. PERIODIZATION

The capitalist mode of production (CMP) is characterized, in its extended reproduction, by a two-fold tendency: to reproduce itself within the social formation in which it takes root and establishes its dominance, and to expand outside of this formation; the two aspects of this tendency act simultaneously. For reasons which we shall see, the CMP can only exist in so far as it extends its relations of production and pushes back its limits. Although this two-fold tendency has characterized the CMP since its origins, it assumes a special significance in the imperialist stage. This stage, which intensifies the tendency for the rate of profit to fall, is characterized by the predominance, as far as the outward expansion of the CMP is concerned, of the export of capital over the simple export of commodities. This characteristic is decisive, and is the very foundation of the Leninist conception of imperialism. It in no way means, however, that the tendency towards the export of commodities and the expansion of the world market weakens in the imperialist stage, and this is certainly not the case; it simply means that the export of capital is the fundamental and determinant tendency of imperialism. Finally, the imperialist stage, corresponding to the development of monopoly capitalism, is marked by the displacement of dominance, both within the social formation and within the imperialist chain, from the economic to the political (i.e. to the state).

The imperialist chain is itself characterized by uneven development; each link of this chain reflects the chain as a whole in the specificity of its own social formation. This specificity is a function of the forms that the dominance of the CMP at the international level assumes over the other modes and forms of production that exist within a social formation. In fact, the reproduction of the CMP with this two-fold tendency attests to the fact that the CMP can only exist by subordinating other modes and forms of production, and by appropriating their elements (their labour-power, and means of labour). Uneven development is produced by the articulation within the social formations between the CMP, as it reproduces itself, and these other modes and forms of production.

This dominance of the CMP has complex effects of dissolution and conservation (for a class struggle is involved here) on the other modes and forms of production that it dominates.[1] The differential form that these effects assume on the international scale delineates the phases of the imperialist stage; these thus correspond to specific forms of capital accumulation, or even to specific forms of global relations of production and of the international imperialist division of labour.

Ever since the beginnings of imperialism, the imperialist chain has been characterized by a fundamental cleavage, separating, on the one hand, the imperialist metropolises, and on the other hand, the social formations dominated by and dependent on imperialism. This cleavage, based on the very structure of the imperialist chain, is radically different from the colonial type of relationship that characterized the beginnings of capitalism, as well as from the later type of commercial capitalism. These were both based on the establishment of the world market and the export of commodities. These relations do continue to coexist in the imperialist stage, with the specific characteristics given them by imperialism, and under its dominance. There are no longer independent social formations whose relations among themselves are relatively external. The process of imperialist domination and dependence henceforth takes the form of the reproduction, within the dominated social formations themselves, and in the forms specific to each of them, of the relation of domination which binds them to the imperialist metropolises.

It is especially important for our purpose here to attempt to define this situation in more detail. A social formation is dominated and dependent when the articulation of its specific economic, political and ideological structure expresses constitutive and asymmetrical relationships with one or more other social formations which enjoy a position of power over it.[2] The organization of class relationships and state apparatuses within the dominated and dependent formation reproduces within it the structure of the relation of domination,

1. N. Poulantzas, *Fascism and Dictatorship*, NLB, 1974; Charles Bettelheim, 'Theoretical Comments' in Arghiri Emmanuel, *Unequal Exchange*, NLB, 1972.

2. M. Castells, *La Question urbaine*, Paris, 1972, pp. 62 ff.

and thus expresses in a specific manner the forms of domination that characterize the class or classes in power in the dominant social formation(s). This domination corresponds to forms of exploitation that are both indirect (because of the place of the dominated formation in the imperialist chain) and direct (through direct investments), in which the popular masses of the dominated formations are exploited by the classes in power in the dominant formations: an exploitation linked to that which they experience from their own ruling classes. Each phase of imperialism is characterized by different forms in which this domination and dependence is realized.

By taking these factors into account, it is possible to outline the periodization of the imperialist stage into phases. I must make clear right away that the periodization involved here is not one of a necessary 'succession' according to a linear schema of 'chronological stage-ism'. The phases that I have attempted to distinguish in the basic features of the extended reproduction of capitalism are the historic effect of the class struggle.

On the other hand, I have to raise here a supplementary question posed by the periodization of imperialism, this being itself a particular stage of capitalism. Imperialism is certainly located in the extended reproduction of the CMP; however, the periodization of imperialism cannot be dissolved into a periodization of the capitalist mode of production in general, save at the risk of blurring the cleavages produced by imperialism itself as a stage in the reproduction of the CMP. (As we shall see, this is the case with those theories which see the CMP as 'imperialist from its beginnings', or make a distinction between 'archeo-imperialism' and 'neo-imperialism'.) The periodization of imperialism itself into phases is legitimate in so far as the CMP exhibits the peculiarity, as compared with 'pre-capitalist' modes of production, of being characterized by two stages, distinguished by a different articulation of its structure. This occurs precisely in its relation to the other modes and forms of production which it dominates in social formations through its extended reproduction. This indicates that the periodization of imperialism must be undertaken with a view to its relations both with 'pre-capitalist' modes and forms of production, and with the 'pre-imperialist' stage of capitalism, which I will call, for the sake of convenience, 'competitive capitalism'. In fact the characteristics of this stage still coexist with those of the imperialist stage, under the dominance of the latter, both within each particular social formation (monopoly capitalist/competitive capitalist relations) and in the imperialist chain as a whole (commercial capitalist/imperialist relations of domination and exploitation).

Finally, the various phases of imperialism are themselves marked by steps and turns, and this is particularly important in analysing the present phase of imperialism.

The following phases of imperialism may thus be distinguished:

(i) the *transition phase* from the stage of competitive capitalism to the imperialist stage, lasting from the end of the nineteenth century up till the inter-war period; within the metropolises, this was essentially the period of unstable equilibrium between competitive capitalism and monopoly capitalism. In the 'outward' expansion of the CMP and the establishment of the imperialist chain, this phase was marked by a relative equilibrium between a domination of the dominated formations based on commercial capital and the export of commodities, and a form of domination through the export of capital. During this period, both the imperialist metropolises themselves, and their relations with the dominated formations, were characterized by an unstable equilibrium between the dominance of the economic and the dominance of the political – i.e. of the state.

(ii) the *phase of consolidation of the imperialist stage*: this came into being between the two wars, in particular with the crisis of the 1930s, the stabilization or establishment of fascism and the Roosevelt New Deal. Within the metropolises, monopoly capitalism established its domination over competitive capitalism, and this involved the dominance of the political (the state) within these formations. However, at this period within the contradictory effects of dissolution and conservation that monopoly capitalism imposed, both on pre-capitalist forms (the form of simple commodity production, the traditional petty bourgeoisie, etc.) and on competitive capitalism (non-monopoly capital), the conservation effects still prevailed over the dissolution effects within the imperialist chain, the export of capital prevailed over the export of commodities, and it was the political aspect that prevailed in relations between the metropolises and the dominated and dependent formations.

It must still be pointed out here, however, that during these phases, though to an uneven extent, the CMP, which characterized the imperialist chain, dominated the dependent formations chiefly by inserting them into this chain. Imperialism's social division of labour between the metropolises and the dominated formations was still to all intents and purposes one between town (industry) and country (agriculture). It was this that made possible the domination of the CMP over formations within which modes of production other than the CMP often continued to predominate, and it was in the form of this predominance (for example feudal predominance, the domination of 'feudal' landed proprietors) that the relation of domination which bound it to the metropolis was reproduced within the dependent formation.

During these phases, relations between the imperialist metropolises were marked by inter-imperialist contradictions which often gave rise to an alternating predominance of one metropolis over the others: by Great Britain, Germany, or the U.S.A. But this predominance was essentially based on the type of domination and exploitation that this metropolis imposed on its own 'empire' of dominated formations, and on the rhythm of development of capitalism in its homeland. The only line of polarization structurally relevant to the imperialist chain was that dividing the metropolises and the dominated formations.

(iii) the *present phase of imperialism*, gradually established after the end of the Second World War, and itself marked by various stages of class struggle. Within the imperialist metropolises, it is by way of the dissolution effects prevailing over the effects of conservation that monopoly capitalism exercizes its domination over pre-capitalist forms and over competitive capitalism during this phase, though of course not always to the same degree; the CMP in its monopoly form certainly does not tend to become the 'exclusive' form of production in the metropolises. Other forms continue to exist, but now only in the form of 'elements' (traditional petty-bourgeoisie, small-holding peasantry, medium capital) that are re-structured and directly subordinated ('subsumed' in Marx's term) within the reproduction of monopoly capitalism.

This phase corresponds to modifications in the relation between the metropolises and the dominated formations. The CMP no longer just dominates these formations from 'outside', by reproducing the relation of dependence, but rather establishes its dominance directly within them; the metropolitan mode of production reproduces itself, in a specific form, within the dominated and dependent formations themselves. This does not prevent conservation from continuing to prevail over dissolution, to a greater or lesser extent, and contrary to the effects within the metropolises of this two-fold tendency which the domination of the CMP imposes on other modes and forms of production. What also characterizes this phase is that this induced reproduction of the CMP within these formations extends in a decisive way to the domain of their state apparatuses and ideological forms. This internalized and induced reproduction, in so far as it is related to modifications in the imperialist chain, also has its effects in the reverse direction, from the dependent formations on the metropolises: in the case of labour-power, this takes the form of immigrant labour.

The contemporary forms of this dependence, including the 'development of under-development', peripheral industrialization and economic blockages, the internal dis-articulation of social relations, etc., have been widely studied in recent years.[3] What have received less attention are those modifications in the imperialist chain that involve the relations of the metropolises among themselves. In fact the forms of capital accumulation and the international division of labour that are at the root of this extended reproduction of capitalism in the relation between metropolises and dominated formations are bringing about a major modification in the present phase. While the line of demarcation and cleavage between the metropolises and the dominated formations is becoming sharper and deeper, a new dividing line is also being drawn within the metropolitan camp, between the United States on the one hand, and the other imperialist metropolises, in particular Europe, on the other. Relations between the imperialist metropolises themselves are now also being organized in terms of a structure of domination and dependence within the imperialist chain. This United States hegemony is not in fact analogous to that of one metropolis over others in the previous phases, and it does not differ from this in a merely 'quantitative' way. Rather it has been achieved by establishing relations of production characteristic of American monopoly capital and its domination actually inside the other metropolises, and by the reproduction within these of this new relation of dependence. It is this induced reproduction of American monopoly capitalism within the other metropolises, and its effects on their modes and forms of production (pre-capitalist, competitive capitalist) that characterizes the present phase: it similarly implies the extended reproduction within them of the political and ideological conditions for this development of American imperialism.

But this duplication of dividing lines is none the less asymmetrical. This new dependence cannot be identified with that which characterizes the relations between metropolises and dominated formations, and can absolutely not be treated as if it were analogous to the latter, in so far as these metropolises continue to constitute independent centres of capital accumulation, and themselves to dominate the dependent formations. It is particularly the under-estimation of this latter element which characterizes the theories of ultra-imperialism.

3. See among others, Samir Amin, *L'Accumulation à l'echelle mondiale*, Paris, 1970, and the various works of E. Faletto, T. Dos Santos, A. Quijano, E. Torres Rivas, F. Weffort, R. Mauro Marini, etc. F. H. Cardoso, *Notes sur l'état actuel des études de la dépendance*, in mimeograph, August 1972, should in particular be consulted.

In fact American imperialism and the imperialism of the other metropolises are locked in struggle for the domination and exploitation of these formations. We need only mention here that one of the most important contradictions between the United States and the E.E.C. at the present time involves the various 'preferential agreements' between the E.E.C. and numerous Third World countries: this indicates the importance that the domination of the dependent formations assumes within inter-imperialist relations.

As a function of the above characteristics, this present phase of imperialism is marked by an upsurge of struggle by the popular masses, which though it takes various different turns, is affecting both the peripheral formations and the metropolises, particularly Europe. It is this accumulation of struggles which gives certain determinate conjunctures of this phase the character of a crisis of imperialism as a whole. One must be careful not to use the term crisis in an economist and over-general sense, for example applying it to an entire phase. This was the fault of the Comintern's analyses in the inter-war period, which, in the characteristic spirit of 'economist catastrophism', considered imperialism itself as a stage of 'general crisis of capitalism', and we can see it again today in a different form in the analyses of the western CP's who characterize 'state monopoly capitalism' in general as the 'crisis of imperialism'. If this is the case, one could just as well say that capitalism has always been in crisis, ever since its origins. What these analyses imply, in their underestimation of the conjunctures of class struggle to which alone the term crisis can properly be applied, is that imperialism or capitalism will somehow collapse by themselves, by virtue of their own 'economic contradictions'. But just as it is the class struggle which gives certain determinate conjunctures of capitalism and imperialism the character of crises, so the outcome of these crises, including a possible restabilization, depends on this struggle.

Our periodization thus directly involves a whole series of epistemological assumptions. The periodization, both into stages and into phases, is applied at the level of the social formations, i.e. the forms of existence of a mode of production, in this case the capitalist: it does not derive from the supposed 'tendencies' of the mode of production itself, this being simply an abstract object. It is only social formations that can be periodized, since it is in them that the class struggle is enacted: a mode of production only exists in the specific conditions – economic, political, ideological – which determine its constitution and reproduction. This implies in particular a periodization in terms of the articulated relations of this mode with other modes and forms of production, an articulation that is constitutive of its own existence and reproduction.

This in turn implies that social formations are not mere 'concretizations' of a mode of production that already has a prefigurative and abstract existence, in the strong sense of this term: the distinction between mode of production and social formations does not refer to different sites of existence, as in a topographical analogy. Social formations are not, in other words, the spatialization of modes of production that exist already as such and are then 'stacked' one on top of the other. Social formations are in actual fact the sites of the reproduction process; they are nodes of uneven development of the relationship of modes and forms of production within the class struggle. This means that the site where the CMP is reproduced in the imperialist stage is the imperialist chain and its links. Thus the stages and phases of periodization refer to modifications in the reproduction process, so long as it is understood that these modifications are not measurable by reference to an ideal and pre-existing model. The mode of production is not a model but a concept; what is involved are modifications in the mode of production such as it exists in certain determinate conditions.

The reason why I see these clarifications as particularly important is that current discussions on this subject show certain confusion.

On the one hand, certain writers[4] consider that the site of the reproduction of the CMP is an alleged 'process' of this mode taken as such, in the abstract. They see social formations merely as a concretization and spatialization of the 'moments' of this process, which is thus emptied of the class struggle. This position often takes the form, in the context of their analysis of the present phase of imperialism, of a theory of a 'world capitalist mode of production', with the social formations being only the spatialized moments of this. This leads directly to the ideology of 'globalization', in other words that of an abstract process whose uneven development would be simply the 'dross' of its concretization into social formations. But uneven development is not a residue or an impurity due to the concrete combination of modes of production reproduced in the abstract; it is the constitutive form of the reproduction of the CMP in the

4. In particular Christian Palloix, *Les Firmes multinationales et le procès d'internationalisation*, Paris, 1973, pp. 100 ff. My criticisms of Palloix are in no way intended to detract from the importance of his writings, which are indispensable for an understanding of contemporary imperialism. This tendency on the author's part is none the less significant, particularly in so far as his analyses are based on the extremely structuralist and economist text by Balibar in *Reading Capital*.

imperialist stage in its relations with other modes of production and social formations. In fact the internationalization of capitalist relations can be understood only in relation to its own location, that is in the reproduction of the CMP in the social formations (the imperialist chain). This is precisely the sense in which this internationalization is not a mere 'integration' of the various social formations; it is not the product of a pre-existing global CMP and a self-sufficient process which is merely concretized in its 'moments', the formations. This notion ends by concealing the existence of the imperialist chain. In actual fact internationalization consists in the induced reproduction of the CMP of the metropolises within the dependent and dominated formations, that is, in the new historic conditions of its reproduction.

Among certain other writers such as Philippe Herzog,[5] however, we still find the old empiricist identification of mode of production and social formation, the CMP, in Herzog's words, being no more than the 'synthesis of the various capitalist economic and social formations'. Ultimately this is a notion derived from a comparative collection of the 'features' of these formations. This empiricist position thus goes directly together with the notion of an imperialist ensemble composed of social formations that are simply juxtaposed and added together. However, the imperialist chain is no more just the sum of its parts than it is an abstract model-process of the CMP, its links simply being the concretization of this mode. The imperialist chain is neither more nor less than the reproduction of the CMP in the social formations under certain determinate economic, political and ideological conditions, with the links of this chain – the social formations – forming the sites of this process.

2. THE INDICES OF AMERICAN CAPITAL'S DOMINATION

Before analysing this situation in more detail, it will be useful to present its fundamental features in the light of the above considerations.

    1. The first striking fact is the continuous increase, ever since the Second World War, of the proportion of American capital within the overall volume of foreign capital investment. In 1960, U.S. foreign investment already accounted for 60 per cent of the world total, while in 1930 it was only 35 per cent. During the period 1960–1968, for which we have comparative statistical information, this

5. *Politique économique*, op. cit., pp. 27 ff., and his contribution to the CERM conference on 'Mode de production et formation économique et sociale', printed in the special number of *La Pensée*, October 1971.

tendency has continued even if at a less spectacular pace, and the gulf between the United States and the other imperialist metropolises has widened still further.[6] In 1960 the real value of direct investments controlled by American firms, on a world basis, came to 30 thousand million dollars. In 1972, the value of these investments was estimated at more than 80 thousand million dollars, on a very conservative assessment.

2. What is still more important, however, are certain new features of these investments. In this period, it is no longer the peripheral formations but rather the European imperialist metropolises that have become the preferred investment area for American capital. In money terms, American direct investment in Europe quadrupled during the years 1957–67, while it did not quite double in Canada, and hardly increased at all in Latin America. The proportionate share of Europe in American foreign investment, which was 15·6 per cent in 1955, has steadily leapt forward since that time: 20·5 per cent in 1960, 28 per cent in 1965, around 31 per cent in 1970. This has been particularly marked in the case of the E.E.C.: in 1963, American investment in the Common Market overtook that in Great Britain, where it had always been considerable, and in 1970 direct American investment in the E.E.C. had caught up with that in the rest of Europe together (Great Britain included).[7] This corresponds, moreover, to the general tendency for metropolitan capital to be invested within its own boundaries.

3. At the same time, considerable differences have emerged in the forms of investment of this capital. Direct investment has come to an increasing extent to predominate over portfolio investment. Although this is in fact a relative and not an absolute distinction, it provides an important index, since it corresponds directly to modifications in the relations of production. Direct investment includes both investments in fixed capital and those that involve, or tend sooner or later towards, taking control of firms and enterprises; although percentages vary depending on statistics and the different institutional arrangements, investment is generally considered direct if it comes to more than 25 per cent of the share capital of a company. Portfolio investment, on the other hand, involves the simple purchase of shares, or short-term stock-exchange or financial operations. At the present time, direct investment forms some 75 per cent

6. J. Dunning, 'Capital Movements in the Twentieth Century', in *International Investment*, London, 1972, a symposium; G.-Y. Bertin, *L'investissement public international*, Paris, 1972, pp. 26ff.; 'Les Investissements directs des États-Unis dans le monde', *La Documentation française*, pp. 7 ff.

7. C. Goux and J.-F. Landeau, *Le Péril américain*, 1971, pp. 24 ff.

of the export of private capital from the principal industrial countries, as against 10 per cent before 1914.[8]

Now, while the overall investment flow from Europe to the United States almost balances that of the United States to Europe (an argument given great play by Mandel, Rowthorne, etc.), some 70 per cent of American investment in Europe takes the form of direct investment, as against only a third of European investment in the United States.[9] This also means that American capital in Europe is effectively multiplied by its cumulated value and by the reinvestment of profits on the spot. In fact, contrary to the situation in the peripheral formations, a considerable portion of these profits (some 40 per cent) is reinvested on the spot or within the same zone.

4. A growing proportion of the foreign investment of the developed countries is allocated to manufacturing industries, and not to extractive industries and the service sector, commerce, etc. This is especially clear in the case of American capital. As far as manufacturing industry is concerned, the proportionate increase of American capital in Europe in relation to the overall export of American capital is still more striking: while in 1950 Europe only received 24·3 per cent of this type of American capital exports, by 1960 it received 40·3 per cent. At the same time, while the overwhelming majority of American direct investment in Europe involved manufacturing industry, and therefore directly productive capital, only a small section of European direct investment in the United States (about a third) involved directly productive capital, the greater part going into the 'service' sector, insurance, etc.[10]

5. These American investments in Europe are linked to the concentration and centralization of capital. They originate from the most concentrated branches and sectors in the United States.[11] In Europe, too, they are directed into sectors and branches with a high degree of concentration, and they thereby contribute to accelerating the pace of concentration. European subsidiaries of American companies are for the most part situated in highly concentrated branches, in which the subsidiary most frequently occupies a dominant position.[12] Finally, the sectors and branches invested in are those

8. J. Dunning (ed.), *The Multinational Enterprise*, London, 1971.

9. B. Balassa, in *La politique industrielle de l'Europe integrée*, edited by M. Bye, Paris, 1968.

10. *La Documentation française*, loc. cit.; Balassa, loc. cit.

11. S. Hymer, 'The Efficiency Contradictions of Multinational Corporations' in *The Multinational Firm and the National State*, Toronto, 1972; C.-A. Michalet, *L'Entreprise plurinationale*, 1969.

12. J. Dunning, *American Investments in British Manufacturing Industry*, London, 1958.

which have the most rapid rate of expansion and enjoy the most advanced technology; hence they exhibit the highest productivity of labour and the dominant features of an intensive exploitation of labour by means of the increased organic composition of capital. Eighty-five per cent of American investment in manufacturing industry is in the metal and engineering industries, chemical and synthetic products, electrical goods and electronics, etc. The rate of growth of this capital is somewhere between 9 and 12 per cent per annum, i.e. twice that of the European gross national product (GNP), and more than twice the growth rate of the American GNP. The rates of increase of the European GNP's, which seem to make such an impression on certain contemporary 'futurologists', are appreciably heightened by the growth of American capital in Europe. Finally, if one examines the direction of development of this investment, it is clear that in a majority of cases it involves raking over licences and patents from European firms, and undertaking the direct exploitation of these technological advantages.

6. Similarly, the export of capital and the hegemony of American capital involves the centralization of money capital, of the big banks and of financial holdings proper. The number of branches of American banks in Europe, which increased from 15 to 19 between 1950 and 1960, rose from 19 to 59 between 1960 and 1967. Within the banking sector 'subsidiary corporations' dominated by American capital increased from a world total of 15 in 1960 to 52 in 1967.[13] One of the results of this situation has been the role that the dollar played for a long time in the monetary domain, and which is now being replaced by the Eurodollar market. It should also be noted that this tendency has taken on major proportions with the entry of Great Britain into the E.E.C., since London is the preferred financial centre for American branch banks in Europe; in 1970, 50 per cent of Eurodollars were held in London, the majority by American banking establishments.[14]

The tendency for industrial and banking capital to merge into finance capital, characteristic of the monopoly capitalist stage, does not abolish the distinction between the concentration of productive capital and the centralization of money capital within capital's expanded reproduction cycle. In this cycle, both the accumulation of capital and the rate of profit are determined by the cycle of productive capital, which alone produces surplus value. This is contrary to the widespread theory which identifies 'finance' capital with banking capital, and draws the conclusion from this that the banks

13. Magdoff, op. cit., pp. 74 ff. Foreign branches of American banks increased from 303 in 1965 to 1009 in 1972.

14. C. Goux and J.-F. Landeau, *Le Péril américain*, pp. 106 ff.

are dominant in the monopoly capitalist/imperialist stage. In point of fact, finance capital is not, strictly speaking, a fraction of capital like the others, but designates the process of merger and the mode of functioning of the combined industrial and banking fractions.

I will have ample occasion to return to these questions in the following essay.[15] I simply want to stress here that, although the industrialization of capital can only be understood at the level of the reproduction process of the total social capital (productive capital, money capital, and commodity capital as well), yet capital as a social relation is based on the productive capital cycle. This is precisely what is meant by the Marxist proposition that it is production and the relations of production, in the CMP the relations of production and the extraction of surplus-value, which determine the realization of surplus-value and the relations of circulation, the famous 'commodity relations'. It is well-known that Lenin had to deal with one aspect of this question in his polemic with Rosa Luxemburg. The Leninist theory of imperialism, and the role of the export of capital in this, is based on the determining role of the cycle of productive capital. This is what explains the predominant place allotted to this in our analysis of the modifications of the present phase of imperialism.

There is good reason to mention this problem at this stage, in the light of certain current interpretations of imperialism, from those of Gunder Frank and Arghiri Emmanuel to those of Christian Palloix, G. Dhoquois and Pierre-Philippe Rey, all of which are based, in the last analysis, if to an uneven extent, on the pre-Marxist conception of the primacy of the cycle and the realm of circulation over that of the relations of production.[16] By radically undermining the Leninist theory, they make it impossible rigorously to periodize the CMP into stages; either they argue for a 'capitalism that has been imperialist from its origins', as with Frank, or for a distinction between 'archeo-imperialism' and 'neo-imperialism' as with Palloix, Dhoquois and Rey; they also make it impossible to periodize imperialism itself into phases.

The modifications involved in the present phase of imperialism also

15. I should like to remind the reader that certain conceptual analyses in this essay, which establish a general frame of reference, will be gone into in more detail in the following essay.

16. André Gunder Frank, 'The Development of Under-Development', *Monthly Review*, September 1966, and *Capitalism and Under-Development in Latin America*, New York, 1969; A. Emmanuel, *Unequal Exchange*, op. cit.; Palloix, op. cit.; G. Dhoquois, *Pour l'histoire*, Paris, 1972; P.-P. Rey, *Les Alliances de classe*, Paris, 1973.

have certain effects on the organization of world trade, i.e. on the export of commodities. There is an inherent tendency in capitalism for the market to expand, and although this is dominated in the imperialist stage by the export of capital, this does not mean that it in any way weakens. The share of trade between the 'developed countries' in world trade as a whole is increasing in relation to trade between these countries and those of the periphery. Trade within the metropolitan zone rose from 46 per cent of world trade in 1950 to 65 per cent in 1965, and is increasing far more rapidly than trade between the centre and the periphery (up 17·5 per cent in 1969). This development also corresponds to the growing share of manufactured products in world trade: these formed around 66 per cent of world trade in 1969, as against less than 50 per cent before 1963.[17]

That said, however, it is none the less the case that, within the imperialist countries, U.S. commodity exports are tending to decline relative to those of other imperialist countries, and particularly of Europe. This gives the Mandel tendency its chief argument for the end of American supremacy in the near future. I shall have a few things to say about this phenomenon in my conclusion, but would like to remark straight away:

(a) that what is decisive, as far as imperialism is concerned, is the export of capital:

(b) that Mandel's argument firstly does not take into account commodities produced and consumed directly in Europe by firms under American control, commodities which in this way 'substitute' for American exports; secondly, he counts as 'European' exports the exports of American-controlled firms in the European countries. The full importance of this becomes clear when one realizes that American investment in Europe has been very extensive in those sectors which are themselves oriented towards exports, including so-called 're-imports' into the United States under a European label. Dunning estimates that a third of the increase in European exports of advanced technological products between 1955 and 1964 was accounted for by firms controlled by American capital, and that in 1980 around a quarter of all British exports will be accounted for by such firms. Moreover, a pamphlet published in 1970 by the French DATAR organization, calling for the implantation of American capital in France, emphasized that investment projects would be particularly welcome if, among other things, 'they provide exports, thus helping us to adjust the French balance of payments'.

To come back to the question of American capital exports. The

---

17. S. Amin, op. cit., pp. 85 ff., and also Magdoff.

facts presented above are particularly important as indications of the changes currently affecting the relations of production, in the form of the international concentration of social capital, and of the labour process, in the form of the imperialist social division of labour on the world scale. It is in this perspective that their true significance can be assessed.

This significance can in no way be reduced to the question of the percentage increase of direct American investment in the European countries in relation to the overall increase of investment in these countries (including indigenous investment), although this form of reasoning is dear both to the Mandel tendency and also to various bourgeois specialists. This percentage may well be an index of the fact that the European countries are far from being simple colonies of the United States, though it is not indicative of the new process of dependence if it is taken in isolation. To just dwell on it for a moment, this percentage, as given by official statistics, seems quite small, an average of 6·5 per cent for Europe as a whole (this is based on figures for 1964, although it has increased considerably since then).

There is, however, good reason to suspect that these data are calculated in such a way as to give a very conservative estimate. First of all, in the majority of European countries, the figures only take into account American investment in the form either of flows of new capital from the United States, or reinvestment by the self-financing of American subsidiaries in Europe. The operations of American capital both on the European capital market (the issue of Euro-bonds) and on the Eurodollar market are neglected, even though two-thirds of the growth of real American investment in Europe is at present financed in this way. Moreover, although investment is generally considered direct only if it accounts for more than 25 per cent of the share capital of a firm, far less than this is often sufficient for American capital to ensure control, given the present concentration of capital and the socialization of the labour process. The figures given also relate to direct investment in the economy as a whole, while if the industrial sector (i.e. productive capital) is taken separately, the percentage is considerably higher. Finally, and most important, these figures do not take any account of American investment that is made in Europe under cover of firms that are legally 'European', but actually under American control and economic ownership. This is particularly the case with Switzerland and Swiss investment in the E.E.C. countries. The significance of this can be seen by considering the fact that, between 1961 and 1967, American investment formed 30 per cent of total foreign investment in France, while Swiss investment formed a further

29 per cent. F. Braun, director of the E.E.C. Commission, adds these two figures together to arrive at a figure of 59 per cent for direct American investment.[18] It is clear that this phenomenon will assume considerable dimensions with the entry of Great Britain into the E.E.C.

If we now go on to examine the actual pattern of American investment within the enlarged E.E.C., then in 1970 the prize for absolute volume must still go to Britain; the economic features of this formation, which combines the features of a leading economic power with close dependence on American capital, are well known. They have been emphasized even by those who hoped that the entry of Great Britain into the E.E.C. would liberate it from this dependence. Great Britain is closely followed in this respect by Belgium and the Netherlands, France together with Italy following behind but quickly catching up. It is in West Germany, however, that American investment is growing most rapidly and massively, and it seems that Germany will replace Great Britain in the lead. Without going so far as C. Goux, who claims that by 1980 Germany will have become the 'Canada of Europe', it is particularly important to note this, in view of the fact that the currently observable close relationship between 'German positions' and 'American positions' is most frequently attributed either to the importance of German exports to the United States, or to the presence of American forces in Germany; everything seems to show, however, that this presence functions more and more as a simple screen for economic penetration. It is even more important to note it at a time when German economic domination within the E.E.C. is being ever more strongly asserted, and when Germany is setting itself up as the champion of 'European integration'.

I would like to repeat once again that what is involved here is not a mere question of percentages. We must therefore go on to deal now with the present modifications in the international constitution of capital and the imperialist social division of labour. What characterizes the present changes in the imperialist chain, and in the relations between the United States and Europe, is the action of new forms of world relations of production on the labour process.

18. F. Braun, in *La Politique industrielle*, op. cit.

3. THE INTERNATIONAL SOCIALIZATION OF THE LABOUR PROCESS AND THE INTERNATIONALIZATION OF CAPITAL

1. The new forms of the international imperialist division of labour (the socialization of the productive forces) correspond to the direction that the present concentration of capital (the relations of production) stamps on the labour process and on the productive forces at the world level. The concentration of capital on an international scale, and the construction of financial empires, dates from the beginnings of the imperialist era. This involved, just as was the case with the process of concentration within a social formation, a distinction between formal legal ownership and real economic ownership (joint-stock companies), which has been referred to ideologically as a 'separation of ownership and control'. This distinction is still valid; the important changes now in progress bear on the contemporary articulation of economic ownership and possession, that is to say, on the forms of the actual relations of production.

In point of fact, the form of concentration which prevailed subsequent to the gradual extinction of the 'capitalist entrepreneur' was either that of international cartels and financial holdings, or else that of one capital controlling either a distinct unit of production (centre of appropriation of nature) in a foreign country, or several 'separate' units of production in various countries. This dominant form thus meant that the relations of possession (direction and control of a specific labour process) and of economic ownership (power to assign the means of production and to allocate resources and profits to this or that usage) were relatively distinct and only partially overlapped; this form of ownership concentrated several separate units of production (and possessions) under a single control. As opposed to this, the present phase of imperialism is characterized by the establishment, under a single centre of economic ownership, of what are effectively complex production units[19] with labour processes that are closely articulated and integrated (integrated production), and divided between various establishments in several countries. This integrated production in no way inhibits the diversification of finished products, quite the contrary, and is not restricted to a single branch. Exchanges between these various establishments are not carried out on the basis of market prices, but are rather 'internal' to these units (at transfer prices). What we are faced with here is the closure, in a new form, of the gap between economic ownership and

19. See on this subject C. Bettelheim, *Calcul économique et Formes de propriété*, Paris, 1971.

possession, but this does not prevent there being new distinctions within the plurality of powers that these relationships involve and their exercise by different bearers and agents.

The closure of this gap must be understood at the level of the overall process: branches, industries, inter-branch relations, as well as in the upstream (raw materials) and downstream (marketing) sectors of production. It has the general result of pushing back, or even sometimes breaking down, the traditional limits between enterprises at the international level; one particular effect is the setting-up of multinational industrial firms (a recent GATT study showed that 30 per cent of international trade took the form of exchanges internal to these firms). This is only one effect, for the multinational firms are only one form of the unification of complex units of production by branch and industry. These firms nevertheless provide an excellent example of the current integration of the labour process. It is changes such as these, in particular, which explain the predominance of direct over portfolio investment.

The international integration of the labour process within a firm can take several different forms. The integration may be vertical, each subsidiary in one particular country being responsible for one stage of production or for a series of components and parts of a product or group of products – the classic example being IBM. Alternately, integration can be horizontal, each establishment or subsidiary specializing in all stages of the production of certain products, which are then exchanged between them – as is the case with Ford. Integrated production is also frequently achieved, to a letter or greater extent, across several branches in the various current forms of conglomerate. In any case, these forms of socialization of labour, even if they do not yet constitute the dominant form of international concentration of capital, are certainly the most pronounced tendency,[20] they form in fact part of a much larger process of international socialization of labour.

2. This socialization of labour on the international scale is not due chiefly to 'technical' factors (the 'technological revolution') but is rather a function of major changes in the global relations of production. It can only be properly understood, in its full import, as part of the imperialist social division of labour, by way of the present forms of internationalization of capital. It is necessary to be very careful here, because of the various ideologies hung onto interpretations of the multinational firms. What are the specific

20. This is the conclusion of the Harvard research project presented by R. Vernon, 'International investment and international trade in the product-cycle', in the *Quarterly Journal of Economics*, May 1966.

features of this internationalization in the present phase, of which these firms are only one of the effects?

(a) The development of bases of exploitation for a particular capital, or a combination of several capitals, in a number of different countries – in other words the extension of the site on which this capital establishes itself as a social relation.

(b) The pronounced tendency towards the combination, in the form of a single economic ownership, of capital coming from several different countries. The 'origin' of this capital is not a question of its nationality (for capital is not a thing), but rather of the place where the original and/or dominant social relations which compose the capital are constructed. In point of fact, capital that does not have a dominant base, in terms of social relations, in a definite country, is a very rare exception.

It must immediately be added, however, that, in the great majority of cases where legal and economic participation of capital from several nations is involved, this internationalization is brought about under the decisive domination of capital originating from one single country: it is this capital which concentrates in its hands the unified economic ownership. The proof of this is that 'joint ventures' which are supposed to represent an egalitarian merger of ownership between capitals from different countries and have a legal expression, remain quite exceptional (examples being Royal Dutch-Shell, Dunlop-Pirelli, Agfa-Gevaert).

This follows from the very nature of capitalist relations of production, such as they are expressed in the present process of concentration, since capital is not (we repeat) a thing, but a relation of production; it is the place defined by the relations of economic ownership and possession that determines the various powers that result from it. The occupation of this place by different capitals, reproducing themselves both within a social formation and outside it, has nothing friendly about it, but depends on a balance of forces; contradictions and competition continue between the components of a concentrated capital. This is in fact so much the more so in that the tight correspondence which is at present being established between economic ownership and possession, and which is the counterpart of the current process of international concentration, militates precisely in favour of a unified control and a central directing agency under a specific capital.

(c) This internationalization of capital is taking place under the decisive domination of American capital. As far as productive industrial capital is concerned, 55 per cent of the assets held by multinational firms outside their country of origin, in 1968, belonged to American capital, 20 per cent to 'British' capital, and the remainder was divided between the Europeans and Japanese. It is also the case that around 40 of the 50 largest multinational firms are American.

This is accompanied, contrary to what Mandel argues, by a widespread tendency for European capitals to merge with American capital, rather than to merge among themselves; the E.E.C. has only accelerated this tendency. Between 1962 and 1968, for instance, there were calculated to be some 109 international take-overs and mergers in the E.E.C., half of which involved capital belonging to a 'third country': 1180 cases of a share being taken in a company, of which 800 involved such foreign capital; 625 cases of common subsidiaries of two Common Market enterprises being set up, but 1124 cases of common subsidiaries set up by a Common Market firm plus a 'third country' one. This 'third country' capital is in the great majority of cases American, either directly or under camouflage.[21] As far as productive capital is concerned, things are even clearer; production subsidiaries set up in 1967 and 1968 in the E.E.C. include 202 set up by capital from another E.E.C. country, and 216 set up by American capital. We need hardly mention here the striking fact that British investment in France, which was massively accelerated with the entry of Britain into the E.E.C., is almost entirely concentrated in distribution and property. To give some idea of the figures involved, we can note that in France, taking the first six months of 1967 and the flow of investment alone, the increase of foreign capital invested was of the order of 167 million francs originating from within the Community, and 442 million francs coming from 'third countries', of which 316 millions were of direct and declared American origin;[22] we have already seen what is often concealed behind other 'third country' investment, or even investment formally originating from within the 'Community'.

Finally, and most important: even in the case of an amalgamation of European capital, what is involved is rarely an actual merger, and still more rarely integrated production; far more common are various kinds of 'understanding' (for example Fiat/Citroën), limited association or exchange of securities. The situation with concentrations under the aegis of American capital is precisely the reverse.[23] In this case, what is most frequently involved is an effective shift of overall powers of economic ownership and possession in favour of American capital, as a result of the balance of forces between

21. 'L'Europe des communautés', 1972, in *La Documentation française*, op. cit.

22. Y. Morvan, *La Concentration de l'industrie en France*, Paris, 1972, p. 397.

23. J. Dunning, in *The Multinational Enterprise*, op. cit., pp. 19, 297 ff.

American and European capital. This is in no way explained, as
several writers would have it, by the 'legal obligations' which
American legislation 'imposes' on its capital (in particular, the fact
that mere participation of this capital in a foreign enterprise can
bring it under the jurisdiction of the anti-trust laws, while subsidiaries which are completely under the legal ownership of American capital escape this).

4. THE IMPERIALIST SOCIAL DIVISION OF LABOUR AND THE ACCUMULATION OF CAPITAL

These are the changes that mark the new forms of the imperialist
social division of labour and the relationships between the imperialist
metropolises; they correspond to new forms of capital accumulation
on a world scale. In fact, by adding to the old dividing line between
metropolises and dominated formations the new dividing line between the imperialist metropolises themselves, and by shifting the
bases of exploitation and accumulation towards the metropolitan
zone, these changes must be understood as a capitalist strategy
designed to counter the circumstances under which the tendency of
the rate of profit to fall now expresses itself. While the export of
capital previously appeared to be chiefly bound up with the control
of raw materials and the expansion of markets, it is now essentially
a response to the need for imperialist monopoly capital to turn to its
account every relative advantage in the direct exploitation of labour.
(This does not mean that the need to expand markets is absent, for
example in the case of American capital's direct investment in
Europe.) The changes that we are concerned with here, involving
the domination of American capital over that of the other metropolises, tend essentially towards one single goal: towards raising the
rate of exploitation, so as to counteract the tendency for the rate of
profit to fall.[24] This, in particular, is the underlying reason why the
reproduction of the dominant capital has become internalized within
the 'external' bases of exploitation themselves, and also the reason
for the new forms of articulation between economic ownership and
possession. These correspond to the current forms of domination of
monopoly capitalism over the other modes and forms of production

24. It should be understood that this is not a short-term tactic concerning
rates of profit alone, but a long-term strategy of the dominant fraction of
international capital aimed at ensuring a social control of the global productive process. On this subject, see the remarkable article by C. Leucate:
'Les contradictions inter-impérialistes aujourd'hui', in *Critiques d'économie
politique*, October–December 1973. See also A. Granou, 'La nouvelle crise
du capitalisme', in *Les Temps Modernes*, December 1973.

at the international level, in other words to current forms of exploitation.

This increase in the rate of exploitation is the resultant both of the level of wages and of the productivity of labour – which includes the degree of technological development, the particular skills involved in the current development of the productive forces, etc. The wage level and the productivity of labour are, in the long run, closely related. In other words, the rate of exploitation and of surplus-value is not measurable simply in terms of the wage level. It also involves the intensive exploitation of labour: i.e. new technical processes, the diversification of products, the intensification of labour and its rhythm. A higher wage, in money or even real terms, may correspond, according to the development of the productive forces, to a smaller proportion of the value produced, and thus to a more intense exploitation, than a lower wage in the context of a lower productivity of labour.

Of course, while the wage level in the dominated countries is lower than that in the imperialist countries, the productivity of labour is considerably higher in the metropolises. But this does not explain the shift in the bases of capital's exploitation towards the metropolises; this can only be explained in terms of the shift in the relative weight of exploitation, in the present phase of imperialism and at the level of world accumulation, towards the intensive exploitation of labour. This shift is itself a function of the main characteristic of monopoly concentration: the rise in the organic composition of capital, that is to say, the increase of constant capital in relation to variable capital (wage costs), and the decrease of living labour in relation to 'dead labour' (embodied in the means of labour). Since the rate of profit is in inverse ratio to this increase in the organic composition of capital, it is here that we find the reason behind the present tendency towards technological innovation. But labour still remains, as ever, the basis of surplus-value, and it is this that explains the current tendency towards raising the rate of exploitation chiefly by means of an intensive exploitation of labour, directly linked to the productivity of labour (relative surplus-value).

The new forms taken by these global relations of production and by the international socialization of the labour process, which are precisely concurrent with this intensive exploitation of labour on the world level, are thus focused in new forms of the imperialist social division of labour. This division within the structure of exploitation does not merely involve the traditional dividing line between 'town-industry-metropolises and countryside-agriculture-dominated formations'. It is now complemented by a division *within* the industrial sector of productive capital itself, at the same time as agriculture itself undergoes a process of 'industrialization' on the international level; it is here that we meet with the shift in the export of capital towards direct investment and manufacturing industries, and thus the importance of manufactured goods in foreign trade.

This new imperialist social division of labour does of course also affect relations between metropolises and dominated formations. It corresponds to the 'development of under-development', and produces dislocations and deformations of a new type within the dependent formations. Capital investment in these formations is generally confined to light industry and has a lower level of technology, while labour-power remains predominantly unskilled; labour is exploited chiefly through the low level of wages, although there are also isolated sectors with high concentrations of capital and labour productivity. But the new division of labour chiefly involves a new division between the United States on the one hand, and the other imperialist metropolises on the other. It has important effects on the wage differences between these formations, the disparity between the United States and Europe in particular playing a special role. It has similar effects on the level of skill and the distinctions between skilled and unskilled labour within these formations, as well as on the spread of wage differentials, this spread being more 'open', and the differentiation of wages within the working class being more significant, in Europe than in the United States. This is analogous to the process taking place in relations between the metropolises as a whole and the dominated countries. It also has effects on technological disparities, on forms of unemployment, current European unemployment being to a great extent due to the tremendous 'restructuring' of the European economies that is currently in progress, and on such things as the role of immigrant labour.

This new division of labour and the shift of dominance towards the intensive exploitation of labour thus finds expression in different forms of exploitation according to the two lines of division. The exploitation of the popular masses of the dominated formations by the ruling classes of the metropolises is chiefly carried out in an indirect manner, that is to say through the place occupied by these formations in the imperialist chain and its polarization, and only secondarily in a direct way, i.e. by foreign capital directly invested in them. On the other hand, the exploitation of the popular masses in Europe by American capital is chiefly carried out directly, and only secondarily in the indirect form.

5. THE FORMS OF EUROPEAN DEPENDENCE

I do not intend here to analyse the various aspects of the new division of labour within the imperialist metropolises, but rather to illustrate the dependence that they involve. If the new division of labour is taken into account, it is clear that the domination of American capital cannot be assessed in terms of the percentage of the means of production that it formally controls within each European nation, nor even in terms of the role of multinational firms under American control. These firms are only one of the effects of the present process and only reflect this domination in a very one-sided manner. A few examples will serve as indications.

First of all, direct American investments in Europe take on a quite different significance if their international concentration is analysed according to the different industrial branches, and if we take account of the fact that they are chiefly oriented to certain branches over which they tend to exert preponderant control.[25] This control, however, is not measurable simply in terms of the importance of American firms in Europe in these branches of production, and the new division of labour cannot be reduced to one established 'within' the multinational firms and their establishments in the different countries. In point of fact, these branches are generally those in which the process of socialization of labour and the international concentration of capital are most advanced. In this context, we are often faced with a 'standardization of basic products' on a world scale, patently so in the case of the engineering and electrical industries, although this does not prevent a certain variation and diversification in the case of finished products. This standardization, which is far from corresponding to mere technical requirements, is most often imposed by the dominant American industry in these branches. A 'European' firm that desires to be competitive in their field has to 'restructure' its production and its labour processes in the light of this standardization, and on the basis of the internationalization of this branch. Very often, however, this is how it comes to be inserted into the process of dependence, and it is led to various forms of sub-contracting for American capital, even if it is not legally absorbed by an American firm. In the same context, this dependence extends to the fact that, in these branches and sectors in which American capital has left its mark on the whole process of production, European capital is invested in the purchase of patents and licences carefully selected by American capital.

25. On the following, see C. Palloix, *Firmes multinationales . . .*, op. cit., the first chapter, and the various publications of the IREP.

This assumes greater importance if we take into account the fact that the current socialization of labour processes and the concentration of capital are not measurable simply within one particular branch, but extend to various industrial branches; this is because American capital is able to establish its domination over several branches by way of its predominance in one. The clear case of this is in the electronics industry. E. Janco has recently shown how the use of computers on their present scale by European industry, a field in which the predominance of American capital is well known, does not correspond to any technical requirements; their use often proves to be superfluous or even on economic.[26] This use, however, is associated with the control by American capital of certain labour processes, and indeed increases this domination. It is certainly not confined to the field of computers alone, but extends, by this means (such as the use of American software), to other sectors where these computers are employed on a massive scale.

The international imperialist division of labour is thus related above all to the social division and organization of the entire labour process.[27] and we can thus see how the present division in favour of American capital is not confined to a division 'within' the American multinationals. There is in fact every reason to believe that, in certain respects at least, the new forms of social division which are currently being extended to sectors and branches of European industry, in particular the reproduction of the division between mental and manual labour in new forms, the forms of qualification and disqualification of labour and the place of engineers and technicians in relation to a certain application of technology, the new forms of authority and the division of decision and execution within the advanced European enterprises (the celebrated problem of their 'modernization'), are the symptoms of an objective process which strengthens the hold of American capital over the entire labour process.

Finally, in the context of the concentration of capital, it should be noted that in certain branches and sectors, such as electrical engineering for example, the internationalization of the cycle of productive capital finds expression in the process (and its forms) that American productive capital firms (such as Westinghouse, General Electric) imposes on the concentration of European productive capital: a movement of 'domestic' restructuring of European capital to conform to the extended reproduction of American

26. E. Janco and O. Furjot, *Informatique et Capitalisme*, Paris, 1972.

27. A. Gorz, 'Technique, techniciens et lutte de classes', *Les Temps Modernes*, August–September 1971; 'Le despotisme d'usine et ses lendemains', in *Les Temps Modernes*, September–October 1972.

capital, which must eventually lead to its incorporation. This also shows how illusory are the theories according to which a more intense 'domestic' concentration by a European country, or even by European capital as a whole, would be the best means of resisting American penetration. This forward flight often serves only to throw those involved into the arms of American capital.

There is perhaps no more striking example than that of France; we shall see in the following essay how France came to exhibit a specific backwardness in regard to the concentration of capital and industrial 'modernization'. For a certain period of time this found its expression in the Gaullist policy of 'nationalism', which corresponded to the interests of a bourgeoisie that was behindhand in the process of internationalization; even the formation of the Common Market met with resistance on the part of certain fractions of the French bourgeoisie. But in the last few years the concentration of capital in France has accelerated significantly, in perfect correlation with the penetration of foreign capital, and American capital in particular.[28] This correlation has taken the form either of a concentration at the direct instigation of this foreign capital, or of a concentration having as its effect the dependence of certain branches and sectors on American capital.

But there is more to it than that, and this can be clearly seen in the current Sixth Plan: (a) this plan is put forward not merely as a plan for the accelerated concentration of the French economy, but also as a plan for an 'industrial restructuring' and for the 'modernization of production'; (b) it corresponds to the policy of a 'European opening' (entry of Great Britain into the E.E.C.) and to an aid policy oriented to the international financial expansion of French big capital: a section of this capital has already attained the scale of the multinational firms, its internationalization having been accelerated since 1969.

What must also be noted here is how French policy towards American investment changed between the Fifth and Sixth Plans. According to the Fifth Plan,

> The present situation in which foreign investment in France is growing steadily from year to year cannot be considered satisfactory. It is essential to modify this development in the next few years in the direction of a restriction of direct investment from abroad, in order to safeguard the basic long-term interests of the French economy.

28. Y. Morvan, *La Concentration de l'industrie en France*, Paris, 1972, pp. 271 ff.

Five years later, however, the Sixth Plan put it differently:

> As far as direct investment by non-residents is concerned, the Committee's forecasts assume the continuation of a very open attitude on the part of the authorities in relation to foreign investment in France, if not a still more open attitude. In these conditions, American direct investment could well double by 1975, taking the years 1964–67 as the basis of reference.

Such examples could be multiplied: Europe's dependence on the American oil majors for energy is a case in point. It is clear, moreover, that the full scope of these developments can only be realized by taking into account the international centralization of money capital and the role of the great American banks. By way of summary we can say that, besides the shifts in the relation of economic ownership towards American capital, under cover of the maintenance of 'autonomous' European legal ownership ('minority control'), the following phenomena are also often present today:

(a) A shift, under cover of the maintenance of 'autonomous' European ownership, of certain powers deriving from economic ownership in favour of American capital (the case of the various and complex types of 'sub-contracting'); this can sometimes go so far as to amount to de facto expropriations which are nevertheless invisible and whose effects only make themselves felt in the long run.

(b) A shift, even when 'autonomous' European ownership is maintained, of certain powers deriving from the relation of possession (direction and control of the labour process) in favour of American capital. Given the present tendency towards closing the gap between economic ownership and possession, this also in the long run leads to a shift of economic ownership in favour of American capital.

These processes can thus only be understood by taking account of the reduction, or even the breaking down, of traditional boundaries between firms and enterprises on the international level.

These factors, however, which are related to the extended reproduction of the dominant imperialism within the other imperialist metropolises themselves, involve more than the relations of production: they assume the expansion of the ideological conditions of this reproduction into these metropolises. In order to understand what is involved in this, it is necessary to realize that ideology does not just consist of 'ideas' (articulated ideological ensembles) but is concretely embodied in a series of practices, know-how, customs and rituals which extend to the economic domain as well.[29]

29. L. Althusser, 'Ideology and Ideological State Apparatuses', in *Lenin and Philosophy*, NLB, 1971.

This is doubly important, in so far as it also bears on the differences between the ideological dependence of the dominated formations on the metropolises, and that of the metropolises themselves on the United States. In the case of the dominated formations, as a result of their original dependence on the metropolises and the ideological under-determination of their own bourgeoisies, the expansion into them of metropolitan ideological forms leads to a deep dis-articulation of their ideological sectors in general, which is the phenomenon that has been referred to incorrectly as a 'dual society'.

In the case of the relationship of the other imperialist metropolises to the United States, this expansion chiefly involves practices, rituals and know-how that are articulated to production. We need only mention the celebrated problems of know-how (aptly rendered in French as *savoir-faire*), of management, of the techniques of organization, and the whole gamut of rituals centring around information processing – these alone would make up a long list. In fact, these practices do not correspond to any technological rationality. What is often involved in them are ideological forms coinciding with the complex dependence of the metropolises on the dominant imperialism, with the effects mentioned above on the social division of labour.

2

The Nation State

We can now return to the question of the nation state in the imperialist metropolises, and see in what way the various positions on this question mentioned at the beginning of this essay are in fact false.

I. THE STATE AND THE PROBLEM OF THE NATIONAL BOURGEOISIE

Here once again we have to expose certain myths that die hard, even within Marxist analysis: common formulations of the very problem such as 'what can – or cannot – the state do in the face of the great multinational firms?', 'how far has the state lost its powers in the face of these international giants?' (formulas dear to Servan-Schreiber), are fundamentally incorrect, in so far as institutions and apparatuses do not 'possess' their own 'power', but simply express and crystallize class powers. The problem is therefore shifted; it becomes, in the first instance, one of the relations between the European bourgeoisies and American capital. And by asking which particular bourgeoisies are involved, we raise the problem of the national bourgeoisie.

In general, the national bourgeoisie is distinguished from the comprador bourgeoisie (we shall define this in a moment) on other levels besides the economic; the national bourgeoisie can only be defined if the political and ideological criteria of its class determination are also taken into account. It cannot be understood simply as an 'indigenous' capital radically distinct from 'foreign' imperialist capital, and uniquely by reference to the economic contradictions that divide the one from the other. In point of fact the imperialist stage, ever since its origins, has been marked by a tendency towards an international interpenetration of capital. Nor does the distinction between national and comprador bourgeoisie coincide, as is often believed, with that between industrial capital and commercial capital. It cannot even be defined by reference to market criteria, the national bourgeoisie being the indigenous bourgeoisie active on the home market; one can discover sections of both the industrial bourgeoisie and of this commercial bourgeoisie that are completely subordinated to foreign capital, just as one can also find, in certain Latin American countries for example, classes of capitalist landed proprietors based on monoculture for export (coffee, for instance) which even so exhibit the characteristics of national bourgeoisie. Finally, what is even more important, the distinction between comprador and national bourgeoisie does not coincide with that between monopoly capital (big capital) and non-monopoly capital (medium capital); there are big monopolies that function as national bourgeoisies, as well as sectors of medium capital completely subordinate to foreign capital.

I do not mean that the economic contradictions between foreign capital and indigenous capital do not play a determining role in defining the national bourgeoisie, simply that this in itself is not enough. In fact, what should be understood by national bourgeoisie is that fraction of the indigenous bourgeoisie which, on the basis of a certain type and degree of contradictions with foreign imperialist capital, occupies a relatively autonomous place in the ideological and political structure, and exhibits in this way a characteristic unity. This place is part of the structural class determination, and is not reducible to class position; rather, it has its effects on this. The national bourgeoisie is capable of adopting, in certain specific conjunctures of the anti-imperialist and national liberation struggle, class positions which make it part of 'the people'; it can therefore be brought into a certain type of alliance with the popular masses.

What is traditionally understood by comprador bourgeoisie, on the other hand, is that fraction of the bourgeoisie which does not have its own base for capital accumulation, which acts in some way or other as a simple intermediary of foreign imperialist capital (which is why it is often taken to include the 'bureaucratic bourgeoisie'), and which is thus triply subordinated – economically, politically and ideologically – to foreign capital.

It is thus clear that this conceptual pair is not suitable for analysing the bourgeoisies of the imperialist metropolises in its relation to American capital, in the present phase of imperialism. To stick to this single distinction inevitably leads in this case, both to its reduction in an economist direction, and to false conclusions.

(a) On the one hand, there are held to be contradictions of economic interest between sections of the indigenous bourgeoisie and foreign imperialist capital, particularly in so far as this indigenous bourgeoisie disposes, both within its social formation and abroad, of its own industrial foundation and bases of accumulation, and the conclusion is drawn from this that these are genuine national bourgeoisies (we shall see that this is the case with the tendency represented by Mandel and the Communist Parties).

(b) Alternatively, it is to start with maintained that these bourgeoisies are such that they cannot adopt class positions that would lead them to form part of the people. The conclusion is then immediately drawn that they can only be comprador bourgeoisies, that is, simple intermediaries between the national economy and foreign capital (this is the case with the 'ultra-imperialist' tendency).

What is necessary, then, is to introduce a new concept enabling us to analyse the concrete situation, at least that of the bourgeoisies of the imperialist metropolises in their relationship with American capital. Provisionally, and for want of a better word, I shall use the term 'internal bourgeoisie'. This bourgeoisie, which exists alongside sectors that are genuinely comprador, no longer possesses the structural characteristics of a national bourgeoisie, though the extent of this of course differs from one imperialist formation to another. As a result of the reproduction of American capital actually within these formations, it is, firstly, implicated by multiple ties of dependence in the international division of labour and in the international concentration of capital under the domination of American capital, and this can go so far as to take the form of a transfer of part of the surplus-value it produces to the profit of the latter; secondly, what is more, it is affected, as a result of the induced reproduction of the political and ideological conditions of this dependence, by dissolution effects on its political and ideological autonomy *vis-à-vis* American capital.

On the other hand, however, it is not a mere comprador bourgeoisie. The domination of American capital does not affect the economies of other metropolises in the same fashion as it affects those of the peripheral formations, and the internal bourgeoisie maintains its own economic foundation and base of capital accumulation both within its own social formation, and abroad. Even at the political and ideological level it continues to exhibit its own specific features, linked both to its present situation and to its past as a 'self-centred' imperialist capital; this distinguishes it from the bourgeoisies of the peripheral formations. Through 'peripheral industrialization', nuclei of a domestic bourgeoisie may even appear within peripheral formations, and although these bourgeoisies scarcely match up to the national bourgeoisies of the previous phases of imperialism, they can certainly not be reduced to what Gunder Frank terms 'lumpen-bourgeoisies'. Significant contradictions thus exist between the internal bourgeoisie and American capital. Even if these cannot lead it to adopt positions of effective autonomy or independence towards this capital, they still have their effects on the state apparatuses of these formations in their relations with the American state.

By considering the current forms of alliance (including contradictions) between the imperialist bourgeoisies and American capital, under the latter's hegemony, we can go on to discuss the question of the nation state. The current internationalization of capital neither suppresses nor by-passes the nation states, either in the direction of a peaceful integration of capitals 'above' the state level (since every process of internationalization is effected under the dominance of the capital of a definite country), or in the direction of their extinction by the American super-state, as if American capital purely and simply directed the other imperialist bourgeoisies. This internationalization, on the other hand, deeply affects the politics and institutional forms of these states by including them in a system of interconnections which is in no way confined to the play of external and mutual pressures between juxtaposed states and capitals. These states themselves take charge of the interest of the dominant imperialist capital in its development within the 'national' social formation, i.e. in its complex relation of internalization to the domestic bourgeoisie that it dominates. This system of interconnections does not encourage the constitution of effective supranational or super-state institutional forms of agencies; this would be the case if what was involved was internationalization within a framework of externally juxtaposed states (a framework which had to be superceded). It is rather based, in the first instance, on an induced reproduction of the form of the dominant imperialist power within each national formation and its state.

It is principally by direct means that these states take responsibility for the interests of the dominant capital. Support for American capital is often of the same type as is granted to indigenous capital (public subventions, tax concessions), but it also comprises the support needed by American capital for its further extension outside this formation, and thus it acts as a staging-post. This support can go so far as to help American capital circumvent the American state itself (the anti-trust legislation, for example). The international reproduction of capital under the domination of American capital is supported by the various national states, each state attempting in its own way to latch onto one or other aspect of this process.

This support for the dominant capital is also given indirectly, via industrial policies of states that seek to promote the concentration and international expansion of their own indigenous capital.

* * *

There are still, of course, important contradictions between the domestic bourgeoisies of the imperialist metropolises and American capital, on a whole series of points, and it is these that the various national states take up when they give support, as is most often the case, to their own domestic bourgeoisie (this is also one aspect of the E.E.C.).[1] But it is necessary to go further here and say that these antagonisms do not at present form the principal contradiction within the imperialist ruling classes. The currently dominant form of 'inter-imperialist' contradictions is not that between 'international capital' and 'national capital', or between the imperialist bourgeoisies as juxtaposed entities.

In point of fact, the dependence of indigenous capital on American capital cuts across the various fractions of indigenous capital itself; this is precisely the source of its internal dis-articulation, since the contradictions between American capital and the domestic bourgeoisies are often the complex form in which the contradictions of American capital itself are reproduced within the domestic bourgeoisies. In other words, the contradictions of indigenous capital may be the contradictions of American capital extrapolated via complex mediations, so that today the domestic bourgeoisie is composed of heterogenous and conjunctural elements. The distinction between domestic bourgeoisie and comprador bourgeoisie coincides even less today than was formerly the case with the national bourgeoisie, either to the distinction between non-monopoly capital and monopoly capital, or to that between productive (industrial) capital and banking capital, or finally to that between a bourgeoisie confined to the 'home market' and a bourgeoisie with an expansionist international strategy. (Sectors of this former bourgeoisie can be completely subordinated to American capital and form the spearhead of its penetration into this market, while sectors of the latter, including 'multinational firms' that are predominantly French – Renault, Michelin, etc. – Dutch or even British, may well exhibit a characteristic autonomy towards American capital, and have significant contradictions with it.) This distinction between domestic and comprador bourgeoisie cuts across these others in a direction that depends upon the conjuncture, as is shown by the fluctuations of Gaullist policy. The concept of domestic bourgeoisie is related to the process of internationalization, and does not refer to a bourgeoisie 'enclosed' within a 'national' space.

The national state thus intervenes, in its role as organizer of

---

1. One contemporary form of this support by the national state for its domestic bourgeoisie is provided by the nationalized sector. It would, however, be wrong to believe that this sector functions as an effective national capital: in fact it is also involved in the process of internationalization.

hegemony, in a domestic field already structured by inter-imperialist contradictions, and in which contradictions between the dominant fractions within its social formation are already internationalized. If the state intervenes in favour of certain major indigenous monopolies against others, in favour of certain sectors of indigenous medium capital against others, or in favour of certain fractions of European capital against others, this often amounts simply to indirect intervention in favour of certain fractions or sectors of American capital against other fractions or sectors of American capital, on which the various fractions and sectors of indigenous and European capital depend. Thus the principal contradiction within the imperialist bourgeoisie may, according to the conjuncture, either run within the contradictions of the dominant imperialist capital and the internationalization that this imposes, or it may run within the domestic bourgeoisie and its internal struggles, but it only rarely opposes the domestic bourgeoisie as such to American capital.

It is this dis-articulation and heterogeneity of the domestic bourgeoisie that explains the weak resistance, limited to fits and starts, that the European states have put up to American capital. The new means of real pressure that the American multinationals can exert on the European states (tax evasion, monetary speculation, misuse of customs barriers) are only a secondary element, despite the claims of the dominant ideological tendency that poses the problem in terms of 'national state versus multinational firms'.

This analysis provides the basis for an examination of the problem of the current class configuration of the power bloc, the specific alliance of the politically dominant classes and class fractions, in the imperialist metropolises. On the one hand, this power bloc can scarcely be located any more on a purely national level; the imperialist states take charge not only of the interests of their domestic bourgeoisies, but just as much of the interests of the dominant imperialist capital and those of the other imperialist capitals, as these are articulated within the process of internationalization. On the other hand, however, these 'foreign' capitals do not directly participate as such, i.e. as relatively autonomous social forces, in each of the power blocs involved; the American bourgeoisie and its fractions, the German bourgeoisie and its fractions, are not directly present as such in the French power bloc or vice versa, even if they do act, through various channels, within the French state apparatuses. Their 'presence' in the French power bloc is rather ensured by certain fractions of the French bourgeoisie and by the state of internationalization that affects these, in short, by their internalization and representation within the French bourgeoisie itself, and by the induced reproduction of the dominant imperialist capital in the imperialist metropolises. It is this that explains a whole series of dislocations at the level of hegemony within these power blocs; the hegemonic fractions of the power blocs in these imperialist metropolises are not necessarily those which have the most ties with American capital, although this does not mean that American capital is not present in these power blocs.

We can now specify what it is that distinguishes our conception both from that of 'ultra-imperialism', and from the conceptions of Mandel and the western CP's. As far as the two latter are concerned, they both accept the existence of a national bourgeoisie in the European countries, though they do not define it in the same way. To each, it would seem, his own national bourgeoisie.

For Mandel, this national bourgeoisie is the agent of the great 'European' monopolies, as opposed to what is happening to European medium capital:

> The era of national big capital and of the nation state has not yet been superseded in Western Europe . . . the growing desire to resist American competition, manifest not only in 'autonomous state capitalism' but also clearly expressed by the great European concerns, the increasing consolidation of the E.E.C., and the growing force of supranational state organs within it, are all parallel processes.[2]

It is all here, and it is in no way surprising after these assertions, belied by the facts, that Mandel falls in with the whole current bourgeois propaganda of 'European unity'. However, this in no way prevents him from stating two pages later what he calls a 'paradox':

> Extra stimulus to do this [i.e. to counteract the relapses in European economic integration (sic!) caused by the indecision of national government] is provided by the fact that when European capital interpenetration is lacking, U.S. concerns stand, paradoxically, to profit more from the Common Market than those of Western Europe.

To give him his due, we should note that Mandel has not been the only one to fall into this position. More recently still, we have had the case of two young French 'futurologists', supposedly defending – with reservations – the thesis of the inevitable and imminent demise of American hegemony in the face of 'European power'. To explain the same 'paradox' they fall back on the following facts:

2. E. Mandel, op. cit., pp. 87–8.

'The linguistic obstacles [between the European bourgeoisies] are real ones. But the most important obstacles are institutional: there is still no legislation for European enterprises . . .'[3] (*sic*)

In fact, if we examine the European situation in the light of the above analysis, we shall see that no such 'paradox' results from technical incompetence, legal inadequacies or incompatibilities of temperament. If the European bourgeoisies do not cooperate and do not coordinate their activity *vis-à-vis* American capital, this is a result of the long-run effects on them of the new structure of dependence on American capital itself. The relations of these bourgeoisies among themselves are decentred ones, in so far as they proceed by way of the internationalization of American capital within the bourgeoisies themselves. In fact, each national European state simultaneously defends the interests of the other European bourgeoisies, allowance being made for their competition with its domestic bourgeoisie, but assuming throughout their common state of dependence in relation to American capital.

The arguments of the European Communist Parties, on the other hand, and particularly those of the PCF and its theorists, insist on the interpenetration of the big monopolies and on the domination of American capital. This is an important item to their credit. In the words of Philippe Herzog:

> These points indicate that we should be careful not to characterize the new step as a struggle of 'national' capital against trans- or multinational capital . . . At the present time, the major national monopolies have certain common interests with foreign capital, and both 'resistance' and 'competition' have lost their 'national' character. The groups that confront one another have interests that are partially bound up together, and are in the process of becoming cosmopolitan.[4]

However, the problem here is simply shifted; the PCF still has its own national bourgeoisie, only this is non-monopoly capital or medium capital. This is not the point at which to go into this in detail, but it is quite clear from the PCF argument, which considers that the only currently dominant fraction is that of the big monopolies; these are globally 'cosmopolitan', and exclude medium capital. This medium capital is classified as part of national 'small capital', or even as part of the petty bourgeoisie, and the PCF seeks an alliance (of 'sincere democrats and patriots') with it in order to

3. A. Faire and J.-P. Sebord, *Le Nouveau Déséquilibre mondial*, 1973, p. 156.

4. op. cit., p. 148.

establish an 'advanced democracy' capable of standing up to American capital.[5] Among other things, this analysis ignores the effects of the socialization of the labour process and of how concentration now renders medium capital dependent on big capital.

2. STATE AND NATION

If the state in the imperialist metropolises, though at present undergoing certain modifications, still maintains its character as a national state, this is due among other things to the fact that the state is not a mere tool or instrument of the dominant classes, to be manipulated at will, so that every step that capital took towards internationalization would automatically induce a parallel 'supranationalization' of states. The task of the state is to maintain the unity and cohesion of a social formation divided into classes, and it focuses and epitomizes the class contradictions of the whole social formation in such a way as to sanction and legitimize the interests of the dominant classes and fractions as against the other classes of the formation, in a context of world class contradictions. The problem we are dealing with, therefore, cannot be reduced to a simple contradiction of a mechanistic kind between the base (internationalization of production) and a superstructural cover (national state) which no longer 'corresponds' to it. Superstructural transformations depend on the forms assumed by the class struggle in an imperialist chain marked by the uneven development of its links.

Now we have already seen that the internationalization of capital does not give rise to a genuine transnational merger. This, however, is only one aspect of the problem. Also relevant is what is happening on the working-class side in the European countries. And here, while the struggles of the popular masses are more than ever developing in concrete conjunctures determined on a world basis, and while the establishment of world relations of production and the socialization of labour are objectively reinforcing the international solidarity of the workers, it is still the national form that prevails in these struggles, however international they are in their essence. This is due for one thing to uneven development and the concrete specificity of each social formation; these features are of the very essence of capitalism, contrary to the belief upheld by various ideologies of 'globalization' The particular aspects that these forms assume today, however, are due to the organizations (parties, unions) that are dominant in the European working classes.

We must also take into account, firstly, the petty bourgeoisie

5. This position is expressed by the entire analysis of the *Traité* quoted above: see the following essay.

(which is reproducing itself today in new forms) and the various peasant classes, whose support is indispensable to these states and actively sought by them, and whose class situation leads to a quite specific form of nationalism; secondly, the social categories of the state apparatuses (such as the administrative bureaucracies, personnel of the political parties), for whom the national state remains a source of privileges.

We thus come up against the problem of the persistence of the national state via the effects that it produces on the 'national forms' of class struggle. However, the question of the relation between state and nation which is raised by the national state is not thereby resolved. In fact, if the nation is constitutively bound up with the existence of capitalism, including its imperialist stage, Marxism-Leninism has never confused the state with the nation; it has simply upheld the thesis of the emergence of the 'national state' and the 'national social formation' under capitalism. The problem is now being raised from a different angle: if the current internalization of production and the emergence of world relations of production in no way eliminates the national entity, does this not at least modify the space of the social formation, that is to say, the configuration of the sites of the reproduction process, to the point of breaking up the national social formation and thus severing the ties between state and nation (supra-national state)? In other words, are the sites on which the extended reproduction of the capitalist mode of production takes place, and the nodes of uneven development, still the national social formations? This question is directly related to the problem of the political and ideological conditions of reproduction in the field of class struggle.

In point of fact, the ties between state and nation are not broken, and the basic sites of reproduction and uneven development are still the national social formations, in so far as neither the nation nor the relation between state and nation are reducible to simple economic ties. The nation, in the full complexity of its determination – a unity that is at the same time economic, territorial, linguistic, and one of ideology and symbolism tied to 'tradition' – retains its specific identity as far as the 'national forms' of class struggle are concerned, and in this way the relation of state and nation is maintained. The changes in progress today only affect certain of the elements of this determination, at least in the imperialist metropolises, and they do so to an uneven extent; these thus take the form of modifications of a state that remains, in its inner core, the national state. These modifications are none the less considerable, and they put in question the legal conception of national sovereignty. This involves questions such as: the role that different states assume in the repression of class struggle internationally (NATO, etc.); the extraterritoriality of the functions and interventions of states, which extend into the formations abroad where their capital is deployed; changes in the internal legal systems of each state that are required to cover the internationalization of its interventions; and political and ideological changes in those state apparatuses that are, *par excellence*, based on the structure of the national state, in particular the army.[6]

That being said, there are nevertheless certain currently visible strains between state and nation in the imperialist metropolises with which we are dealing, although not in the sense generally understood by the supranationalization of the state. What we are faced with is not the emergence of a new state over and above the nations, but rather with ruptures of the national unity underlying the existing national states; this is the very important contemporary phenomenon of regionalism, frequently expressed in the form of nationalist resurgences (Brittany, the Basque country, Acquitaine, etc.), which demonstrates that the internationalization of capital is leading more towards a fragmentation of the nation, such as it is historically constituted, than to a supranationalization of the state. This phenomenon is all the more characteristic of the present period in that, far from resulting from the supposed supranational cooperation of European capital against American capital, it corresponds to the extended reproduction of international capital under the domination of American capital within the European countries themselves, and to the new structure of dependence. This leads to a tendency to the internal dis-articulation of the European social formations and of their economies (the accentuation of 'poles of development') which can even lead to cases of domestic colonization under various labels of regional planning.[7] This dis-articulation is what is at the root of the disintegration of the capitalist national unity.

3. THE INTERNATIONALIZATION OF THE STATE AND ITS ECONOMIC ROLE

The current internationalization of capital and the emergence of 'multinational giants' alongside the state cannot be discussed in terms of two entities 'possessing' power and redistributing it. In particular, to argue that the more 'economic power' increases and

6. Alain Joxe, 'La crise générale de la stratégie', in *Frontieres*, no. 9, September 1973, pp. 71 ff.

7. Michel Rocard and others, *Le Marché Commun contre l'Europe*, 1972; and the debate around this book in *Critique socialiste*, October–November 1973.

is concentrated, the more it takes away power from the state, is not only to fail to understand that the state does not possess any power of its own, but also the fact that it intervenes decisively in this very concentration. The current development in no way encroaches on the dominant role of the state in the monopoly capitalist stage.

This dominance of the state corresponds to the considerable growth of its economic functions that is absolutely indispensable to the extended reproduction of big capital. But this is only part of the problem, and in particular it fails to explain why this economic intervention essentially continues to have the national states as its supports. Could it not be said that these economic interventions, while remaining the same in nature, are changing their support, and that the national state is nowadays being deprived of implementing these interventions, to a great degree, in favour of super-state institutions or even an embryonic supranational state?

There can be no doubt that forms of 'coordination' of the economic policies of different states have proved to be a contemporary necessity (various international institutions, including the E.E.C.). But these institutional forms do not in fact amount to apparatuses supplanting the national states or superimposed on them. And the reasons for this include one that we have not so far touched on, i.e. that these economic interventions by the state are not, as a well-established tradition would have it, neutral technical functions imposed by the necessities of a 'production' that is itself considered as neutral in character. The economic functions of the state are in fact expressions of its overall political role in exploitation and class domination; they are by their nature articulated with its repressive and ideological roles in the field of class struggle of a social formation, which brings us back once more to the points made above. It is impossible to separate the various interventions of the state and their aspects, in such a way as to envisage the possibility of an effective transfer of its 'economic functions' to supranational or super-state apparatuses, while the national state would retain only a repressive or ideological role; at the very most, there is sometimes a delegation in the exercise of these functions.

In fact, by looking in this direction, one loses sight of the real tendencies at work: the internalized transformations of the national state itself, aimed at taking charge of the internalization of public functions on capital's behalf. One thus ends up by defending one's 'own' national state against 'cosmopolitan institutions'. In fact, however, these international institutional forms are in no way 'added on' to the national states (an expression dear to the PCF),[8] but are

8. J.-P. Delilez, 'Internationalisation', op. cit., p. 69.

precisely the expression of their internalized transformations. These transformations do not just involve the economic interventions of the national state, but also the repressive and ideological aspects by which these interventions are accomplished.

This conception of the neutral and technical 'economic functions' of the contemporary state is nevertheless that of the Western CP's, particularly the PCF (the state as an organic factor of production, the state forming part of the economic base, etc.),[9] in their theory of 'state monopoly capitalism'. These functions, which in themselves are held to be neutral, are seen as currently 'misappropriated' in favour of the big monopolies alone, but capable of being utilized, by a simple change in state power and without the state machine being smashed, in favour of the popular masses. One would imagine that this analysis would have led the PCF to adopt the theory of the supranational state in the context of an internationalization of production; if this has not happened (or at least not yet), it is because the PCF sees the imperialist chain as a simple juxtaposition and addition of the various national state monopoly capitalisms. The PCF thus insists that 'international capital' inserts itself into each national social formation 'by embracing and adapting to the specificities of its state monopoly capitalism', while in reality it is the specific structure of each social formation that is reorganized with regard to the internationalization of capital. In the PCF version, the functions that the national state performs with regard to the internationalization of capital are not themselves seen as deeply transforming and changing this state, but simply as added on to its 'national' functions. It follows that, by a defence of the national state, supported by the 'national bourgeoisie/medium capital' against 'cosmopolitan' capital, these state functions can be used for a genuine 'international cooperation' imposed by the requirements of production, without the state apparatus being smashed.

To return to our own problem, capital which overflows its national limits certainly has recourse to national states – not only to its own state of origin, but to other states as well. This gives rise to a complex distribution of the role of the state in the international reproduction of capital under the domination of American capital, which can lead to the exercise of the state functions becoming decentred and shifting among their supports, which essentially remain the national states. According to the conjuncture, any one or other of the metro-

9. In particular Herzog, in his *Politique économique* already quoted, pp. 35, 65, 139 ff. See the following essay.

politan national states may assume responsibility for this or that
international intervention in the reproduction process, and for the
maintenance of the system as a whole.

4. THE ROLE OF THE STATE IN THE INTERNATIONAL
REPRODUCTION OF SOCIAL CLASSES

The various state functions that we have been concerned with so far
all focus on the extended reproduction of the capitalist mode of
production; the determinant moment of this reproduction involves
the extended reproduction of social classes, of social relations. The
state has a specific role of its own in this process, intervening on the
one hand in the reproduction of the places of the social classes, on
the other hand in the 'training and subjection' of agents to render
them suitable for occupying these places, and thus in the distribution
of agents among these places.

Now if it is certainly the national state that still fulfils this role,
and if this role still depends on the specificity of the social formation
and the class struggle, it is none the less the case that it is nowadays
accomplished to an ever greater extent in the context of the
imperialist social division of labour and a capitalist reproduction
of social classes that is global in scale. The role of the European
national states in this respect (in such matters as the educational
apparatus, retraining) has among other tasks that of reproducing the
new forms of division of labour established between the United
States and Europe. The forms of extended reproduction of the
working class, its skills and its composition (into labourers, semi-
skilled workers, etc.), the forms and rhythms of reproduction of the
new petty bourgeoisie (e.g. technicians, or engineers), of the exodus
from the countryside or of immigrant labour in Europe, and the role
of the European national states in this respect, to give only some
examples, depend closely on this division of labour between the
United States and Europe, which consists of technological gaps,
differences in wage levels and differentials, forms of the socialization
of labour within integrated production, in which the aspect of disqualification of labour which accompanies the present aspect of
highly skilled labour tends to become located outside of the United
States, with Europe moreover being confined to relatively inferior
forms of technology.

These examples do no more than indicate the problem; but they
do lead us to a more general thesis, in so far as they demonstrate the
limitations of a conception that is very widespread today (represented in particular by Baran and Sweezy) which sees the United
States as the model or prefigured pattern of the future towards

which Europe is inevitably and unambiguously tending. This theory is valuable only as an analogy, since it neglects the new cleavages of dependence which have been inserted between Europe and the United States. To take, for example, the celebrated 'expansion of the tertiary sector' in the United States, over which a good deal of ink has flowed, it is clear that the rhythms and forms of this development, which are quite different in the United States and in Europe, are due to the place that the United States currently enjoys as the world's administrative centre, and not to a mere 'delay' on the part of Europe along the American path, such that it is bound sooner or later to catch up. In order to examine the social classes and state apparatuses in the imperialist countries, one cannot limit analysis to the case of the United States and simply treat this formation in the same exemplary fashion as Marx did in his time with Great Britain; the other imperialist metropolises, and Europe in particular, form a specific field and object.

One final question should be mentioned here, in view of its importance and implications. The changes in the role of the European national states, designed to take charge of the international reproduction of capital under the domination of American capital, as well as the political and ideological conditions of this reproduction, involve decisive institutional transformations in the state apparatuses. There can be no doubt that, on the one hand, the particular forms of 'strong state' (authoritarian police-state) that are in the process of being established, to a greater or lesser extent, throughout Europe, and on the other hand, the accumulation of conditions for a possible process of fascisization, are the expression both of the class struggle within these formations and of their place in the new structure of dependence.

3

Conclusion:
The Present Stage and its
Perspectives

A few final points are necessary.[1]

1. The first point concerns the stages of the present phase of imperialism, and more particularly its current stage. We must refer first of all to the historical establishment of American hegemony, and the forms that it has assumed. Dating as it did from the Second World War, it took on the concrete characteristics of the period. American hegemony, established in a period in which the European economies were destroyed, thus exhibited certain peculiar features which are now in the process of being eliminated (for example the role of the dollar). Since that time, the European economies have been 'reconstructed' and have progressively acquired a power that they did not previously enjoy. In this context, it is clear that American hegemony is today 'declining' in relation to the exceptional forms that it assumed during the preceding step.

On the other hand, political factors have assumed a decisive importance here, precisely in so far as the role of politics is a quite particular one under imperialism. The smarting defeat of the United States in Vietnam, and the upsurge of national liberation struggles in the dominated formations in general, have contributed significantly to the present decline in certain forms of American hegemony.

2. But let us look more closely at this decline, with particular reference to the foundations of American hegemony in Europe.

In point of fact, the current decline in this hegemony is only

1. The preceding essay, including this conclusion that follows it, was published in *Les Temps Modernes* in February 1973, in the very midst of the 'dollar crisis' and before the 'oil crisis' broke out. Subsequent events have fully confirmed my analysis.

relative to the quite exceptional step of the relative destruction of the European economies and its aftermath. These steps must, however, be considered within the periodization of the present phase, and its principal features. In other words, the decline must be understood in the context of an entire phase of American hegemony. It should certainly not be seen as revealing a uniform tendency that, projected exponentially as it is by various contemporary 'futurologists', would signal the end of American hegemony here and now, or even its inevitable end in the short run.

In this respect, it is necessary to select the determinant criteria, and these can only be those of the export of capital, chiefly productive capital. Although American hegemony is generally declining in comparison with the exceptional forms that it previously assumed, it has, however, become stronger from this point of view; to tell the truth, it has advanced *pari passu* with the reconstruction of the European economies. This was certainly the main factor in reactivating inter-imperialist contradictions, which previously seemed to have more or less 'subsided'. But this reactivation in no way signified, in itself, the end of American hegemony. It is only in the theory of ultra-imperialism that this hegemony is identified with the complete absence of inter-imperialist contradictions and a 'pacification' of the imperialist metropolises under American hegemony, such that one could speak of the end of this hegemony as soon as contradictions were reactivated.[2] All indications are, on the contrary, that this reactivation of inter-imperialist contradictions at present signifies only a turn in American hegemony in relation to the preceding stage, with Europe coming to reoccupy the place of a secondary imperialism which has fallen to it in the present phase.

These features must lastly be located in a global context, and I should like to mention here just one element of considerable importance: the tremendous economic agreements recently concluded between the U.S.A. and U.S.S.R., an index of the strengthening of American hegemony over Europe, which long enjoyed a monopoly of trade with the Soviet bloc.

I do not intend to spend more time here refuting the various futurological analyses of the relative 'strength' or 'weakness' of the American and European economies, analyses which pose the question of inter-imperialist contradictions in terms of the 'competitive-

---

2. There is no better example of this than Sweezy himself, who, after the first devaluation of the dollar, completely reversed his position, and is now preaching the imminent end of American hegemony. We can now see how these successive devaluations play the role of an offensive weapon for American imperialism.

ness' and actual 'competition' between 'national economies'. In general, these arguments are restricted to 'economic criteria' which, considered in themselves, do not mean very much (rates of growth, of increase in GNP, etc.), and extrapolate from these in a quite arbitrary manner, particularly in so far as they ignore the class struggle. The question that now has to be considered is rather that of the present crisis of imperialism. What is currently in crisis is not directly American hegemony, under the impact of the 'economic power' of the other metropolises, whose rise would, according to some people have erected them automatically into 'equivalent counter-imperialisms', but rather imperialism as a whole, as a result of the world class struggles that have already reached the metropolitan zone itself. In the present phase of the internationalization of capitalist relations, this crisis does not either automatically or inevitably put in question the hegemony of American imperialism over the other metropolises, but rather affects the imperialist countries as a whole, and thus finds expression both at their head, and in the sharpening of inter-imperialist contradictions. In other words, it is not the hegemony of American imperialism that is in crisis, but the whole of imperialism under this hegemony.

It follows that there is no solution to this crisis, as the European bourgeoisies themselves are perfectly aware, by these bourgeoisies attacking the hegemony of American capital. The question for them, faced with the rising struggle of the popular masses in Europe itself, is rather to reorganize a hegemony that they still accept, taking account of the reactivation and intensification of inter-imperialist contradictions; what the battle is actually over is the share of the cake. The recent vagaries of the E.E.C. have shown this perfectly well. What we have seen over the last two years, and particularly with the dollar crisis, is a process which, as all observers agree, resembles a series of successive withdrawals by the E.E.C. in the face of American 'demands'; there is no need here to go over these in detail (monetary policy, attitudes towards the 'oil crisis', etc.). These withdrawals are generally interpreted as an 'offensive by American capital designed to restore its tottering hegemony', and several observers have been quite carried away with conjectures and forecasts about the coming 'rounds', meticulously counting up the points scored by the 'adversaries'. In fact, however, there is nothing of the kind, and these people simply cannot see the wood for the trees; American capital has no need to re-establish its hegemony, for it has never lost it. This hegemony is indeed the basis of all the contemporary developments, which can only be understood in this light. The E.E.C.'s apparent progress of one step forwards, two steps back, means nothing more than a certain reorganization of this hegemony in the present context of the intensification of inter-imperialist contradictions. I would even go so far as to say that what is at present taking place, far from signalling an attempt by American capital to 're-establish' its hegemony, is rather an offensive on its part to undermine even the place of a secondary imperialism that Europe had succeeded in occupying under its hegemony.

This leads us directly to a further assertion: the issue of this crisis, and there are crises that die hard, will depend on the struggle of the popular masses. And in this struggle, given the present phase of imperialism and the current conjuncture, it is the struggle of the popular masses in Europe against their own bourgeoisies and their own state that is fundamental.

Part Two

The Bourgeoisies: their Contradictions and their Relations to the State

The Problem as it Stands Today

The previous essay has shown that the bourgeoisies of the imperialist metropolises, and the European bourgeoisies in particular, can only be analysed in the context of the internationalization of capitalist relations that characterizes the present phase of imperialism. Although the domestic bourgeoisies of these metropolises are caught up in the extrapolated relations of American capital, this does not mean that they do not constitute a specific field, with its own internal contradictions, in their relationship to the state. It is this aspect on which we now have to focus, and it will enable us to explain in more detail a series of questions that were no more than raised in the previous section. These questions will now be examined with regard to the present phase of monopoly capitalism, which is simply the present phase of imperialism as it appears within each social formation and its own field of specific contradictions.

It is only in their unity and their concrete articulation that these two aspects of the problem, the relationship between the domestic bourgeoisies and American capital on the one hand, and the specific contradictions of the domestic bourgeoisies on the other, can explain the reality of a social formation. It is nevertheless legitimate to discuss each of these two aspects in relative separation from the other; the basic characteristics of the present phase of imperialism are no more just the transposition, onto the level of international capitalist relations, of the specific characteristics of the present phase of monopoly capitalism within each imperialist metropolis, than the latter are the mere expression of this internationalization.

I

In the stage of 'competitive capitalism', the cycle of the extended reproduction of social capital involved the differentiation of distinct fractions of this capital, thus giving rise to distinct 'moments' of the reproduction process – productive or industrial capital in the strict sense, banking capital and commercial capital. The effect of this was to divide the capitalist class into different fractions, the industrial bourgeoisie, banking bourgeoisie and commercial bourgeoisie, a situation that corresponded to definite forms of the capitalist relations of production in this stage.

The important point to note here is the existence of contradictions and struggles between these various fractions of the bourgeoisie in those capitalist formations, which were characterized by the dominance of the competitive stage. This was all the more the case in that large landowners deriving their incomes from ground rent were also to be found in this stage, and were often present on the terrain of political domination: this stage was that of the establishment of the dominance of the capitalist mode of production (CMP) over other modes and forms of production in the capitalist social formations, which meant that the effects of conservation still prevailed over the dissolution effects that the CMP imposed on these modes and forms. The large landowners were thus generally met with in two forms: (a) either as a class distinct from the bourgeoisie, a derivative of the feudal mode of production which existed alongside capitalism in these formations (the classic cases being East Prussia and Southern Italy); (b) alternatively, when the dissolution effects were sufficiently advanced as a result of the introduction of capitalism in agriculture, as a distinct fraction of the bourgeoisie (this was the English case).[1] The existence of these contradictions and struggles already had certain consequences at the level of economic class domination. It is certainly true that from the time that the CMP establishes its dominance over the other modes and forms of production in a capitalist formation, it is the cycle of productive/industrial capital, which produces surplus-value and within which the capitalist relations of production are constructed, that determines the overall features of the reproduction of capital in such a formation; this is precisely the meaning of Marx's reproduction schemas in *Capital*. But this does not prevent the preponderant place in economic domination being occupied, according to the different stages, and often alternately, by one or the other fraction of the bourgeoisie: the industrial bourgeoisie itself, the commercial bourgeoisie or the banking bourgeoisie. On this domination will depend the concrete

1. I showed previously, together with certain other writers, that the big landowners based on ground rent, whom Marx wrongly treated in the final chapter of *Capital* vol. III as an autonomous and distinct class deriving from the CMP, do not in fact belong to this (*Cahiers marxistes-léninistes*, 1967; *Political Power and Social Classes*, pp. 168–9, 231).

path, the demeanour and the rhythm that the development of capitalism in this formation will follow.

As far as the terrain of political domination is concerned, this is also occupied not by one single class or class fraction, but by several dominant classes and fractions. These classes and fractions form a specific alliance on this terrain, the power bloc, generally functioning under the leadership of one of the dominant classes or fractions, the hegemonic class or fraction. This class or fraction, which can in no way be identified with that which holds the preponderant position in economic domination, can itself vary with the different stages; it may be the industrial bourgeoisie, the commercial bourgeoisie or the banking bourgeoisie, depending on the concrete stages and turns of the class struggle.

We must now make an important point about certain current interpretations of the periodization of the CMP in its extended reproduction.[2] According to these interpretations, this periodization would be based on the determining role, in the reproduction cycle of the social capital, first of commercial capital, then of industrial capital, and finally of banking and financial capital. This infallibly leads to a conception of 'phases' marked by the necessary successive domination and hegemony first of the commercial bourgeoisie, then of the industrial bourgeoisie, and finally of the banking bourgeoisie, thus also compounding, in the latter case, the old error of identifying monopoly capitalism with the domination and hegemony of the banks. Besides the fact that this interpretation ultimately obscures imperialism as a specific stage of capitalism,[3] it leads to accepting the possibility of the entire process of reproduction of social capital on an extended scale being determined by the cycle of commodity capital, and thus, during a certain 'period' of this extended reproduction, by the cycle of commercial capital. This entails radically undermining Marx's analysis of the determining role of production. In fact, this particular interpretation is based on a more general characteristic of such theories: on the privileged (or even principal) role that they attribute, contrary to Marx, to circulation. It is precisely this that leads them to allot a privileged place to the cycle of money capital in monopoly capitalism.

* * *

2. Among others, that of C. Palloix, *L'Économie mondiale capitaliste* and *Firmes multinationales et procès d'internationalisation*, op. cit. See also the works cited by G. Dhoquois, P.-P. Rey, etc.

3. The most typical example of this is Gunder Frank and the role he attributes to the expansion of 'market relationships' at the beginning of capitalism.

This is a problem of decisive importance, and we must dwell on it for a moment. It is of course true that the process of valorization of capital cannot be understood in terms of the immediate production process alone, as Marx shows in the second volume of *Capital*: this would lead to the very 'productivism' that Marx criticizes, particularly in his remarks on the Physiocrats. This process can only be understood in terms of the reproduction of the aggregate social capital, in which, via the mediation of the market, the various fractions of capital appear as 'moments' of the reproduction process. Capital as a social relation cannot be apprehended in a production process considered in isolation from the process of circulation: the conversion of productive capital into money capital and back again by the mediation of commodity capital.

This being so, it is none the less true that the reproduction of the social capital as a whole is based, for Marx, on the determining role of 'production', understood as the articulation of the relations of production onto the labour process, thus marking out the places of social classes and the class struggle. Social classes, as they first appear in the process of circulation and realization (Marx's few sentences on social classes in *Capital*, classes related to ground-rent, profit and wages) are based, in their structural determination, on the relations of production. In other words, capitalist exploitation in the form of the production of surplus-value, which is realized by way of commodities, and by the existence of labour-power itself as a commodity, is based on the relations of production specific to capitalism; it is precisely there that the place of these classes, their reproduction and the class struggle, can be read off and deciphered.

The determining role of productive capital in the reproduction of the aggregate social capital has decisive implications for the determination of social classes, as we shall see fully in the following essay. In fact, it is only in terms of this role that Marx's analysis of the working class can be understood, a class that is not defined by wage labour (purchase and sale of labour-power, i.e. the 'wage-earning class'), but by productive labour, which under capitalism means labour that directly produces surplus-value. This is why, in Marx's theory, it is only those wage-earners who depend on productive capital who form part of the working class, since it is only productive capital that produces surplus-value. Wage-earners who depend on the sphere of the circulation and realization of surplus-value do not form part of the working class, since these forms of capital, and the labour that depends on them, do not produce surplus-value.

Those writers, on the other hand, who defend the principal role of circulation in the reproduction of the social capital (C. Palloix, P.-P. Rey, etc.) and who are thereby linked with A. Emmanuel and

A. Gunder Frank, are necessarily led to the conclusion that class relations only appear as such, in the last analysis, in the circulation of capital, in market relationships (in the purchase and sale of labour-power).[4] It is clear that this conclusion leads, among other things, precisely to the theory of the 'wage-earning class', i.e. to including in the working class all non-productive wage-earners.

To return to the problem in hand. For Marx, the determinant role of productive capital depends on the fact that it is this alone that produces surplus-value. This is of course the result of a very complex process of reasoning on Marx's part, through which he extricated himself from the 'superficial' sphere of market relationships and the whole pre-Marxist political economy based on the 'space of circulation'. In *Capital* Marx says:

> The first theoretical treatment of the modern mode of production – the mercantile system – proceeded necessarily from the superficial phenomena of the circulation process as individualized in the movements of merchant's capital, and therefore grasped only the appearance of matters. Partly because merchant's capital is the first free state of existence of capital in general. And partly because of the overwhelming influence which it exerted during the first revolutionizing period of feudal production – the genesis of modern production. The real science of modern economy only begins when the theoretical analysis passes from the process of circulation to the process of production.

And again:

> Industrial capital is the only mode of existence of capital in which not only the appropriation of surplus-value, or surplus-product, but simultaneously its creation is a function of capital. *Therefore with it the capitalist character of production is a necessity. Its existence implies the class antagonism between capitalists and wage-labourers* . . . (my emphasis: N.P.) Money-capital and commodity-capital, so far as they function as vehicles of particular branches of business, side by side with industrial

4. C. Palloix, *Firmes multinationales*, pp. 112 ff. and 146 ff., who follows in this respect P.-P. Rey: 'The ultimate secret of the capitalist relation of production is that it has got itself incorporated as a simple moment of a sub-ensemble of the circulation process', 'Sur l'articulation des modes de production', in *Problèmes de Planification*, no. 13–14, p. 95; the effect of this on Rey is that he pays exclusive attention to the wage-form. Confusions such as these also have wider repercussions: for example, the various current critiques of the so-called 'consumer society', critiques centred around the commodity-form (particularly, in France, the analysis of Baudrillard).

capital, are nothing but modes of existence of the different func-
tional forms now assumed, now discarded by industrial capital in
the sphere of circulation – modes which, due to social division of
labour, have attained independent existence and been developing
one-sidedly.[5]

It would be easy enough to give several quotations along the
same lines, but the matter is already perfectly clear. We should
particularly note the role that Marx attributes to the cycle of commercial capital (commodity capital) in the phase of transition from
feudalism to capitalism, a phase that Marx refers to elsewhere as the
period of manufacture. Precisely during this phase, however, there
is no extended reproduction of capital; this only comes about after
the transition to capitalism is achieved, being contemporary and
co-substantial with the establishment of the dominance of the CMP
over the other modes and forms of production, i.e. with the transition
from the formal 'subsumption' of labour-power and means of labour
to capital to its real 'subsumption', and to the control by capital of
the political and ideological conditions of its reproduction. This
extended reproduction, which opens the first *stage* of capitalism,
competitive capitalism as distinct from the transitional manufacturing phase, is characterized by the determination of the overall
circulation of capital by the cycle of productive capital.

However, the determinant role of productive capital in the
extended reproduction of capital and in the valorization of the social
capital as a whole, does not mean that the commercial bourgeoisie
may not predominate, both in economic domination and political
hegemony, at the competitive stage of the social formations in which
the CMP has established its dominance. During this same stage, this
role may also fall to industrial capital in the strict sense, or to banking capital. Marx himself demonstrated this in his political works,
and particularly those on France (*The Class Struggles in France*,
the *Eighteenth Brumaire*, *The Civil War in France*).

We can thus see the real distance separating these analyses from
those current ones that we have mentioned. It is not by chance that
these latter lead to a radical subversion of Leninism, in this case the
Leninist conception of imperialism and monopoly capitalism,
generally taking the form of a common rejection of both Lenin and
Rosa Luxemburg, under cover of an alleged 'return' to Marx. I am
of course aware here of simplifying problems that are exceedingly
complex: problems that include Lenin's ambiguous relationship
with Hilferding, his relationship to Rosa Luxemburg's arguments,
and also certain problems in Marx himself. All these are problems

5. *Capital* vol. III, p. 331 and vol. II, p. 55 (Moscow editions).

that in many respects remain open, and which it is not the purpose of the present text to dwell on. But despite this note of caution, which is not merely verbal, I still hold to what seems to me the essential point. Lenin's analysis is distinct from that bf Rosa Luxemburg, who gives a privileged place to circulation and commodity capital, and also – despite his ambiguities – distinct from that of Hilferding, who gives a privileged place to banking capital, identifying this with finance capital. Lenin's analysis is based on the determinant role of productive capital. Lenin in fact advanced Marxist theory – not simply the theory of imperialism, but Marxist theory in general – by extricating it completely from a certain conception of the 'market' and of 'market relationships', which is sometimes ambiguously present even in Marx.

Furthermore, by ascribing this decisive importance to the relations of production and to the social division of labour that they involve, it is possible to arrive at the fundamental question: the reproduction of capital is not merely the circulation of the aggregate social capital (the celebrated 'economic space'), but also involves the reproduction of the political and ideological conditions under which this reproduction takes place. To criticize the technicist conception of the productive forces does not mean restoring in any form the primacy of circulation and thus falling back into pre-Marxist conceptions; it means restoring the primacy of the relations of production in their direct relationship to the political and ideological conditions of their reproduction. In other words, the reproduction of capital as a social relation is not simply located in the 'moments' of the cycle: productive capital – commodity capital – money capital, but rather in the reproduction of social classes and of the class struggle, in the full complexity of their determination.

II

We can now raise the first important question involving the role of the capitalist state as this existed in the stage of competitive capitalism, i.e. in its most simple form. On a terrain of political domination occupied by several classes and class fractions and divided by internal contradictions, the capitalist state, while predominantly representing the interests of the hegemonic class or fraction (itself variable), enjoys a relative autonomy with respect to that class and fraction as well as to the other classes and fractions of the power bloc. One reason for this is that its task is to ensure the general political interest of the power bloc as a whole, organizing the 'unstable equilibrium of compromise' (Gramsci) among its components under the leadership of the hegemonic class or fraction; the other reason is that it organizes this hegemony with respect to the social formation as a whole, thus also with respect to the dominated classes, according to the specific forms that their struggles assume under capitalism. This relative autonomy is inscribed in the very structure of the capitalist state by the relative 'separation' of the political and the economic that is specific to capitalism; it is in no way a function of the intrinsic nature of the state or 'political instance' as such, but rather derives from the separation and dispossession of the direct producers from their means of production that characterizes capitalism. In this respect, this relative autonomy is simply the necessary condition for the role of the capitalist state in class representation and in the political organization of hegemony.

The correspondence between the state on the one hand, which ensures the social formation's cohesion by keeping the struggles that develop it within the limits of the mode of production and by reproducing its social relations, and the interests of the hegemonic class or fraction on the other hand, is not established by means of a simple identification or reduction of the state to this fraction. The state is not an instrumental entity existing for itself, it is not a thing, but the condensation of a balance of forces. The correspondence in question is established rather in terms of organization and representation: the hegemonic class or fraction, beyond its immediate economic interests which are of the moment or at least short-term, must undertake to defend the overall political interest of the classes and fractions that constitute the power bloc, and thus its own long-term political interest. It must unite itself and the power bloc under its leadership. In Gramsci's profound intuition, it is the capitalist state with all its apparatuses, and not just the bourgeois political parties, that assumes an analogous role, with respect to the power bloc, to that of the working-class party with respect to the popular alliance, the 'people'.

The power relations within the power bloc are thus crystallized by way of the concrete articulation of the branches of the repressive state apparatus and the ideological state apparatuses, in the specific relationships that these maintain with the various dominant classes and fractions. On this articulation depends, among other things, the forms assumed by the capitalist state. These forms thus depend, in this respect, on the precise relations between the dominant classes and fractions, which are themselves the effects of the principal contradiction, that between the bourgeoisie and the working class.

The basic question is thus already raised. Are these characteristics of the power bloc and the capitalist state, together with the analyses of the Marxist classics on this subject, valid only for competitive capitalism? Now although substantial modifications have taken place with the monopoly capitalist stage, and especially in its present phase, this is not the case. This is what I shall try to demonstrate, by considering the current modifications more closely.

The monopoly capitalist stage, the stage of imperialism, is certainly marked by important changes in the general role of the state, with particular reference to what are referred to as the state's 'economic functions', that is to say its role in the reproduction of the relations of production themselves.

In order to come to grips with these changes, a few preliminary points must be clarified:

1. As against a simplistic conception of the role of the state, which bases the distinction between the repressive state apparatus and the ideological state apparatuses on the fact that the state has only a repressive role (exercise of political violence) and an ideological one (inculcation of the dominant ideology), performed predominantly by the repressive and the ideological apparatuses respectively, it must be stressed that the state always has a direct economic role in the reproduction of the relations of production: direct insofar as it is not limited to simple cases of repression and ideological inculcation in the economic sphere. However, this economic role is not a technical or neutral function of the state; it is always governed by political class domination. It is in this sense that it is always exercised under the principal aspect of either political repression or ideological inculcation, by way of the repressive apparatus or the ideological apparatuses, and it is precisely in this way that it is possible to uphold the distinction between these apparatuses. Thus to speak of the state's repressive apparatus and ideological apparatuses in no way means that the state has no role other than a repressive and an ideological one. This is why it is not legitimate to add to these apparatuses a state 'economic apparatus' distinct from the others (for example the planning commission in contemporary France). This would be necessary to provide in some way for the economic functions of the state if one considered that the repressive apparatus had only a repressive role, and the ideological apparatuses only the role of ideological inculcation. This would lead precisely to the position that there are on the one hand the state's functions of ideology and political repression, and on the other hand neutral and technical state functions; but this conception is just as false as that of considering that the state has only a repressive and an ideological role.

2. In the competitive capitalist stage the capitalist state (the liberal state) always played an economic role; the image of the

liberal state being simply the gendarme or night watchman of a capitalism that 'worked by itself' is a complete myth. This myth is part of the same error that gives rise to an economist reading of Marx's writings on reproduction in the second volume of *Capital*, according to which the reproduction of capitalism would be restricted to an 'economic space' functioning somehow 'by itself', by simple self-regulation. From taxation through to factory legislation, from customs duties to the construction of economic infrastructure such as railways, the liberal state always performed significant economic functions, though of course not to the same degree in all the capitalist social formations – the role of the state was far more important in Germany and France than in Great Britain, for example. Marx himself outlines in *Capital* the shadowy presence of the liberal state's interventions in the economy.

If it is possible to speak of a specific non-intervention of this state into the economy, this is only in order to contrast it with the role of the state in the stage of monopoly capitalism, the 'interventionist state' which Lenin already had in mind in his analysis of imperialism. The difference between this and the state of competitive capitalism is not, as we shall see, a mere quantitative one. In the stage of monopoly capitalism, the role of the state in its decisive intervention into the economy is not restricted essentially to the reproduction of what Engels termed the 'general conditions' of the production of surplus-value; the state is also involved in the actual process of the extended reproduction of capital as a social relation.

Furthermore, as soon as it is accepted that the reproduction of capitalist relations is not confined to the economic space, the very notion of the 'conditions' of production is put in question. This notion tends to imply that under capitalism, political and ideological relations (the *conditions*: the state) and the economic space (the relations of production) are in principle external to each other in a water-tight fashion.[6] This idea of the 'conditions' of production must in fact be located in the context of Marx's analysis, where he posited, as specific to the capitalist mode of production (CMP) in relation to 'pre-capitalist' modes (particularly the feudal), the characteristic 'separation' of the political and the economic, whereas these appeared in pre-capitalist modes as closely interwoven. This separation, however, does not imply any kind of constitutional

6. Engels in fact writes of the 'general external conditions' (*die allgemeine äussere Bedingungen*) of production: *Anti-Dühring*, Marx-Engels-Werke vol. 20, p. 260 (English edition, Moscow, 1962, p. 380). On this subject, see also J. Hirsch, in Hirsch and others, *Probleme einer materialistischen Staatstheorie*, 1973.

externality under capitalism, including its competitive stage, between politics and ideology (the conditions) and the economic (relations of production). This separation is simply the necessary and specific form, in the reproduction of capitalism through all its stages, of the presence of politics and ideology *within* the relations of production.

This relation of 'separation' is itself modified, though not abolished, in the monopoly stage, a stage that involves certain shifts in the limits between politics and ideology, on the one hand, and the economic space on the other; the extended reproduction of capitalism transforms the actual sites of this process. In other words, these modifications affect the very configuration and constitution of the fields in question, i.e. those of the economic space and of its 'conditions' respectively. A whole series of domains and functions which, in the competitive stage, formed part of the 'conditions' of production (which does not mean that they were in any sense genuinely external to it), now directly belong to the valorization of capital and its reproduction on an extended scale. The state's contemporary interventions in this respect, e.g. in 'living conditions' outside of work, thus form so many direct economic interventions by the state in the reproduction of the relations of production. If we are at present witnessing a characteristic expansion of the domains of politics and state intervention, this is precisely insofar as these coincide with the expansion of the space of capital's valorization.[7]

The effect this has is to alter the state's role, and such a change defines the stages into which the CMP's structure is periodized, most specifically the break between competitive and monopoly capitalism. I had indicated this problem by pointing out that monopoly capitalism is characterized by the displacement of dominance within the CMP from the economic to the political, i.e. to the state, while the competitive stage is marked by the fact that the economic played the dominant role in addition to being determinant.[8]

It is evident that the displacement of dominance must be seen in its relation to the CMP's structure in particular, because it is in its very reproduction that the displacement arises and marks the division into stages. This displacement cannot be located in the same way as the difference between determination and dominance in other modes

7. See below, pp. 156 ff.

8. *Political Power and Social Classes*, pp. 51 ff. See also Bettelheim, 'Preface' to the French edition of Baran and Sweezy, *Capitalisme monopoliste*, and 'Theoretical Remarks' in Emmanuel, *Unequal Exchange*, p. 314.

of production, as for example in the feudal; here the economic is determinant, while the religious aspect of ideology is dominant. This displacement does not remove the separation which is typical of the CMP between the political and the economic, in contrast to what is argued by certain analyses of state monopoly capitalism, namely that the state is today part of the base. The implications of this view will be seen in a moment.[9]

Taking into account the specific structure of the CMP and the relations of production that characterize it, the dominant role is assigned as a function of the extended reproduction of capital and its valorization; it is the decisive intervention of the state in this process that confers on it the dominant role. In other words, it is the very functioning of the economic relations of the CMP (the extended reproduction of capital) and their own contradictions that determines, in the monopoly capitalist stage, the shift of dominance towards the state. This means that this shift and the 'economic role' of the state in monopoly capitalism are related:

(a) to the changes in the capitalist relations of production that characterize monopoly capitalism and its phases;

(b) to the type and forms of intensive domination that the CMP, in the stage of monopoly capitalism and according to the different phases of this stage, has to exercise over other modes and forms of production, including that of competitive capitalism, both within each social formation and on the international scale, in order to suppress its contradictions and assure its reproduction.

By examining these factors it will be possible to establish and elucidate the dominant role of the state in the stage of monopoly capitalism.

III

These transformations in the role of the state are thus articulated to changes that have overtaken the bourgeoisie itself in the stage of monopoly capitalism. Contrary to how a very widespread line of thought would have it, these transformations cannot be analysed by a direct examination of how the state is related to the 'economic system', but only by way of the changes in class relations. In this respect, a whole series of points can be raised: what are the new forms of contradiction and division into fractions that have affected the bourgeoisies, and to what extent do they undermine the various

9. This is, moreover, the reason for keeping the term 'intervention' to describe the state's action in the economy, on condition that this term is not understood in the sense of an essential externality between state and economy.

fractions of the bourgeoisie that existed in the stage of competitive capitalism? Can one still speak, in the monopoly capitalist stage, and in particular in its present phase, of a power bloc comprising several bourgeois fractions which occupy the terrain of political domination? Can one as a result still speak of a relative autonomy of the state in relation to a hegemonic fraction, with the state guaranteeing, under new forms, the general political interests of this power alliance?

These questions are of paramount political importance. We may get some idea of them by briefly reviewing (necessarily schematically) the current positions of the western CP's, and particularly the PCF, on the subject, i.e. on 'state monopoly capitalism'.[10] These positions serve as a basis for the current strategy of an 'anti-monopoly alliance' and of an 'advanced democracy'. This analysis makes the same type of error as that which we met with in the previous essay with respect to its position on the internationalization of capitalist relations, this time in relation to the domestic bourgeoisie and its relationship to the state. But the error now shows through much more clearly, and it is therefore at this point that we should pause to consider it. It has three main aspects to it:

(a) Contemporary changes, and particularly the 'merging' of capital and the massive domination of big monopoly capital, mean that one can no longer speak of a power bloc. The terrain of political domination is seen as currently occupied by the big monopoly capitalist fraction alone; the rest of the bourgeoisie, being excluded, is thus placed alongside the dominated classes. In point of fact, the PCF analysis deals almost exclusively with the single hegemonic fraction, big monopoly capital, and practically passes in silence over the other dominant bourgeois fractions. By thus failing to distinguish between the hegemonic and the dominant fractions, it ends up considering that the place of political domination is now occupied by big capital alone, and that the other bourgeois fractions, in particular non-monopoly capital, are henceforth excluded.

Of course, the question is not usually presented in such a blunt fashion: it is, however, no less clear than would otherwise have been the case, as can be seen from the recent *Traité marxiste d'économie politique*.[11] Every time that political domination is under discussion, it is only the big monopolies that are mentioned. On the other hand,

10. I am confining myself here to the analyses of the PCF. But the same analyses are to be found, with only minor variations, in texts published in the GDR (*Zur Theorie des staatsmonopolistischen Kapitalismus*, Berlin, 1967), in Italy by the PCI, and elsewhere.

11. I have already noted these theories in my article 'On Social Classes', *New Left Review* 78. See also J. Lojkine, 'Pouvoir politique et lutte des classes' in *La Pensée* no. 166, December 1972, etc.

every time that any capital other than 'big capital' is discussed, what is brought up first and foremost is 'small capital', with which an alliance is sought. These terms must be clearly understood. If 'small capital' is taken to mean the petty bourgeoisie of craftsmen and shopkeepers, then the search for this alliance is correct, for in fact this petty bourgeoisie does not belong to 'capital' as such, i.e. to the fractions of the bourgeoisie; in this sense, however, the term 'small capital' is wrongly applied. But the use of the term 'small capital' in fact fulfils a quite different function here. By speaking only of the 'big monopolies' and 'small capital', and thus conjuring away non-monopoly or medium capital, the impression is given that all those who do not belong to the 'big monopolies', the sole dominant fraction, are automatically part of 'small capital', capable of an alliance with the working class; 'small capital' is thus taken to include also medium capital, which is thus assimilated to the petty bourgeoisie. On the rare occasions that the *Traité* speaks of medium capital, it is to locate it on the same side as small capital, in their alleged common contradiction to 'big capital'.[12]

This analysis has clear implications for the strategy of an 'antimonopoly alliance', an alliance stretching to include all fractions of the bourgeoisie except the 'big monopolies', which are seen as alone occupying the terrain of political domination. It is equally clear how this analysis is tied up, in the mind of the PCF, with that of the 'national bourgeoisie/non-monopoly capital' noted above.

(b) This analysis is combined with a specific analysis of the state under state monopoly capitalism. The decisive role that the state fulfils in the present stage is quite correctly emphasized. What must be questioned here, however, is the very conception of the 'production process' in which the state intervenes. The production process is firstly considered as composed of two separate instances, the productive forces and the relations of production, and secondly as based on the primacy of the productive forces;[13] the necessary consequence of this is the conception of a neutral and autonomous

---

12. *Traité* . . . vol. I, pp. 223 ff., etc. Also P. Herzog, *Politique économique et Planification*, op. cit., pp. 66 ff.

13. 'In the reciprocal action of the productive forces and relations of production, it is the productive forces that play, in the last analysis, a determining role . . .', *Traité*, op cit., vol. I, p. 183. The *Traité* certainly speaks of a unity of relations of production and productive forces. But this is merely a verbal formula: in fact, such a unity can only be based on the production process, a process which is precisely the form of the domination of the relations of production over the productive forces. In other words, to attribute primacy to the productive forces inevitably means jettisonning the very unity of the relations of production and the productive forces.

'level' of development of the productive forces. State intervention is seen as to a large extent technical and neutral, an indispensable requirement of the 'development of the productive forces'. The state is thus conceived, as far as this aspect is concerned, as 'forming part of the base' and as an 'organic factor of the process of social production' (as in the *Traité*'s analysis of the French Plan). Naturally, the state is still seen as related to the interests of the 'big monopolies', but this relationship is understood simply as a misappropriation of the economic functions of the state, themselves neutral, in favour of the big monopolies. Current state intervention would thus have, as it were, two sides to it: the good side, corresponding to the celebrated 'socialization of the productive forces', since every 'socialization' (they do not ask which one) must in itself be good; and the bad side, corresponding to the private appropriation of the means of production. The two sides are seen as dissociable, since they correspond to two levels considered as distinct.[14]

The political consequences of this position, which is bound up

14. P. Herzog, op. cit., pp. 35 ff. and 45 ff. These positions are also related to other theoretical errors. It would be useful here to recall: (a) that it is scarcely possible to envisage an economic space as such, possessing intrinsic and immutable limits regardless of the mode of production; these limits are rather themselves variable according to the mode of production and even with the stages of the capitalist mode; (b) that, contrary to the economist illusion of a 'self-reproduction' of the economic, the capitalist state has always intervened in the economy; (c) that the particular and decisive form of these interventions at present does not prevent the reproduction of the relative 'separation' of state and economy in the present stage and phase, although this should not be understood as an actual externality of the two. The thesis of state monopoly capitalism, on the other hand, implies: (a) that capital only functions 'normally', as it were, without state 'intervention' (the self-regulation of the economy), as it supposedly did in the competitive stage: the decisive intervention of the state at the monopoly stage is already the index of a 'structural crisis' of capitalism; (b) that this intervention abolishes the relative separation of the capitalist state and the economy (the state as an 'organic factor of production' and 'part of the base'). Now, these positions are contradictory, since, based on false assumptions, they imply on the one hand that the current state intervention is by itself the index of a 'structural crisis' of capitalism, but that on the other hand, the state is managing to control, organize and plan capitalist reproduction: in fact, if one believes that this intervention abolishes the relative separation of state and economy, it is impossible to understand the limits of this intervention, and so the formulations of the theorists of state monopoly capitalism converge, as we shall see, with those of the defenders of an 'organised capitalism' (on certain aspects of these questions, see also M. Wirth, 'Zur Kritik der Theorie des staatsmonopolistischen Kapitalismus', in *Probleme des Klassenkampfs*, no. 3, 1973).

with an 'economist-technicist' conception of the production process and the productive forces, are particularly serious and should not be concealed. It is implied that the transition to socialism requires the conservation of the present state in its good aspect and its neutral economic interventions in the 'development of the social production process', merely purifying it of its bad aspect, and that it is possible to prevent this intervention from being misappropriated in favour of the monopolies by a simple change in state power. The Leninist thesis of the necessity of smashing the capitalist state apparatus is thrown overboard, and cheerfully attributed to 'ultra-left deviationists'. It is clear, however, as the experience of Chile has recently demonstrated yet again, that what is involved here is no mere academic question.

(c) Finally, and less paradoxically than might appear at first sight, the state is simultaneously conceived as a mere tool or instrument, manipulable at will by the fraction of big monopolists, a fraction which is considered 'integrated' and to which is attributed a 'unity of will'. This is the thesis of the 1960 Moscow conference of the 81 Communist parties, ill accepted even by the PCF in its extreme form, of the 'fusion of the state and the monopolies in a single mechanism'.[15] Precisely in so far as it is no longer possible to speak of a power bloc, but only of a single dominant fraction, the big monopolies, themselves considered as a metaphysical entity, abstractly unified by the 'merging' of different capitalist fractions, it is not accepted that the state apparatus has any relative autonomy as a political unifier, either for the monopoly fraction itself or for the power bloc as a whole. The dual political effect of the instrumentalist conception of the state, which is necessarily bound up with an idealist/economist conception, is extremely clear here; a tool or instrument possesses a neutral, technical utility, and can thus be manipulated at will by its holder.

This thesis not only leads to a dubious analysis of the contemporary state apparatus, but it also implies that, once the handful of 'usurpers', i.e. the big monopolists, are ousted from power, this state, in its present form, can be used in a different way, to serve the interests of socialism.

IV

In the light of these interpretations, it is clear that the decisive question at present is that of the class relations among the bour-

15. cf. the paper by F. Lazard given at the conference of Choisy-le-Roi, and reprinted by *Économie et Politique*, special numbers 143–4 and 145–6, 1966, on 'Le Capitalisme monopoliste d'État'.

geoisie in the stage of monopoly capitalism, and particularly in its present phase. What are the current contradictions and fractions within the bourgeois camp?

This question directly refers back to the formation of finance capital in the monopoly capitalist stage, as the product of a process of 'merger' chiefly between industrial and banking capital, a merger which subordinates commercial capital, and which gives birth to the monopolies. There are in fact several sides to this question:

(1) Does this 'merger' of industrial and banking capital establish an effective unification of these fractions, or does it reproduce their contradictions in a new form, even giving rise to new ones? What, moreover, is the precise status of the concepts of finance capital and monopoly capital?

(2) What is the status and the significance of the differentiation between monopoly capital and non-monopoly capital, which are often referred to more descriptively as big capital on the one hand, and medium and small capital on the other? What are the relationships between these forms of capital?

These are the questions that I shall be analysing in the following pages, trying to locate them in their proper place and to solve a series of theoretical problems on which the answers to these questions depend. I would like to make one preliminary point here, which will have to be taken into account in the following analysis: the forms of contradiction among the dominant classes and fractions always depend on the forms of the principal contradiction, which is that between the bourgeoisie as a whole and the working class.

This involves firstly, the actual constitutive forms of the process of concentration and centralization of capital. The essential features of this process, and even its efficient causes, such as the tendency of the rate of profit to fall, are nothing more than the direct expression of the struggle of the working class and the popular masses, i.e. of the class struggle. The falling rate of profit is the outward sign of the resistance (i.e. struggle) of the working class against its exploitation. Looked at historically, the process of concentration, which is the 'response' to this tendency, is 'provoked' and precipitated by popular struggles, both on the national and the world levels. In other words, the changes in the bourgeoisie, and the changes in the relations of production and the exploitation of labour, are in the last instance simply responses by the bourgeoisie to the struggle of the working class and the popular masses. The extended reproduction of capital is nothing other than the class struggle, the contradictions within the dominant classes and fractions being only the effects, within the power bloc, of the principal contradiction.

It also involves, therefore, the particular forms of the historic process within each concrete social formation. The demeanour and rhythm of this process, the particular forms of these secondary contradictions, the concrete configuration of the power bloc and the hegemony of this fraction or that over the others, all depend, in the last analysis, on the forms of the principal contradiction in these formations.[16]

16. Naturally, a dialectical process is still involved here. These fractions within the bourgeoisie, the effects of the principal contradiction, may in their turn have fractioning effects on the working class: for example, there are differences in the working class, particularly important in France, according to whether it depends on monopoly capital (which is concentrated) or on non-monopoly capital. On this subject, see M. Castells and F. Godard, *Grandes Entreprises, appareils d'État et processus d'urbanisation*, 1974.

The Contradictions Among the Bourgeoisie Today

I. MONOPOLY CAPITAL

I shall first deal with those questions that directly raise the problem of the relations and contradictions within finance or monopoly capital.

I

To put forward certain theses that are still to be demonstrated: what is referred to as the 'merging' of industrial and banking capital need not present the features of a combination that is closely integrated and henceforth exempt from contradictions and division into fractions; both of these are in fact to be found within monopoly capital in a new form. On the one hand, finance capital is not a fraction of capital in the same sense as industrial or banking capital; it is the form assumed by their relationship within the process of their merger itself, through which they are reproduced. This means, on the other hand, that finance capital is not the same as banking capital, contrary to the impression given by a certain confusion of terminology. The merging of industrial and banking capital does not necessarily imply the takeover of industry by the banks and the domination of the banking sector.[1]

Let us say for the moment that the process referred to as a 'merger' involves and reproduces, in a specific form, the distinction between productive capital and money capital established by Marx in *Capital*, as the form of extended reproduction inherent in the

1. One of the first to have indicated this problem, in his remarkable studies on the history of capitalism in France, is of course J. Bouvier; see his recent article 'Rapports entre systèmes bancaires et enterprises industrielles dans la croissance européenne au XIXe siècle' in *Studi Storici*, October–December 1970, and especially *Un siècle de banque française*, 1973, pp. 116 ff.

social capital under capitalism. This is a side of things which Lenin insists on in his *Imperialism*, even though he speaks of a 'merging or coalescence', and this is precisely because of the determinant role that he attributes, following Marx, to productive capital. Lenin goes so far as to say:

> It is characteristic of capitalism in general that the ownership of capital is separated from the application of capital to production, that money capital is separated from industrial or productive capital, and that the rentier who lives entirely on income obtained from money capital, is separated from the entrepreneur and from all who are directly concerned in the management of capital. Imperialism, or the domination of finance capital, is that highest stage of capitalism at which this separation reaches vast proportions.[2]

The term 'merger' refers to a two-fold process, with two aspects that are united but relatively distinct:

(a) The process of concentration of industrial-productive capital, on the one hand, and the process of centralization of money capital (banking capital) on the other;

(b) The forms of interpenetration and the relations between these two aspects.

'Mergers' within productive capital (concentration) and within money capital (centralization), which go to form monopoly capital, are already themselves 'merged' processes, in the sense that the centralization of one is involved in the concentration of the other, and vice versa. What is at issue here, however, is the contradictory cycle of the reproduction of the aggregate social capital, with its distinctions between productive capital and money capital. It is thus possible to speak quite rigorously of a reproduction cycle dominated by the concentration of productive capital, and a reproduction cycle dominated by the centralization of money capital. This is important to note, for we shall return to this differentiation in the form of the contradictions between predominantly industrial monopoly capital and predominantly banking monopoly capital, which I shall refer to for the sake of simplicity as industrial monopolies and banking monopolies. The determinant role in this process of merger, however, falls to the concentration of productive-industrial capital; the reproduction of the aggregate capital is determined by the cycle of productive capital. But this does not mean, any more than in the case of competitive capitalism, that the process of merger cannot take place under the economic aegis and political hegemony of banking capital, as well as under that of industrial capital itself.

2. Collected Works, vol. 22, Moscow, 1964, p. 238.

II

The concentration of industrial capital involves productive capital in the strict sense, and this alone produces value; this forms the real basis of capitalist accumulation and of the extraction of surplus-value.[3] Monopoly capital is chiefly the outcome of the concentration of industrial capital, in particular of the amalgamation of several production units and productive capitals under a single economic ownership. It is true that the capital that forms these monopolies is already, in the form of joint-stock companies, a composite capital, which involves the centralization of money capital which is re-organized so as to function as a single productive capital. But the principal aspect, as far as the reproduction of the productive capital is concerned, falls to the concentration of capital, i.e. to the pattern that the new forms of the relations of production stamp on the labour process and the social division of labour.

This directly raises the question of the 'criteria' of this concentration, or the measure of its 'degree'. This is of particular importance for us, since it partially coincides with the boundary between monopoly and non-monopoly capital, as also with their contradictions. This question cannot be resolved by a mere listing of isolated technical criteria, but only at the level of the relations of production in their relation to the labour process. In point of fact, these various 'criteria' are simply so many indices and effects of the actual transformations in the relations of production.

The reason for this is that these transformations directly correspond to the tendency of the rate of profit to fall which is characteristic of monopoly capitalism, and to its principal counter-tendency, the rising rate of exploitation. Monopoly capital is in fact characterized by a rise in the organic composition of capital. The proportion of constant capital (= fixed capital, i.e. machinery, as well as a certain part of the circulating capital) in the organic composition is significantly higher in relation to that of variable capital (wage costs), which signifies a relative decline of living labour in relation to past or 'dead' labour. But the rise in the organic composition of capital inversely affects the rate of profit. This makes it necessary for monopoly capital to heighten the rate of exploitation, not chiefly by altering the wage level but by the intensive exploitation of labour,

3. On certain aspects of the questions that I examine below, I would cite, while taking into account the criticisms that I have made of them elsewhere, P. Herzog, *Politique économique et Planification*, op. cit.; J.-P. Delilez, *Les Monopoles*; P. Salama and J. Valier, *Une introduction a l'économie politique*, 1973; C. Palloix, *L'Économie mondiale capitaliste*, 1971, and *Firmes multinationales et procès d'internationalisation*, op. cit.

including increasing the productivity of labour; also to fully valorize capital by taking every advantage of the differences in rates of profit between branches and sectors of social production. This is essentially what is behind the transformations in the relations of production and the new forms of social division of labour.

To return to the question of the indices of concentration of capital and of monopoly capital, beginning with the most visible, the size of enterprise, as seen in the 'giant enterprise' and the 'big industrial firm'. This concentration can assume several forms. In the form of vertical concentration, it is effected by the amalgamation, under unified control, of various phases of material production, and the expansion of the production unit up- and down-stream to include labour processes that previously devolved upon separate production units. This expansion also most frequently involves the circulation of capital, which implies the subordination of commercial capital to industrial capital; the industrial monopolies, aiming at monopoly control of the market, possess their own trading networks. This extension further involves domains upstream from production which were previously separate, and dependent on an economic control of their own, notably natural resources, raw materials and research. Industrial concentration also takes on a horizontal form when it involves the extension of a production unit to several labour processes belonging to one and the same phase of production.

These features are the product of the articulation of the relations of production (economic ownership and possession) and the labour process, and of their effects on the boundaries of the production units. These can not be directly apprehended via quantifiable empirical criteria, which can only serve a very relative role as indices. This is particularly the case with the criterion of the size of enterprise, assessed in terms of the number of workers employed, a favourite criterion for statistical distinctions between 'big', 'medium' and 'small' enterprises. This criterion completely disregards the question of the productivity of labour, which is a correlate of the increase in the organic composition of capital, varying with the various branches of production. A petrochemical enterprise employing a certain number of workers might involve monopoly capital, while a textile enterprise employing the same number of workers was controlled by non-monopoly capital. This is all the more the case in that monopoly capital is characterized by the tendency towards a proportionate decline in living labour as compared to dead labour.

But we cannot rely principally on a measure of degree of concentration according to the various branches of social production, one that refers to the proportionate share of certain firms in the production of each branch. Given the socialization of the labour process and the need for monopoly capital to take advantage of the unequal rates of profit in different branches, monopoly capital is often spread over several branches; the firm of Pechiney, for example, produces both aluminium and chemical products. By confining one's attention to branches of industry, one would necessarily underestimate the degree of concentration and mistake the boundaries between monopoly and non-monopoly capital. The same objection applies to a measure of concentration according to the share of various firms in certain products; one of the characteristics of the big industrial firm is precisely the constant diversification of the finished products that it puts on the market. We can go still further: even the criterion of the percentage that the production of a firm forms in the national product is a very approximate index, since not only does it entirely ignore the differentiation according to branches, but it also neglects the process of internationalization of capital; and the criterion of the percentage of assets held by firms often confuses legal property with economic ownership.

What about the criterion of the position of monopoly capital on the market? The Marxist theory of monopoly capital is not located on the terrain of the relation between capitals in the market; market factors and the circulation of capital are only an effect of the extended reproduction of capital based on the production cycle. The existence of monopolies with a dominant market position does not abolish market competition, but merely reproduces it at a different level. The objections to the theory of monopoly capitalism that are put forward from the standpoint of the market, claiming that there are in fact no such things as monopolies but merely 'oligopolies', that there is no abolition of competition but rather an 'imperfect competition', are both situated on a different terrain from Marxist theory, and attribute to it positions that are foreign to it. The position of a firm on the market is only a mere index of the concentration of capital, an index that can only be used with great precaution.

Finally, the ability to realize super-profits, which monopoly capital enjoys by virtue, among other things, of its dominant market position, as well as the need for selective investment in the most profitable branches and domains, are reflected in the utilization of profit. Monopoly capital enjoys quite remarkable possibilities of accumulation and extended reproduction by the summation of its own proceeds, i.e. by self-financing. The rate of self-financing correlates with the degree of concentration. But on this level too, the boundary between monopoly and non-monopoly capital is completely relative, given the involvement of money capital or banking capital in the concentration of productive capital.

III

Before going on to analyse the relations of production, we must pause to consider the role of the centralization of money capital in the reproduction of social capital. This centralization can itself be understood only in terms of its relation to the concentration of productive capital, which remains the determinant moment of the reproduction process. The possibilities of self-financing, i.e. the accumulation and profitable use of the proceeds directly obtained from production, present certain limits, by virtue of the unevenness between the flow of profit and the extension of productive capital.[4] The profit flow may prove insufficient to launch new lines of business, while in other cases, it enables the formation of 'reserves', which must themselves bring in a profit until they are needed for the expansion of the enterprise. In any event, even if the formation of complex production units by concentration transforms the significance of the exchanges between the component production units, so that these are no longer 'external' exchanges between units under separate control, but 'internal' exchanges within the complex unit, these exchanges continue to take place, exhibiting irregularities tied to the ups and downs of investment. Finally, given the need for rates of profit to be equalized in the interests of profit maximization, the unevenness between branches and sectors require rapid transfers of capital from one branch or sector to others.

This is precisely where the role of credit comes in, i.e. of money capital or banking capital as a financial intermediary; the centralization of money capital that gives rise to banking monopoly capital (the 'big banks') is directly bound up with the concentration of productive capital. But in the concrete historic process, and according to the forms of the principal contradiction, this centralization may have a rhythm that precedes, accompanies or follows this concentration, according to whose aegis – that of industrial capital or banking capital – the formation of monopoly capital is accomplished under in the country in question. In concrete formations at various steps, it is possible to discern different forms and degrees of industrial concentration and banking centralization, i.e. advances or

4. For example, the rate of self-financing of industrial investment in France is between 65 and 70 per cent; in the United States, after a spectacular increase, it fell back to 75 per cent between 1965 and 1970.

delays of one in relation to the other; in France in particular, banking centralization has tended at each stage to precede industrial concentration. Finally, in the formation of banking monopoly capital, the profits directly realized by productive capital are involved alongside funds from public saving.

It should already be clear that finance capital, which is the mode of functioning of the amalgamation or 'merging' of industrial capital and money capital in the reproduction of the social capital, is firstly established in the forms of the intervention of the centralization of money capital in the formation of industrial monopolies, and the intervention of the concentration of productive capital in the formation of banking monopolies. This process of merger, however, does not stop at this point; it extends to the growing interdependence of industrial monopoly capital and banking monopoly capital, which gives rise to the emergence of what are generally referred to as the great 'financial empires'. These exhibit a higher level of the merger process between big industrial firms and big banks. This step, which represents the amalgamation, under a single economic ownership and control, of big industrial firms and big banks, may appear either in the form of industrial capital creating or controlling its own banks, or of banking capital creating or controlling its own industrial firms. Here again, this aspect of the merger process may in a particular country either precede, accompany or follow the rhythm of concentration and centralization. In other words, the process of merger referred to as finance capital involves both the relations between the elements that enter into the combination, and, as a result of this, these elements themselves; but, nevertheless, it does not imply a pure and simple extinction of these elements, by their 'integration' into a metaphysical entity called finance capital. These points are very important if we are to grasp the contradictions that run through monopoly capital at every moment of its reproduction, and hence to reveal the fissures in the merger process.

At the same time, however, (a) the formation of industrial monopoly capital (concentration) and the formation of banking monopoly capital; (b) the manner and form of their interdependence; and (c) the relations between monopoly capital and non-monopoly capital – in short, the present relations and contradictions within the bourgeoisie, can only be understood by examining how the relations of production affect the labour process.

This examination of the relations of production and their present transformations is the principal aspect of the problem, given the primacy of the relations of production over the productive forces; it is precisely the action of these transformed relations on the labour process that has as its effect the present forms of capitalist social-ization of the productive forces.[5] At this point I shall pause for the time being, stressing as the main thing the impact of the present transformations of the relations of production actually within monopoly capital.

2. THE PHASES OF MONOPOLY CAPITAL AND THE MODIFICATIONS IN THE RELATIONS OF PRODUCTION

I

Although the extended reproduction of capitalism produces certain transformations in this mode that are to be understood as stages and phases, there is still an invariant core of production relations that characterizes it, and this is why these transformations are only the 'transformed forms' of a mode of production that remains capitalist. Capitalist relations of production are characterized by the fact that both the relation of economic ownership (ability to assign the means of production and to allocate resources and profits to this or that use) and the relation of possession (direction and relative control of a certain labour process) are functions of capital; the direct pro-ducers (the proletariat) are here 'dispossessed' of everything except their labour-power, which itself becomes a commodity, resulting in the extraction of surplus labour under the specific form of surplus-value.

1. The first problem that this raises is that the competitive and monopoly stages, located in the 'extended' reproduction of capital-ism, are to be distinguished from what Marx refers to as the period of manufacture, or simple commodity production. This is because during the period of manufacture (formal subordination or 'sub-sumption' of labour to capital), the direct producers were not yet dispossessed of their means of production, although the ownership of these was already in the hands of capital.

Thus the relation between these two stages of capitalism, com-petitive and monopoly, is not at all the same as that between both of these, on the one hand, and the manufacturing period on the other, contrary to the arguments of the PCF which, basing itself

5. The celebrated socialization of the productive forces, which several contemporary Marxist analyses use as a real magic formula in their explana-tions, is not in fact an immanent tendency of the labour process as such; it refers rather to the process that the relations of production stamp on this. This means that there is, strictly speaking, no such thing as a neutral 'socialization' of the labour process: under capitalism, there can only be a capitalist socialization of the labour process.

chiefly on the 'socialization' of the productive forces, periodizes capitalism into three 'stages': the manufacturing period, competitive capitalism and monopoly capitalism.[6] In fact, there are no modifications in the labour process between competitive capitalism and monopoly capitalism comparable to those that distinguish manufacture from the extended reproduction of capitalism, despite all talk of the 'scientific and technical revolution'. The labour process is only socialized under the domination of determinate relations of production, and these have an invariant core during both these two stages of capitalism. The manufacturing period, however, forms rather the transition, in the strict sense of the term, between feudalism and capitalism, while the two stages in question both relate to the extended reproduction of capitalism itself.

2. It is no less true, however, that the stages of capitalism are characterized by differential forms of the dominant capitalist relations of production (and this is sometimes true even of the phases into which each stage is divided in relation to the process whereby capitalist relations, or of one of their forms, dominate the other relations or forms of capitalist production – both within a social formation and internationally). What exactly do these differential forms involve?

These modifications involve the forms of appropriation of surplus-value; they do not alter the expropriation and dispossession of the direct producers from their means of production, i.e. the place of the workers in the relations of production. These differential or 'transformed' forms involve the particular forms in which relations of economic ownership and relations of possession are articulated within the place of capital itself. They have very significant effects on the socialization of the labour process and the patterns that they give this, but they do not alter its structure.

3. These transformations essentially correspond to a rise in the rate of exploitation (intensive exploitation of labour, relative surplus-value) designed to counteract the tendency for the average rate of profit to fall. By 'essentially', I mean that this exploitation bears directly on the principal contradiction (bourgeoisie/working class), and it is for this reason that I am concentrating on this question. It is clear, however, that the transformations in the relations of production actually involve a very complex network of factors. To give just one example, which is particularly important at the present time: these transformations are particularly designed to enable monopoly capital to counteract the tendency of the rate of profit to fall that

6. J.-P. Delilez, *Les Monopoles*, etc., op. cit., pp. 117 ff.; P. Herzog, *Politique économique*, op. cit., pp. 49 ff.; P. Boccara, *Études sur le capital-isme monopoliste d'État*, 1973, pp. 21 ff.

follows from the increase of constant capital in relation to variable capital, not just by raising the rate of exploitation, but also by devaluing a part of constant capital itself. In the relation between capitals, it is precisely the changes in the relations of production that we have discussed that make this possible, and thus these transformations are equally designed to enable capital in general, as well as its various components, to function in the new conditions in which the average rate of profit is established under monopoly capitalism. Nevertheless, this complex network of factors, and the changes within it, all come back in the last analysis to the contradiction of labour and capital, in other words, to exploitation.

These transformations in the articulation of economic ownership and possession within the place of capital:

(a) are expressed in concrete relationships between the various powers that they bear;

(b) give rise to different degrees of economic ownership and possession on the part of these various fractions of capital, according to the stages and phases of capitalist development.

The transformations are thus directly reflected:

(a) in changes in legal ownership;

(b) in changes in the boundaries of production units ('enterprises');

(c) in differentiations between the agents who, occupying the place of capital or directly dependent on it, exercise the plurality of power of the relations that define this place.

II

The current transformations may be better understood by contrasting them with the typical form of these relations in the stage of 'competitive capitalism'. This stage was characterized by a coincidence of boundaries between the relations of economic ownership and of possession. The individual capitalist was both the economic owner of the unit of production, and controlled and directed the labour process that went on within it. This coincidence, which corresponded to a degree of capitalist socialization of labour processes that were still separated from one another, gave rise to the classic image of the production unit as an 'individual enterprise'. It was also extended to the 'individual' legal ownership that the private capitalist enjoyed. The individual entrepreneur and his direct agents concentrated in their hands the exercise of the plurality of powers deriving from economic ownership and possession.

In contrast to this, one of the most striking changes, throughout the monopoly capitalist stage, consists in the relative dissociation between economic ownership and legal ownership introduced by joint-stock companies.

The joint-stock company, a form of legal ownership corresponding to the concentration and centralization of capital, is one of the major ways in which this process is effected. On the one hand, this is true actually within the processes of the concentration of productive capital – the merger and take-over of industrial firms – and the centralization of money capital; on the other hand, it is so in the growing interdependence between these two movements, i.e. between industrial monopolies and banking monopolies. The industrial monopolies, while they often create their own complexes of dependent banks and financial holding companies, themselves receive capital from the banking groups; the latter hold portfolios of shares through the system of participation characteristic of joint-stock companies. Conversely, the banking monopolies themselves, by the same system of participation, often directly receive capital from the industrial monopolies. In short, joint-stock companies are a form of legal ownership that implies a certain socialization of the latter (a 'private' one) within the bounds of the capitalist class.

There is of course a relative dissociation between economic ownership and legal ownership: not every share or interest taken by a shareholder in a firm's capital corresponds to an equivalent or proportionate share in economic ownership and real control. This ownership is wielded as a whole by a few large shareholders, not necessarily a majority, who by various means that have been well enough studied, concentrate in their hands the powers that derive from it.

But although this shows how ludicrous are a whole series of old myths about 'social capitalism' (and more recently, that of 'participation' by a 'shareholding democracy'), it only affects one aspect of the relative dissociation between economic and legal ownership. The more remote effects can only be understood in terms of a modification in economic ownership itself in the monopoly capitalist stage, which for the time being I shall simply mention: the disappearance of the figure of the individual entrepreneur, the increasing concentration bound up with the socialization of the labour process, corresponds to a dissociation of the various powers belonging to economic ownership. Instead of integral and separate units of economic ownership, we have the growth of various degrees of economic ownership and of powers corresponding to these degrees, according to the various moments of concentration of capital and its various fractions. This tendency is effected by way of the dissociation between legal and economic ownership.

This dissociation, articulated with the dissociation of the powers and degrees of economic ownership, has the following effects that directly concern us here:

(a) the processes of concentration and centralization, and their interdependence, are effected under forms that are often hidden by legal ownership;

(b) further, this legal ownership conceals in a quite special way the real contradictions that divide monopoly capital beneath its unified façade.

In short, by taking account of these dissociations, we provide ourselves with the means of examining the contradictions within the bourgeoisie itself in the monopoly capitalist stage.

This involves, firstly, the specific process of merger in the cycles of productive and money capital. This process can in fact be achieved, to varying degrees, in the form of a legal autonomy of the enterprises involved; the legal control or take-over of one firm by another is only one of the possible forms or outcomes of this process. There are in fact a whole range of ways in which economic ownership can be concentrated while the firms involved retain their distinct legal independence; minority control, in which one firm takes a minority interest in the share capital of another, but one which is sufficient to give it real economic ownership, either fully or in part, is only one of these ways. Sometimes, it is not even necessary to take a financial interest; a large industrial company can subordinate another production unit by means of various types of sub-contracting agreements, either taking over some of the powers deriving from economic ownership, in which case the latter firm experiences a contraction in the degree of its economic ownership in favour of the former, or taking over these powers in their entirety, in which case a real expropriation is involved – and all this not simply under cover of legal autonomy, but of a legal ownership that is entirely separate and distinct.

These effects can also be seen in the forms of interdependence and contradiction *between* the concentration of productive capital and the centralization of money capital. In order to take over economic ownership of an industrial firm, as a whole or in part, and thus the powers that derive from this, it is not necessary for a banking group to hold the majority of the share capital of this firm (legal ownership) nor even to hold any. It is often sufficient for the banking group simply to be selective in its financing and to differentiate in credit conditions, given the specific circumstances of the flow of profit, for it to impose its real control on the assignment of the means of production and the allocation of resources by this enterprise. This even affects the big monopolies, given the limits of their self-financing and their need for a rapid turnover of capital, as much as it does non-monopoly industrial capital. There is finally no need to dwell here on the various forms of 'agreements' and 'understandings' of industrial or banking monopolies among themselves, or between industries and banks, forms which often correspond to new steps in the monopolization process under a mask of autonomous legal ownership.

The effects of these dissociations between legal and economic ownership, on the one hand, and between the plurality of powers of economic ownership on the other, can also make themselves felt in the reverse direction. A single legal unit – a large industrial firm, a big bank, or a financial holding company – may often conceal, under the façade of elements that have been 'taken over', either relatively distinct economic units, or more often, various degrees of economic ownership of the capitals that make it up. An industrial or banking monopoly, or a financial group, can be divided by internal contradictions between the capitals of which it is composed, even though these appear as legally 'integrated'.

However, this dissociation of the powers deriving from economic ownership is only the counterpart of the tendency towards the concentration and centralization of capital under a single ownership. It in no way indicates some sort of egalitarian or proportional distribution of power or economic ownership among the capitals that have been concentrated. This dissociation coincides with the contradictions among these capitals and the struggles between the capitalist fractions, and must be understood in fact as a means by which the powers of certain capitals are undermined, and their economic ownership degraded, in favour of other capitals which concentrate in their hands these powers and degrees of ownership. This contradictory process of dissociation and concentration in fact characterizes the whole range of relative expropriations that take place in the extended reproduction of monopoly capital, tending towards the amalgamation of capitals under a single economic ownership, and thus equally marks the resistances to this process; the merging of capitals has nothing friendly or cooperative about it.

III

Furthermore, under the façade of a relative stability of the forms of legal ownership throughout the development of monopoly capitalism (i.e. the joint-stock company), the monopoly relations of production themselves undergo change. These changes amount to so many new forms of the capitalist relations of production corresponding to monopoly capitalism; they involve in particular the dissociation and concentration of economic ownership in its connection

with the relationship of possession in the labour process. The central
site of these changes is thus the actual cycle of productive capital,
and they are expressed in significant changes in the social division of
labour and in the forms of enterprise.

The division of monopoly capitalism into phases that I shall
follow here is the same as that presented in the previous essay as a
periodization of imperialism:[7] (a) the transition phase from competitive capitalism to monopoly capitalism; (b) the phase of the consolidation of monopoly capitalism; (c) its present phase. By dealing
with the modifications in the relations of production 'internal' to
the metropolises according to these phases, I hope to make the
preceding analysis more precise.

The relationship of possession, closely articulated to the labour
process, refers to the possibility of putting means of production to
work in a centre of appropriation of nature, and thus depends on
the degree of control of a determinate labour process (or series of
processes) and of the conditions of its reproduction. The relationship
of possession carries a series of specific powers, distinct from those of
the property relationship, and which relate in particular to the
direction and internal organization of the labour processes within
the social division of labour.

A production unit (an 'enterprise'), as a form in which the relations of production are articulated to the labour process, is defined
first and foremost in relation to possession. In this respect, what
characterizes the specific cohesion of a particular production unit in
relation to others is the close interdependence of the labour processes that are carried out in it, and this is what determines the
effective ability to use the means of production. This interdependence
of labour processes which do not have a specific autonomy has nothing to do with the 'physical' proximity of various establishments;
labour processes that are practically inextricable may very well be
carried out in various establishments that are geographically
separated. Each labour process which can be centralized in a distinct
establishment is involved in a determinate transformation by virtue
of the interdependence of these processes. Thus products that circulate between these processes do not constitute 'external' exchanges,
are not properly speaking 'bought' and 'sold', but are rather
exchanges internal to the production unit (at transfer prices), forming a continuous flow. The production unit thus presupposes a
central directing instance for the relationship of possession; in the
capitalist mode of production this is 'separate' from the workers,
and governs the social division of labour.

7. See above, pp. 45 ff.

In the capitalist mode of production the possession relationship is a function of the place of capital, which also concentrates in it economic ownership. A capitalist production unit (an 'enterprise') also presupposes an economic ownership of the means of production that are used in this unit. Whenever the production process involves certain interdependencies between labour processes that are carried out on means of labour belonging to different owners, then we have relations between distinct production units. In other words, a capitalist production unit is the concrete form of the relation between an economic ownership and a possession that both belong to capital.

This analysis of the production unit, which presumes a radical break with all 'institutionalist' conceptions of the enterprise, enables us to elicit two guiding lines: (a) given the growing socialization of the labour process that corresponds to the process of concentration of capital under monopoly capitalism, it becomes clear that the very boundaries of the production units are shifted; (b) this shift in boundaries is governed by the patterns that the concentration of capital stamps on the socialization of the labour process, and thereby, on the social division of labour. It is not the result of any technical necessity of the labour process in itself. The labour process only exists under the social conditions in which it is carried out.

Now, the precise articulation of economic ownership and possession assumes different forms according to the phases of monopoly capitalism.[8]

During the phases of transition and consolidation, monopoly capitalism took root and established its domination in the social formations of the metropolises, in particular over the forms of competitive capitalism (non-monopoly capital). These phases correspond to specific forms of the expansion of monopoly capitalism in the face of very strong resistances on the part of non-monopoly capital and of small-scale production based on the form of simple commodity production (i.e. of the commercial and artisanal petty bourgeoisie). In the contradictory effects of dissolution and conservation that the domination of monopoly capitalism imposes on these forms, it is the effects of conservation that still win out; monopoly capitalism does not yet manage entirely to subordinate ('subsume' in Marx's term) these forms. This has its consequences on the reproduction of monopoly capitalism itself: in the rise in the rate of exploitation designed to counteract the falling rate of profit, the dominant form is not yet shifted towards the intensive exploitation of labour. The organization

8. See the table on pp. 134-5.

of the labour process and the social division of labour has not yet passed as a whole into the hands of monopoly capital.

What we are faced with here is a relative advance in the concentration of economic ownership over the socialization of the labour process. This is in fact a general historical tendency within the process of domination of one mode or form of production over others, which we find here in a specific form in the relation between the two stages of capitalism. It is in fact the concentration of economic ownership based on the social conditions of production and reproduction that is today stamping its patterns and its rhythm, with its inevitable dislocations, on the socialization of the labour process.

These forms of the expansion of monopoly capitalism, historically accomplished by the advancing concentration of economic intervention, themselves involve a dissociation, this time between economic ownership and possession. The dominant form that replaces competitive capitalism, i.e. individual economic ownership and individual capitalist possession in a determinate production unit, is that of a single, concentrated economic ownership embracing several separate production units, i.e. an economic ownership subordinating ('subsuming') relatively distinct relationships of possession. The typical form found here is that of the holding company or trust, which, with its concentrated economic ownership, can control extremely diversified production units, extending to the most diverse and distant branches, and whose labour processes exhibit a characteristic autonomy; the German Stinnes empire of the inter-war period is the classic example of this. Even in the case of a concentration within one industrial branch (metal industries, chemicals), the boundaries of the production units, or even the relative autonomy of their labour processes and the organization of these processes, resist the concentration of economic ownership; there has not yet been the transition to the 'restructuring' phase.

It is in these phases in particular that we find on a massive scale the phenomenon of dissociation of the powers deriving from economic ownership itself. This corresponds to these forms of expansion of monopoly capitalism, and precisely makes this expansion possible by means of an advance of economic ownership. Monopoly capitalism not only rapidly concentrates economic ownership in its hands, whole sections at a time, but simultaneously accumulates powers deriving from ownership units that still remain formally independent of it.

It should now be clear why this dissociation of powers deriving from economic ownership, which enables a real expropriation (in varying degrees) in favour of monopoly capital, is made possible by the dissociation, during these phases, between economic ownership and possession. Monopoly capital takes on certain powers of the economic ownership of another capital, while certain other powers remain, during this process of struggle and resistance, in this other capital's hands, to the extent that the predominant form of concentration does not yet break the limits of the production units and extend onto the separate units of possession; the capitalist who sees himself deprived of certain of his powers of ownership can still retain important powers of possession. Any degree of economic ownership under capitalism must involve powers of possession, given the way in which the place of capital is precisely defined by these two relationships. However, the dissociation between economic ownership and possession, involving the concentration of separated possessions under a single ownership, does not imply the possibility of a degree of ownership, or of certain powers of ownership, without powers of possession.

IV

In this respect, however, the present phase of monopoly capitalism is characterized by significant modifications in the relations within the imperialist metropolises. During this phase, it is the effects of dissolution that are prevailing over the effects of conservation, in these contradictory effects that the denomination of monopoly capitalism imposes on the other modes and forms of production. Monopoly capitalism imposes its direction on the whole range of labour processes, and imposes a social division of labour on the whole of the social formation. This reorganization of the labour process is nowadays expressed by the massive socialization (a quite specific one) of the labour process; it corresponds to the shift in dominance towards the intensive exploitation of labour (relative surplus-value).[9]

In these conditions, the dominant form of concentration of productive capital in the present phase is that of integrated production, as already signalled; this requires a restructuring of the labour process in the direction of a socialization and a social division in conformity with the concentration of economic ownership. The labour processes that are conducted within the various production units under a concentrated and single ownership are now closely

9. It also corresponds, however, to a balance of forces between capitals in the constant process of the devalorization of a section of capital, a devalorization which also contributes towards counteracting the tendency of the rate of profit to fall.

articulated. This has the gradual effect of setting up complex production units which have the various sub-units of which they are composed, the elementary production units, as their organic elements; this is what is involved in the emergence of big industrial corporations or giant enterprises. The classic case is that of petrochemicals, where technological innovations in the treatment of petroleum products have given rise, within the same economic ownership, to a close articulation between labour processes that originally belonged to two different branches (petrol and chemicals). The traditional boundaries of the production units are receding to the point of coinciding with the boundaries of economic ownership; this is the celebrated question of the 'restructuring' or 'modernization' of enterprises. This integration of labour processes, and the recession of the boundaries of production units, involves concentration within one branch just as much as concentration between branches; parallel to this, in fact, the boundaries of the branches of social production are themselves becoming blurred. Exchange between the elementary production units of one complex production unit becomes exchange 'internal' to the letter. It is thus apparent how this integration of the labour process prevents neither the diversification of investment areas, nor the constant diversification of the finished products offered by the giant firm.

This current direction of concentration of capital thus involves a tendency for the gap or dissociation between ownership and possession which characterized the previous phases of monopoly capitalism to close once again. Monopoly capitalism achieves the real and extended subsumption of the means of labour and labour-power by way of the massive dissolution of other forms of their relations. The various units of possession subordinated to concentrated ownership dissolve, concomitantly with the recession of the boundaries of the production units, into a single possession; the complex production units require a central directing instance to command the integration of the labour process and regulate the continuous flow between the elementary production units. The powers that derive from this single possession are concentrated in the economic ownership of the giant firm. This concentration of powers of possession is, however, effected in several ways – among others, by the domination of one elementary production unit over others within the complex production unit, in particular when this unit provides the others with common basic products which they in turn diversify.

This tendency for the gap between economic ownership and possession to close again has its effects on economic ownership itself. While increasing the interdependence of labour processes and capitals, it reproduces even more intensely – and this is what concerns us here – the contradictions between the various capitalist fractions. It thus leads to a necessary closure of the dissociation between the various powers deriving from economic, and to an increased concentration of the 'degrees' of economic ownership that are distributed between the various production units. The absence of an integrated production made it possible for an industrial monopoly to take over a whole series of production units, by means of partial expropriations, but to leave certain powers of ownership (some of the various types of sub-contracting) to distinct capitals, because of the resistance by the established boundaries of possession and production units within the labour processes. But the increased socialization and integration of the labour processes, as well as the concentration of the direction and control of these processes, lead inevitably to an intense struggle for the concentration of the powers of ownership into a single centre.

This process affects not just relations between monopoly and non-monopoly capital, which we shall come back to later, but also relations within monopoly capital itself. This is proved not only by the repeated failures of joint undertakings, and of the subsidiaries set up by several monopoly groups together, but also by the intense struggle between the monopolies for exclusive and sole control of whole firms and sectors. It also affects relations within one single concentrated capital or monopoly group; the various 'understandings' which often gave rise to various degrees of economic ownership shared between the various capitals thereby amalgamated under the dominance of one of them, tend more and more to give way to the exclusive concentration of all powers of ownership in the hands of one alone.

In short, this increased tendency towards the merger of capitals, which is expressed in the present phase in the tendency for the dissociations between economic ownership and possession, and between the various powers and degrees of economic ownership, to close, only increases the contradictions and struggles between the capitalist fractions; this is the first conclusion that is directly important for us here.

V

I shall have occasion to return to this argument in examining the relation between monopoly and non-monopoly capital in the present phase; we shall see in particular that the present modifications in the monopoly relations of production go far beyond the mere formation of complex production units, which is only one small effect of these modifications. For the time being, I shall restrict myself to three particular points.

1. The phases of monopoly capitalism that have been analysed above must in no way be seen in terms of a unilinear stage-ism of chronological succession. In degrees that vary according to the concrete social formation involved, monopoly capitalist relations of the consolidation phase still coexist with those of the present phase, in a very special manner. In so far as what we are dealing with here is a *stage* of capitalism (monopoly capitalism), it is necessary to grasp thoroughly the significance of Lenin's statement that this stage is not the 'superstructure' of the 'old capitalism'; in point of fact competitive capitalism (non-monopoly capital) still constantly reproduces itself under monopoly capitalism and its various phases, although in a dependent fashion. What this means is that even in its present phase, monopoly capitalism exhibits in its relations of production characteristics which relate to its domination or require its 'extension' over a non-monopoly capital which continually resurrects itself. Moreover, given the unevenness of profit rates between different branches and sectors, and the necessity for monopoly capital to maximize its super-profits, the tendency towards concentration in the form of holding companies, without an effective integration of labour processes or closure of the gap between economic ownership and possession, is a permanent tendency in the extended reproduction of monopoly capital.

It is none the less the case that in the present phase, this form of expansion assumes specific characteristics, for it is taking place actually within the new coordinates of this phase: concentration in the form of holding companies currently assumes, in the main, the form of the conglomerate. Even if these conglomerates include extremely diverse labour processes, without effective integration, it is still the case, in the words of Y. Morvan,[10] that 'conglomerates are not "holding" companies in the traditional sense of the term; in the majority of cases, the traditional holding companies confined themselves to taking a greater or lesser share in the capital of the companies they controlled, without attempting to exercise overall responsibility for their management. The conglomerates, however, are not content simply to hold shares in the capital of their subsidiaries; they attempt rather to run them, and thus appear more like true industrial firms.'

In short, the periodization of capitalism into stages, and the effects of dissolution and conservation that monopoly capitalism imposes on competitive capitalism, cannot be seen in the same terms

10. Y. Morvan, *La Concentration de l'industrie en France*, 1972, p. 112.

as the relations between the capitalist mode of production on the one hand and other non-capitalist modes and forms of production on the other. These two stages have a form of articulation that is all their own, in so far as monopoly capitalism amounts to the extended reproduction of the capitalist mode of production as a whole, and thus reproduces the general contradictions of the reproduction cycle in a new form. This is even more true for the periodization of monopoly capitalism itself into phases: the present phase, which has specific characteristics of its own, does not simply conserve the characteristics of the 'preceding' phases of monopoly capitalism, but constantly reproduces these in a new form. As a result of all this, the forms followed by the 'merger' process in the concentration cycle of productive capital and the centralization cycle of money capital, as well as their interdependencies and interrelations, are extraordinarily complex. The only way to elucidate them is by a concrete analysis of the way that these various phases are articulated in a concrete social formation; this is particularly apparent in the case of France, while until the last few years was relatively backward in capital concentration.

2. The periodization established on the world scale, regarding the internationalization of capitalist relations, does not exactly coincide in time with the periodizations of the various capitalist metropolises. We must not forget here that the imperialist chain is not the mere sum of the parts of which it is composed, and that the links of this chain exhibit an uneven development. There can thus be chronological dislocations both between the phase of the imperialist chain as a whole and the 'corresponding' internal phase of one particular imperialist metropolis, and between the concrete phases that the various metropolises are experiencing at a particular moment in time. It is still the case, however, that if one metropolis shows itself to be 'backward' in relation to the phase of the imperialist chain globally, it is this chain that will impose on the metropolis in question its transition to the corresponding internal phase. Here again the characteristic backwardness of France is an obvious case; it is only recently, with the 5th and 6th Plans, that France has moved into the present phase of monopoly capitalism, and this is precisely under the impulse given by the internationalization of capitalist relations.

3. The analysis we have given so far of the changes in the relations of production according to the phases of monopoly capitalism, of the connections between the relationships of economic ownership and possession and between the powers that derive from these, all involved the *place* of capital and of its fractions. A quite different problem is that of the *agents* who exercise these powers, i.e. those who occupy the place of capital or depend directly on it. It is clear

that the changes in these relations have had the effect of diversifying the categories of agents who exercise these powers: the famous questions of the managers and of the technostructure only form one of the aspects of this problem. These modifications have also had their effects on the institutional structure of the 'firm', giving rise to the tendency of centralization/decentralization of 'decision-making' in the giant firms, to the bureaucratization of the modern enterprise, etc. These questions certainly have their importance, but they are in the last analysis secondary, since they are only an effect of the changes in the relations of production. This has to be pointed out, in view of the institutionalist tendency that is currently dominant, and which sees the problem as centring on the changes in the organizational structure of the 'firm'.

3. CONTRADICTIONS WITHIN MONOPOLY CAPITAL

This section is concerned to emphasize the fact that, under its unified exterior, finance capital reproduces in a new form, and in an extended manner, the contradictions inherent in the reproduction process of capital. The 'merger' of capitals that gives rise to finance capital is, beneath its legal appearance, a divergent and contradictory process; finance capital is not an integrated capital, but refers to the mode of functioning of the capitalist fractions in their growing interdependence, and to the relations between them in this process.

I shall analyse first of all these contradictions and fractional divisions of monopoly capital, as a component of the domestic bourgeoisie of the imperialist metropolises.

I

In the first place, these contradictions involve relations between the industrial monopolies on the one hand, and the banking monopolies on the other, distinguished by the respective domination of the concentration of productive capital and the centralization of money capital. Each of these two have already been produced by the process of the merger of industrial and banking capital, and they reproduce in their turn the contradictions between productive capital and money capital. Thus finance capital exhibits within itself the constitutive contradictions of the bourgeois class. In this connection, we could speak of the 'internalization' of contradictions within finance capital, as long as it is clearly understood that what is involved here is neither an integrated whole, finance capital, nor mere contradictions between 'financial groups' each of which already formed an integrated whole, but rather contradictions within the very elements entering into the process of finance capital – industrial capital and banking capital – elements which are already modified in and by their participation in this process.

Contrary to what is very often believed, the term 'finance capital' is not synonymous with that of 'banking capital'. This is certainly the meaning that it sometimes acquires, and very clearly so in the case of Hilferding; Lenin, however, although there are certain slips in this respect in his *Imperialism*, is careful not to sanction this confusion. As against Hilferding, Lenin constantly upholds the determining role of productive capital,[11] as well as the reproduction under imperialism of the distinction between this and money capital, and in this respect he follows Marx. It is nevertheless necessary to be doubly careful here, for the meaning that Lenin gives to the term finance capital is different from that of Marx; in comparison to Lenin's use, this term remains for Marx a descriptive one, used to refer to a series of different practices that involve either commercial capital or banking capital.[12]

Finance capital, therefore, which designates the process of merger between industrial capital and banking capital, does not at all imply, even though it indicates a new and very important role for banking capital and for the cycle of money capital, that this merger necessarily takes place under the aegis of banking capital and by way of the domination of banking over industry, which would be the case if finance capital was identified with banking capital. This confusion is very serious, and it has two effects in particular:

(a) Those who reject the Leninist theory base their claim that this theory has not been verified on the grounds that by way of

11. I do not mean to go into a comprehensive analysis of this question here; let me simply confine myself to one example, but a highly significant one, from Lenin's *Imperialism* (op. cit., p. 226). Lenin himself quotes Hilferding, seeming to adopt the definiton that the latter gave of finance capital, i.e. identifying it with banking capital: 'This bank capital, i.e. capital in money form, which is thus actually transformed into industrial capital, I call "finance capital".' However, Lenin immediately adds: 'This definition is incomplete insofar as it is silent on one extremely important fact – on the increase of concentration of production and of capital to such an extent that concentration is leading, and has led, to monopoly . . . The concentration of production; the monopolies arising therefrom; the merging or coalescence of the banks with industry – such is the history of the rise of finance capital and *such is the content of that concept*' (my italics: N.P.).

12. On this subject, see Suzanne de Brunhof, *La Politique monétaire*, 1973, pp. 113 ff.

self-financing, industry has 'since' escaped from the control of the banks.[13] This does not only attribute to Lenin a theory of the process of monopolization as accomplished under the inevitable aegis of the banks, but by confusing finance capital and banking capital it also underestimates the active and decisive role of banking capital in the merger process, even when this is accomplished under the aegis of industrial capital. This becomes quite clear, however, once finance capital is considered as the way in which industrial and banking capital function 'together'.

(b) This confusion has also had its effects on Marxist writers; certain of these have been led to propose a periodization of the capitalist mode of production according to which capital is dominant in the reproduction of the total social capital: first comes the phase of commercial capital, then that of industrial capital, and finally that of banking capital, which is thus somehow identified with finance capital. Besides the remarks already made on this subject above, this theory on the one hand leads to confusing any periodization of capitalism into stages (this is where the false problem as to whether capitalism has been imperialist since its beginnings, and the distinction between 'archeo-imperialism' and 'neo-imperialism', both arise); on the other hand, and this is particularly important to us here, it inevitably leads to attributing to banking capital the dominant role in the process of merger that gives rise to monopoly capitalism.[14]

Now, right through the cycle of capitalism's extended reproduction, including the imperialist stage, the reproduction of the total social capital is determined by the cycle of productive capital, which alone produces surplus-value. But this does not directly indicate which fraction of capital it is that, in any of these stages or phases, plays the dominant role in the economy, and, according to the conjuncture, enjoys political hegemony.

* * *

13. Among others, Jean Meynaud, *L'Europe des affaires*, 1967, pp. 111 ff. In fact this is the position of all bourgeois authors.

14. 'Imperialism, with its specific features such as the export of capital and the division of the world, is therefore bound up with the internationalization of capital, through the specific role played by money capital. Hence the contemporary dominance of international finance capital, the dominance of the banks and the money market . . .', C. Palloix, *Internationalisation du capital et Stratégie des firmes multinationales*, p. 19. See also the same writer's *L'Économie mondiale capitaliste*, op. cit., and the various articles by G. Dhoquois, and others. I should, however, add that Palloix (in other writings of his) does recognize the nature of finance capital as a merging of industrial and banking capital.

These points are especially applicable in the imperialist stage, and for industrial monopoly capital and banking monopoly capital in particular. Depending on the concrete social formation, the phase and the conjuncture, the merger process and its functioning in the reproduction of capital can take place either under the aegis and economic leadership of industrial capital itself (the case of United States) or that of banking capital (Germany being the classic case), in their mutual struggle for the division of surplus-value.

For a long time in France this process took place under the aegis of banking capital and subject to its dominant economic role; however, contrary to what happened in Germany, this banking capital remained speculative and shied away from industrial investment. It is this that led both to the delay in industrialization and in the merger of monopoly capital in France, and to the specific characteristics of this process; for a long period, there was a divergent process of merger, in the main internal to each fraction (relatively separate concentration and centralization), with an advance of banking centralization over industrial concentration that was reinforced after the 1929 crisis.[15] Even today, there are three French banks among the top ten non-American banks in the world (the Banque Nationale Populaire in 4th place, Crédit Lyonnais in 5th, and Société Générale in 10th), while among the largest non-American industrial firms, Renault, the largest French firm, is only the 18th, Rhone-Poulenc the 27th, and the Compagnie Française des Pétroles the 32nd.

Now although the past few years have witnessed an acceleration of the merger process, the degree of concentration in French industry is still less than that in such other E.E.C. countries as Great Britain, Germany, Holland and even Belgium. This acceleration has this time taken place under the aegis of industrial monopoly capital (in the 5th and especially the 6th Plans), in an economy in which banking monopoly capital still retains, despite the evolution of such groups as the Suez Company or the Banque de Paris et des Pays-Bas, a pronounced speculative character; the special role that speculation in landed property plays in France is something that can only be understood in relation to the strategy being followed by banking monopoly capital. This also explains why, despite the fact that France has entered the present phase of monopoly capitalism under the effect of the internationalization of capitalist relations, and under the aegis of industrial monopoly capital, the tendency towards 'integrated production' still remains less advanced than in other imperialist metropolises. Despite significant changes, portfolio

15. J. Houssiaux, *Le Pouvoir du monopole, essai sur les structures du capitalisme contemporain*, 1958; B. Gille, 'La Concentration économique', in *La France et les Français*, Paris, 1972.

Characteristics features / Periodization	Articulation of modes and forms of production	Relations of production
THE TRANSITION TO CAPITALISM	1. Unstable equilibrium between CMP and 'pre-capitalist' (feudal) modes of production. 2. Forms of petty commodity production.	Economic ownership: capital $\Big\}$ Manufacture Possession: direct producers
THE EXTENDED REPRODUCTION OF CAPITALISM I STAGE OF COMPETITIVE CAPITALISM	1. Establishment of the dominance of the CMP. 2. Conservation effects often still dominant on other modes of production, especially on the form of petty commodity production.	CONSTANT CHARACTERISTIC $\Big\}$ ECONOMIC OWNERSHIP + POSSESSION = PLACE OF CAPITAL *Relations:* a. Economic ownership $\Big\}$ identification b. Possession *Degrees* of economic ownership and possession: no dissociation *Powers* deriving from these relations: no dissociation Individual capitalist entrepreneur
II STAGE OF MONOPOLY CAPITALISM — II. 1. Phase of transition from competitive to monopoly capitalism	1. Appearance and *extension* of monopoly capitalism. 2. Unstable equilibrium between monopoly capitalism and competitive capitalism. 2. Dissolution effects of capitalism on other modes of production. 4. Equilibrium of dissolution/conservation effects of capitalism on the simple commodity form.	CONCENTRATION/CENTRALISATION OF CAPITAL *Relations:* Dissociation Concentrated economic ownership ↓ ↓ ↓ Possession 1. Possession 2. Possession 3, etc. *Degrees:* dissociation Conc. ec. owns'p Conc. possession e.o. 1. e.o. 2. e.o. 3. pos. 1. pos. 2. pos. 3 *Powers:* dissociation $\Big\}$ Conc. e.o. → Powers / Powers / Powers Conc. pos. → Power / Power / Power
II. 2. Phase of the consolidation of monopoly capitalism	1. Dominance of monopoly capitalism, but the dominant aspect still its extension. 2. Dissolution effects dominant on the simple commodity form. 3. Conservation effects dominant on competitive capitalism.	
II. 3. Present phase of monopoly capitalism	1. Dominant *intensive* exploitation of monopoly capitalism over other forms of production, and *extended real subsumption* of their elements by monopoly capitalism. 2. Massive dissolution effects on the simple commodity form. 3. Dissolution effects dominant on competitive capitalist form.	TENDENCY FOR THE GAPS TO BE CLOSED IN A NEW FORM *Relations:* Concentrated economic ownership ↗ ↑ ↖ Possession 1. Possession 2. Possession 3. *Degrees:* Conc. ec. owns'p. Conc. possession ↑ ↑ ↖ ↑ ↑ ↖ e.o. 1. e.o. 2. e.o. 3. pos. 1. pos. 2. pos. 3 *Powers:* Economic ownership $\Big\}$ ←Powers / ←Powers / ←Powers Possession

Legal ownership, relations of production	Labour process	Type of production unit	Agents supporting relations and exercising powers	The State
Dissociations resulting from the equilibrium between modes of production (classic case being landed property).	Formal subsumption of labour to capital: manufacture.		Owners and direct producers.	Transition State: in Europe the 'Absolutist' State.
Capitalist identification of legal ownership and economic ownership: individual capitalist.	1. *Beginnings* of the real subsumption of capital to labour. 2. *Extensive* exploitation of labour dominant. 3. Appearance of intensive exploitation of labour: first effects of co-operation and socialization (machinery and large-scale industry).	Simple and 'separate' production units.	CONSTANT CHARACTERISTIC: POWERS DERIVING FROM THE PLACE OF CAPITAL. Powers concentrated and exercised by the individual capitalist entrepreneur/support of the relations.	1. Determination *and* dominance of the 'economic'. 2. Liberal state.
Capitalist dissociation of legal ownership and economic ownership (the joint-stock company).	Intensive exploitation of labour reinforced.	Concentration of simple production units, concentrated units still endowed with high degrees of economic ownership, of possession and of corresponding powers (trusts). Concentrated economic ownership ↓ ↓ ↓ SPU 1. SPU 2. SPU 3. (SPU = Single production Unit)	1. Dissociation of capitalist agents *supporting* the relations. 2. First dissociation of agents *exercising* powers. (The question of managers)	DOMINANT ROLE OF THE STATE 1. Unstable equilibrium between the dominance of the economic and the dominance of the state. 2. The interventionist state.
				Consolidation of the dominant role of the state.
	1. Intensive exploitation of labour becomes dominant. 2. Extended real subsumption of labour to capital. 3. Extended co-operation and socialization of the labour process. 4. Domination of 'dead labour' over 'living labour'. (Role of technological innovation.)	INTEGRATED PRODUCTION Complex production unit ↑ ↑ ↑ EPU 1. EPU 2. EPU 3. (EPU = *Elementary* Production Unit) Complex production units ↑ ↑ ↑ DPU 1. DPU 2. DPU 3. (DPU = *Dependent* Production Unit)	1. Concentration of the *supports* of the relations. 2. Reproduction of the dissociation of the agents who exercise powers. (The question of the 'centralization/decentralization' of the 'big firm'.)	1. New role of the state in the reproduction and accentuation of its dominance. 2. New form of interventionist state.

(Vertical text in left margin of Labour process column, top to bottom: TENDENCY ... FOR THE RATE ... OF PROFIT ... TO FALL)

DOMINANT/IMPERIALIST SOCIAL FORMATIONS

operations, classic holding companies, and even simple participation in companies with very different activities, are still highly important.[16]

These economic contradictions lead, depending on the specific formation and the moment of the process, to internal struggles between industrial monopoly capital and banking monopoly capital, struggles centred on political hegemony. It is particularly clear that Gaullism and the evolution of the political regime in France, even under Pompidou, can only be explained by reference not only to monopoly capital and its hegemony, but also to the intense struggle for political hegemony between these monopoly capitalist fractions.

The above remarks are thus equally valid for the present phase of imperialism and of monopoly capitalism. Just as the monopoly capitalist *stage* does not necessarily imply the dominance and hegemony of banking monopoly capital, so the present *phase* does not necessarily involve the dominance and hegemony of industrial monopoly capital. The transformations in the relations of production and the social division of labour which we have noted as characteristics of this phase, in no way amount to a differentiation in this sense in relation to the preceding phases, a differentiation that would consist in an inevitable shift of dominance and hegemony in favour of industrial monopoly capital.

Finally, the contradictions within monopoly capital over the division of surplus-value also involve commercial capital. Although this capital exhibits a pronounced tendency to become subordinated to the industrial monopolies, which have often their own distribution channels, it is clear that it is affected by its own cycle of concentration (distribution monopolies, supermarket chains, etc.), a circuit that reproduces within finance capital the contradictions between industrial capital, banking capital and commercial capital. In the latter case, however, we can put forward a general proposition concerning the imperialist stage, and its present phase in particular: the tendential law of the falling rate of profit – which, given the monopoly position of industrial capital on the market, affects the entire social capital – together with the growing autonomy of industrial capital in relation to commercial capital, leads to a characteristic subordination of commercial capital within the finance capital process. Even if commercial capital intervenes in the inter-monopoly

16. Y. Morvan, op. cit., p. 269, and especially J. Bouvier, *Un siècle de banque française*, op. cit.

contradictions, it can have neither economic aegis nor political hegemony. It has in fact hardly ever held this role except in certain cases and moments of competitive capitalism.

II

Inter-monopoly contradictions within the monopoly bourgeoisie involve:

(a) Contradictions between the industrial monopolies. These relate especially to competition for the conquest and control of markets, since monopolization does not suppress competition on the market, and there is never a perfect division of the market between the monopolies. But these contradictions also assume other forms: these include struggles for public finance and state support; for the take-over of medium capital and the amalgamation of individual capitals; for investment in the most profitable sectors and branches; for access to technological innovations.

(b) Contradictions between the banking monopolies. These include struggles for control of the money market, for the most rapid and most profitable turnover of the money capital which they hold, for the biggest share of the cake in financial and monetary speculation.

(c) Lastly, contradictions that divide the various capitals that have been amalgamated and concentrated in several forms, forms which often imply varying degrees of economic ownership unevenly divided between these capitals, and various powers that are relatively dissociated even under a single management. In other words (and this cannot be adequately stressed), the contradictions of monopoly capital do not express themselves simply as 'inter-monopoly' contradictions, i.e. as contradictions between monopolies as integral entities, but also cut through every single monopoly. This is particularly clear in the case of financial groupings in the strict sense, which, while they form an advanced level of 'amalgamation' of industrial and banking capital, at the same time reproduce within themselves the contradictions of the capitals thus amalgamated.

The analysis we have made here clearly shows that monopoly capital, the 'autonomous' form of existence of capital in the finance capital process, is not a fraction of the bourgeoisie in the same sense as those of industrial capital proper, banking capital and commercial capital. The key difference that is relevant for us here is that we are dealing with a fraction of the capitalist class (monopoly capital) which is divided by contradictions and fissures that are far more severe than those that affect each of these other fractions, precisely in so far as monopoly capital reproduces within it the contradictions between these fractions themselves, a conclusion which is of the utmost importance in examing the present role of the state.

This is all the more so in that these contradictions themselves can only be grasped if account is taken of the complex dependence of the domestic bourgeoisie on the dominant imperialist capital, and of the induced reproduction of the contradictions of the latter within it. The internationalization of capitalist relations gives rise to a whole series of strategic oppositions within the domestic bourgeoisie of the metropolises, which in no way necessarily coincide with the degrees of dependence of its components on the dominant imperialist capital. This is particularly the case with the opposition between that monopoly capital which has a strategy of international expansion and that which has a strategy of limited expansion within the national economic field, an opposition which assumed a decisive importance in France under the Gaullist regime. It is still the case, and this is what matters to us here, that it is often the monopoly capital with a strategy of international expansion that enters into the most intense contradictions with the dominant imperialist capital.

4. THE CONTRADICTIONS BETWEEN MONOPOLY CAPITAL AND NON-MONOPOLY CAPITAL

The contradictions within monopoly capital itself, discussed above, are combined in the stage of monopoly capitalism, depending on its particular phases, with the other contradictions within the bourgeoisie as a class, i.e. between monopoly capital on the one hand, and non-monopoly capital on the other.

I

It is first of all necessary for me to explain the terms that I am using in preference to the traditional ones of 'big' and 'medium' capital. Due to their imprecise character, the latter, although they may have a descriptive value in the context of a rigorous analysis of monopoly capitalism, can easily go together with serious political errors.

Such terms, relating to the order of magnitude, may in fact be understood as referring simply to directly visible and measurable empirical criteria, such as the 'size' of the enterprise, or the number of workers employed. These are only very partial indices and effects of the differentiation between monopoly and non-monopoly capital. Even worse, as they appear to imply a graduated and homogenous scale in the order of distribution of various capitals, or even a unilinear and continuous process of capital reproduction and valorization, they may lead to false analyses in either of two contra-dictory directions.

(a) On the one hand, they may blur the dividing lines and the specific contradictions between monopoly and non-monopoly capital, by assuming a progressive and uniform path of transition between the various components of this capital. This reinforces the mythic image of the bourgeoisie as an integrated totality, organized on a continuous series of levels; in the extreme case, by considering the reproduction process as homogenous in space and time, some people are led into denying the concepts of monopoly and non-monopoly capital any scientific status. What is left, as far as the bourgeoisie of the monopoly stage is concerned, is an abstract analysis in terms of industrial capital and banking capital, with finance capital abstractly denoting their 'amalgamation' into a uniform and continuous pro-cess. In this context, moreover, even the use of the terms 'big' and 'medium' capital becomes superfluous.

(b) On the other hand, the terms 'big' and 'medium' capital can lead to blurring the class dividing lines between, on the one side, capital as such, i.e. the bourgeoisie, and on the other side small-scale manufacturing and handicraft production, i.e. the petty bourgeoisie. This is effected by the surreptitious introduction, in this scale of magnitude, of the term 'small capital' to denote the petty bour-geoisie. The term 'big capital' is kept to refer to monopoly capital, seen as alone constituting the bourgeoisie, and by the term 'non-monopoly strata' a continuous line is drawn to include both 'medium capital' (the remainder of the bourgeoisie) and 'small capital' (the petty bourgeoisie), giving it to be understood that all who do not form part of 'big capital' no longer belong to the bourgeoisie. In this way medium capital is supposed to have the same type of contradictions in regard to big capital as the petty bourgeoisie has in regard to the bourgeoisie, and hence to present the same possibilities as the petty bourgeoisie as far as alliance with the working class is concerned; this is of course the current political line of the PCF with its 'anti-monopoly alliance'. However, this theoretical con-fusion is also found with other writers, as for example A. Granou. He does not flinch from expressly separating the 'medium bour-geoisie' from the bourgeoisie proper, in such expressions as: 'The bourgeoisie must ensure the unreserved support of all strata of the petty and medium bourgeoisie.'[17] This amounts to sanctioning the myth of a union of 'small and medium-size enterprises', which is in fact only a means by which non-monopoly capital subordinates the petty bourgeoisie by obtaining its support in its own struggle against

17. *Les Temps Modernes*, January 1973, p. 1215.

monopoly capital, and creating in the petty bourgeoisie the illusion of a community of interest. We need only recall that the federation of small and medium-size enterprises in France includes 'firms' with anything up to 300 empolyees.[18]

In short, the use of terms referring to a graduated and uniform scale may on the one hand mask the split within the bourgeoisie between monopoly and non-monopoly capital, while on the other hand it may obliterate the class barrier between capital in general and the petty bourgeoisie, under cover of the term 'small capital'.

The same theoretical line may be taken still further. It may be assumed that the contradictions within the bourgeoisie, on both sides of the dividing line between monopoly and non-monopoly capital, coincide with groupings definable in the relative order of their magnitude or size. If this were so, nothing would stand in the way of there being contradictions between big and small monopolies, or, among non-monopoly capital, between enterprises defined according to their respective size and magnitude.

As far as the distinction between monopoly and non-monopoly capital is concerned:

1. The movement of concentration and centralization of capital is a constant process. It follows that the boundaries between monopoly and non-monopoly capital are variable and relative. They depend both on the phase of monopoly capitalism and on its concrete forms (branches, sectors, etc.) within a social formation. In point of fact, non-monopoly capital is based in the stage of competitive capitalism, such as this continues to function in a formation dominated by monopoly capitalism. This mode of functioning is itself transformed as a function of the domination of monopoly capital. There is in no sense a simple 'coexistence' of two separate water-tight sectors. The criteria by which non-monopoly capital is defined are always located in relation to monopoly capital and its specific characteristics in a given phase: these criteria are not those intrinsic to a competitive capitalism such as this would have been able to function before the dominance of monopoly capitalism.

Thus, to take up some more examples of the series of indices and

18. P. Bleton, *Le capitalisme français*, 1966, p. 84. It is apparent here that the identification of non-monopoly capital with the petty bourgeoisie ('small and medium-size enterprises'), which in the case of the 'anti-monopoly strategy' gives rise to a right opportunism, can also give rise to left opportunism: this identification can lead to the petty bourgeoisie, under the label 'small capital', being considered as forming part of non-monopoly capital (the bourgeoisie), and thus to ruling out, *a priori*, those possibilities for alliance with it by the popular forces which occur in certain conjunctures.

effects that we already mentioned above in analysing the concentration of capital: the organic composition of capital is significantly lower in the case of non-monopoly capital, which does not exhibit in any clear fashion the shift of dominance towards intensive exploitation of labour (relative surplus-value). However, because the reproduction of non-monopoly capital is located in the general context of monopoly capitalism, it should not be thought that this form of capital still remains as it was at the stage of competitive capitalism. If there are differences in this respect in relation to monopoly capital, it is none the less the case that the intensive exploitation of labour, by raising the productivity of labour and by technological innovations, affects non-monopoly capital as well. Moreover, where non-monopoly capital does not manage to extend its economic ownership on to the socialization of the labour process, its production units are most often confined to one single branch. But this is not a general rule, for non-monopoly capital can often be involved in this socialization, and may thus sometimes extend over several branches. Finally, non-monopoly capital does not exhibit the amalgamation of industrial capital and money capital characteristic of monopoly capital. But even here, industrial capital does not appear in a totally separate form, and the legal form of the joint-stock company, in particular, is adopted by non-monopoly capital itself.

2. The basis of the differentiation between monopoly capital and non-monopoly capital lies in the specific relations of production which characterize these two forms of capital in their articulation with the labour process. In the realm of productive capital in particular, even while the interdependence of labour processes is on the rise in the social formation as a whole, non-monopoly capital does not manage to extend this integration under a single economic ownership, so that its typical production unit is generally restricted to a specific labour process, or a series of definite processes. The relationships of economic ownership and possession do not exhibit the type of dissociation characteristic of monopoly capital. Economic ownership and possession closely coincide, and legal ownership most frequently amounts to economic ownership. These are relevant when considered in relation to the distinguishing features of monopoly capital, although they should not be seen in terms of the individual entrepreneur of the period of competitive capitalism.

II

The relations and contradictions between monopoly capital and non-monopoly capital thus depend on the phases through which monopoly capitalism is passing, in the concrete forms that these assume within the social formations. They go closely together with the forms assumed by the contradictory effects of dissolution and conservation which the domination of monopoly capitalism imposes on competitive capitalism and even on non-monopoly capital. During the phases of transition and consolidation the conservation effects prevailed over the dissolution effects, while in the present phase, the balance has clearly shifted in favour of the latter.

The dominance of the dissolution effects in the present phase, however, does not amount to the radical elimination of non-monopoly capital by way of a pure and simple take-over by monopoly capital; the principal path taken by this dissolution is not that of a formal expropriation of non-monopoly capital. This can be formulated by saying that the dissolution effects are quite compatible, not only with the persistence of a transformed sector of non-monopoly capital (secondary conservation effects) but even with a reproduction of this sector in a new form. The overall super-accumulation of capital by monopoly capital, and the dominant role of the latter in the valorization of capital, still maintains a specific margin of accumulation for non-monopoly capital. This is expressed among other things in the fact that a number of non-monopoly enterprises exhibit a high rate of profit, sometimes even higher than that of monopoly capital, although uneven rates of profit, both between enterprises and in time, are also more pronounced in this case than in that of monopoly capital.[19]

There are a series of economic reasons which explain the usefulness for monopoly capital of preserving and reproducing a restricted sector of non-monopoly capital:

(1) Non-monopoly capital occupies sectors that are of limited profitability in a given period and enables monopoly capital to choose the moment of its expansion, by virtue of the selectiveness it must apply in its investments in the context of the falling rate of profit tendency and of unevenness in the tendency for rates of profit to be equalized.

(2) Monopoly capital often leaves non-monopoly capital the possibility of pioneering new sectors of production, intervening itself only when the risks are minimized; this was the case, to a certain extent, with the electronics and computer industries in the United States and Japan.

(3) Non-monopoly capital enables monopoly capital to recoup technological innovations at lowest cost. Monopoly capital does not

19. J. Parent, *La Concentration industrielle*, 1970, pp. 172 ff.

have to finance these in their entirety; several innovations in fact derive from non-monopoly capital, but since this cannot itself apply them, it hands them over to monopoly capital in the form of patents. The classic case here is that of United Steel, the dominant giant in the United States metal industry, which has scarcely been responsible for any innovations in this branch, but has simply taken over the innovations of small firms.

(4) Given the disparities in the labour market and non-monopoly capital's low level of labour productivity, this capital is also useful for channelling and bringing into use workers with a low level of training who come from the rural exodus or from the proletarianization of the traditional petty bourgeoisie. In this case, this capital functions as a staging-post in the process of subjecting labour-power to monopoly capital.

(5) Non-monopoly capital is also useful, particularly in the context of integrated production, for secondary lines of production that do not enter into the continuous and large-scale flow of complex production units; this is for example the case with automobile accessories.

(6) Finally, these are reasons connected with price formation. Since non-monopoly capital is in general faced with higher production costs, by virtue of its lower level of labour productivity, monopoly capital can fix its monopoly prices by reference to those of non-monopoly capital, thus hiding its super-profits.

These examples should be ample enough. We should recall, however, that even outside those cases where the survival of non-monopoly capital is advantageous for monopoly capital, the persistence of the former is also due to the fact that competitive capitalism constantly reproduces itself under the domination of monopoly; there is a process of constant and 'spontaneous' resurgence of new non-monopoly capital, parallel to the continuous dissolution of the old. What we are faced with are two stages, competitive and monopoly, of the same capitalist mode of production. The dissolution effects of one of these stages on the other do not take the same forms as in a periodization of different modes of production. Non-monopoly capital is not a simple form that is preserved or conserved, as in the case of feudal forms surviving within capitalism, but a form reproduced under the domination of monopoly capitalism. This is the reason why those sectors marked by a characteristic reproduction of non-monopoly capital, in particular where the number of new non-monopoly enterprises surpasses that of the enterprises of the same kind that are eliminated, often have a high rate of expansion: in France, examples are rubber products and plastics, and electrical construction. To sum up, nothing could be more false than the analysis that is often currently made of French society, on the model of the false conception of the 'dual society' in the dependent countries, in terms of 'two sectors', a 'backward', 'retrograde', 'traditional' sector on the one hand (small and medium-size enterprises), a 'modern' and 'advanced' sector on the other (the monopoly sector). In fact, both of these belong to the same structure of extended reproduction of monopoly capital.

These reasons, however, are still far from sufficient to explain either the current persistence of non-monopoly capital, or the fact that the dissolution effects, at the present time especially, follow the indirect paths of dependence of this capital on monopoly capital, rather than the direct paths of pure and simple take-over and liquidation. In fact, the concrete rhythms and forms of the concentration process closely depend on the political struggles in the social formation, and particularly on the forms assumed by the principal contradiction.

In considering the history of the relationship between monopoly and non-monopoly capital in the imperialist metropolises, it appears that, confronted by the struggles of the popular masses and the resistance of non-monopoly capital, monopoly capital has been led to a selective strategy involving indirect forms of subordination of non-monopoly capital, so that it can avoid serious fissures in the power bloc in the face of the dominated classes; this strategy has sought to avoid sudden political and ideological jolts. Current forms of dependence are, as Baran and Sweezy rightly point out,[20] distinct from the 'wild' forms of take-over and liquidation of non-monopoly capital that were particularly characteristic of the first phase of monopoly capitalism; these forms led to the belief in a pure and simple elimination, in the short term, of non-monopoly capital. These changes of strategy, of which anti-trust legislation in the United States was only one aspect, must be interpreted as concessions by monopoly capital to non-monopoly capital within the power bloc itself; the reality of these concessions is undeniable, though of course it is far different from the ideological picture presented.

The main significance of these strategic compromises must be understood; they should not be taken in the abstract, in a static fashion, but rather within the general context of capital concentration. Thus they do not amount to sudden checks or reverses in the process of capital merger, nor are they, as the current and static interpretation has it, positive measures in favour of non-monopoly capital; they are not real measures in defence of the economic and

20. *Monopoly Capital*, op. cit., p. 62.

political independence of non-monopoly capital against monopoly capital. What they essentially affect is the rhythm (acceleration and deceleration, temporary 'pauses') and forms, i.e. the profile, of the concentration process.[21] They also have their effects on the distribution of the total surplus-value – the division of the cake – between monopoly and non-monopoly capital. For example, a slower and more regular concentration process, forms of dependence rather than straightforward elimination or take-over, while they are not 'positive' for non-monopoly capital in the strict sense (they cannot be calculated in the abstract, and concentration still takes place), are nevertheless often concessions made by monopoly to non-monopoly capital. They are positive in the context of the balance of forces, in the sense that the effects of the concentration process are not as negative for non-monopoly capital as they would have been without these compromises.

A characteristic example of this strategy, effected by way of the state as the decisive organizing factor of hegemony, is provided by the preliminary discussions around the 6th Plan in France. 'Modern' big monopoly capital organized in the Comité National des Patronats Français, which dominated the 6th Plan's Industrial Commission, was thinking of a rhythm of expansion and growth along 'Japanese' lines, of around 7·5 to 8 per cent per year. One consequence of this, as Michel Bosquet correctly stressed, would have been 'the closing down of thousands of small and medium-size enterprises'; these proposals also corresponded to an offensive by monopoly capital against non-monopoly capital. The state later fixed on a growth rate of around 6 per cent, the reason being not only fear of working-class reactions in the face of the negative effects that the growth rate originally conceived of would have brought for them, but also the need for a compromise with small and medium-size enterprises, i.e. with non-monopoly capital. There was clearly an extremely lively debate here between the C.N.P.F. and the small and medium-size enterprises.[22] But this certainly did not mean that the disintegration of non-monopoly capital was in any way stopped by the 6th Plan – quite the contrary!

These points are essential to bear in mind if we are to grasp the concrete patterns of the concentration process as it develops in the

21. I should like to recall here that the concentration and centralization of capital should in no way be seen, in its real historical development, as a gradual, unilinear and homogenous process. In certain periods, generally brief, this process can even undergo relative retreats.

22. Michel Bosquet, *Critique du capitalisme quotidien*, Paris, 1973, pp. 122 ff.

different phases of monopoly capitalism and in the concrete social formations, and hence the exact relations between the various fractions of the bourgeoisie. It is particularly mistaken to believe that the forms in which non-monopoly capital persists and is maintained can be explained exclusively by the fact that they fit perfectly in with the temporary interests of monopoly capital, or that they exist only to the extent that they are economically useful to monopoly capital; this would be to take up the same position as the bourgeois economists who account for this persistence in terms of supposed 'technico-economic limits' intrinsic to the concentration process. What should not be forgotten is that we are dealing here with a political balance of forces within the bourgeoisie itself, in the context of its confrontation with the working class (the principal contradiction). The forms and tempo of the concentration process, as expressed in the forms of persistence of non-monopoly capital, are often simply strategic measures that serve the political interests of monopoly capital, by ensuring its political hegemony over the bourgeoisie as a whole and maintaining the political cohesion of the power bloc in the face of the working class. This balance also helps to explain the dislocations involving the 'advance' or 'delay' of the concentration process in the various social formations. The long period of French backwardness in this respect cannot be entirely explained by the 'structural economic' weaknesses of French capitalism; rather, what is seen as the 'weakness' of French capitalism was no intrinsic characteristic, but was based precisely on this balance of forces. This weakness was in fact related to the particular type of compromise that French monopoly capital was forced to make with non-monopoly capital, and also – until the last few years – with the petty bourgeoisie, for political reasons related to the struggle of the working class.

These remarks lead us to go more deeply into the question of the relations between monopoly and non-monopoly capital in the present phase, in which the dissolution effects on non-monopoly capital prevail over the conservation effects. These dissolution effects are essentially taking place through the indirect and diverse forms of dependence of non-monopoly capital on monopoly capital, although this is always accompanied by forms of legal absorption through formal expropriation (as after bankruptcies). Under the appearance of a maintenance of independent legal ownership by non-monopoly capital, the powers deriving from economic ownership are frequently taken over, in whole or in part, by monopoly capital; this is particularly so in the case of many sub-contracting agreements, as a result of which non-monopoly capital scarcely retains any powers of its own regarding the employment of the means of labour and the allocation of the resources of its enterprise.

This can be taken even further if account is taken of the socialization of the labour processes themselves and the direction and control of these processes as a whole by monopoly capital in the present phase. One effect of this situation, as we have seen, is integrated production and the formation of complex production units under both the ownership and the possession of big capital. But the new forms of social division of labour are in no way confined to the inside of these units. In fact, apart from what is happening in relation to economic ownership, it is now evident that the direction and control even of the labour processes conducted in non-monopoly 'enterprises' progressively escape from the control of non-monopoly capital and are taken over by monopoly capital. There is a shift taking place in the powers deriving from possession, or at least in certain of these, in favour of monopoly capital. This follows several paths, including: standardization of basic products and of norms of work organization imposed on the labour process as a whole by monopoly capital; technological dependence of non-monopoly capital on monopoly capital through patents and licences; subjection of non-monopoly capital to a social division of labour which to a considerable extent confines it to sectors with a low level of productivity and an inferior technology. There is no need to dwell on the fact that the limited margins for self-financing disposed of by non-monopoly capital render it especially dependent, in the general context of a necessarily rapid turnover of capital, on money capital and its centralization, by the leonine controls that the big banks impose as a condition of granting credit.

These developments can only be understood in their full scope if account is taken of the current tendency for the dissociations between economic ownership and possession on the one hand, and between the powers deriving from economic ownership on the other, to close again. The on-going loss of possession by non-monopoly capital of the control and direction of its labour processes leads directly to the concentration of economic ownership in the hands of monopoly capital, in such a way that, behind the legal façade or the façade of a retention by non-monopoly capital of independent economic ownership, the very boundaries of its 'enterprises', i.e. its production units, are progressively being dissolved. Many non-monopoly enterprises are in fact dependent production units; while these are to be distinguished from the elementary production units that form part of a complex production unit, they scarcely any longer form independent units run by the individual entrepreneur, of the type characteristic of the competitive stage, or even as he functioned in the previous phases of monopoly capitalism.[23]

III

By taking account of these two aspects of the process, both the characteristic dependence of non-monopoly capital on monopoly capital and the strategy followed by the latter of avoiding the brusque elimination of the former, it is possible to discern the relation of non-monopoly to monopoly capital in the present phase of monopoly capitalism. This phase reproduces the contradictions between monopoly and non-monopoly capital on an extended scale; however, what we are most concerned with is to understand the current forms of these contradictions.

During the phases of transition to and consolidation of monopoly capitalism, these contradictions actually assumed particularly sharp forms, manifesting themselves on the political scene by deep fissures in the power bloc and by severe political crises. Non-monopoly capital, by way of its political parties and the forms of state and regime of the time, often functioned as an autonomous social force, challenging step by step the economic domination of monopoly capital in its abrupt and untamed forms. Non-monopoly capital still possessed appreciable strongholds in the economic domain, and frequently even occupied the political foreground by way of its political organizations; in this case non-monopoly capital formed the governing fraction (this was the case in France up till the first years of Gaullism), while monopoly capital had already conquered real political hegemony.[24] In the context of this intense struggle, both monopoly and non-monopoly capital often sought the support of the popular classes in order to counter the designs of their opponent.

However, things are no longer the same in this respect. The complex subordination and dependence of non-monopoly capital on monopoly capital is today largely an accomplished fact in the imperialist metropolises. The reproduction of their contradictions is itself located within this relationship of subordination, by the

23. See the table on pp. 134–5.

24. For the concepts of the power bloc and hegemony, see pp. 24 ff. above. By the *governing* class or fraction, I mean that class or fraction that generally provides the political personnel and the 'heads' of the state apparatus, and which, by way of its own organizations, occupies the political foreground. As Marx himself showed, the governing class or fraction may be different from the hegemonic class or fraction, whose interests the state especially serves. These questions are analysed in *Political Power and Social Classes*.

development and consolidation of multiple networks of dependence. Not only are the production and labour processes of non-monopoly capital closely intertwined with those of monopoly production, but even the large-scale enterprise can no longer serve non-monopoly capital as an ultimate escape route to refloat its business. Monopoly capital's transition from a strategy of elimination to a strategy of dependency for non-monopoly capital precisely indicates that it has in fact already capitulated to monopoly capital, in the sense that henceforward it is only struggling to survive and only seeking to adjust its dependence on monopoly capital. This does not contradict the fact that the latter retains a portion of the total surplus-value, if a progressively limited one (transfers of surplus-value in favour of monopoly capital), since its accumulation margins are restricted in the face of monopoly super-accumulation. The very fact that every major crisis of monopoly capital is chiefly reflected, in the first instance, in the 'security zone' which monopoly capital has been able to create around it by preserving a non-monopoly sector, makes the class solidarity between the two even stronger. In short, in considering monopoly and non-monopoly capital in the present phase, we must bear in mind their new relationship of organic interdependence. This in no way means that the contradictions between monopoly and non-monopoly capital have now been 'superceded', quite the contrary. It simply means that we should not expect a political expression of these contradictions in the form of a break by non-monopoly capital as a social force with its class front.

To understand properly this class solidarity which now more than ever characterizes the contradictory relationships between monopoly and non-monopoly capital, we have to take into consideration the form currently assumed by the principal contradiction, that between the bourgeoisie as a whole on the one hand, and the working class and popular masses on the other; one of the main characteristics of the present phase is that of the rise of working-class and popular struggles in the imperialist metropolises themselves. And it is extremely significant in this respect that these working-class struggles often have their most severe effects on non-monopoly capital, given the fragile margins for accumulation and manoeuvre that this enjoys in the context of its dependence on monopoly capital. In fact, if we take the situation of the last few years, in France in particular, it is plain to see that non-monopoly capital has put up stronger resistance to the concessions 'extracted by force' by the working class than has monopoly capital; we need only mention the negotiations, during and after the Grenelle agreements, on the raising of the S.M.I.G. [guaranteed minimum wage]. Monopoly capital is in a position to pass wage increases directly onto prices, and to make up for them by increasing the productivity of labour, a possibility that non-monopoly capital does not always enjoy, or not to the same extent. Furthermore, we know that the big employers often take refuge in their struggle against the working class behind the 'difficulties of small and medium-size enterprises', a class solidarity which, beneath its ideological mask, does correspond to certain actual facts. It is one of the stronger points of the strategy of monopoly capital that it has managed to unite *non-monopoly capital* closely with it, using the latter, having driven it back into the 'security zone', as a protective shield and a rampart in its struggle against the working class, passing directly onto non-monopoly capital the effects of the working-class struggle against itself which is the core of the contemporary struggles.

This does not prevent monopoly capital, in its contradiction with non-monopoly capital, from playing off the working class to some extent against non-monopoly capital, in appropriate specific conjunctures. One reason why monopoly capital sometimes shows itself to be 'understanding' in regard to certain concessions made to the working class is the fact that these precipitate the disintegration of non-monopoly capital, which cannot afford them in the same way that monopoly capital can. This could be recently observed in France in the attitude of the 'modernizing' and 'social' tendency of the big employers of the C.N.P.F. (Ambroise Roux, Martin, etc., or even the policy of Chaban-Delmas and his social policy 'advisers'), in contrast to that of the small and medium enterprises.[25]

The above analysis points to one decisive fact; the increased dependence of non-monopoly capital on monopoly capital, and the transfer of a growing part of the total surplus-value from the former to the latter, in no way means that non-monopoly capital is 'exploited' by monopoly capital, as G. Mury and M. Bouvier-Ajam made out at the time that the PCF's strategy of an anti-monopoly alliance was being worked out:[26] 'An entire section of the bourgeoisie is rejected, reduced and even exploited by the other.' To uphold this position is in fact to reproduce, at the level of the national social formation, the same type of theoretical errors as have been made by A. Emmanuel at the international level when he locates the global relation of exploitation as one between 'rich nations' and 'proletarian nations', implying that the bourgeoisies of the dependent countries are themselves exploited by the bour-

25. G. Martinet, *Le Système Pompidou*, 1973.

26. *Les Classes sociales en France*, 1963, vol. I, p. 96 (Éditions sociales). This book, now out of print, contains some excellent analyses.

geoisies of the imperialist metropolises. Both these analyses lead to a similar political result: in the one case, to a supposed class solidarity between the popular masses of the dependent countries and their own bourgeoisies ('the exploited nations') against the imperialist bourgeoisies; in the other case, to a supposed class solidarity between the popular masses of the imperialist countries and their non-monopoly bourgeoisies ('exploited bourgeoisies') against monopoly capital. In fact, however, the relationship of exploitation is that between the bourgeoisie as a whole and the working class and popular masses.

5. NON-MONOPOLY CAPITAL AND THE TRADITIONAL PETTY BOURGEOISIE

It is clear enough that the arguments I have given above are intended to refute those of the Western CP's, which, by using the terms 'non-monopoly strata' and 'small-scale capital', exclude non-monopoly capital from the bourgeoisie and from economic and political domination, by identifying it in practice with the manu-facturing, artisanal and commercial petty bourgeoisie, and thus including it among the dominated classes (non-monopoly strata). Let us say right away that there is a decisive difference here, which is in fact a class barrier. The petty bourgeoisie is not a bourgeoisie smaller than the others; it is not part of the bourgeoisie at all, since it does not exploit, or at least is not chiefly involved in exploiting, wage labour. The difference between a craftsman in an artisanal or even 'semi-artisanal' enterprise, and a small employer who exploits ten workers, is not of the same order as that between the latter and an employer who exploits twenty workers; there is a class barrier involved which cannot be reduced to a difference in 'magnitude'. To ignore this is to fall completely into the myth of the 'small and medium-size enterprises'.

This also entails that the contradictions that divide the petty bourgeoisie from monopoly capital are completely different in type to those which divide non-monopoly capital from monopoly capital. Although statistics only give an incomplete picture, these show that the dissolution effects imposed by monopoly capital on the tradi-tional petty bourgeoisie, especially in the present phase, are in sharp contrast to those imposed on non-monopoly capital. In the case of the traditional petty bourgeoisie, these effects actually do assume the forms of an accelerated process of liquidation and elimination.

French statistics, generally based on the number of workers employed by an 'enterprise', include a general category of firms with fewer than five employees which is particularly relevant for us, though they do not distinguish more precisely within this category. Cross-checking in various ways makes it possible to say that it is here that the petty bourgeoisie in the strict sense is to be found, that which does not employ any wage-workers, or which does not in the main employ wage labour, or which is located in a transitional position between artisanal and semi-artisanal forms. It is precisely this category that is affected, far more severely and significantly than the others, by liquidation effects; between 1954 and 1966, 127,500 artisanal enterprises employing five workers or less closed down, while the number of those employing between six and nine workers increased by 73,000.[27] This is expressed in the quite characteristic decline in the absolute number of petty-bourgeois 'small enterprises' in relation to the decline of non-monopoly capital; statistics by sectors show that what are classed as 'manufacturing enterprises' in France declined by an annual average of 9,000 between 1962 and 1967, followed by a decline of around 800 to 1000 for textiles and wood and furniture. An analysis of the economically active population by establishments (which differs from analysis by firms) shows that between 1954 and 1966 the percentage working in establishments with no wage labour fell from 6 to 4 per cent, the percentage in establishments employing from one to four workers fell from 13 to 10 per cent, that in establishments employing between five and ninety-five workers remained stable (at around 6 per cent), while the percentage in establishments in all other categories rose.[28] Finally, there was a decrease in the number of heads of firms, between 1954 and 1968, of some 90,000, these being for the most part firms with no wage labour.

It is thus quite possible to speak of a massive process of pauperization and proletarianization of this petty bourgeoisie, quite different to the forms of domination of monopoly capital over non-monopoly capital. But even in the case of this petty bourgeoisie, the tempo and forms of its subjection to monopoly capital depend on the precise role of the state in managing the 'unstable equilibrium of compromise', as is illustrated by the recent Royer law in France.

As far as relations between monopoly and non-monopoly capital are concerned, i.e. relations within the bourgeoisie itself, the schematic picture of a radical internal polarization between a few giant monopolies on the one hand, and a mass of small firms on the other, corresponds even less either to the real situation in the imperialist metropolises in general, or even to the French social

27. J. Chatain, 'Concentration dans le secteur des métiers', in *Économie et Politique,* October 1970.

28. Y. Morvan, op. cit., pp. 228 and 249.

formation in particular; the latter, for certain historic reasons, still contains an appreciable number of small-scale enterprises. In fact non-monopoly capital covers a wide and diverse range, including in several branches and sectors a good number of medium-size enterprises which are also affected by a growing dependence on monopoly capital. In short, the picture of a non-monopoly bourgeoisie massively polarized from below is far from corresponding to reality.

In this case, too, we see the fallacious character of the use of terms implying an order of magnitude. In the case of the non-monopoly bourgeoisie, for example, our objection to the theories of state monopoly capitalism is not simply that we wish to limit more closely the section of the bourgeoisie that should be considered as effectively pauperized. It is not a question of seeing only the 'smallest' section of the bourgeoisie, instead of non-monopoly capital as a whole, as forming part of the dominated classes, and including 'medium capital' in the dominant class. It is non-monopoly capital as a whole that is located by a class barrier on the side of the bourgeoisie. Nothing proves, moreover, that the sharpness of the contradictions between non-monopoly and monopoly capital exactly coincides with divisions of magnitude. There is no reason why a 'small' capitalist enterprise should have greater contradictions with monopoly capital than a 'medium-size' one. The process of liquidation and elimination does not just affect the small capitalist, even if mortality rates appear to be greater for small capitalist enterprises than for medium-size. Those who are affected by this process are above all the small trader and the craftsman, and as all empirical evidence shows, the significant division in this respect is that between the small capitalists (part of the bourgeoisie) on the one hand, and the petty bourgeoisie on the other hand.

6. CONTRADICTIONS WITHIN NON-MONOPOLY CAPITAL

The contradictions within monopoly capital, or those between monopoly and non-monopoly capital, are not the only ones that currently divide the power bloc; there are also contradictions within non-monopoly capital itself, for example contradictions between industrial, banking and commercial non-monopoly capital.

In this context we may note a phenomenon that is analogous, although of less overall significance, to that affecting the relationships between the dominant imperialist capital and the domestic bourgeoisies. This derives from the very structure of the dependence involved: contradictions within non-monopoly capital tend more and more to reproduce and reflect, at their own level, contradictions within monopoly capital itself. In other words, the contradictions within the dependent sector reproduce in their own fashion the contradictions of the dominant sector. Sections of non-monopoly capital, even though they are not absorbed by monopoly capital, can nevertheless very often depend on one monopoly firm or another, either through sub-contracting constraints, or, as often happens, through their actual labour process. The contradictions between these monopoly firms are thus directly reflected in contradictions between non-monopoly firms dependent on the monopolies involved, these contradictions thus acquiring an induced and over-determined character.

This can often produce contradictory effects, leading to non-monopoly capital suffering the extrapolation of monopoly capital, the directing centre of capital accumulation, to a breach in the homogeneity of non-monopoly capital in the face of monopoly capital, and finally to a decline in its unitary resistance to monopoly capital. The contradiction between monopoly and non-monopoly capital is directly affected by this induced reproduction of the specific contradictions of monopoly capital within non-monopoly capital. A non-monopoly firm is at once united with non-monopoly capital in its contradiction to monopoly capital, and united with the monopoly on which it depends in the latter's contradictions with other monopolies, which also have other non-monopoly firms dependent on them. The dissolution effects that non-monopoly capital experiences are finally expressed here in a dissolution of its political unity in resisting monopoly capital, which from then on prevents it from functioning as an effective social force.

The contradictions within monopoly capital are not only reproduced within non-monopoly capital, but also in the relations between monopoly and non-monopoly capital; this or that fraction of monopoly capital (the predominantly industrial or the predominantly banking fraction), this or that sector of monopoly capital, often follow different strategies and tactics towards non-monopoly capital. These strategies and tactics are largely related to the contradictions that affect monopoly capital and to the balance of forces between its various components. In France in particular, banking monopoly capital, with its general attitude of reservation towards industry, has often followed a more conciliatory strategy towards non-monopoly capital, being content to exercise control in an indirect form by way of credit decisions, while industrial monopoly capital, through the current transformations in the relations of production ('industrialization', 'modernization', etc.) has taken a more aggressive position. This has often enabled banking monopoly capital, by way of its political representatives, to present itself as the defender of small and medium-size firms (e.g. the role of the Independent Republicans, who thus continue an old tradition of the traditional big bourgeoisie in France), both in relation to working-class demands and to the 'appetites' of the modernizing tendency (industrial monopoly capital) of the big employers in France. The latter on the other hand have sought a policy of compromise towards the working class, in the context of their own contradictions with banking monopoly capital and non-monopoly capital – witness the contradictions between Giscard d'Estaing and Chaban-Delmas.

The above analysis already permits us to draw an initial political conclusion: just as non-monopoly capital cannot be seen, under the label of the 'anti-monopoly strata', as currently excluded from economic and political domination and from the power bloc, so it cannot be considered as a fraction of the bourgeoisie that can form part of the people in an imperialist metropolis, and can thus be won for an alliance with the popular classes in the process of transition to socialism. If this was true in the previous phases of monopoly capitalism, it is all the more true in the present phase, given the way that non-monopoly capital has been cemented into the common front of the bourgeoisie, and given the end of its autonomy as a social force. This is especially so since, as we indicated in the previous essay on the internationalization of capitalist relations, non-monopoly capital can in no way be seen as part of a national bourgeoisie confronting a monopoly capital that is entirely comprador, the lines of division between the domestic bourgeoisie and the dominant imperialist capital rather cutting through both monopoly and non-monopoly capital.

This of course does not mean that in isolated cases 'small capitalists' cannot come over to the side of the working class, nor that the strategy of the popular masses in the transition to socialism should put non-monopoly capital, or the domestic bourgeoisie as a whole, in the same basket with monopoly capital, which is the main enemy, and treat them in the same fashion. It is clear that at certain stages in the process, certain forms and degrees of 'compromise' with non-monopoly capital are going to be necessary on the part of the working class and its allies, i.e. of the 'people'. But it is equally clear that this has very little in common with an 'anti-monopoly alliance'.

3

The Contemporary State
and the Bourgeoisies

I. THE DEBATE

The role of the state in monopoly capitalism, and particularly in its present phase, must be located in relation to the above analysis of the contemporary forms assumed by the contradictions within the bourgeoisie. The following discussion, however, which locates the state in relation to the domestic bourgeoisie, must itself be seen in the context of the role of the state in the framework of the internationalization of capitalist relations. Finally, an exhaustive examination of the state is only possible if the class struggle as a whole, and therefore the dominated classes as well, are taken into consideration. While it sanctions and legitimizes class domination, the state also provides the cohesive factor of the entire social formation, and in reproducing the social relations of this formation it condenses in itself all of the formation's contradictions.

I

It must be said straight away that the analyses of the capitalist state made by the Marxist classics are not confined, as is often said, to the role of the state in 'competitive capitalism', or in the nineteenth century. This is the basic criticism that, in one form or another, has been levelled against my arguments in *Political Power and Social Classes* and *Fascism and Dictatorship* by P.C.F. writers: from L. Perceval and J. Lojkine through to P. Herzog, M. and R. Weyl, A. Gisselbrecht, and others.[1]

1. L. Perceval has written long criticisms of both my earlier books, in *Économie et Politique* no. 190, May 1970 and no. 204–5, July–August 1971; J. Lojkine, 'Pouvoir politique et Luttes des classes', article cited from *La*

The reasons for referring here to my earlier arguments and these criticisms of them is that the very heart of the differences between our positions is involved here. Although there are certain variations between these writers themselves, which expose very well the contradictory positions they have retreated into, their criticisms can be summed up as follows. The analyses of Marx, Engels, Lenin and Gramsci on which I based myself were certainly correct in terms of the specific situation that the latter confronted, but they are no longer applicable to the state of state monopoly capitalism, which according to the P.C.F. exhibits the features indicated at the beginning of this essay.

These criticisms appear to me to be groundless, though not because the form of state present under monopoly capitalism does not have its specific features. Rather, not only do the analyses of the capitalist state made by the Marxist classics bear on all forms of this state, including its present form, but it is only on this basis that the modifications currently taking place can be understood.

1. To start with the essential point, the analysis of the 'fusion of the state and the monopolies in a single mechanism' in the present phase ('state monopoly capitalism'), which implies on the one hand that monopoly capital is the only dominant fraction and that non-monopoly capital is excluded from the terrain of economic and political domination, and on the other hand that monopoly capital is itself a fraction abstractly 'unified' by its own means, is simply wrong. Today, as always, the state plays the role of political unifier of the power bloc and political organizer of the hegemony of monopoly capital within the power bloc, which is made up of several fractions of the bourgeois class and is divided by internal contradictions. The relation between the state and the monopolies today is no more one of identification and fusion than was the case in the past with other capitalist fractions. The state rather takes special responsibility for the interests of the hegemonic fraction, monopoly capital, in so far as this fraction holds a leading position in the power bloc, and as its interests are erected into the political interest of capital as a whole *vis-à-vis* the dominated classes.

We have already seen, in fact, that monopoly capital, the product

---

Pensée; P. Herzog, *Politique économique*, op. cit.; M. and R. Weyl, 'Ideologie juridique et Lutte des classes', *Cahiers du CERM*; A. Gisselbrecht, 'Le Fascisme hitlérien', *Recherches internationales à la lumière du marxisme*, 1973.

of finance capital, does not constitute a unified or 'integrated' fraction; it is divided by the internal contradictions that we have briefly reviewed. In its relation with monopoly capital, the state takes responsibility for the interests of monopoly capital as a whole; it does not concretely identify itself with any one of its components, no more than with this or that particular monopoly, but rather works by way of its various interventions to organize monopoly capital politically and give it political cohesion, imposing these interventions, as it were, on specific components of this capital. Short of accepting the completely false position that monopoly capital forms an 'integrated and fused' ensemble possessing in an extraordinary fashion its own prerequisites of economic and political organization, and hence drawing the inevitable conclusion of an overall 'weakening' of the contemporary state in the face of this 'monopoly power' (state and monopolies being conceived as entities exchanging 'power'), it must be acknowledged that the contemporary state is not a simple tool or instrument that can be freely manipulated by a single coherent 'will', any more than it has been in the past.

In this sense it is still possible to speak of the contemporary state's relative autonomy in relation to monopoly capital. This relative autonomy is registered both in the principal contradiction (bourgeoisie/working class), and (which is particularly important for us here) in the struggles and contradictions within monopoly capital itself. It is thus simply the expression of the state's role in the political cohesion of monopoly capital and the organization of its hegemony. It should be understood of course that this relative autonomy cannot be taken in the sense of the state being the arbiter of inter-monopoly contradictions, nor the locus of a coherent and rational policy 'external' to monopoly capital. If we reject the analysis of a 'fusion of the state and the monopolies in a single mechanism', this is not at all in order to uphold the position of an 'independence' of the state in relation to the monopolies, but to refute a problematic which, whether under the label of 'fusion' or under that of 'independence', poses the relations between the state and the hegemonic fraction as relations between separate entities, such that the state could 'possess' its own 'power', and that one side could 'absorb' the other (take away its 'power', leading to fusion) or 'resist' it (leading to independence or arbitration). Moreover, by maintaining that there is today such a fusion, the conclusion must be drawn that in the past the state was independent or played the role of arbiter, which is just as false. The state does not have its own 'power', but it forms the contradictory locus of condensation for the balance of forces that divides even the dominant class itself, and particularly its hegemonic fraction – monopoly capital.[2]

The specific contradictions of the P.C.F. theorists must also be noted. These indicate the dead ends to which the official thesis of fusion (or 'amalgamation') and the single mechanism leads, as expressed by the Conference of 81 parties, the P.C.F. Colloqium at Choisy-le-Roi, and the *Traité du capitalisme monopoliste d'État*. Although this thesis can be found in its pure form in certain of the criticisms that L. Perceval and J. Lojkine level against me, a rather different tune is sometimes to be heard from other quarters. P. Herzog, for example, after himself repeating the ritual criticisms of my position, can nevertheless write, without retreating in the face of his own incoherence:

> The state of the monopolies cannot be conceived as a fusion between the two terms . . . We have said that public intervention reflects and consolidates a balance of forces; there can be no question for us but that today the thrust of this intervention reflects above all the interests of the financial oligarchy. As we have seen, however, the balance of forces also opposes the monopolies themselves; although the state tends to be their common property, it does not belong to any single one of them . . . *The absence of fusion* between state and monopolies corresponds to a three-fold reality . . . despite the internal struggles within the oligarchy, the necessary search for relative coherence in state intervention leads to actions which in general do not directly reflect the interests of this or that group, and which are to a certain extent imposed on each of them . . .[3]

If this is the case, however, the very concept of state monopoly capitalism is open to question. Did not H. Claude, an eminent

2. It is interesting to note that this same false conception of the relation between the state and social groups is found, in just the same form, among a whole series of writers who pose the question in instrumentalist terms as one of external entities one of which (social groups) would influence and subordinate the other (the state); this links up with an old tradition of bourgeois empiricism. This was already true of the many theories about 'pressure groups' versus the state in the 'decision-making process', particularly that of R. Dahl, *Who Governs?* We come across it today in the progressive tendency represented by G. McConnel, *Private Power and American Democracy*, New York, 1966; W. Domhoff, *Who Rules America?*, New York, 1971; J. Lowi, *The End of Liberalism*, New York, 1969, and finally J. K. Galbraith himself, *The New Industrial State*, New York, 1972. These points are made quite clear by C. Offe, *Strukturprobleme des Kapitalistischen Staates*, 1972, pp. 66 ff.

3. op. cit., p. 68.

P.C.F. theorist, recently assert once again that, given the important role of the state ever since the beginnings of imperialism, the only new element that sanctions the concept of state monopoly capitalism is quite specifically that of the fusion of the state with the private monopolies, which Claude for his part considers an accomplished fact?[4]

2. The second aspect of the question relates to the fact that this monopolist fraction, itself divided, is not the only dominant fraction; it is the bourgeoisie as a whole that is the dominant class. Non-monopoly capital, itself deeply divided into fractions, also takes part in the power bloc, in which monopoly capital simply forms the hegemonic fraction.[5] If non-monopoly capital participates in this way in bourgeois class domination, this of course does not mean that there is today, any more than in the past, an effective sharing of power between the dominant but non-hegemonic fractions and the hegemonic fraction; just as in the past, the state overwhelmingly serves the interests of the hegemonic fraction. But what is involved here in the last analysis is the long-term political interest of monopoly capital. This implies, in the particular sense that we have seen, a strategy of compromise towards non-monopoly capital, and a specific role for the state in this respect – it being understood that this does not refer to an explicit, coherent and 'rational' strategy, but to the resultant of a balance of forces.

At the same time the various state interventions, corresponding to the interests of monopoly capital, are thus concerned with the extended reproduction of capital, i.e. of the whole of the social capital. It is already false from this point of view to say that the state is in the 'exclusive' service of the 'big monopolies'. But there is more to it than that. The state's economic interventions in favour of monopoly capital are not simply 'technical' interventions deriving from the requirements of 'monopoly production', but like any state economic intervention, they are political interventions. In their specific forms and modalities, they generally take account of non-monopoly capital and the need for cohesion on the part of the power bloc, and in this way non-monopoly capital finds expression in certain *pertinent effects* within the very structure of the state's monopolist 'economic policy'.[6] Finally, we should remember that several

4. H. Claude, 'Le Capitalisme monopoliste d'État', *Cahiers du CERM*, no. 91, 1971, p. 21.

5. Here again, however, as we have seen, it is still necessary to make clear exactly which component of monopoly capital is involved: banking or industrial.

6. By 'pertinent effects' I mean the specific expression at the political level of a class or class fraction that exists in its own right but without constituting a social force (*Political Power and Social Classes*, pp. 77 ff.).

examples of state intervention 'in favour' of non-monopoly capital can be cited, even though they are limited in scope, and these include the domain of credit and public finance, and of taxation. These are not of course effective measures by the state to aid the survival or resistance of non-monopoly capital *vis-à-vis* monopoly capital, but rather the result of the resistance of non-monopoly capital to being purely and simply taken over by monopoly capital. If the state is no longer in such cases the arbiter between monopoly and non-monopoly capital, it nevertheless represents the condensation of their contradictory relationship; this is moreover one of the reasons for the internal contradictions of the state's 'economic policy'.

It is also in this context that we find the current limits of the state's relative autonomy *vis-à-vis* monopoly capital and the power bloc as a whole. This relative autonomy here refers to the specific role of the state and its various apparatuses in elaborating the political strategy of monopoly capital, in organizing its hegemony in the context of its 'unstable equilibrium of compromise' *vis-à-vis* non-monopoly capital, and establishing the political cohesion of the class alliance in power. The scope of this relative autonomy can be grasped by contrasting it to the thesis of fusion and the single mechanism. Just as the state does not belong to this or that monopoly group, as Herzog puts it, nor does it tend to be their 'common property', for the state is not a thing but a relation, more exactly the condensation of a balance of forces. The relative autonomy of the state must be understood here as a relationship between the state on the one hand, monopoly capital and the bourgeoisie as a whole on the other, a relationship which is always posed in terms of class representation and political organization.[7]

I have tried to show this concretely, as it operates in the context of

7. To regard the state in this way as a relation (more precisely the condensation of a balance of forces) is to avoid the false dilemma in which contemporary discussion of the state is trapped, between the state as a thing and the state as a subject. The state as a thing involves the instrumentalist conception in which the state is a passive tool in the hands of a class or fraction; with the state as a subject, the state's autonomy, now considered as something absolute, is related, as we shall see, to its own will in the form of a rationalizing instance of 'civil society'. In both cases, the relationship of the state to the classes is seen as a relation of externality. However, and we shall also come back to this, the relative autonomy of the state is in fact inscribed in its very structure (the state is a relation), in so far as it is the resultant of the class struggle and class contradictions as they are expressed and concentrated, in a specific manner, within the state itself. This also enables us to locate precisely the specific role of the bureaucracy.

monopoly capitalism, in the case of fascism. I will just say a few words here on the contradictions of the P.C.F. theorists in their criticisms of my position. I see these as particularly important in so far as these theorists all consider fascism, and German Nazism in particular, as a 'prefigurative' but typical case of state monopoly capitalism. Critics such as M. and R. Weyl, L. Perceval, J. Lojkine, etc., have constantly reproached me for not having seen the 'exclusive' relationship between the state and monopoly capital in a period when monopoly capital is the *only* dominant fraction, for opposing the conception of the fascist state as a simple agent at the command of monopoly capital alone, in short for rejecting the thesis of fusion and the single mechanism.[8] Here again, however, some different notes are struck, which show· once more the dead ends that this thesis leads to. A. Gisselbrecht in particular, someone who is well informed on the concrete problems of fascism, states, after the habitual criticisms of my arguments:

It would in fact go against the Marxist theory of the state to present the fascist power as the 'direct' domination or 'creature' of the monopolies, their mere organ of execution. The state is rather the 'executive committee' of the interests of the capitalist class *as a whole*, which thus leaves room *both* for contradictions between the groups that compose it *and* for a certain active role on the part of the state's own organs of decision.[9] (Gisselbrecht's emphases.)

Gisselbrecht even goes so far as to say that 'the naive idea of the fascist state as a purely passive agent or emanation of the monopolies . . . is foreign to Marxist theory.'[10] We did not make him say this. It is quite clear that this is precisely the case with the thesis of fusion and the single mechanism.

Finally, Lojkine himself, when he analyses the role of the state in monopoly capitalism in another context, does not shy away from contradicting himself completely when he asserts:

The bourgeois state, the political organization that serves the bourgeoisie (and not simply monopoly capital), has a duel function: 1) to maintain the *cohesion* of the social formation; 2) to enforce directly the domination of the bourgeoisie. The first function implies the second in so far as the domination of the capitalist class presupposes the existence of *an organism inde-*

8. Lojkine, op. cit., p. 152.
9. ibid., p. 17, note 53.
10. ibid., p. 31.

pendent of society [Lojkine's emphases] and able to 'regulate' and 'normalize' the class struggle.[11]

We have here a quite remarkable reversal of Lojkine's positions; the proud guardian of the thesis of fusion and the single mechanism actually sets himself up as defender of the old error, deriving from the writings of the young Marx, of a state 'independent' from society, something that I took great care to guard against in discussing the relative autonomy of the state and its role as the factor of cohesion for the social formation as a whole.

What is involved here are not simply the inconsistencies of one theorist, nor even just the contradictions of the thesis of fusion and the single mechanism: the contradictions go further. For the same instrumentalist/idealist conception of the state that underlies this position, simultaneously legitimizes the position of a real independence of the state *vis-à-vis* social classes. An 'instrument' is at the same time totally manipulable by the person who wields it and entirely independent of him, in the sense that it can be used, just as it is, by someone else (the working class). And at this point we link up again with Herzog's other arguments, already mentioned, on the neutral state as 'organic factor of production', and the inevitable implications of this for the transition to socialism, which would thus be possible without the destruction of the state apparatuses.

3. The complex relationship between state and power bloc in the present phase has important effects within the very state apparatuses of the imperialist metropolises. It should be noted here that, on the one hand, the thesis of the fusion of the state and the monopolies in a single mechanism, presupposing as it does the existence of a single dominant fraction itself abstractly unified, prevents any analysis of the internal contradictions of the contemporary state. On the other hand, and more generally, the instrumentalist thesis implies that the contradictions between the fractions in power only take the form of external pulls (influence) on the pieces of the state-instrument, this metaphysical entity, each of these fractions trying to take more than its 'share'. In actual fact, these contradictions are inscribed in the very structure of the capitalist state apparatuses. The contradictory relations between fractions of the power bloc under the hegemony of monopoly capital exist in the relationships between branches of the repressive state apparatus, between the ideological state apparatuses, and in the relations involved within each one of these. The balance of forces within the power bloc, precisely in so far as it

11. J. Lojkine, 'Contribution à une théorie marxiste de l'urbanisation capitaliste', in *Cahiers internationaux de Sociologie*, January–June 1972, p. 141.

is a balance of power is expressed in contradictory relations actually within the state and its apparatuses, the privileged seats of one or other fraction of the power bloc, and is also expressed in the form of internal contradictions between the various interventions of the contemporary state. Hence the relative autonomy of the state does not imply a coherent and rational will on the part of the agents of the state, as an intrinsic entity; it exists concretely as the contradictory 'play' within the state apparatuses, or even as the resultant of the balance of forces which is condensed in the state.

Thus the contradictory relations that currently exist within the political apparatus (parties, parliament, senate, etc.), within the central and local government apparatuses, within the various ideological apparatuses (educational, cultural, information, etc.), as well as between these apparatuses, are not just the effect of the struggle of the dominated classes, but also express the contradictions of the power bloc itself. As far as the power bloc is concerned, contrary to the effects that the struggle of the dominated classes has on the state apparatuses, the relations between the bourgeois fractions often take the form of the apparatuses becoming the seats and bastions of contradictory powers.

We must repeat again here that even so, there is no question of there being separate 'pieces' of the state, or of an effective division of state power between the fractions that compose the power bloc. The capitalist state is characterized, today just as in the past, by a specific internal unity of its apparatuses, which is simply the expression of the interests of the hegemonic fraction, and of its own role as the factor of cohesion of the power bloc.

This unity of the state power, condensed into an institutional unity of the state apparatuses, is not established in a simple fashion, either by some kind of united act of will on the part of the monopolies, or because the monopolies have got a physical stranglehold on the state-instrument as a whole, where this is seen as having an intrinsic instrumental unity. It is rather established in a complex fashion, depending on the class contradiction, by means of a whole chain involving the subordination of certain apparatuses to others which particularly condense the power of the hegemonic fraction; involving under-determinations, short-circuits and doublings-up of certain apparatuses by others; displacements of 'function' between apparatuses and dislocations between real power and formal power; shifts of apparatuses from the ideological field to the field of the repressive apparatus and vice versa; finally, significant cleavages within each apparatus itself.[12]

12. In the field of studies of political institutions, to which I shall confine myself here, we have an appreciable and constantly growing number of

2. ON THE PRESENT ROLE OF THE STATE

Despite these specifications, it is still true that important modifications have taken place, not only in the establishment of the interventionist form of state as against the 'liberal' state of competitive capitalism, but also within the interventionist state itself according to the different phases of monopoly capitalism. The specific characteristics of each of these phases (transition, consolidation, and the present phase), i.e. modifications in the capitalist relations of production, the effects of these on other modes and forms of production, the degrees of internationalization that mark these phases and which are transposed into specific relationships within the power bloc, all have their effects on the 'economic functions' of the state, the displacement of dominance in favour of the state, and the relation between the state and class hegemony, according to the different phases of monopoly capitalism.[13]

There is thus no doubt that we are witnessing the emergence within the imperialist metropolises, in the present phase of imperialism, of important changes in the interventionist state, which can only be understood by taking account of the entire field of class struggles in the metropolises. The state's 'economic interventions',

---

concrete analyses of this process. However, it must be noted that there are most often directly interwoven with political analyses and struggles, and do not always appear in the form of 'books' or review articles. Simply by way of example, I would mention the following here: in France, besides the works of M. Castells, F. Godard, D. Vidal, J.-M. Vincent, and others already mentioned, those of M. Amiot on cultural policy and the ideological apparatuses, of J. Ion on urban policy, and the CERAT-IEP team in Grenoble on municipal institutions. Internationally (and here also simply by way of example) there are in the French language the works of M. Van Schendel, C. Saint Pierre, G. Bourques and N. Frenette in Quebec; those of the journal *Contradictions* (particularly by A. Corten) in Belgium; those of *Bandiera Roja* in Spain which have recently appeared in *Les Temps Modernes*. Among texts not translated into French, I would mention those of G. Therborn in Sweden, those of certain members of the *New Left Review* group in Great Britain and of the journal *Kursbuch* in Germany; several in Italy, in particular those of the journal *Inquiesta*, as well as some in Greece; the works of J. Solé-Tura in Spain, E. de Ipola in Argentina, E. Villa in Mexico, F. Weffort in Brazil, and A. Quijano in Peru. Finally, there are those of several of our Chilean comrades, in particular around the former Latin-American School of Social Sciences in Santiago.

13. The interventionist role of the state is in fact no more a gradual, unilinear and homogenous process here than in the process of capital concentration. In the course of establishment of the state's dominant role, certain

in particular, have never been so pronounced as in the present phase, nor has the displacement of dominance in favour of the state. This role of the state in the present phase (in favour of monopoly capital), as well as affecting its traditional functions, also relates to certain other decisive functions that it performs:

(1) its functions in the current form of internationalization of capitalist relations by the induced reproduction of the dominant imperialist capital actually within the metropolises, in the parallel expansion abroad of its own bourgeoisie, and in the reproduction of the new forms of the imperialist social division of labour: the functions that were analysed in the previous essay.

(2) its functions in the current forms of the closure of the gap between economic ownership and possession, corresponding to the expansion of monopoly exploitation and to the dominant forms of intensive exploitation of labour: it is here that we find, among other things, the present role of the state in financial centralization, but also in industrial concentration by way of 'restructuring' and 'modernization', a role that is particularly clear in France with the 6th Plan; also, in a certain sense, its role as a customer, including military expenditure.

(3) its functions in the current dominance of the dissolution effects of monopoly capital on other forms of production: the role of the state in the elimination of the traditional petty bourgeoisie, in the domination of monopoly capital over non-monopoly capital, in the penetration and expansion of monopoly capital in agriculture and the rural exodus; it is here in particular that we come across the role of public financing.

(4) finally, its functions in directly setting under way the main counteracting tendencies to the falling rate of profit tendency, including:

a. the present forms of intensive exploitation of labour by way of state intervention in the productivity of labour and the extraction of relative surplus-value: the role of the state in scientific research

---

of its economic functions show accelerations, decelerations, and sometimes even relative 'retreats'. As S. de Brunhof correctly points out: 'The economic power of the state is not marked by an irreversible process of growth . . . Far from expanding in a continuous fashion, the strength of state capitalism can undergo regressions . . .' (*Capitalisme financier public; influence économique de l'état en France 1948–1958*, 1965, pp. 202 ff.). J. Bouvier has shown very well how the financial role of the state as banker was reduced in France in the Fifth Republic as against the Fourth, and he pertinently adds: 'The role of the qualitative, i.e. the political, should be emphasized in the history of state intervention, 'planning', and the public banking and financial institutions.' (*Un siècle de banque française*, op. cit., p. 153.)

and technological innovation, in the reproduction of labour-power by way of educational 'training' (the school system, retraining, etc.), town planning, transport, the 'health' service and other public facilities;[14]

b. the parallel devaluing of certain sections of constant capital, in the new conditions of establishment of the average rate of profit: this is one aspect of 'industrial modernization', and of public investments.

In other words, we have here a series of modifications that indicate the role and place of the state, and that characterize the current forms of extended reproduction of capital. The above points are not intended to give an exhaustive list of current state interventions. The problem is to isolate the chief structural modifications that govern these interventions, rather than to provide a descriptive enumeration of them. We could in fact mention a whole series of other state interventions, also very important, going from those affecting the labour market (an 'incomes policy') to those in the domains of distribution, and of 'collective consumption';[15] all these, however, in the last instance depend on and derive from the modifications that I have just indicated.

This brings me to a further point. Not all the new state interventions we are discussing here always or directly take the form of 'economic interventions', in the narrow sense that this term had in the stage of competitive capitalism – interventions on the 'market' or in the construction of 'economic infrastructure', of railways for example. This fact has led to several theories according to which there is supposedly at the present time a decline in the state's 'economic interventions', these being taken over directly by private monopolies (as in market organization, or the construction of motorways), and an increase in its 'social' and 'political' interventions.[16]

This seems to me to be wrong, particularly in so far as these arguments apply unaltered terms taken from a field of application which is that of competitive capitalism.[17] In this stage, marked by the dominance of the economic and the extensive exploitation of labour, it was still possible to make a relative distinction between, on the one hand, state intervention in the extended reproduction of

14. M. Castells, *Néo-capitalisme, consommation collective et contradictions urbaines*, mimeographed, Centre d'étude des mouvements sociaux, 1973.

15. A. Granou, *Capitalisme et Mode de vie*, 1973; P. Mattick, *Marx and Keynes*, New York, 1969.

16. Among others, the general report by E. Maire to the most recent congress of the CFDT, pp. 26–7 (June 1973).

17. See above, pp. 118 ff.

the conditions of production, and on the other hand, state intervention that was directly economic, though this does not mean that the latter form of intervention was in this stage neutral and dissociated from the state's political and ideological interventions. In the monopoly stage, however, and in its present phase in particular, marked as these are by the dominant role of the state and the displacement of dominance towards the intensive exploitation of labour, this is no longer the case. The political and ideological 'conditions' of production are themselves directly involved in the process of capital's extended reproduction; they are the very forms of reproduction's existence.

In other words, what we have is a new relationship between politics, ideology and the economic, one that transforms the very field and content of these terms, in the sense that the space of production is reorganized as a 'function' of the political and ideological conditions of reproduction, so that state intervention in this respect is already as such economic intervention.[18]

It is thus incontestable that, in so far as these formations are marked by the increasingly dominant role of the state, and as the economic domination and political hegemony of monopoly capital is being overwhelmingly asserted, the contemporary state tends more and more to reflect this situation. The play of its relative autonomy *vis-à-vis* the hegemonic fraction, monopoly capital, takes place within far more confined limits than was the case in the past. From the point of view of the power bloc, the restriction of these limits is simply one effect, among others, of the dependence of non-monopoly capital on monopoly capital, which is largely an accomplished fact, and of the fact that non-monopoly capital has henceforth ceased, except in very rare and particular conjunctures, to play the role of an autonomous social force.

II

Precisely by establishing the current relationship between the state and the field of class contradictions, we can resolve a whole series of adjacent problems concerning the present role of the state:

18. As I have already pointed out, what is involved here is a shift in the boundaries between the state and the economic, and not an abolition of their relative separation, which is specific to capitalism. This therefore implies that the state's present economic interventions cannot transgress certain limits that are co-substantial with capitalism itself; the permanent fiscal and financial crisis of the present state is one of the clearest indices of these limits (on this subject, see J. O'Connor, *The Fiscal Crisis of the State*, 1973).

1. Firstly, it becomes clear that this present role of the state can in no way be taken to imply some kind of 'organized capitalism', which, by way of a 'rationalizing instance', would have overcome the specific contradictions of what is generally referred to as the 'anarchy of production', and which is in fact nothing more than the crystallization of class contradictions. The state certainly fulfils the general role of factor of cohesion of the social formation, i.e. a general 'organizing' and 'regulating' role, but this role is not something distinct from its functions in relation to the class struggle: it is the concentrated expression of class hegemony. This comes back to the problem of refuting the whole series of conceptions (which were already those of Keynes) specifically those concerning capitalist planning. Such planning, for example the French plan, was seen as the 'rational' and 'coherent' policy of an apparatus that is in part 'technical' and 'neutral', and has succeeded in neutralizing or reconciling capitalist contradictions. These conceptions, which have affected the workers' movement by way of the whole tendency of 'revolution from above', i.e. belief in a transition to socialism by means of the state alone (the providential state, or even state socialism), can take several different forms.

It is not enough here to recall, against the current technocratic arguments of the Galbraith type, that capitalist competition is constantly reproduced under monopoly capitalism, and that the state administrative apparatus (the bureaucracy) cannot be conceived as endowed with a will and power of its own, imposing its policies on society as a whole. We have to go further and stress, against the very conception of state monopoly capitalism:

(a) the contradictions within the power bloc, which are effects of the principal contradiction, and which precisely make it impossible to see the terrain of class domination as occupied by one fraction alone, the big monopolies, itself abstractly unified and integrated, and practising an unambiguous and coherent policy by means of the state-instrument;

(b) the fact that there can be no such thing as a 'rational kernel' in capitalist planning, corresponding to some intrinsic level or other of the productive forces, such that class contradictions would simply overdetermine the intrinsic rational aspect by misappropriating it. Capitalist planning, in the sense of an effective control of the contradictions of capitalist reproduction, is actually unthinkable (the myth of organized capitalism).[19] This is, however, what the state monopoly

19. See also, among others: E. Altvater, 'Zu einigen Problemen des Staatsinterventionismus', in Janicke: *Herrschaft und Crise*: J. Hirsch, 'Funktionsveränderungen der Staatsverwaltung in spätkapiatlistischen Industriegesellschaften', in *Blätter für deutsche u. intern. Politik*, February 1969;

capitalism argument threatens to lead to, even if its authors expressly reject this conclusion. In point of fact, let us repeat, the present role of the state and its interventions are the contradictory condensation of a balance of forces, as against the old but prodigiously tenacious conception of bourgeois idealism which, from Hegel through to Weber and Keynes, sees in the state the rational kernel of 'civil society'. To support my argument by a concrete example, I would just signal the contemporary functioning of the nationalized sector, a perfectly capitalist one.[20] This certainly does not mean that capitalist planning is an illusion: it expresses both the logic of monopoly reproduction, and the present policy of the state as a political apparatus.

2. Secondly, however, and partly as a reaction to the theses of state monopoly capitalism, there are a whole series of analyses current on the left, which I have already alluded to, that simply reject the decisive role that the state plays today. These see the state as 'drained' of its 'power' in the face of the 'concentrated power' of the monopolies. We cannot conceal the fact that this threatens to lead to a very questionable political position, one partly concealed behind the current debate on 'self-management', a term that has several different political aspects to it. According to this position, the principal objective of political struggle should no longer be the state, but simply the power of capital in the enterprises. I certainly would not say that the self-management thesis necessarily coincides with these positions; however, it is necessary to state that positions on 'self-management' and on the contemporary 'decline' in the role of the state often go together.

III

These points, taken together with the present forms of the principal contradiction (bourgeoisie/working class) and the upsurge of class struggle on the part of the popular masses in Europe, can also explain a series of important contemporary phenomena.

(a) To start with, it can explain the developing crisis of hegemony

---

Muller-Neusüss, 'Die Sozialstaatsillusion', in *Sozialistische Politik*, 1970; U. Jaeggi, *Kapital und Arbeit in der Bundesrepublik*, 1973; J. O'Connor, 'Scientific and Ideological Elements in the Economic Theory of Governmental Policy', in *A Critique of Economic Theory*, ed. E. Hunt and G. Schwartz, Penguin, Harmondsworth, 1972; Flatow-Huisken, 'Zum Problem der Ableitung des bürgelichen Staates', in *Probleme des Klassenkampfs* no. 7, May 1973; Braunmühl and others, *Probleme einer materialistischen Staatstheorie*, op. cit., in particular Hirsch's contribution.
20. P. Brachet, *L'État-patron, théories et réalités*, 1973.

that currently affects the European bourgeoisies. We have established that at the level of the class struggle and the power bloc, the European bourgeoisies are composed of heterogenous and conjunctural groupings in their contradictions with American imperialist capital. This is already an important factor making for instability of hegemony, given the internalization of the contradiction of imperialist capital present within each 'national' European power bloc. Parallel with this, the internal contradictions of these power blocs are becoming sharper, and this precisely in a period in which the role of the state is more and more important and the restriction of its relative autonomy is becoming an imperious necessity for monopoly capital. Now if it is not true that the contemporary state is being transformed into a simple instrument of the monopolies, it is still the case that it is less and less able, in this context, to play its role as organizer of hegemony effectively. State policy often amounts to a series of contradictory and temporary measures which, if they express the logic of monopoly capital, also reveal the fissures and dis-articulations of the state apparatuses, reproducing the contradictions of the power bloc in the face of a decline in the hegemonic capacities of monopoly capital. At a time when the role of the state is more crucial than ever, the state seems affected by a crisis of representativeness in its various apparatuses (including the political parties) in their relations to the actual fractions of the power bloc: this is one of the reasons behind the controversies over 'state control', 'regionalization', and 'decentralization', at least in the form that they assume within the bourgeoisie itself.

(b) Added to this is an additional phenomenon, connected with the new and close articulation that has been established between the economic, the state and ideology. If the contemporary state seems to have managed to regularize the 'wild' character of capitalist economic crises, at least to a certain extent (though this has nothing in common with the myth of an 'organized capitalism'), it has done this by way of an apparently paradoxical route: it has only managed it at the cost of directly transforming economic crises into crises of the superstructures – of the state, including its ideological apparatuses. One reason for this, among others, is that the state, by directly taking charge of the extended reproduction of capital and regularizing the economic crises, has itself assumed certain of the functions fulfilled by these 'crises': the decrease in value of certain sections of capital, together with the inflation and unemployment directly orchestrated by the state (i.e. structural or rampant inflation).[21]

21. It is in fact impossible to consider the 'economic crises' of capitalism as 'dysfunctional' moments of the economic 'system' which the state, as rationalizing instance, simply attempts to 'avoid', as the whole of bourgeois

The state has thus been transformed from a buffer or safety valve on economic crises into a sounding-box for the reproduction crises of social relations. In fact, the very relationship between economic and political class struggle is now transformed; in the present phase, every economic struggle objectively confronts, in a more or less direct fashion, functions and apparatuses, branches and sub-branches of the state. What is more, the expansion of the process of valorization of capital and of state intervention into a whole series of domains ('living standards' and 'life-style') which are now directly part of the extended reproduction of capital, leads to a remarkable politicization of the various struggles over the quality of life, struggles which are all the more important in that they do not simply question the production 'conditions', but also, in a more or less direct fashion, the very reproduction of the relations of production.[22] This is the reason why a certain political consensus, based on the state as guarantor of expansion and expressed in particular by the whole ideology of Keynesianism, is no longer effective. The state's subordination to the logic of monopoly capitalist reproduction, which is thus experienced as 'its' inability to respond to the needs of the masses, has never been more flagrant than it is at a time like the present, when the state is intervening in all the domains in which these needs present themselves. It is entirely symptomatic of this that the bourgeoisie finds itself for the first time obliged to put forward a real programme, at a moment when it can less than ever carry this out.

---

ideology on this subject maintains. The economic crises of capitalism are organic moments of the reproduction of social capital. These crises, while they may find expression at the political level as political crises and revolutionary situations, i.e. as possibilities for the overthrow of capitalism, also function at the same time to focus tendencies counteracting the falling rate of profit tendency (massive devalorizing of capitals, destruction of productive forces, etc.). Thus these 'economic crises' also play the role of a 'purge' of capitalism and are in fact the very conditions of its extended reproduction and perpetuation. This should be sufficient to counter the economist errors that see in economic crises a mechanical factor of capitalism's dissolution. What is even more important here, however, is the present role of the state in this respect: by intervening to 'regulate', at least to a certain extent, the 'wild' economic crises of capitalism, the state must at the same time take in hand the organic functions that these crises play in the extended reproduction of capital. There is thus no question of the state having managed to 'avoid' these crises; rather the crises are orchestrated from above by the state itself, which simply attempts to regulate their 'wild' side. This is directly reflected in the internal crisis of the state apparatuses and in the permanent contradictions between its various economic functions.

22. See above, pp. 27 ff.

In the face of this situation, the contemporary state really seems to be characterized by an inability stably to manage, in the long run, the bourgeoisie's developing crisis of hegemony.

(c) The bourgeoisie's strategy towards this state of affairs is one of proceding, whatever happens, to make certain readjustments in the processes of legitimation, involving the relationship between current forms of the dominant ideology and the reorganization of the state apparatuses,[23] together with an increase in political repression. I do not intend here to go into this question in depth. I would simply point out that these readjustments in legitimation, which can certainly not be reduced to a simple adjustment of the relations between parliament and the executive, but can neither be identified with a process of fascisization in the strict sense, relate to certain considerable transformations in bourgeois legitimacy, given the way this has presented itself till now. This also goes together with the ideological crisis that is today affecting these formations. There is a whole range of transformations involved here, from a shift away from the legitimacy of popular sovereignty towards a legitimacy of the state bureaucratic administration, through to a change in the role of political parties and ideological apparatuses and the breakdown of the legal/ideological boundaries between 'private' and 'public' (the subversion of the very domain of basic liberties, for example). It would thus seem that not only the traditional form of parliamentary democracy, but even a certain form of political democracy as such, has already had its day as a result of the structural transformations of contemporary capitalism. However this may be, the principal objective of these transformations of legitimacy's to hide from the masses the present role of the state and the nature of the political power that it embodies, under the guise of a technical and neutral instance, with the ideology of technocracy supplanting the legal/political region in the dominant position within bourgeois ideology. The ideology of the 'pluralist' state as 'arbiter' between the interests of 'social groups' and bearer of the 'general will' of the 'individual citizens', has been supplanted by that of the state as 'technical' instance in relation to the intrinsic 'requirements' of 'production', 'industrialization' and 'technical progress'.

There is no doubt that the present state is succeeding to a certain extent (though for how much longer?) in this ideological operation

23. On this, see J. Habermas, *Legitimationsprobleme im Spätkapitalismus*; C. Offe, *Strukturprobleme des Kapitalistischen Staates*, op. cit.; I. Balbus, *Politics as Sports: An Interpretation of the Political Ascendancy of the Sports Metaphor in America*, mimeographed, 1973; M. Duverger, *Sociologie de la politique*, 1973.

of reproducing the privatization of 'individuals' within the new 'public' domain. In fact, although the economic struggle of the popular masses is now directly coming up against the state, we need to realize the present limits of this objective politicization. Violent confrontation with the state, which is nowadays so noticeable, often goes together with a trust, on the part of those challenging the state, in the right wing that commands the governing levers. In France, in particular, we see how it is perfectly possible to burn tax offices and attack C.R.S. men while still voting for the U.D.R. This amounts to saying that the current ideology of technocracy is still so dominant that it often dominates even the struggles of the popular masses, who confront a 'technocratic power' which is omnipresent but whose political nature they do not always understand, even in their opposition to it.[24]

The case of Servan-Schreiber reminds us that the bourgeoisie can even set itself up at the head of these movements in order to lead them astray.

24. These are in fact only partial effects of this ideological operation, in contrast to the view held by many theories of the 'technocracy'. The latter consider, in one form or another (e.g. H. Schelsky, 'l'État technique' in *Auf der Suche nach Wirklichkeit*, 1965 or H. Marcuse, *One-Dimensional Man*, London, 1964) that the present 'technological transformations' are leading to an effective depoliticization (supercession of the class struggle) or even to a 'technical alienation' ('manipulation') of the individual. We must note here that, despite their apparently opposed conclusions, these writers base themselves on assumptions that are quite similar to those of the protagonists of the 'scientific and technical revolution' which we shall be discussing fully in the third part of this book.

4

Some Notes on the Bourgeois Personnel

I. THE PROBLEM OF THE MANAGERS

The principal aspect in the preceding arguments has been that of the Marxist theory of social classes, the aspect of the places assigned to these classes in the social division of labour, places which we referred to in the Introduction by the term 'structural class determination'. In so far as capital is concerned, I stressed the forms assumed by the articulation of the two relationships (economic ownership, possession) that delimit in a definitive manner its place (which also extends to political and ideological relations) and the various powers that derive from this place. In point of fact, to define certain agents as bourgeois is not to ascribe to them some kind of intrinsic quality such as their class origin, but is rather a reference to the place that these agents occupy, i.e. their situation in relation to the relationships that define the place of capital, and in relation to the powers that they exercise and that derive from these relationships in a constitutive way.

I

We may see the full scope of this problem if we consider a series of arguments by modern sociologists and economists who, in their study of 'contemporary society', radically separate the relationships in question and the powers that in fact derive from them, as well as seeing the problematic of social classes essentially in terms of agents (social classes allegedly being the sum of the individual agents of which they are composed).

These theories can take several forms; that which is most important for us here is centred around the theme of the managers. It gave rise to a great deal of writing in the years following the Second World War, and is continually being resurrected, the latest variant being Galbraith's 'technostructure'.

At the bottom of it all is the desire to refute the Marxist theory of social classes, which, as the same old story has it, was correct for the nineteenth century, but no longer corresponds to modern, 'post-industrial', 'techno-bureaucratic', etc., society. This conception is based on several assumptions: the big corporation of today is supposedly based on a radical separation between 'ownership' of the means of production and 'powers of decision'; the latter are supposedly exercised by managers (technostructure) radically distinct from owners, and these managers are often seen as the new dominant 'class'. This is then alleged to have important consequences as far as the motivations of managerial behaviour are concerned, these being different from those of the owners. The managerial mind is not moved by profit, as was formerly the case with the owners, but rather by the power and expansion of the firm, so that contemporary society is no longer based on the logic of profit.

If this is in very broad lines the problematic of the managers/technostructure, its two epistemological assumptions, i.e. on one side the rupture between relations of production and powers of decision and, on the other, the problematic of classes based on agents, are also found in a whole series of related conceptions:

(a) that of Dahrendorf,[1] whose roots go back to Max Weber and which I have criticized elsewhere. Dahrendorf sees the constitution of classes, or rather of 'social groups', as deriving originally and fundamentally from 'power relations', essentially defined as relations of 'command' and 'obedience' in institutions of the 'authoritarian' type, with ownership being only one possible consequence of these power relationships. This is in the last analysis the traditional objection to the Marxist theory of social classes.

Touraine's positions,[2] at least in certain of their aspects, ultimately derive from the same tendency, even though he was one of the first to indicate that the principal ideological danger today is that of the various forms of 'organization theory', and though his arguments are incontestably of a different stature to those of Dahrendorf. This is not the place to go into a detailed critique of Touraine's particular theories; I would simply point out that, with him, this tendency assumes the conceptual form of a division of 'post-industrial society' into a class of those who command and decide (possessors of 'knowledge' as opposed to owners) and a class of those who execute;

1. *Class and Class Conflict in Industrial Society*, London, 1959. For a Marxist critique of Max Weber, see the seminal articles of J.-M. Vincent in *Fétichisme et Société*, 1973; see also M. Lowy, *Dialectique et Révolution*, 1973.

2. *Post-Industrial Society*, London, 1972.

(b) that which examines the present ruling class in terms of groups of agents, i.e. of power elites. This conception is particularly to be found in the work of C. Wright Mills, Jean Meynaud, and others, for whom, 'parallel' to the owners who form one of the elite groups, there is another equivalent elite group of managers, a conception which Ralph Miliband has also now taken up, at least to a certain extent.[3] It is found very clearly in the work of Pierre Bourdieu (hardly surprising, given his impenitent Weberianism), who has recently discussed the question of the dominant class. Despite the fact that he uses, instead of the term elite, that of class fraction (a case of 'Marxism *oblige*'), these 'fractions' are found to coincide with the 'socio-professional categories' of the INSEE (*Institut National des Statistiques et Études Nationales*). In point of fact, Bourdieu informs us that 'the different fractions of the ruling class' are:

(1) teachers; (2) administrators in the public sector; (3) members of the liberal professions; (4) engineers; (5) managerial staff in the private sector; (6) industrial employers; (7) commercial employers.

The managers identified with the 'administrative and managerial staff', are here seen as a fraction of the 'ruling class'.[4]

Although these conceptions do base themselves on certain transformations specific to monopoly capitalism, already mentioned by Marx in the context of his remarks on joint-stock companies, they display several confusions.

The first confusion is that of identifying legal ownership and economic ownership, the latter being the real relation of production. Now if there is, certainly under monopoly capitalism, a relative dissociation between these two types of ownership, since not every 'share' carries an equivalent portion of economic ownership, it is none the less true that real economic ownership is still a function of the place of capital.

3. *The State in Capitalist Society*, Weidenfeld and Nicholson, London, 1969. See my controversy with Miliband in *New Left Review*, 58 and 59.

4. Pierre Bourdieu, 'Reproduction culturelle et reproduction sociale', in *Informations sur les sciences sociales*, UNESCO ed., April 1971, particularly p. 59. This does not prevent Bourdieu from talking five pages further on (p. 64) of the 'dominant fraction of the dominant classes: the business bourgeoisie'! This leads me to indicate at this point a problem to which I shall return later on, concerning the characteristic arbitrariness of the INSEE's classification by socio-professional categories according to 'profession'; the managers and the heads of the state apparatuses in particular whom we are concerned with here do not exactly coincide with the various 'higher managers' of the INSEE.

But this still does not solve the problem of the managers. Who exactly are these managers, and what is their structural determination or class membership? Are they or are they not part of the capitalist class, on what grounds and why? If they are, then do they form a distinct fraction, and what would be the basis of this distinction? This raises the question of the relation between the places of the social classes and the agents that occupy them.

Certain solutions to the problem of the managers have been proposed, on the basis of empirical material, but these do not close the matter. The first holds that, in their great majority, the agents/supports of the powers deriving from the relationships of ownership and possession (the managers, directors, chief executives and top officials of enterprises) are practically identical with the agents of economic ownership itself. And this is not merely because they all swim in the same 'social milieu', or share the same 'cultural capital', in a formula favoured by Bourdieu, but rather because they generally themselves hold an appreciable number of shares, giving them a high degree of economic ownership. If managers belong to the capitalist class, this is directly because they are the immediate supports of the relations of legal and economic ownership.[5]

The second answer is directly located in a problematic of agents as subjects, with social classes considered as the sum of the individuals of which they are composed. In this problematic, which is particularly clear in Miliband's case, and even with Baran and Sweezy, the ultimate criterion of class membership would reside in the agents' behavioural motivations. These writers thus do all they can to show that the managers themselves well and truly obey the logic of profit 'imposed' by the 'system'; this gives rise to a whole series of very scholarly analyses full of evidence that enterprises controlled by managers are just as much oriented towards profit as those directly controlled by members of the owning 'families'. The managers, moved by the 'lure of gain' just as much as the actual owners, would for this very reason belong to the dominant class. However, since their motivations and their mentality still exhibit certain peculiarities in relation to those of the owners, they would constitute a distinct elite or fraction of this class.

These two answers are both unsatisfactory. The first, while it casts light on the connections that the manager-agents have with ownership, still neglects the sure distinction that there still is in very many cases between the agents/supports of the relationships of ownership and possession on the one hand, and those who exercise

5. See in particular the very interesting article on this by Robin Blackburn, 'The New Capitalism', in *Ideology in Social Science* (ed. Blackburn), London, 1972.

the powers deriving from these on the other. If there is not the shadow of doubt that the managers 'do good business', they are still not physically and personally identifiable with the agents who concentrate in their hands the real economic ownership of the enterprises that they direct.

As far as the second answer is concerned, it ignores the fact that the criterion of class membership is not one of behavioural motivations: even Max Weber recognized very well that the criterion of membership of the capitalist class was not the 'lure of gain'. Profit is not a behavioural motivation, but an objective category referring to one form in which surplus-value is realized.

There is still more to it, however. This conception, based on a problematic of agents, necessarily poses the dual question of class membership and the differentiations within the dominant class in terms of social groups and the individuals who compose them. Instead of a differentiation of the dominant class in terms of the fractions of capital, we have here a differentiation in terms of elites or power groups. We are thus led to consider, on the basis of so-called 'sociological' criteria, that the managers are a distinct elite (fraction) of the dominant class, with the owners (undifferentiated) being only one fraction among a whole series of other groupings of agents. The unity of these elite groups as parts of a dominant class is ultimately deduced from a set of criteria such as their common participation in the 'decision-making process' (divisions between those who decide and those who execute), their common 'culture', and their inter-personal relations.

II

Marx already indicated that the modifications represented by the joint-stock company involved a differentiation between the agents who were the supports of the relationships of ownership and possession, and the agents who exercised the powers that were directly attached to these. In fact, while in the capitalist mode of production 'the work of directing . . . becomes one of the functions of capital',

the capitalist mode of production has brought matters to a point where the work of supervision, entirely divorced from the ownership of capital, is always readily obtainable. It has, therefore, come to be useless for the capitalist to perform it himself. An orchestra conductor need not own the instruments of his orchestra . . . To say that this labour is necessary as capitalistic labour, or as a function of the capitalist, only means that the *vulgus* is unable to conceive the forms developed in the lap of

capitalist production, separate and free from their antithetical
capitalist character.[6]

Marx's argument is clear: while the various powers of ownership
and possession belong to the place of capital (they are 'functions' of
capital), they are not necessarily fulfilled by the owner-agents themselves; they are not 'functions' of the capitalist owners.

This argument could be developed further in the same direction.
It is the place of capital, defined as the articulation of relationships
that bear certain powers, that determines the class membership of
the agents who fulfil these 'functions'. This refers us to two interconnected aspects of the problem:

(a) The powers involving either utilization of resources, allocation
of the means of production to this or that use, or the direction of
the labour process, are bound up with the relationships of economic
ownership and possession, and these relationships define one particular place, the place of capital.

(b) The directing agents who directly exercise these powers and
who fulfil the 'functions of capital' occupy the place of capital, and
thus belong to the bourgeois class even if they do not hold formal
legal ownership. In all cases, therefore, the managers are an integral
section of the bourgeois class. It may be surmised that there is no
question here of delimiting in empirical-statistical fashion the
'numerical' boundaries of the 'group' of managers, or even of
deciding to which 'socio-professional category' these directing agents
belong, nor yet of saying who exactly exercises these functions in
this or that particular case.

In referring to these functions attached to the place of capital,
and to the powers that derive from this, we see clearly that this place
is defined on the basis of the social division of labour as a whole. It
is not confined to the relations of production, but extends to the
ideological and political relations that these relations of production
entail, which are thus also a constitutive factor of structural class
determination. The directing role of the managers, the fact that they
fulfil functions of capital and that they exercise directly the powers
of these functions, is bound up with their situation in the hierarchical authority of the despotic organization of work in the factory,
and also with their situation in relation to the 'secrecy of knowledge' and 'bureaucratic secrecy' in the division between mental
and manual work. These situations, in the precise forms that they
assume in this case, are also so many determinants of the bourgeois
class. This objective place of the managers in political and ideological relations cannot be reduced to simple characteristics of

6. *Capital*, vol. I, p. 331; vol. III, pp. 379–80.

'culture' or 'social milieu'; it is embodied in the specific ideology of these agents, which, in its form of 'economic rationality', 'efficiency of returns' and 'expansion', in short in the form of technocracy, is the currently dominant variant of bourgeois ideology.

This enables us to conclude that the managers, who belong to the capitalist class by virtue of the place of capital that they occupy, cannot constitute a distinct fraction of this class, e.g. a fraction distinct from the owners. On the one hand, the managers do not have a place or a relationship of their own; the dissociations that we have analysed between the relationships of economic ownership and of possession (i.e. of the direction of the labour process) do not in any way mean that the latter, exercised by the managers, has become separated from the place of capital. On the other hand, if a distinction is established between the various 'agents' who support the relationships of capital, and those who exercise its powers, this in no way means some kind of separation between the place of capital and its powers (capitalists against managers), or more precisely some kind of separation between the relationships of economic ownership and of possession on the one hand, and the powers that derive from these on the other. This or that manager or set of managers belongs to the fraction of capital whose place he occupies: industrial capital, banking capital, commercial capital. In other words, the managers themselves do not possess a specific unity as a class fraction, contrary to what is currently maintained by several theories, particularly in France, which most often base the 'sociological unity' of managers and 'techno-bureaucrats' on their educational formation and their common culture, on for example their training in the Grandes Écoles – the Polytechnique, the ENA, and the Centrale.

This latter type of analysis, however, also has still more wide-ranging effects. Do we not read on all sides that, in order to decide whether to approve of the investment of foreign capital, particularly American capital, in a European country, one must know whether the controlling positions in the subsidiary corporation are or are not entrusted to 'indigenous' executives? This assumes that the national origin of these managers, together with their 'autonomy of decision', will have effects on the functioning of this capital in favour of the national economy. It may be relevant here to mention that the policy of 'indigenous directors' is a particular characteristic of the notorious ITT. In the same line of thought, of course, the economic policy of Gaullism has often been ascribed to the 'industrial choices' of École Normale graduates.

In point of fact, the various phases of monopoly capitalism, the differential forms of articulation of the relations of economic ownership and possession and of the powers that derive from them, have become transposed, depending on these phases, into characteristic forms of dissociation of the agents/supports of these relationships who exercise these powers. This development has generally been studied by contemporary sociologists and economists under the rubric of 'centralization and decentralization' or 'bureaucratization and debureaucratization' of the big firms, in terms of the 'organizational model' or form of 'decision-making process' in the large enterprise and multinational firm. What must be emphasized here is that these are secondary effects of the forms assumed by the relations of production, and by the process of the reproduction of social relations, within the production units. They are not the result of any technical factors, such as, for example, the use of computers. They are definitely effects, despite what is implied by the institutionalist tradition and its modern version 'organization theory' who with their notion of the 'enterprise' argue that it is ultimately the specific structure of the enterprise as an institution that determines the relations that are constructed there: relations which then become 'power' relations between those who 'decide' and those who 'execute', independent of the relations of production and exploitation.

One last point: at best, information about the individual agents, their physical identification and their inter-personal relationships, can provide simple indices of the fundamental processes involved, on condition that this index role and its often distorting character is clearly borne in mind. For example, the tendency for industrial and money capital to become amalgamated into finance capital has often as its effect the physical and personal interpenetration of their agents. It is quite well known that the boards of directors of big industrial firms include directors and owners of the banking monopolies, and vice-versa: we also have the contemporary phenomenon of the interchangeability and mobility of the directing personnel of various capitalist fractions. From a study of the composition of these boards we can certainly draw certain indications as to the concrete forms of the process of capital merger in certain particular cases (scrutiny of the various editions of *Who's Who?* is a currently fashionable method in sociology). However these indices can often be deceptive, and in particular they may hide the fundamental processes and strategies of the various fractions of capital. Just to take one example, the presence of representatives of the big banks on the boards of directors of large enterprises is found both in France and in Germany, but it does not have the same significance in each case. In Germany in particular, banking monopoly capital has always had a direct policy of intervention and investment in industry, while banking capital in France has even today an extremely speculative character (stock-exchange operations or massive investments in landed property).

2. THE 'HEADS' OF THE STATE APPARATUS

I

We encounter the same problematic of agents as subjects in a series of analyses of the current relations between the ruling class and the state apparatus: from certain PCF writings on state monopoly capitalism through to those of Miliband, and of Galbraith in *The New Industrial State*. The chief purpose of these analyses is to show the relationship between the hegemonic fraction of monopoly capital and the state apparatus by physical identity, identity of class origin, or inter-personal relationships between the agents of the monopoly capitalist fraction and the 'heads' of the state apparatus (top civil servants, cabinet members, political personnel in the broad sense). For the PCF in particular, the fusion of the state and the monopolies into a 'single mechanism' is proved by the physical identification of the 'individuals' who control it. A typical example of this kind of analysis is that which talks of 'Pompidou the banker'.[7]

This aspect of the question, however, is contingent and secondary. In point of fact, the hegemonic fraction has often been distinct from the *governing* class or fraction, and is so today in certain social formations, the governing class or fraction being that from which the higher members and political personnel of the state apparatus are recruited (class origin) and sometimes still belong. This phenomenon has, however, in no way prevented an objective correspondence between state policy and the interests of the hegemonic fraction. To seek such a correspondence at all costs in a supposed identity between the hegemonic fraction and the governing class or fraction, is bound to lead, in cases where there is a clear distantiation between the two, to considering the governing class as the hegemonic only; this was the root of the social-democratic errors about fascism, which was considered as the 'dictatorship of the petty bourgeoisie' because of the petty-bourgeois class origin of the top personnel of the state apparatuses under fascism.

To return to the contemporary state. The argument outlined, which can only be very approximate in character, may also lead to

7. E.g. the recent book by H. Claude, *Le Pouvoir et l'Argent*, 1972, which nevertheless includes some remarkable insights.

concealing class hegemony. We can see how at present, under certain social-democratic governments (Germany, Austria, Sweden, Great Britain under Wilson), the hegemony of monopoly capital is accomplished by way of a political personnel largely arisen from the ranks not just of monopoly capital, but also from the petty bourgeoisie, and even often from the labour aristocracy by way of the trade unions and the social-democratic or labour parties. It is precisely this that the apologists for these governments present as proof of the absence under their regime of monopoly capitalist hegemony.[8]

However:

(a) All this does not mean that members of the hegemonic class or fraction do not directly participate in the apparatuses of the capitalist state (in government, as top personnel of the political parties, and as heads of the state administration); this has always been the case with every form of the capitalist state, in the past as much as at present. We may even say that this phenomenon is more pronounced than previously in the state apparatus of the present phase, both because of the decisive role of the contemporary state's economic intervention, and because of the expansion of the nationalized sector of the economy which monopoly capital is involved in controlling, the particular dependency of non-monopoly capital on monopoly capital, and finally the institutional transformations of the state itself. This phenomenon, however, which can thus serve as an index, remains secondary and cannot in any way be interpreted as a 'physical stranglehold' of the 'monopolists' over a state which previously still retained the virginal 'purity' of an 'arbiter' through an 'honest' civil service.

(b) I should like to add one more word on the French case. The phenomenon of the direct presence of members of the monopoly fraction within the state apparatuses, which has been so pronounced in the last decade, has been especially striking in comparison with certain specific features of the French past, bound up with the 'Jacobin' tradition of the Third or even the Fourth Republics. The Fifth Republic has not only made up for its backwardness in this respect, but even overtaken certain other metropolitan states in exhibiting a real tendency towards the colonization of the state by actual members of the monopolist fraction. This, however, is bound up with certain peculiar features of the Gaullist regime – or even of the character of the Gaullist movement/party and the institutions of the Fifth Republic – as it has functioned in a country in which

8. This is of course only a secondary aspect of the problem of social-democratic governments, which I cannot go into in depth here.

the economic intervention of the state is particularly important (the apparatus of the Plan was a real haven for the colonization of the state by members of monopoly capital) and the nationalized sector particularly extensive.

(c) It should not be forgotten that this phenomenon is counterbalanced, even in France, by the civil service and the Grandes Écoles, providing as these do a political personnel that still to an appreciable extent comes from the ranks of non-monopoly capital, the liberal professions and even from the petty bourgeoisie.[9] But even this element, which refutes a false identification of the members of the monopoly fraction and the state apparatuses in terms of class origin, is taken up in other ways by the ideological theory of elites and managers. In this case it is the common training and 'culture' of the Grandes Écoles graduates that is stressed, being oriented as these are towards the administration of business enterprises and the state apparatuses and exhibiting a high degree of interchangeability and mobility of functions by way of the nationalized sector of the economy and all sorts of informal networks. What has been completely thrown overboard, meanwhile, is the hegemony of monopoly capital, and this has been replaced in these theories by the all-powerful techno-bureaucratic 'caste', 'elite' or 'class' that is supposed to wield the real levers of command in the economy and the state.

II

Finally, the arguments that allege a physical identification of the members of the monopoly fraction and the capitalist class as a whole with the members of the state apparatus, or reduce the latter mechanically to a common denominator with respect to their origin or even their class membership, entirely conceal an important problem: the existence and specific mode of functioning of the social category to which members of the state apparatus belong, i.e. the state bureaucracy. The state functionaries constitute a social category: this is determined by the relation of these agents to the state apparatuses and by the fact that they perform objective functions on behalf of the state.

What is the essential fact here which the argument about the fusion of the state and the monopolies into a single mechanism conceals? Precisely that the functioning of this category cannot be reduced to the class origin or even the class membership of its members; if this were the case, then the problem of bureaucracy, which

9. According to an INSEE investigation (*Études et Conjonctures*, February 1967).

was so important for Marx, Engels, Lenin and Gramsci, could not even be posed.

This social category, whose members are generally of different class origins and belong to different classes, often exhibits, despite this diversity, a specific internal unity, which is simply the effect on these agents of the unity of state power and the institutional unity of the state apparatuses (in particular their 'centralism'). This social category can certainly serve, as a group, the interests of classes and fractions other than those which its 'heads' belong to, or from which they originate. The classic case that Marx analysed, the English one, was that of a state bureaucracy whose heads belonged to the landed nobility and which functioned in the service of the bourgeoisie; that analysed by Lenin was the case of the 'bourgeois specialists', originating from the bourgeois class, but in the service of the Soviet state. There is also the case of the fascist bureaucracy in the service of monopoly capital, or again that of the political personnel from the petty-bourgeois class in France under the Third Republic, who served the bourgeoisie despite their own Jacobin tradition.

What is more, in certain specific conjunctures, this social category can function as an effective social force. In this case, it intervenes in the political field and the class struggle with a weight of its own; it is not purely and simply 'in tow' either to the hegemonic class or fraction, or to the class or fraction from which it originates or to which it belongs.

It is thus clear that the social category of the agents of the state apparatus, the bureaucracy in the broad sense of the term, assumes a specific role particularly within the limits of the capitalist state's relative autonomy.[10] It is, however, still necessary to say a few more words on the class membership of the agents of this social category. In fact, the class question for this social category cannot simply be reduced to that of their class origin. A social category, just like a stratum or a fraction, is not a 'group' alongside, outside, or above classes. Its agents do not just have a class origin, as if, from the moment that they join the state bureaucracy, they cease to form part of social classes. It should be stressed all the more that the present

10. The specific role of the bureaucracy is to intervene within the relative autonomy of the capitalist state. This role is, however, neither the cause nor the principal factor in this autonomy, contrary to how all idealist conceptions present it; they see the state as a subject, and ascribe its 'autonomy' to its 'rationalizing will', the bureaucracy being the embodiment of this (Hegel, Weber, etc.). On the contrary, it is the relative autonomy of the state, inscribed in its very structure (see above), that makes possible this specific role of the bureaucracy.

position of the PCF, less paradoxically than might appear at first sight, considers these agents of the state as a 'group' that escapes belonging to any class. It is as if there were, in the state apparatuses, on the one hand the massive and direct presence of the 'monopolists' themselves, and on the other hand, radically distinct from the former, 'civil servants' who in so far as they formed a grouping of their own, escaped from class determinations and simply constituted one of the celebrated 'anti-monopoly strata'.[11] The latter, it will be recalled, are seen as located on the margin and outside of classes.

In actual fact, unless we are to abandon the Marxist theory of social classes for some kind of conception of 'stratification', then the fact that the state agents function as a social category should not suppress or conceal the question of the class determination of this category and its agents. The latter indeed derive from various classes: generally the heads of the state apparatuses come from the bourgeoisie, the intermediate and subaltern levels from the petty bourgeoisie. Let us concentrate for a moment on the heads of these apparatuses. These generally belong to the bourgeois class, not by virtue of their inter-personal relationships with the members of capital itself, but chiefly because, in a capitalist state, they manage the state functions in the service of capital.

However, this class determination of the heads of the state apparatuses, precisely to the extent that it is bound up with their role as a social category, is neither direct nor immediate. It takes place by way of the state apparatus, which is what establishes these agents as a social category. It follows that, if one should not see these heads as a distinct fraction (elite) of the bourgeois class, there can be no question either of asking which fraction of the capitalist class they belong to. As against the managers, who themselves occupy the place of capital, the bourgeois class membership of the heads of the state apparatus is refracted and mediated by the role of the state in the cohesion and reproduction of the social relations of a capitalist formation. It would be more exact to say that the division of the bourgeoisie into fractions is indirectly reflected within the heads of the state apparatus, i.e. by way of the differentiations and dislocations between the various branches and apparatuses of the state, which (within the limits of the unity of the state power) reproduce the contradictions of the power bloc.[12]

11. *Traité* . . . , *le capitalisme monopoliste d'État*, op. cit., vol. I, pp. 233 ff.

12. These guiding principles enable us to analyse the present situation correctly. In fact, to the extent that the present role of the state involves a shift of the functions of representation and organization from the political parties towards the state administration, the present contradictions of the power bloc are expressed above all within the state apparatus proper. These

Far more than in the case of the managers, therefore (for what we are dealing with here is a social category), the situation of these agents in the political and ideological relations plays an important role in their structural class determination. These agents are directly attached to the state apparatuses, in charge of 'operationalizing' the role of the state in the reproduction of the social division of labour, more specifically in the reproduction of the relations of political and ideological domination and subordination. Now the state, while it assumes this role in the reproduction of the social division of labour within the social formation, at the same time concentrates and represents this social division in and by its own apparatuses; the state, as both Engels and Lenin said, epitomizes social contradictions within itself. In other words, these agents carry out the role that the state has to play in this social division, while being themselves, as members of its apparatuses, located in this division in the form in which it is institutionalized by the state: this determines the situation of these agents in organized physical repression, the exercise of legitimate authority, and the institutionalization of the division between mental and manual labour and between the tasks of 'decision' and those of 'execution'. This has decisive effects on the specific ideology of these agents. This ideology, even though it is sometimes distinguished from that of the managers in the form of 'serving the general interest' and 'the state authority over and above particular interests' still constitutes a form of bourgeois ideology.[13]

This structural class determination of the heads of the state apparatus is, however, distinct from the quite unique case of the state

---

assume on the one hand the form of internal contradictions between its different branches and institutions (the various 'ministries' and 'departments', the central and local apparatuses, etc.), on the other hand the form of contradictions between the state's various interventions. Hence the phenomenon, so characteristic today, of constant permutations of the various state functions between apparatuses and branches, and the constant overlap of their 'spheres of competence'. This shift in the state's role as organizer of hegemony towards the administration has contradictory effects: (a) a growing politicization of the top administrators of the state apparatuses (on this subject see J.-P. Chevenement, in Chevenement and Motchane, *Clefs pour le socialisme*, 1973); (b) the centrifugal tendencies of an 'autonomization' of the state administration within narrow limits which the present phase imposes on the state's relative autonomy. This gives rise to attacks by the bourgeoisie itself against state centralism and *dirigisme*.

13. See the contributions by A. Cottereau, J.-M. Vincent, J. Sallois, etc. in the volume *L'Administration*, edited by Sallois, due to appear shortly in the collection 'les Sciences de l'action'.

bourgeoisie, which can in fact constitute a distinct class or class fraction. It is possible to speak of a state bourgeoisie in cases in which there has been a radical rationalization and state-ization of the economic sector without the workers themselves having real control of production, and with the state remaining an institution distinct and 'separate' from the popular masses. In cases such as these, the heads of the state apparatus occupy, by way of the state, the same place of ownership (here state-ized) and possession of the means of production 'separate' from the workers, exercising the powers that derive from this: the exploitation and extraction of surplus-value is shifted towards the heads of the state apparatus itself. This is the process of state capitalism in the strict sense.

To return to the question of the class membership of the members of the state apparatus which is particularly important in so far as it can affect the political functioning of the bureaucracy. The fact that this social category can function, in specific conjunctures, in a 'unitary' fashion, and that it presents certain characteristic dislocations not only in relation to the classes from which its members originated, but also to those to which they still belong, does not mean that this class membership has no effects. These effects are expressed in the form of characteristic breaks actually within the bureaucratic body of the state, and by dislocations between the bourgeois heads, on the one hand, and the petty-bourgeois subaltern and lower levels on the other. These breaks and dislocations assume their full importance in the particular case of a political crisis.

Part Three

The Petty Bourgeoisie,
Traditional and New

Theoretical and Practical Relevance of the Problem Today

1. GENERAL REMARKS

The question of the petty bourgeosie stands not only at the centre of current debates on the class structure of the imperialist metropolises, but also of debates on the dominated and dependent 'peripheral' formations, as is shown by various analyses of the problem of marginality. This question is certainly a crucial aspect of the Marxist theory of social classes. It has now assumed a decisive importance, both in the imperialist and in the dominated social formations; it was on this question, among others, that, as we now know, the socialist development in Chile came to grief.

I

Before we begin to examine this problem, it will be useful to mention certain current theories and the premises on which they are based.

These theories are based on a real fact, the exact significance of which we shall assess later on. The considerable increase, throughout monopoly capitalism and its various phases, of the number of non-productive wage-earners, i.e. groups such as commercial and bank employees, office and service workers, etc., in short all those who are commonly referred to as 'white-collar' or 'tertiary sector' workers. The first line of thought to which this has given rise is one that expressly attempts to refute the Marxist theory of social classes, and with it the theory of class struggle. It is generally based on, or at least tainted with, the general notion of a dissolution of class boundaries and the class struggle within present society, and this process is allegedly marked by a generalized 'embourgeoisement', i.e. by an 'integration', of the working class.

It is particularly interesting to note the various forms that this line of thought takes, in so far as these often influence current Marxist analyses of the question. I would say very generally that these analyses are often concerned to refute one particular form that this tendency takes, that of the middle class as third force, without seeing that the same tendency can just as well manifest itself in another form, which I shall deal with first.

1. In its first form, this tendency denies the class specificity of these new wage-earning groupings, dissolving them into the bourgeoisie and the working class. It generally considers either that the overwhelming majority of these groupings form part of the bourgeoisie, or that they form part of the working class, although it sometimes divides them into those belonging to one class and those to the other. I would like to stress that these conceptions all share one common theoretical position, i.e. that the groups in question have no class determination of their own *vis-à-vis* the bourgeoisie and the working class, but are subject to the determination of either the one or the other. It is not by chance that the criteria of class determination involved in most of these conceptions, following an old bourgeois tradition, are based on relations of 'power', 'hierarchy', or 'authority', with the economic situation of the agents being seen as only the effect on this.

(a) The first version of this tendency is that which maintains, after the fashion of Renner, Croner, Bendix and others,[1] that the overwhelming majority of these new wage-earning groupings belong to the bourgeoisie; this is one variant of the conception of the 'embourgeoisement' of advanced industrial society. The bourgeoisie is defined here quite independently of the relations of production, by reference to 'entrepreneurial functions' and the exercise of hierarchical 'authority' in society. The 'functions' performed by these groupings – in the expressly functionalist sense of this term – are seen as directly emanating from the decomposition of the tasks and roles of the 'entrepreneur', and of 'clerks' and 'services', which were previously all directly fulfilled by the controlling bourgeoisie itself. These groupings would thus now belong to the bourgeoisie through a process of delegation of these functions and of the authority that is attached to them.

(b) The second version of this tendency is that which maintains that these wage-earning groupings belong for the most part to the working class, either (i) through the claim, following an old social-democratic tradition, that the determining criteria of the working class are the mode of distribution, i.e. wages, and, in opposition to

1. K. Renner, *Wandlungen der modernen Gesellschaft*, 1953; F. Croner, *Soziologie der Angestellten*, 1962.

the bourgeoisie, the lack of ownership of the means of production: this is of course the concept of the wage-earning class, which we shall come back to later; or (ii) by maintaining, in addition to the previous criteria, that there are a 'plurality' of extremely varied criteria for defining the working class, which include 'low level of income', or the absence of bourgeois 'status', or of the exercise of authority, the latter being monopolized by the power elites. What is stressed here, by Theodor Geiger, C. Wright Mills and others,[2] is the similarity in this respect between the 'conditions' of the working class and those of these wage-earning groupings. The conclusion is therefore drawn that the latter have been merged into the working class.

(c) The third version, represented by Dahrendorf in particular,[3] tries to split the difference, by claiming that one section of these new groupings belongs to the bourgeoisie, the other to the working class. The determinant criterion here is precisely the place of these groupings in relation to the exercize of 'power' and 'authority', in the Weberian sense of these terms. Thus according to Dahrendorf, the dividing line cutting through these groupings is located, within the contemporary social 'organizations' which distribute relations of 'legitimate' authority (*Herrschaftsverbände*), between those who decide (the bourgeoisie) and those who execute (the working class).

The ideological operation involved in these conceptions is quite clear, and ultimately coincides with that of the middle class as a third force, even though these conceptions are explicitly presented as critiques of the latter position.

In point of fact, however, by denying the class specificity of these wage-earning groupings, and thus dissolving them into the bourgeoisie and the proletariat, i.e. by clinging to the 'dualist' image of society which has often, quite wrongly, been ascribed to Marxism, they end up precisely by dissolving the concepts of bourgeoisie and working class, and denying the class struggle. No-one has expressed this better than Dahrendorf himself:

It follows from our analysis that the emergence of salaried employees means in the first place an extension of the older classes of bourgeoisie and proletariat. Both classes have become, by these extensions, even more complex and heterogenous than their decomposition has made them in any case. By gaining new elements, their unity has become a highly doubtful and precarious

2. T. Geiger, *Die soziale Schichtung des deutschen Volkes*, 1932; C. Wright Mills, *White Collar*, New York, 1951.

3. 'The Service Class', in *Industrial Man* (ed. T. Burns), 1969.

feature. White-collar workers, like industrial workers, have neither property nor authority, yet they display many social characteristics that are quite unlike those of the old working class. Similarly, bureaucrats differ from the older ruling class despite their share in the exercise of authority. Even more than the decomposition of capital and labour, these facts make it highly doubtful whether the concept of class is still applicable to the conflict groups of post-capitalist societies. In any case, the participants, issues, and patterns of conflict have changed, and the pleasing simplicity of Marx's view of society has become a nonsensical construction.[4]

There can, however, be other aspects to this ideological operation. In particular, while accepting the reality of the class struggle, the hegemonic and directing role of the working class may be questioned, in favour of, among others, various groups affected by 'institutional conflicts'. If this is coupled with the conception of institutions as the basis of social relations, then it leads directly to the conclusion that the principal struggle today is not that over exploitation, but over 'institutions' (anti-institutional struggles); these are of course the arguments of someone like Ivan Illich, which are very fashionable at the moment.

2. The second form of this tendency, which also has diverse variants to it, is the theory of the middle class.

Although it appears to be opposed to the first, this form in fact fulfils the same ideological function. In its dominant aspect it is bound up with an old conception of traditional political and socio-logical theory, that of the 'third force', directly relayed by the social-democratic tradition into the strategy of the 'third road' (between capitalism and socialism). In the face of the antagonism between the bourgeoisie and the working class, the 'middle class' is seen as the mediating pillar and the basic 'stabilizing' factor of bourgeois society. This 'middle class' is not only considered as on the same footing as the bourgeoisie and the working class, but it is also conceived as the central axis of social development, i.e. as the region where the class struggle is dissolved.

The essential problem here is thus not directly that of the analytical pertinence of treating these wage-earning groupings as a single class, but rather the theoretical and political conception that governs this, and which commands the actual analysis of the middle class that this tendency makes. The 'middle class' is here considered as a 'homogenous group', defined in general on the basis of income

4. R. Dahrendorf, *Class and Class Conflict in an Industrial Society*, pp. 56–7.

criteria, and criteria of mental attitudes and of psychological motivations. It is supposed to be the result of a progressive dissolution of the bourgeoisie and the proletariat in contemporary capitalist societies into a common stew: the 'embourgeoisement' of a larger and larger section of the working class, and the 'declassing' of a larger and larger section of the bourgeoisie. This 'class' is thus supposed to form the stew in which classes are mixed together and their antagonisms dissolved, chiefly by forming a site for the circulation of individuals in a constant process of 'mobility' between the bourgeoisie and the proletariat. This group thus appears as the dominant group in contemporary capitalist societies.

I choose the word group, since to use the term class to apply to a grouping that dissolves the class struggle would be quite pointless. As far as this tendency is concerned, it uses the term 'middle class' to mean that classes no longer exist. This is also what is maintained, by extension of these arguments, by those writers whose studies turn on the celebrated question of the tertiary sector and the 'tertiarization' of present society. It is evident that, by basing itself on the distinction between 'industry', 'agriculture' and the rest, and combining this with the ideology of 'professions' and 'socio-professional categories' (as do INSEE and in fact all bourgeois statistics), this conception lumps together in the 'tertiary' sector big commercial magnates, the banks and the media, shopkeepers great and small, handicraftsmen and 'liberal professions', managing directors and higher executives, workers in commerce, 'offices' and 'services', and all civil servants from the President of the Republic down to the postman. We would not only go along with R. Fossaert and M. Praderie in asserting that this 'tertiary' sector does not form a class, but go so far as to state clearly that, if the 'traditional' Marxist conception of social classes is maintained, then the members of the tertiary sector must be considered as belonging to various different classes: to the bourgeoisie, petty bourgeoisie, and working class.[5] Of course, if the very existence of the tertiary sector as third force proves that social classes and the class struggle no longer exist, then the use of the term class itself becomes superfluous.

II

There is good reason for laying emphasis on this last theory, as we shall see. Let us now turn to a solution to the problem that is nowadays proposed by the PCF, with its arguments about state monopoly capitalism. This argument, clearly put forward in the *Traité* already

5. Fossaert, *L'Avenir du capitalisme*, 1961; Praderie, *Les Tertiaires*, 1968.

mentioned, is presented as an explicit criticism of the 'middle class/ third force' tendency. It displays, however, a whole series of confusions and false principles, which are the same as those that underlie the political strategy of the 'anti-monopoly alliance'.

The PCF argument, while it rejects the dissolution of the wage-earning groupings into the working class, still denies their class specificity, or even their membership of a class as such.

> The intermediary strata do not form one or more classes in the strict sense of the term. There is not a single middle class, but rather a series of differentiated social strata located in an intermediate position.[6]

The theoretical foundation is thus that these strata are seen as belonging to no class. In fact, in a chapter of the *Traité*, nevertheless entitled 'Class Membership of the Intermediate Wage-Earning Strata', all we find is formulations of the following kind:

> From a class point of view, salaried employees, technicians, engineers, research workers etc. are located in an intermediate position which brings them ever closer to the working class, although they should not . . . at the present time be confused with the latter.[7]

Nowhere does the *Traité* answer the question: what class are these groupings strata of, what exactly is their class membership?

We must pause here, for this involves a very basic question, of great importance for the Marxist theory of social classes and the class struggle in general. Marxism indeed admits the existence of fractions, strata, and even social categories ('state bureaucracy', 'intellectuals'). But this in no way involves groupings alongside, marginal to or above classes, in other words external to them. Fractions are class fractions; the industrial bourgeoisie, for example, is a fraction of the bourgeoisie. Strata are class strata; the labour aristocracy is a stratum of the working class. Even the social categories, as we have seen above in relation to the state bureaucracy, have their class membership.

This is a basic point of distinction between the Marxist theory of social classes and the various conceptions of bourgeois sociology. The great majority of non-Marxist sociologists indeed speak of social classes, and are even ready to define them, if in ways which are most often quite fantastic. But they consider that this division into classes is a simple and partial subdivision of a more general

6. loc. cit., vol. I, p. 204.
7. ibid., p. 236.

stratification, which also comprises other groups parallel and external to classes. This was already the case with Max Weber (classes *and* status groups), and it is found today in several forms (particularly that of social classes *and* political elites). Moreover, in these sub-divisions, these sociological tendencies generally ascribe to other groups a more important role in society than they do to social classes. The Marxist reply to these tendencies cannot simply be to maintain that classes are the basic groups in the 'historic process', while admitting the possibility that other groups exist parallel and external to classes, at least in a 'synchronic' cross-section of a social formation. The division of society into classes precisely means, both from the theoretical and methodological point of view and from that of social reality, that the concept of social class is pertinent to all levels of analysis: the division into class forms the frame of reference for every social stratification.

III

It is still necessary to go further, for, even if the above point is accepted, it is still possible to legitimize in another way the concep-tion of certain social groupings external to classes, unless we clarify certain theoretical aspects of the question.[8]

1. Social class is a concept that refers in particular to the overall effects of the structure on the field of social relations and on the social division of labour. It would, however, be quite false to see social class as a 'model'; this would precisely lead to accepting the possibility of the existence, in the reality of a social formulation, of certain other groupings external to classes, as the effect of a 'richness' of the 'concrete reality' which overflows its 'abstract model'. In this view, social class would be simply a schematization of the reality, a kind of skeleton of it, extracted from the real by a simple operation of abstraction, so that the groupings external to classes are precisely the richness of the determination of the concrete which escapes this 'grid' of intelligibility. This is of course an old nominalist conception of social classes, ultimately deriving from an empiricist theory of knowledge and of the relations between the abstract and the con-crete.

2. A social formation is the locus of existence of an articulation of several modes and forms of production. This is expressed: (a) in the existence within a social formation of other classes besides the two classes based on the dominant mode of production, classes which derive from other modes and forms of production present in that

8. For the general conceptual framework of the following discussion, see above, Introduction, pp. 13 ff.

formation; (b) in the effects of class decomposition and restructuring, of the over- and under-determination of class, i.e. by effects of the articulation of these modes and forms of production on the classes which derive from them in a social formation.

The effects of this articulation, however, cannot involve the emergence of social groupings external to classes, groupings which are thus as it were 'atypical' or 'anomic'. This would mean returning to the empiricist conception of 'residues' or 'impurities' in the concrete reality, conceived as a mere stew into which 'abstract' modes and forms of production are thrown, with these groupings being as it were the scraps. Here again we come across the false conception of the 'abstract model', this time in the context of the relations between modes of production and social formations. Social formations are not in fact the concretization and spatialization of modes of production existing already in a state of abstract purity, but rather the particular form in which the modes of production exist and are reproduced. The classes in a social formation are not the concretization of classes in the various modes of production, such that these could give rise, in the course of this concretization, to a concrete fall-out that would escape them; they are rather the form of existence and reproduction of the classes of the various modes of production involved (the class struggle).

3. We come now to the final facet of the question. The class struggle in a social formation takes place within the basic context of a polarization of various social classes in relation to the two basic classes, those of the dominant mode of production, whose relationship constitutes the principal contradiction of that formation. Could it not be the case, either that old social classes come to be dissolved into social groupings 'external' to classes, or that similar new social groupings emerge, as the effect of the class struggle and of the polarization in question? And could such groupings not then be located in a specific relation to the two basic classes without themselves having a class membership of their own, since their 'relational' connection to these two classes in the class struggle would have as its particular effect the absence, or elimination, of a specific class place? This is sometimes how the PCF's theory of the 'intermediate strata' is presented.[9]

In point of fact, this polarization plays a very important role not just in so far as class position is concerned, but also in the structural class determination. However, the conception outlined above is untenable. It in fact assumes that classes firstly exist as such, in isolation, and only then enter into relations of struggle, so that this class

9. J. Lojkine, 'Pouvoir politique et luttes des classes', in *La Pensée*, December 1972.

struggle would then have as its effect, by way of the polarization it involves, the dissolution of certain classes into social groupings without class membership, even without the relations of production on which these classes were based being undermined. It must be stressed, however: (a) that social classes can only exist in the form of class struggle, and that the places of social classes coincide with class practices (social relations); (b) that the determination of class by the class struggle still does not mean that classes (or certain social groupings) only exist in a 'relational' form, in the sense that their situation would change according to the class struggle, which would thus be conceived here after the Tourainian model of 'social movements'. This would in fact mean reintroducing, under an 'anti-structuralist' façade, the idealist conception of a reduction of objective class determination to class position. But the adoption of class positions converging with those of the bourgeoisie or the working class no more eliminates the structural class determination or place of these social groupings than the adoption of bourgeois class positions by a certain stratum of the working class (the labour aristocracy) eliminates *its* class determination and transforms it into an 'intermediate stratum'.

In brief, the class struggle and the polarization it involves does not and cannot give rise to groupings alongside of or marginal to classes, groupings without class membership, for the simple reason that this class membership is itself nothing more than the class struggle, and that this struggle only exists by way of the existence of the places of social classes. Strictly speaking, it actually makes no sense to maintain that there are 'social groupings' that are external to the classes but are nevertheless involved in the class struggle. The problem of the real elimination of certain classes or fractions in the extended development of capitalism (the traditional petty bourgeoisie, the small-holding peasantry) is of course a quite different question. In these cases, what we are faced with is not at all a process of reabsorption of these classes into social groupings without a class membership ('intermediate self-employed strata'), but rather a process of gradual elimination of these classes themselves (what residue there is still forming classes).

IV

These questions are important enough to warrant some additional remarks. Confusions of this kind can also be found in certain current analyses of the peripheral formations, articulated around the problematic of marginality (the 'marginal masses'). What is broadly re-referred to by this term is the phenomenon, in the peripheral formations, of a 'mass of individuals' produced by the massive rural exodus, who are concentrated in the urban zone where they live off occupations that are allegedly 'parasitic'. This conception is closely bound up with that of the 'dual society', i.e. a social formation composed of two heterogenous sectors, a traditional agrarian and a modern industrial one, each with their own class structure, so that marginality would be a characteristic of certain social groupings without a class membership, groupings that are seen as located in the space between (in the margin of) these two separate sectors.

This theory in fact dispenses with a rigorous analysis of the effects, in the present phase of imperialism, of the induced reproduction of monopoly capitalist relations of the metropolises within the peripheral formations. In particular it ignores such phenomena as the transitional forms in which labour-power comes to be subsumed by these relations, the constitution of this labour-power into a reserve army for imperialism, and concealed unemployment. What is even more interesting is to examine the objections to this theory of marginality put forward by certain Marxist writers. These have most commonly been concerned to refute the theory of the dual society (i.e. that there are not in fact two separate sectors), stressing on the one hand that the emergence of these social groupings without class membership is a structural effect of the domination of monopoly relations over other modes and forms of production in the peripheral formations, and co-substantial with this, and that on the other hand these 'atypical' groupings are in fact not marginal at all, since their political role can be extremely important.[10] The objections are correct, but they still miss an essential point and also dispense with a class analysis of this grouping. The structural effect of the present phase of imperialism in the dominated and dependent formations is not such as to generate 'social groups' alongside classes or external to them. In maintaining this position, and thus retaining the problematic of groups marginal to social classes, the real problem is concealed, i.e. the process, which is certainly an extraordinarily complex one, in which social classes are decomposed and reorganized in the peripheral formations, a process of over- and under-determination.

What ultimately underlies both the analyses of marginality and the objections mentioned, at least from a theoretical point of view, is the empiricist conception of social classes as the sum of the individual agents of which they are composed. Social classes are here examined in the first instance not according to their places in the social division of labour, but according to the concrete individuals

10. In particular R. Stavenhagen, *Sept Thèses erronées sur l'Amerique latine*, 1973.

who participate in them. The question thus becomes: to what class does this or that individual or 'mass' of individuals belong, and it follows that in cases where it is difficult to give a precise answer, while these 'individuals are seen as disqualified in class terms. They are classified as belonging to 'groupings' that are marginal to the classes, it is in fact the question that has been wrongly posed. There is a clear epistemological collusion here between the nominalist/idealist conception of social classes (of classes as an 'abstract model') and this empiricist conception, with both leading to the same results: in one case, it leads to social groupings which fall outside the class grid, and in the other, to individuals and groupings that do not take part in the composition of classes, and are seen as sums of individuals.

What is more, this problematic makes it impossible to pose a perfectly legitimate question, that of the agents who occupy the places of the social classes; this is particularly bound up with that of the reproduction of social classes. In fact, the question of agents is quite different from that of the 'individuals' whose sum would comprise the social classes, in so far as it is posed within a different problematic. The agents are not 'individuals' who are regrouped to give birth to various 'groupings', so that classes would only be one of these possible assemblages; classes are rather reproduced according to the reproduction of the places of social classes in the class struggle.

All the points we made previously concerning the principal aspect of social classes, that of their places, and the reproduction of these places in the social division of labour, were designed to exclude the possibility of social groupings existing alongside or outside of the class struggle. This problem, however, is still relatively separate from that of the reproduction (training/subjection/distribution) of the agents among the places. It is apparent that, in this process of the reproduction of agents, it is possible to isolate a whole series of phenomena, ranging from transitory situations to contradictory class membership, and even the effective 'declassing' of agents. The capital difference, however, is that a sum of 'declassed' agents can never amount to a pertinent social grouping in the field of class struggle; this is brought out by Marx in all his analyses of the lumpenproletariat. In any case, it is clear that the question of the new wage-earning groupings cannot be treated on the level of an assemblage of declassed agents.

V

To return to the current PCF position on state monopoly capitalism and the 'intermediate wage-earning strata'. This argument actually goes together with a very precise political strategy, that of the 'anti-monopoly alliance', which here shows itself to be an unprincipled one. In point of fact, every class alliance of the popular masses (the 'people') involves a series of real contradictions between the interests of the various classes in the alliance, contradictions which have to be taken seriously into consideration and resolved correctly; these are the 'contradictions among the people'. There can be no doubt that certain of the contemporary wage-earning groupings outside of the proletariat form part of the people. But recognition of their class membership, which differentiates them from the working class, is nevertheless essential in order to establish a correct basis for the popular alliance, under the leadership and hegemony of the working class. We shall return to this later. By expressly denying the class membership of these groupings, their differentiation from the working class is hidden, i.e. the possibility that they have class interests that are relatively distinct from those of the working class is concealed. By imputing to them interests identical to those of the working class, the long-term interests of the working class itself, which is the only class that is revolutionary to the end, are distorted so that they can be amalgamated with those of these other groupings, while the real problem is precisely that of leading groupings with their own specific class membership to take up the positions of the working class. The proponents of the state monopoly capitalism theory may well stress the fact that these shifting classless strata do not belong to the working class, but in their political conclusions they increasingly converge with the social-democratic error of the 'wage-earning class'.

2. THE TRADITIONAL PETTY BOURGEOISIE AND THE NEW PETTY BOURGEOISIE

The particular question of these new wage-earning groupings will form the chief object of the following analysis. I shall refer to them as the new petty bourgeoisie, for what I am seeking to show here is that they belong together with the traditional petty bourgeoisie (small-scale production and ownership, independent craftsmen and traders) to one and the same class, the petty bourgeoisie. I shall thus have to discuss the traditional petty bourgeoisie as well, and raise a series of more general theoretical problems, as follows:

(a) What precisely defines the petty bourgeoisie in its structural class determination, i.e. its place in the social division of labour, including not only relations of production but also relations of political and ideological domination/subordination? What is its particular position in the process of the reproduction of social classes? It will become clear, in fact, that the petty bourgeoisie cannot be placed on the same footing as the two basic classes of a capitalist formation, the bourgeoisie and the proletariat, among other reasons because of its polarization. This raises another question: how, and on what basis, can social groupings that apparently have different places in economic relations belong to one and the same class, the petty bourgeoisie?

(b) What principles should govern the analysis of the petty bourgeoisie into class fractions? Do these fractions of the petty bourgeoisie have the same significance as the fractions of the two basic classes, bourgeoisie and proletariat? Can economic relations alone suffice to define the class fractions of the petty bourgeoisie? And besides the key differentiation between the traditional petty bourgeoisie and the new petty bourgeoisie, what are the class fractions of the new petty bourgeoisie itself?

(c) What political positions divide the petty bourgeoisie? Can the petty bourgeoisie have an autonomous class position of its own in the long run? To what extent, if any, do the various political positions that divide it coincide with fractions of the petty bourgeoisie as defined by their structural class determination; and what, moreover, is the role of the conjuncture in this respect?

I

To begin with the first question, I would like to pick up again a thesis that I have already put forward elsewhere, and which is particularly relevant to the problem of the traditional and the new petty bourgeoisie belonging to the same class; the principles governing this thesis, however, have much wider implications. If certain groupings which at first sight seem to occupy different places in economic relations can be considered as belonging to the same class, this is because these places, although they are different, nevertheless have the same effects at the political and ideological level. I must now go into the thesis in greater detail, and also rectify it somewhat.

I can only do this by referring to the phenomenon of polarization. Class polarization, while it certainly cannot generate social groupings without a class membership, still has a considerable importance in the actual determination of social classes. This polarization results from the fact that the class struggle in a capitalist social formation is centred around the two basic classes of this formation (the principal contradiction), the bourgeoisie and the working class.

This class polarization has as its initial field of application the actual structural class determination of the petty bourgeoisie, i.e. the place that the groupings that comprise it occupy in the social division of labour. In point of fact, if it is true that class position in the conjuncture must not be confused with class determination, it is still the case that the latter itself involves class practices, since social classes only exist in the class struggle. In other words, the phenomenon of polarization does not mean that the various petty-bourgeois groupings, already with their own determinations, simply take up class positions that converge either with those of the bourgeoisie, or with those of the working class (polarization of class position), but rather that their structural class determination itself can only be grasped in their relation, within the social division of labour, to the bourgeoisie and the working class (polarization of class determinations).

This already involves the economic relations of this class determination, economic relations which play the principal role here just as they do for every social class. In fact, from this point of view, the traditional petty bourgeoisie (small-scale production and ownership) and the new petty bourgeoisie (non-productive wage-earners) both have in common the fact that they neither belong to the bourgeoisie nor to the working class. This is a common criterion which appears to be wholly negative. However, this factor assumes a quite different role according to whether it is considered 'in itself', i.e. as defining in isolation the places of the petty bourgeoisie or whether, as is in fact correct, it is considered in the context of class polarization. The question then arises as to what are the effects of this negative criterion. Small-scale production and ownership on the one hand, and non-productive wage-labour on the other, only assume their significance in relation to what is happening to the bourgeoisie and to the working class in this respect. This common negative criterion can certainly not be transformed into a positive criterion, in the strict sense, simply by considering it in the context of the polarization of the two basic classes. The fact that these groupings, as far as economic relations are concerned, neither from part of the bourgeoisie nor part of the proletariat, is not sufficient to define a common place for them in economic relations, i.e. a determination by simple extrapolation. On the other hand, however, in looking at the question from the specific aspect of this polarization, it is clear that this negative criterion does not just have a simple excluding role; it actually produces economic 'similarities' which have common political and ideological effects. In other words, although the exclusion of these groupings from certain places (bourgeoisie, proletariat) does not suffice to locate their specific situation, this exclusion still indicates, even at the level of economic relations, the outlines of their places, which are reaffirmed by the political and ideological relations.

II

This phenomenon of polarization does not only involve economic relations, but also the ideological and political relations of the structural class determination of these groupings: i.e. the common features of these groupings with regard to the political and ideological relations that specify the places of the bourgeoisie and the working class in the social division of labour. The full importance of this is particularly apparent in relation to the specific features of the petty-bourgeois ideological sub-ensemble.

We are faced here, however, with certain particular problems:

(a) Reference to political and ideological relations is absolutely indispensable in order to define the place of the petty bourgeoisie in the structural class determination. This is not only in order to provide a foundation for the common class membership of the traditional and the new petty bourgeoisie, but also and above all in order to grasp the place of the new petty bourgeoisie in relation to the working class, and the fractions of this new petty bourgeoisie. This does not mean that as far as the two basic classes are concerned, the bourgeoisie and the working class, their places in the social division of labour are exhaustively determined by the relations of production; the structural determination of every social class involves its place both in the relations of production, and in the ideological and political relations. This question, however, acquires a quite special significance for classes other than the two basic classes, particularly for the petty bourgeoisie. Since the latter is not at the centre of the dominant relations of exploitation, i.e. the direct extraction of surplus-value, it undergoes a polarization that produces very complex distortions and adaptations of the political and ideological relations in which it is placed. The fact that examination of political and ideological relations is particularly important in the case of the petty bourgeoisie does not mean that these relations are important only for this class (and not for the bourgeoisie and the working class), nor is it the sign of a conceptual difficulty, such that the Marxist criteria of economic class determination would be 'uncertain' in its case, and the balance would have to be swayed by taking refuge in ideological and political criteria. If these relations have to be stressed in this case, it is because of the real situation of the petty bourgeoisie in the class struggle within a capitalist formation.

(b) These political and ideological relations here involve the structural class determination of the petty bourgeoisie, something that must be distinguished from its class positions. To refer to these relations is not to reduce class determination to class position. These relations (place in the division between mental and manual labour, in relations of power and authority, etc.) certainly have their effects, particularly on the class positions of the new petty bourgeoisie. But if reference to politics and ideology could be reduced to class position in the conjuncture, this would mean, in the final analysis, that every time that petty-bourgeois groupings adopted bourgeois class positions they would belong to the bourgeoisie, while every time they adopted working-class positions they would belong to the working class. This would mean rejecting the objective determination of social classes. It can never be sufficiently stressed that the distinction between structural class determination and class position is not a distinction between an economic determination and a political/ ideological position. Class determination involves objective political and ideological places just as much as class position involves conjunctures of economic struggle. The distinction here is defined by the space of the conjuncture (class position).[11] We shall come back to this problem when we examine the effects of polarization on the class positions of the petty bourgeoisie.

III

Finally, in analysing the petty bourgeoisie we shall also have to take into account, just as in the case of the bourgeoisie, its reproduction, and in particular its reproduction in the present phase of monopoly capitalism. This involves both the reproduction of its place, which is the principal aspect, and the reproduction of its agents. We must simply note here that the question of reproduction is particularly important in the case of the petty bourgeoisie: (a) in so far as the reproduction of its place is concerned, because of the accelerated elimination of the traditional petty bourgeoisie in the present phase, and because of the accelerated expansion in this phase of the new bourgeoisie; (b) in so far as the reproduction of agents is concerned, because of the conditions of training and subjection of its agents and of their distribution, which are quite special in the case of the new petty bourgeoisie.

11. See the Introduction, pp. 14 ff.

2

Productive and Unproductive Labour: The New Petty Bourgeoisie and the Working Class

We must now examine the new wage-earning groupings that are referred to as the new petty bourgeoisie – new in the sense that it is in no way destined to follow the traditional petty bourgeoisie, threatened with extinction, and that its development and expansion are conditioned by the extended reproduction of capitalism itself, and the latter's transition to the stage of monopoly capitalism. We shall start by investigating the various components of its structural class determination, in order to arrive at the effects of this determination at the level of political practice. This requires that we examine the place of these groupings not only in economic relations, but in the social division of labour as a whole.

It is, however, the place of these groupings in economic relations that we must dwell in first, since it is this place that plays the principal role in their class determination. The first point to note is that these groupings do not belong to the bourgeoisie, in so far as they have neither economic ownership nor possession of the means of production. On the other hand, they do present the phenomenon of wage-labour, remunerated in the form of a wage or salary. The basic question that is raised here, therefore, is that of their relationship to the working class, a question that can in the first instance be formulated as that of the boundaries and limits of the working class in capitalist relations of production.

In point of fact, the criterion of ownership of the means of production only assumes the significance it does in so far as it corresponds to a determinate relation of exploitation, a relation that is itself located in the relationship between the direct producers (the specific exploited class of the mode of production in question) and the means and object of labour, and hence with the owners of the latter. Now in the case of capitalism, as Marx puts it, if every agent belonging to the working class is a wage-earner, this does not necessarily mean that every wage-earner belongs to the working class. The working class is not defined by a simple and intrinsic negative criterion, its exclusion from the relations of ownership, but by productive labour: 'Every productive worker is a wage-earner, but it does not follow that every wage-earner is a productive worker.'[1]

Marx's distinction between productive and unproductive labour is a particularly difficult question; although he intended to deal with this in Volume IV of *Capital*, he never presented it in a systematic way. There are a few fragments on the subject in *Capital*, but the subject is developed in greater detail in texts that Marx did not himself publish: chiefly *Theories of Surplus-Value*, the *Grundrisse*, and the *Results of the Immediate Production Process* (the unpublished chapter of *Capital*, vol. I). Of course, these analyses can only be reconstituted in a coherent form by locating them in the corpus of Marx's work as a whole and the different steps of its development; a whole series of scholars have already applied themselves to this task, and research and debate on this subject still remains open. Here I shall simply confine myself to indicating certain general themes within Marx's analyses.[2]

I

Productive labour always refers to labour that is performed under definite social conditions, and thus is directly dependent on the social relations of exploitation of a given mode of production. The productive or unproductive character of labour does not depend either on certain intrinsic characteristics, or on its utility. It is in this sense that one should understand Marx's argument, according to which the definitions of productive and unproductive labour are

1. 'Results of the Immediate Production Process', in *Capital* Vol. I, Penguin, 1975, Appendix.
2. On this subject, I should also like to mention, firstly the remarkable article by E. Terray, 'Prolétaire, salarié, travailleur productif', in *Contradictions*, no. 2, July–September 1972; also M. Freyssenet, *Les rapports de production: travail productif/travail improductif*', May 1971, a mimeographed document from the Centre de Sociologie Urbaine; no. 10, 'Travail et Emploi', of *Critiques d'économie politique*, particularly the articles by P. Salama and C. Coliot-Thélène; M. Mauke, *Die Klassentheorie von Marx und Engels*, 1970; and M. Tronti, *Operai e capitale*, 1972.

not derived from the material characteristics of labour (neither from the nature of its product nor from the particular character of the labour as concrete labour), but from the definite social form, the social relations of production, within which the labour is realised.[3]

Or again,

If follows that productive labour in no way implies a *specific content*, a particular utility or determinate use-value in which it is materialized. This explains why labour with the *same content* may be productive or unproductive.[4]

Thus what is productive labour in a given mode of production is labour that gives rise to the dominant relation of exploitation of this mode; what is productive labour for one mode of production may not be so for another. In the capitalist mode of production, productive labour is that which directly produces surplus-value, which valorizes capital and is exchanged against capital:

The result of the capitalist production process is neither a mere product (use-value) nor a *commodity*, that is, a use-value which has a certain exchange-value. Its result, its product, is the creation of *surplus-value* for capital . . . for what capital as capital (hence the capitalist as capitalist) wants to produce is neither an immediate use-value for individual consumption nor a commodity to be turned first into money and then into a use-value. Its aim is the *accumulation of wealth*, the *self-expansion of value*, its *increase*; that is to say, the maintenance of the old value and the creation of surplus-value. And it achieves this *specific product* of the capitalist production process only in exchange with labour, which for that reason is called *productive labour*.[5]

We shall see in a moment that this definition of (capitalist) productive labour is not the only one that Marx gives, and this leads to certain major problems; however, we can say for the present that it is sufficient to enable Marx to outline the essential boundaries of the working class. Thus, for example, labour performed in the sphere of circulation of capital, or contributing to the realization of surplus-value, is not productive labour; wage-earners in commerce, advertising, marketing, accounting, banking and insurance, do not produce surplus-value and do not form part of the working class

3. *Theories of Surplus-Value*, vol. I, Moscow, 1969, p. 153.
4. 'Results of the Immediate Production Process', loc. cit.
5. *Theories of Surplus-Value*, vol. I, pp. 387–8; see also *Capital*, vol. I, pp. 508–9.

(productive labour). It is only productive capital that produces surplus-value.

> Merchant's capital is simply capital functioning in the sphere of circulation. The process of circulation is a phase of the total process of reproduction. But no value is produced in the process of circulation, and, therefore, no surplus-value. [Hence,] Since the merchant, as a mere agent of circulation, produces neither value nor surplus-value . . . it follows that the mercantile workers employed by him in these same functions cannot directly create surplus-value for him.[6]

From the standpoint of the individual capitalist, these wage-earners do appear to be the source of his profit. But from the standpoint of the social capital and its reproduction, the profit of commercial and banking capital does not derive from a process of value creation, but from a transfer of the surplus-value created by productive capital. These wage-earners simply contribute towards redistributing the mass of surplus-value among the various fractions of capital according to the average rate of profit. Of course, these wage-earners are themselves exploited, and their wages correspond to the reproduction of their labour-power. 'The commercial worker . . . adds to the capitalist's income by helping him to reduce the cost of realizing surplus-value, inasmuch as he performs partly unpaid labour.' Surplus labour is thus extorted from wage-earners in commerce, but these are not directly exploited in the form of the dominant capitalist relation of exploitation, the creation of surplus-value. It is only for the individual capitalist that their labour is exchanged for variable capital, while from the standpoint of the social capital as a whole and its reproduction, their remuneration is an unproductive expense and forms part of the *faux frais* of capitalist production.[7]

It is necessary to emphasize at this point that this distinction between the process of value production and the process of circulation is not the same as the supposed distinction between 'secondary' and 'tertiary' sectors, nor is it one of an institutionalist kind between the types of 'enterprise' (industrial, commercial) in which this labour takes place. Labour involved in the circulation process (sales, advertising, negotiation, etc.) may well be undertaken by industrial enterprises for themselves, but it still remains unproductive labour, and its agents unproductive workers. On the other hand, certain types of labour may appear to form part of the circulation process,

6. *Capital*, vol. III, Moscow, 1962, pp. 274; vol. II, Moscow, 1961, pp. 287.
7. *Capital*, vol. III, pp. 294 ff.

and may be undertaken by commercial enterprises, while in fact they increase the exchange-value of a commodity on the basis of its capitalist use-value, and thus produce surplus-value, their agents thus forming part of the working class. In Volume II, Chapter VI of *Capital*, Marx analyses 'to what extent the transport industry, storage and distribution of commodities in a distributable form, may be regarded as production processes continuing within the process of circulation'.[8] This last aspect of the question is particularly important in the present phase of monopoly capitalism, as for instance in relation to the productive workers involved in various types of 'after-sales service' (repairs, etc.).

Also to be considered as unproductive labour is that taking the form of services, whose products and activities are directly consumed as use-values and are not exchanged against capital but rather against revenue or income:

> Every time that labour is purchased, not in order to substitute it as the living factor in the value of variable capital, but in order to consume it as a use-value, i.e. a service, this labour is not productive labour and the wage-labourer is not a productive worker ... the capitalist does not confront him as capitalist, as the representative of capital; what he exchanges for the labour is not his capital, but his revenue, in the form of money.[9]

These services, from those of the hairdresser to those of the lawyer, the doctor or the teacher, remain unproductive labour even if, as in the two latter cases, they contribute towards the reproduction of labour-power:

> The particular utility of this service *alters nothing in the economic relation*; it is not a relation in which I transform money into capital, or by which the supplier of this service, the teacher, transforms me into *his capitalist*, his master. Consequently it also does not affect the *economic character* of this relation whether the physician cures me, the teacher is successful in teaching me, or the lawyer wins my lawsuit. What is paid for is the performance of the service as such ... [10]

Moreover, the forms of payment for these services in no way change the nature of the economic relation:

> It ... does not depend on the general relation, but rather on the natural, particular quality of the service performed, whether the

8. ibid., pp. 262–3.
9. 'Results ...'
10. *Theories of Surplus-Value*, vol. I, p. 393.

recipient of payment receives it as day-wages, or as an honorarium, or as a sinecure – and whether he appears as superior or inferior in rank to the person paying for the service.[11]

This grouping of service providers, even including wage-earners in this sector, thus does not belong to the working class.

It is, moreover, essentially in terms of this problem of services that Marx deals with a series of forms of labour that greatly contribute to the reproduction of capitalist social relations, i.e. the labour of the agents of the state apparatuses, the civil servants; it is of course necessary to exclude here that directly productive labour that is performed within the state sector, for instance 'nationalized' industrial enterprises, 'public' transport, and workers in the various 'public services'. Thus Marx says:

> The services that the capitalist purchases from the state . . . for their use-value, whether he does so voluntarily or otherwise, no more become elements of capital than do the commodities that he buys for his private consumption. As a result these services are not productive labour, and their agents are not productive labourers.

This is essentially labour performed by agents of the state apparatuses, which is paid for out of taxation, and taxation is still an exchange on the basis of revenue:

> Certain forms of unproductive labour can be incidentally involved in the productive process; their price may even enter into the price of the commodity in so far as the money that they cost forms a part of the capital advanced. This labour may then give the impression that it is exchanged against capital rather than against revenue. Examples of this would be taxes, the costs of public services, etc. These however are so many *faux frais* of production . . . If for example all indirect taxes were transformed into direct taxes, they would still have to be payed for just the same, although they would no longer represent an advance out of capital, but rather an expenditure of revenue.[12]

It is clear that labour of this kind performed by agents of the state apparatuses is essential for the extended reproduction of capitalist social relations. This, however, does not mean that this labour is directly productive, any more than is labour performed in the circulation process, although this too is necessary to the reproduction of the total social capital.

11. *Grundrisse*, Harmondsworth, 1973, p. 468.
12. 'Results . . .'.

But are the agents providing services themselves exploited? In principle, the exchange of use-values against revenue is an exchange of equivalents, and cannot as such give rise to a relation of exploitation. We must, however, introduce here the essential element of the expansion of the wage form into all sectors of a social formation in which the capitalist mode of production is dominant, and where capital tends to subordinate ('subsume') all labour-power. This expansion of the wage form is particularly great under monopoly capitalism and in its present phase. The exchange of equivalents assumes a seller and a purchaser who remain formally independent of one another at the level of economic relations, but the wage relation and the direct intervention of capital tends to seize hold of the service sector as a whole. From medicine through to the liberal professions (law, architecture, etc.), and including entertainment, and the media, the agents providing services have overwhelmingly become employees of capital, which has seized hold of their activities. This does not mean that these wage-earners have become productive workers. But they too sell their labour-power, their wages correspond to the cost of reproduction of this labour-power and they even provide a portion of their labour without payment. Surplus labour is extorted from them, and this enables capital to cut down on its revenue in order to increase the surplus-value accumulated in relation to surplus-value consumed or spent on *faux frais*.[13] In point of fact, these agents are involved here in the redistribution of surplus-value within the sphere of capital, thus giving rise to transfers of the surplus-value that is produced by productive capital in favour of the capital that appropriates their labour-power. Their exploitation is thus of a similar order to that which wage-earners in the sphere of capital circulation experience.

The case of agents of the state apparatuses and those who perform 'public' services is rather more complex (the latter including teachers in state schools, medical personnel in the state sector, etc.); in this case, capital does not intervene directly to subsume labour-power. The capitalist is present not as capitalist but as buyer of services. These agents also provide surplus labour, which is extorted from them, but they are not involved in a transfer of surplus-value in favour of the state as employer. Their exploitation, in the form of extortion of surplus labour, is essentially a function of the unequal situation in the exchange between them and capital, the latter having a dominant position on the market. This capital, by way of the state, subjects these agents to the wage form and to its control in order to achieve economies of revenue and thus to increase the surplus-value accumulated. That said, however, there are certain particular

13. E. Terray, op. cit., pp. 143–6.

cases bound up with the state's present economic interventions (particularly the training of labour-power) in which these wage-earners are involved, by way of the state, in transfers of surplus-value among the fractions of capital, as a function of the average rate of profit and the role of the state in effecting this.

There is still one final problem regarding the situation of service workers. Not only are these not productive workers, despite their being wage-earners, but they are not all necessarily exploited. The wage form no more coincides with productive labour than it does with exploitation, i.e. the extortion of surplus labour: a well-known lawyer who is the salaried employee of an enterprise that uses his services does not have surplus labour extorted from him. In a case such as this, the wage form conceals a simple exchange of equivalents. In the opposite direction, however, an agent who sells his services without being a wage-earner may have surplus labour extorted from him by virtue of the unequal terms of exchange that result from the dominant position of capital on the market. Such cases have to be examined in terms of the relation of surplus labour to 'socially necessary labour-time'.

II

I have sought to present in the above section Marx's analyses of capitalist productive labour in their most simple form. There are still certain points, however, where Marx's rather unsystematic arguments exhibit ambiguities which can only be straightened out by locating these arguments within the general problematic of his work. This is indispensable if we are to clarify certain particularly contested instances of class membership.

I would like to put forward here one major proposition, and deal with certain problems that it raises. Marx's analyses of capitalist productive labour must be rounded off on one key point, which would seem to be co-substantial with the definition of capitalist productive labour. We shall say that productive labour, in the capitalist mode of production, is labour that produces surplus-value while *directly reproducing the material elements that serve as the substratum of the relation of exploitation: labour that is directly involved in material production by producing use-values that increase material wealth.*

This, however, already raises a problem. What is the precise theoretical status of this 'addition' to Marx's definition? Is it a real 'addition', in other words an element really absent from Marx's analyses? Why is it not explicitly involved in these analyses, and what role should it be given?

The basic ambiguity here is not simply that this element seems to be absent from Marx's analyses of capitalist productive labour, but that Marx even goes so far as to say explicitly that the concrete content of the labour and its use-value are completely indifferent for productive labour. What are the reasons behind this apparent absence, and Marx's assertion? What is actually involved here?

In point of fact, Marx already gives a general definition of productive labour in Volume I of *Capital*:

> In the labour process . . . man's activity, with the help of the instruments of labour, effects an alteration, designed from the commencement, in the material worked upon. The process disappears in the product; the latter is a use-value, nature's material adapted by a change of form to the wants of man . . . If we examine the whole process from the point of view of its result, the product, it is plain that both the instruments and the subject of labour, are means of production, and that the labour itself is productive labour.

And again:

> The labour-process, resolved as above into its simple elementary factors, is human action with a view to the production of use-values, appropriation of natural substances to human requirements; it is the necessary condition for effecting exchange of matter between man and Nature; it is the everlasting Nature-imposed condition of human existence, and therefore is independent of every social phase of human existence, or rather, is common to every such phase.[14]

This being said, should one see here a 'contradiction' in Marx between this general definition of productive labour and that of capitalist productive labour, or alternatively, as several writers believe today, that Marx purely and simply abandoned the first definition when he sought to define capitalist productive labour? These writers hold that the only pertinent definition that Marx gives is that of productive labour under definite social conditions (e.g. capitalist ones).[15] Alternatively again, should one say, as does Emmanuel Terray in particular, that these two definitions are both equally pertinent for Marx, but that they exist in his work in separation from one another, so that one can only attempt to link them in each specific case?

Let us examine the question in more detail. What has to be

14. *Capital*, vol. I, pp. 180 ff.
15. C. Coliot-Thélène, op. cit.

emphasized once again is that it is not possible to speak rigorously of the production process and of productive labour 'in itself', in the sense that this only ever exists under definite social conditions. It is even these social conditions that determine the possibilities of its existence, as we formulated it in stressing the constitutive and dominant role of relations of production over the labour process, and of the social division of labour over the technical division. It is clear however that this does not make it impossible to speak of certain general characteristics of the labour process, the social determinations of this being its conditions of existence. It only precludes us from committing the basic error of considering the labour process and the 'productive forces', and hence the production process as a whole, as a neutral and intrinsic instance, whose abstract 'combinations' and 'elements' would produce the 'social forms' in which they were 'expressed'. This is the sense in which we should understand Marx's dictum, in relation to productive labour, that 'The fact that the production of use-values, or goods is carried out under the control of a capitalist and on his behalf, does not alter the general character of that production.'[16]

How does it happen then that Marx, in his analyses of capitalist productive labour, seems sometimes simply to forget the general character of a use-value that is directly involved in the definition of material production (although we have seen this re-emerge when Marx considers the transport and storage of commodities)? One particular reason for this, in the texts where Marx speaks of capitalist productive labour, and which are essentially texts of criticism in which he attacks false conceptions, is that what Marx is seeking to avoid at all costs is the confusion of productive labour with useful labour, the general utility of labour and its product. The use-value character that is directly involved in material production must not be confused with the notion of 'utility'; 'luxury' products and those of the armaments industry still represent productive labour. These confusions nevertheless continue to this day, as is shown by Baran and Sweezy, who consider armaments as unproductive labour on the grounds that they are not 'useful'.

In fact, however, the general definition that Marx gives of productive labour is in no way 'absent' from his analyses of capitalist productive labour. It is present in two ways.

A. Firstly, it does appear explicitly, but in what I would call an oblique form, by way of the commodity, and this does raise certain problems. In the commodity Marx explicitly 'picks up' what he had not in fact ever left behind, i.e. use-value as the substratum or

16. *Capital*, vol. I, p. 177.

material support of exchange-value, the creation of surplus-value (productive labour) presupposing exchange-value and the commodity, which already means labour performed under definite social conditions. Hence, 'In so far as it produces commodities, labour remains productive; it is materialized in commodities which are simultaneously use-values and exchange-values . . . Thus only labour that is externalized in commodities is productive'.[17] Or again,

> In considering the essential relations of capitalist production it can therefore be assumed that the entire world of commodities, all spheres of material production – the production of material wealth – are (formally or really) subordinated to the capitalist mode of production . . . It can thus be said to be a characteristic of *productive labourers*, that is, labourers producing capital, that their labour realizes itself in *commodities*, in material wealth. And so *productive labour*, along with its determining characteristic – which takes no account whatever of the *content of labour* and is entirely independent of that content – would be given a second, different and subsidiary definition.[18]

But this oblique form of the commodity, by way of which Marx explicitly picks up the general character of productive labour as labour directly involved in the reproduction of the material elements of production, under the social forms of capitalism in particular, still raises a problem. If, as Marx notes elsewhere, all labour directly involved in material production tends under capitalism to take the form of commodities and to be subordinated to or subsumed by capital, it is still the case that, with the generalization of the commodity form under capitalism, labour can take the commodity form without producing surplus-value for capital. This is particularly the case with the work of painters, artists, and writers, which is concretized in a work of art or a book, i.e. in a commodity form, even though what is involved are services exchanged against revenue. Marx himself notes that products can assume the 'price form' and the 'commodity form' without thereby possessing value. In other words, although all capitalist productive labour takes the commodity form, this does not mean that all commodities represent productive labour.[19]

B. Even though Marx only effects an explicit linkage between the general definition of productive labour (labour directly involved in material production) and the definition of capitalist productive

17. 'Results . . .'.
18. *Theories of Surplus-Value*, vol. I, p. 397.
19. *Capital*, vol. I, p. 102.

labour in an oblique form, I would go further and assert that the former definition is in fact always implicitly included in the latter, so that it does not have to intervene as such. This is where I would distinquish myself from Terray, in particular, who, while he (correctly) maintains the pertinence of the general definition of productive labour for capitalist productiove labour, sees there two genuinely distinct definitions in Marx. This leads him to attempt to overcome the difficulty that arises, by 'classifying' types of labour that would be productive according to the general definition of productive labour, and types that would be productive according to the specifically capitalist definition of productive labour, in order to re-establish the articulation of the two 'case by case', according to the contradictory situations in which the various agents find themselves with this perspective. Just to take one of his examples, that of wage-earners in the sphere of circulation. Terray is led to exclude these from the ranks of productive workers on the grounds that they do not perform productive labour in the sense of the general definition (they do not take part in the process of material production), while according to the capitalist definition they would be productive workers, 'because they bring a capitalist surplus-value, whatever might be the origin of this surplus-value and the role of this capitalist'.[20]

I think that this is a false way of proceeding. Not only does it ignore the co-substantiality of the general definition of productive labour in Marx's analyses of capitalist productive labour, but it also falls into the same misunderstanding that I already indicated, that of conceiving the general definition of productive labour as the original one, i.e. as valid 'in itself', alongside social forms that would play a 'supplementary' role, whereas these in fact form the effective conditions of existence for productive labour. The general definition of productive labour does not need to become involved in Marx's analyses of capitalist unproductive labour. To return to the example of wage-earners in the circulation sphere, we do not need the general definition of productive labour here to conclude that these wage-earners are non-productive; if they are not productive workers, this is because according to the capitalist definition of productive labour, and from the standpoint of social capital, they do not create surplus-value. Why should this be deemed 'insufficient', so that one would need to add on the general determination of productive labour, which Marx, in speaking of capitalist productive labour, would allegedly have forgotten *en route*?

It is not insufficient at all. Despite certain ambiguous formulations on

20. E. Terray, op. cit., p. 133.

Marx's part, the capitalist definition of productive labour as he sees it (labour that directly creates surplus-value) already includes the general definition, in the form that this takes in the capitalist mode of production. In other words, if this general definition does not need to be brought in, it is because it is in essentials already present. Marx gives us the reason for this in *Theories of Surplus-Value*, in referring to the extended reproduction of capitalism; it is that, in this extended reproduction, all labour directly involved in material production tends, by being 'really' subsumed by capital, to become directly productive of surplus-value:

> To the extent that capital conquers the whole of production ... it is clear that the unproductive labourers, whose services are directly exchanged against revenue, will for the most part be performing only *personal* services, and only an inconsiderable part of them ... will produce material use-values . . . Consequently only a quite insignificant part of these unproductive labourers can play a direct part in material production once the capitalist mode of production has developed.[21]

In other words, labour producing surplus-value is broadly equivalent to the process of material production in its capitalist form of existence and reproduction. The real subsumption of the labour process by capital, i.e. its extended reproduction (as distinquished from its formal subsumption), contains within it, and directly links up with, the general definition of productive labour, for it is nothing other than the form that this latter assumes in the capitalist reproduction of labour.

III

These remarks are particularly important in so far as Marxist discussion of productive labour has too often been exclusively oriented to exchange-value, neglecting the process of material production. We can here indicate a practical result of this, one that involves in particular the examination of the role of 'science' and its various 'bearers' in the process of material production and in the creation of surplus-value.

In fact, the relationship between productive labour and the process of material production which is involved in all productive labour must be particularly stressed in the case of 'science', because of the current spread of various ideologies of the role of 'science' within the contemporary production process. It is seen as intervening more and more 'directly', as such, in the production process ('the scientific and

21. *Theories of Surplus-Value*, vol. I, pp. 155 ff.

technical revolution'), and the 'bearers of science', in a very broad sense, are seen as forming part of the productive workers and thus belonging to the working class. This is particularly the case with Radovan Richta, for whom, 'in the course of the current revolutions in production, science has become the central productive force in society, and in practice the key factor in the growth of the productive forces'.[22]

We shall have to return to the assumptions involved in conceptions of this kind, particularly that of science being a neutral force in its relationship with the productive forces, conceived as these are in a purely technicist fashion. But the above analysis of productive labour already enables us to clear the ground, before introducing any other considerations. It implies the necessity of making a major distinction, right from the start, among the 'bearers of science': the distinction between, on the one hand, 'research' and the 'production and distribution of information', and the agents of this, and on the other hand, the engineers and technicians directly involved in a material labour process as part of the productive collective worker. The case of these latter presents certain peculiar features. However, the previous analysis suffices to exclude the labour of the former quite clearly from capitalist productive labour. In fact, even if capital bends the whole of scientific work to its requirements, enrolling science 'in its service', as Marx puts it (there is in this sense no 'neutral' science), and even if the role of technical innovations is today more important than in the past (intensive exploitation of labour), this does not by itself make scientific work productive. The work of the first category, the scientists proper, is no more directly involved in the process of material production today than it was in the past. Under capitalism, science remains something separate from the direct producers ('science independent ... of labour') and is involved in this process not as such, but, as Marx puts it, through its 'technological applications', being incorporated in one or other of the factors of the material labour process, labour-power or means of production.[23]

The work of scientific research and the production of information is thus not work that produces surplus-value. Moreover, it is not the agents of this work who produce science, in the strict sense; science, which cannot be localized in a process delimited in time and space, is ultimately based on labour, and on the experience of innumerable direct producers, who are themselves engaged in material labour processes of the most varied kinds, but all separate from 'research'.

22. R. Richta, *La Civilisation au carrefour*, 1969, p. 17. See the criticism of these theories in *Cahiers du Cinéma*, nos. 242–3, January 1973, pp. 24 ff.

23. *Capital*, vol. I, pp. 359 ff. and 371 ff.

This work remains unproductive even if its products assume the commodity form (patents, licences) and have a 'price', for they no more produce value in their own right than do works of art. These scientific 'products' are not reproducible as such.[24] This does not prevent these agents from being able to bring an individual capitalist surplus-value, in particular when, as is the case to a pronounced degree today, capitalists directly invest in this domain, transforming these agents into salaried employees (software and engineering companies, for example); from the standpoint of the social capital, however, what is involved here is simply the tranfer of surplus-value. Finally, the basic position is not changed when this labour, and the activities bound up with it, take place actually within industrial enterprises, as is often the case in the present phase of concentration (around two-thirds of scientific personnel in France today work for industrial enterprises), any more than activities bound up with the circulation and realization of surplus-value are transformed into productive labour when they are performed within this institutional framework.

24. See also the similar arguments of Janco and Furjot, *Informatique et Capitalisme*, 1972, pp. 72 ff., and Bettelheim's note.

3

The Class Determination of the New Petty Bourgeoisie: Political and Ideological Components

We have just been looking at the specifically economic class determinations of the new petty bourgeoisie, in relation to productive and unproductive labour, determinations that already draw the boundaries separating this class from the working class.

However, structural class determination also includes the political and ideological relations that circumscribe the place of a class in the social division of labour as a whole. Reference to these relations is doubly important in this case.

(1) Economic relations such as the distinction between productive and unproductive labour are not sufficient to delimit the class boundaries between the working class and certain fringe sections of the new petty bourgeoisie, i.e. those fringes that are themselves directly involved in a process of material production. This is the case with the supervisory staff and with engineers and technicians.

(2) These political and ideological relations are also decisive for those groupings of the new petty bourgeoisie for which economic relations and the distinction between productive and unproductive labour already draw clear boundaries separating them from the working class. The reason for this is that these relations intervene in the relationships between these groupings and in their common class membership (the new petty bourgeoisie), in their relationships with the traditional petty bourgeoisie, and finally in the fractional division of the new petty bourgeoisie that is a function of the polarization that divides it.

I. THE WORK OF MANAGEMENT AND SUPERVISION

To begin with the first point, which relates to the organization of the actual process of productive labour. I shall confine myself for the time being to the question of the class membership of certain agents such as the 'foremen', for example, in order to pose the general theoretical problem of the 'work of management and super-vision', which has in fact a much larger scope. We are directly faced here with the problem of the articulation between the relations of production and the labour process, in the form of the relation between the technical division of labour (Marx's actual term is 'division within the workshop') and the social division of labour, which is only the way that the question of the articulation between productive labour in general and capitalist productive labour in particular is posed within the actual organization of the labour process. Once again, we might usefully recall certain basic proposi-tions that have governed the whole of our analysis.

1. The labour process does not exist in itself as an autonomous level of the productive forces, but always in definite social forms, in particular articulated to definite relations of production; what gives this articulation the form of a process of production is the domination of the relations of production over the labour process.

2. In the actual organization of the labour process, the social division of labour, directly dependent on the relations of production, dominates the technical division.

3. The social division of labour is directly related to the political and ideological conditions involved in the determination of social classes and their reproduction. In its form as a social division of labour within the production process itself, it is related to these political and ideological 'conditions' in the form that they exist in this process.

4. The implications of this for the agents that occupy the places of the social classes mean that it is the social division of labour with-in the production process that dominates their place in the technical division of labour.

These points are particularly important in analysing certain forms of labour directly involved in the process of material production and the creation of surplus-value. They enable us to clarify Marx's arguments, particularly those on the work of management and super-vision in the production process. I shall say right away that these arguments exhibit certain ambiguities, particularly in so far as Marx examines the aspects of technical and social division of labour 'separately', without always showing how the former is articulated to and dominated by the latter. It would be useless to pretend that this ambiguity, though to a considerable extent a function of Marx's order of exposition, is not also a product of certain 'economist/technicist' residues present in his work, which one can come across in a whole series of problems, but which it is not the place here to go into. Marxism however is not a fixed dogma, and it is clear in particular that the Proletarian Cultural Revolution in China has enabled Marxism to advance decisively in this particular respect.

Let us turn now to Marx's arguments on the 'double nature' of the work of management and supervision ('on the one hand . . . on the other hand'), and the importance that he attributes to the social division of labour:

> The labour of supervision and management is naturally required wherever the direct process of production assumes the form of a combined social process, and not of the isolated labour of independent producers. However, it has a double nature.
>
> On the one hand, all labour in which many individuals co-operate necessarily requires a commanding will to co-ordinate and unify the process, and functions which apply not to partial operations but to the total activity of the workshop, much as that of an orchestra conductor. This is a productive job, which must be performed in every combined mode of production.
>
> On the other hand . . . this supervision work necessarily arises in all modes of production based on the antithesis between the labourer, as the direct producer, and the owner of the means of production. The greater this antagonism, the greater the role played by supervision. Hence it reaches its peak in the slave system. But it is indispensable also in the capitalist mode of production, since the production process in it is *simultaneously* [my italics: N.P.] a process by which the capitalist consumes labour-power.[1]

In this last aspect, supervision represents part of the *'faux frais'* of capitalist production.

Let us place these arguments in the context of the capitalist relations of production. The place of capital is here characterized, in contrast to other modes of production, by the fact that it combines both the economic ownership of the means of production and their possession: the direct producers (the workers) are completely separated from the means and object of their labour, and even dis-

1. *Capital*, vol. II, p. 376.

possessed of these. In the capitalist social division of labour, Marx tells us, the direction of the labour process tends to become a 'function of capital', and capital completely takes over this direction. This is not the effect of chance; it is rather that, under capitalist relations of production (ownership and possession both falling to capital), the organization of the labour process as a whole is bent to the requirements of capital. The separation and dispossession of the workers from their means of production, the characteristic of capitalist exploitation, means that there is no division or coordination of tasks that simply corresponds to purely 'technical' requirements of 'production', and exists as such. The work of management and supervision under capitalism is no more a technical task, than the division of labour within the working class, in particular the minute breakdown of tasks, is the effect of 'machinery' or 'large-scale industry' as such, but rather the effect of their capitalist form of existence.

This domination of the social division of labour over the technical division is the basis of the specific organization of capitalist labour which Marx refers to as the despotism of the factory.

> If, then, the control of the capitalist is in substance two-fold by reason of the two-fold nature of the process of production itself, – which, on the one hand, is a social process for producing use-values, on the other, a process for creating surplus-value – in form that control is despotic. As co-operation extends its scale, this despotism takes forms peculiar to itself.[2]

Here again, Marx seems to ascribe an equal share in this despotism ('on the one hand . . . on the other hand') to the socialization of the 'productive forces' and to the extraction of surplus-value (the relations of production). In the last quoted sentence, he even seems to ascribe a key importance to the former element, insisting on the relation between the development of despotism and that of coopera-tion. In point of fact, this is not at all the case, and this can be seen from the previous quotation on the management and supervision of the labour process. Marx relates this directly to the opposition between the 'owner' and the 'direct producer', telling us that this 'reaches its peak in the slave system', where, however, the 'socializa-tion of the productive forces' is far less developed than in capitalism.

In a word, the despotism of the factory is precisely the form taken by the domination of the technical division of labour by the social, such as this exists under capitalism. The work of management and supervision, under capitalism, is the direct reproduction, within the

2. *Capital*, vol. I, pp. 331–2.

process of production itself, of the political relations between the capitalist class and the working class.[3]

What then is the class determination of those agents whose basic function is determined by this work of management and supervision, such as the foreman and other NCOs of the production process? It is wrong to present this determination in the form of a dual class membership, by reference to the 'double nature' of their work. In these terms they would form part of the working class (of productive labour) to the extent that they perform labour that is necessary to any cooperative process, but would not form part of the working class to the extent that they maintain political relations of exploitation. This is wrong because it does not take account of the articulation of the technical and social divisions of labour that is a function of their class place, with the social division being dominant. Otherwise this argument could equally be applied to the capitalists themselves, for Marx also says:

> Given that he represents productive capital engaged in its valorization process, the capitalist performs a productive function in so far as he exploits productive labour . . . As director of the labour process, the capitalist may carry out productive labour, in that his work is an integral part of the total labour process, and is embodied in the product.[4]

It is thus no more true to say that the foremen and supervisors have a double class membership (working class and capitalist) than that the capitalists themselves do.

The reason why these agents do not belong to the working class, is that their structural class determination and the place they occupy in the social division of labour are marked by the dominance of the political relations that they maintain over the aspect of productive labour in the division of labour. Their principal function is that of extracting surplus-value from the workers – 'collecting' it. They exercise powers that derive from the place of capital, capital that

3. Marx also says, on the question of large-scale industry (the extended reproduction of capital): 'In all these cases, the producers lose their autonomy, the establishment of the specifically capitalist mode of production resulting in a regime of domination and subordination *actually within the process of production*' (Marx's emphasis), 'Results . . .'

These are certainly political relations, but political relations that exist and are reproduced within the production process. Political relations are not limited to those that are located within the state and its apparatuses, although this is the principal locus of these relations.

4. 'Results . . .'

has seized hold of the 'control function' of the labour process; these powers are not necessarily exercised by the capitalists themselves.

> Just as at first the capitalist is relieved from actual labour so soon as his capital has reached that minimum amount with which capitalist production, as such, begins, so now, he hands over the work of direct and constant supervision of the individual workmen, and groups of workmen, to a special kind of wage-labour.[5]

On the other hand, however, these agents must be distinguished from the higher managers discussed in Part II, Chapter IV. With the development of monopoly capitalism, these managers cannot only exercise powers deriving from the relations of possession (control and direction of a labour process) but also certain powers that derive from the relation of economic ownership, even exercising these powers at the top level. They thus occupy the actual place of capital, and hence belong to the bourgeoisie. The agents we are dealing with here, however, are merely subaltern ones. They, too, are exploited by capital; they, too, provide surplus labour, i.e. labour that is in part unpaid (*faux frais*), and sell their labour-power, while the higher managers are essentially paid out of the profits of the enterprise.

This question of the class barrier between the agents who perform the tasks of management and those of supervision of the labour process respectively is indirectly hinted at by Marx's terms 'work of management *and* supervision'. These two terms do not assume a sharp distinction between types of work, since all management work is at the same time supervisory work, and vice versa (hence the combination). However, they do imply a differentiation, within the social division of labour, between controlling instances and subaltern instances (hence the two separate terms, 'management' and 'supervision').

Let us finally return, if it is necessary, to what radically separates these arguments from those of the institutionalist/functionalist tendency with its concepts of power and authority. The political relations dealt with here are only analysed as places in the social division of labour, with the various powers that derive from them being constitutively connected to the relationships that compose the relations of production. The despotism of the factory is the form taken by political relations in the extended production of social classes, actually on the site where the relations of production and exploitation are constructed; the powers that derive from them are in no way a function of 'organizational' relations within the

5. *Capital*, vol. I, p. 332.

enterprise as an institution. The capitalist enterprise is itself only the articulation of the relations of production, political relations and ideological relations within a production unit as centre of appropriation of nature and of exploitation.

2. THE DIVISION BETWEEN MENTAL AND MANUAL LABOUR: ENGINEERS AND PRODUCTION TECHNICIANS

I

We come now to the question of the ideological relations in the social division of labour within material production, and of their articulation with the political relations; this is the problem of the division between mental and manual labour, whch we shall first of all examine in the structural class determination of the engineers and technicians directly involved in material production. The division between mental and manual labour, however, goes far beyond this particular case, and in fact affects the whole of the new petty bourgeoisie in its relationship to the working class.

Marxist theory has long shown a certain uneasiness with respect to the question of the mental/manual labour division. On the one hand, the Marxist classics always emphasized either the decisive role of this division for the 'historic appearance' of the class division as such (Marx, Engles), or alternatively the close relationship between the abolition of the division between mental and manual labour and the suppression of class exploitation, even of class divisions in general (Lenin, Mao). On the other hand, however, this division between mental and manual labour seems to get lost whenever it comes to defining the class determinations of a particular social formation, in particular the capitalist one. We are clearly dealing here with a very important problem, one that has been raised again by the Cultural Revolution in China. And if we take into account the decisive importance that the breakdown of this division has on the road to socialism, we can no longer content ourselves with simple assertions, or dodge the question of the precise role of this division in the actual determination of classes in a capitalist formation.

I would say, quite summarily, that the actual basis of this uneasiness I referred to lies above all in the fact that, for Marxism, the division between manual and mental labour in no way coincides with the division between productive and unproductive labour in the capitalist mode of production. The various fragments of analysis that Marx gives in this respect, i.e. in relation to the productive collective worker in the development of capitalist production, seem quite clear:

Since with the development of the real subsumption of labour by capital, that is of the specifically capitalist mode of production, it is no longer the individual worker but more and more a socially combined labour power that becomes the real agent of the collective labour process; and since the different labour powers involved in the formation of the productive apparatus as a whole participate in very different ways in the immediate process of commodity production . . ., one more with his hand, the other more with his head, one as manager, engineer, or technician, another as supervisor, a third as the actual manual worker . . ., a growing number of functions of labour power fall under the heading of productive labour, and their bearers under that of productive worker, being directly exploited by capital and subordinated to its processes of valorization and production.[6]

Hence,

In order to labour productively, it is no longer necessary for you to do manual work yourself; enough, if you are an organ of the collective labourer, and perform one of its subordinate functions.[7]

These analyses of Marx's have expressly been made use of by the proponents of the 'new scientific and technical revolution' in order to extend the boundaries of the working class to include the new groupings of engineers, technicians, etc. This is not always done in the same way, but the basis of it is always the same, from Richta through to Garaudy's 'new historical bloc', by way of Mallet's 'new working class', and down to the present position of the PCF on state monopoly capitalism. The PCF position is considerably more subtle in its presentation, but still introduces a distinction that does not in fact exist in Marx: that between the collective worker and the productive worker.[8] The engineers, etc., are seen as forming part of the collective worker, without as yet, as the PCF has it, forming part of the productive worker. As quasi-workers, they appear as one of the celebrated anti-monopoly strata so dear to the PCF. There is no need to repeat here what others have quite adequately shown, i.e. that these agents are often assimilated to the working class in the practice of both the PCF and the CGT.

For a long time now, the debate has been centred on the question of whether or not these agents perform, in a 'technical' sense, productive labour. The assumptions of this debate involve: (a) an economist/technicist reduction of the very concept of the production

6. 'Results . . .'.
7. *Capital*, vol. I, pp. 508–9.
8. *Traité* . . ., *le capitalisme monopoliste d'État*, op. cit., vol. I, pp. 211 ff.

process to one of a self-sufficient and neutral process; (b) the view that science and technology are neutral forces, independent of their political and ideological preconditions; (c) an economist reduction of the class determination of these agents, as if the character of their work as capitalist productive labour was enough, independent of their political and ideological determinations, to place them in the working class.

These assumptions lead to an inevitable conclusion: the appearance of the productive collective worker, through making the 'bearers of science' into workers (productive labour), leads, via the celebrated 'socialization' of the labour, to the division of mental and manual labour being 'superceded'. This is the axis of all the current verbiage about the superceding of this division by automation.

These arguments are completely false. If one actually refers to the several texts that Marx devotes to this question, it is clear that, despite certain ambiguities, they all insist on the unity of the two aspects involved, i.e. on the political and ideological conditions under which the productive collective worker is formed. The constant themes in Marx's discussions of this point are as follows:

(1) What gives rise to the productive collective worker is the socialization (extended cooperation) of the labour process under capitalism;

(2) This very socialization at the same time deepens the division between mental and manual labour.

What Marx is talking about throughout is the *capitalist* socialization of labour.

I shall just quote here, by way of example, one single passage from *Capital* on the productive collective worker, which I have already mentioned above. This passage is quite remarkable, since it shows how Marx grasps the two aspects of the question in one and the same sweep of his presentation:

> In considering the labour-process, we began ... by treating it in the abstract, apart from its historical forms, as a process between man and Nature ... We further added: This method of determining, from the standpoint of the labour-process alone, what is productive labour, is by no means directly applicable to the case of the capitalist process of production. We now proceed to the further development of this subject.
>
> So far as the labour-process is purely individual, one and the same labourer unites in himself all the functions, that later on become separated ... As in the natural body head and hand wait upon each other, so the labour-process unites the labour of the

hand with that of the head. Later on they part company and even become deadly foes [*feindliche Gegensatz* in the original text: N.P.]. The product ceases to be the direct product of the individual, and becomes a social product, produced in common by a collective labourer, i.e. by a combination of workmen, each of whom takes only a part, greater or less, in the manipulation of the subject of their labour. As the co-operative character of the labour-process becomes more and more marked, so, as a necessary consequence, does our notion of productive labour, and of its agent the productive labourer, become extended. In order to labour productively, it is no longer necessary for you to do manual work yourself; enough, if you are an organ of the collective labourer, and perform one of its subordinate functions . . .[9]

This is a remarkable passage, for in a single sweep of his presentation, within one paragraph, Marx indicates: (a) that the supports of mental labour tend to become part of the productive collective worker, but that (b) at the same time, and even for the same reasons (capitalist socialization), mental labour separates off from manual labour in an 'antagonistic contradiction'. How should we understand this contradiction between the agents of these two forms of labour, which are separated actually within productive labour itself? This is the whole question.

We must first examine the division between mental and manual labour in more detail, since this is in fact at the centre of the problem. I should like to put forward here the following proposition, as my principal thesis on this subject. Not only is this division between mental and manual labour not simply a technical division of labour, but it actually forms, in every mode of production divided into classes, the concentrated expression of the relationship between political and ideological relations (politico-ideological in this sense) in their articulation to the relations of production; that is to say, as these exist and reproduce themselves, in the particular form of their

9. *Capital*, vol. I, pp. 508–9. For some reason, the French translation differs from the original German text on a decisive point. In J. Roy's version (Editions Sociales, vol. II, p. 183), the sentence 'Later on they part company and become deadly foes' (*Später scheiden sie sich bis zum feindlichen Gegensatz*, *MEW* vol. 23, pp. 531–2), is simply omitted. The impression is thereby given that the appearance of the 'productive collective labourer' represents a 'moment' of capitalist production in which the division of mental and manual labour is superceded. Is this a result of Roy's incompetence, or a sign of certain ambiguities in Marx's own text, since Marx personally revised the French translation?

relationship (politico-ideological), both within the production process itself, and beyond this, in the social formation as a whole. This division between mental and manual labour assumes specific forms in the capitalist mode of production, which is characterized by a quite particular 'separation' of the two.

II

This first rules out any attempt to understand the mental/manual labour division, and the actual content of these terms themselves, in terms of general criteria which necessarily become in this case inadequate empirical ones: in particular, descriptive criteria of a bio-physiological character ('natural movements' and 'thought'), or of the kind: 'hand work' and 'brain work', 'dirty jobs' and 'clean jobs', those who 'actually do things' and those who do not, etc.

We must now draw the full implications of the thesis that the division of mental and manual labour does not coincide with the distinction between productive and unproductive. This is because it is not a distinction of the same order. It is not sufficient to say, as it is for the distinction between productive and unproductive labour, that it only exists under specific political and ideological conditions, since the distinction between mental and manual labour is precisely the concentrated form of these conditions themselves. In fact, while Marx gives a general definition of productive and unproductive labour, the status of which we have already examined, he never gives anything of the same kind for mental and manual labour, but only a few descriptive phrases. Every time that Marx gives the general definition of productive labour as labour directly involved in the process of material production, he takes care to point out that this cannot be identified with manual labour, but he gives no general definition of manual labour itself (similarly, mental labour is not at all reducible, for Marx, to what he refers to as non-material production). Moreover, even when Marx speaks of the form of productive labour specific to a given mode of production, he is still always careful to stress that this does not coincide with manual labour, either because, as in pre-capitalist modes of production, mental labour is directly present within manual labour (not yet 'separated' from it, although we know from other texts by Marx and Engels that the division between mental and manual labour certainly already existed), or because under capitalism, mental labour can form part of the collective worker. Now if it is impossible to give a general definition of this kind, from the standpoint of the production process, and the labour process in particular, this is precisely because, as far as this process is concerned, the division between mental and

manual labour is simply the form taken by the political and ideological conditions of the process within the process itself.

Let us keep this point in mind, as its consequences will soon be
clearly seen. The reproduction of the mental/manual labour division involves a considerably wider field than that which is grasped
descriptively by expressions such as 'dirty jobs' and 'clean jobs', and
assumes far more complex forms.

III

The divisions between mental and manual labour, and its precise
content, thus depends on the given mode of production. How does
it appear in the capitalist mode, and how can we verify the general
thesis we advanced above, particularly in the case of the engineers
and technicians?

Marx's main discussions of the capitalist division of mental and
manual labour are situated in the context of the capitalist socialization of labour, of machinery and large-scale industry, and are
directly bound up with the question of the fragmentation of tasks
(simple and complex labour). These questions have in fact often been
considered as involving a purely technical necessity inherent to
'large-scale industry' as such, while they are actually linked to its
capitalist form. Even Lenin was not free from certain serious errors
in this respect, particularly in his assessment of the 'positive' technical aspects of Taylorism, which he saw as applicable to the
socialist 'enterprise'. For Marx, however, machinery and large-scale
industry is the particular form taken by the extended reproduction
of capitalist relations of production (real subsumption/subjection of
labour by capital), following on from the stage of manufacture which
is the form of transition from feudalism to capitalism (formal sub-
sumption/subjection of labour to capital). The capitalist division of
mental and manual labour is thus directly bound up with the specific
nature of these relations, in particular with the separation and dispossession of the direct producer from his means of production, such
as this is reproduced through the real subsumption of labour by
capital:

> What is lost by the detail labourers, is concentrated in the capital
> that employs them. It is a result of the division of labour in
> manufactures, that the labourer is brought face to face with the
> intellectual potencies of the material process of production, as the
> property of another, and as a ruling power. This separation . . . is
> completed in modern industry, which makes science a productive
> force distinct from labour and presses it into the service of
> capital.

Marx quotes with approval Garnier, the French translator of Adam Smith, for whom,

Like all other divisions of labour, that between hand labour and head labour is more pronounced in proportion as society (he rightly uses this word, for capital, landed property and their State: K.M.) becomes richer.[10]

In these passages Marx makes a connection between mental work and science, both of these being 'separate' from the direct producer and opposed to him. How do we get from here to the role of political and ideological relations in the class determination of the engineers and technicians?

1. First, by way of the relation between science and ideology. This is too vast and important a subject for us to deal with it here from first principles. Let us simply say that this 'science' which we are dealing with, science appropriated by capital, never exists in a pure or neutral form, but always in the form of its appropriation by the dominant class, i.e. in the form of a knowledge that is closely interwoven with the dominant ideology. This is even the case with what is called 'basic research'. It is science as such that is subjected to the social, political and ideological conditions of its constitution, and not only its 'technological applications'. This is all the more so in that there is no essential separation, or at least there has not been since the industrial revolution (machinery and large-scale industry), between science and technique. In the case of the engineers and technicians, however, we are precisely dealing with the 'technological applications' of scientific discoveries in the process of material production, and it is the massive development of this aspect that is responsible for the contemporary expansion of this grouping of agents. Technological applications of science are in the direct service of capitalist production, in so far as they serve the development of capitalist productive forces, since the productive forces only exist dominated by the relations of production. These applications are thus interwoven with ideological practices corresponding to the dominant ideology. The dominant ideology itself, of course, does not just exist in 'ideas', i.e. articulated ideological ensembles, but is embodied and realized in a whole series of material practices, rituals, know-how, etc., which also exist within the production process. The technological applications of science are here directly present as a materialization of the dominant ideology.

We can draw an initial conclusion here regarding the position of the engineers and technicians. Their work of technological application of science takes place under the sign of the dominant ideology, which they materialize even in their 'scientific' work; they are thus supports of the reproduction of ideological relations actually within the process of material production. Their role in this reproduction, by way of the technological application of science, takes the particular form under capitalism of a division between mental and manual labour, which expresses the ideological conditions of the capitalist production process.

There is in fact no intrinsic 'technical' reason deriving from 'production' why these applications should assume the form of a division between mental and manual labour, and it is pertinent here that science itself is in the last analysis the result of the accumulated experience of the direct producers themselves. Of course, scientific work is not this alone; it also involves a specific work of systematization ('general labour' in Marx's formulation) and scientific experiment that is not reducible to 'direct experience'. But this specific work only exists as such in its capitalist form in the context of the division of mental and manual labour. This division is thus directly bound up with the monopolization of knowledge, the capitalist form of appropriation of scientific discoveries and of the reproduction of ideological relations of domination/subordination, by the permanent exclusion on the subordinated side of those who are deemed not to 'know how'.

This is an aspect of the problem that was very well recognized by Gramsci in his characterization of the engineers and technicians as modern intellectuals. For Gramsci, these engineers and technicians were intellectuals, i.e. 'ideological functionaries' in his own expression, in so far as they had a particular relationship to knowledge and science in the capitalist mode of production, and were involved in the capitalist division of mental and manual labour. Gramsci even went so far as to consider the great majority of them to be organic intellectuals of the bourgeoisie.[11]

2. This leads on directly to a second point, concerning the actual content of capitalist mental labour in the production process, which links up with our earlier discussions. Although the technological application of science, in its capitalist ideological forms, is bound up with mental labour, it in no way follows from this that all mental labour under capitalism is connected with these applications. The capitalist division of mental and manual labour is not the product of a separation between science and the direct producers; this separation itself is only one partial effect of the separation of the direct producers from their means of labour, and it is this that is directly

11. Gramsci, 'The Intellectuals', in *Prison Notebooks* [selection], London, 1971, pp. 5 ff. See below, pp. 252 ff.

responsible for the relation between mental labour and the reproduction of capitalist ideological relations. Now on the one hand, there is no such thing as a purely technological application of science; every such application is constitutively bound up with the materialization of the dominant ideology in the form of practical knowledge of various kinds. On the other hand, mental labour also comprises a series of practices that have nothing to do with technological applications; there is a long list of these within the enterprise, from the rituals of 'know-how' to 'management techniques' and various 'psycho-socio-technical' practices.

At this point we can already see the articulation of political and ideological relations breaking through in the specific form of mental labour. Let us concentrate for the moment, however, on the ideological relations. If the practices just referred to have nothing to do with the technological application of science (even as 'ideologized'), they are still legitimized, and not by chance, as being invested with a knowledge which the workers do not possess. We could thus say that every form of work that takes the form of a knowledge from which the direct producers are excluded, falls on the mental labour side of the capitalist production process, irrespective of its empirical/natural content, and that this is so whether the direct producers actually do know how to perform this work but do not do so (again not by chance), or whether they in fact do not know how to perform it (since they are systematically kept away from it), or whether again there is quite simply nothing that needs to be known.

This relationship between knowledge and the dominant ideology which is expressed in the form of the legitimization of a mental labour separate from manual labour and possessing this knowledge, is quite specific to the capitalist mode of production and to bourgeois ideology. It is essentially based on the need for the bourgeoisie to constantly 'revolutionize' the means of production, which Marx explains in *Capital*. This relationship affects every domain of bourgeois ideology. Just to take one significant example: during the transition from feudalism to capitalism, and then in the stage of competitive capitalism, both these being marked by the establishment of the bourgeois state and by the dominance of the legal/political region within bourgeois ideology, this region (politics and law) was explicitly legitimized, from Machiavelli and Thomas More down to Montesqieu and Benjamin Constant, as a kind of scientific technique, on the model of apodictic *episteme*. As against a knowledge legitimized as 'natural' or 'sacred', this knowledge was now legitimized as a 'rational scientific practice', and it established itself, even in the framework of legal/political ideology itself, in opposition to a mode of thought that it called 'utopian'. This was directly expressed in the effects that legal/political ideology had in the establishment of the civil services and centralized 'bureaucracies' of the bourgeois state. The specific separation of mental and manual labour that the establishment of the bourgeois state and its agents as a body 'separate' from society involved, was founded on the encasement of knowledge in legal/political ideology in the form of 'science'.

This relationship between bourgeois ideology and knowledge is, however, considerably reinforced in the stage of monopoly capitalism, marked as this is by the shift of dominance within bourgeois ideology towards the region of economics; this is where we come across the various theories of the 'technocracy'. The same relationship is also found in inverted form in certain aspects of the revolt against this ideology, a revolt which is carried out in a mechanically oppositional fashion (also in a moral form), and is thus still dominated by bourgeois ideology. This is the basis of the various forms of naturalist rejection of science, and of the 'ecological' return to nature.

IV

This, however, is only one aspect of the question of the engineers and technicians, and still only involves ideological relations. These engineers and technicians, however, while intervening in the capitalist production process through the technological application of science, are by that very fact also involved, at least in their great majority, in the political relations of management and supervision of the labour process.

This involvement is in the first place indirect and, occurs through the technological applications themselves, in so far as these are designed for application in a capitalist labour process that already contains these relations. A 'technological application' designed for incorporation in a capitalistically organized labour process already materializes in itself the powers involved in the work of management and supervision:

> The combination of this labour appears just as subservient to and led by an alien will and an alien intelligence – having its *animating unity* elsewhere – as its material unity appears subordinate to the *objective unity* of the *machinery*, of fixed capital, which, as *animated monster*, objectifies the scientific idea, and is in fact the coordinator . . .[12]

But the involvement of these engineers and technicians is also direct; they are often themselves responsible for the work of management

12. Marx, *Grundrisse*, Pelican Marx Library, p. 470.

and supervision; they directly control the 'efficiency' of the workers, and the achievement of output norms.[13]

What is more, they perform this work of direction and supervision through being endowed with specific functions in relation to knowledge. Their mental labour, separated from manual labour, represents the exercise of political relations in the despotism of the factory, legitimized by, and articulated to, the monopolization and secrecy of knowledge, i.e. the reproduction of the ideological relations of domination and subordination. It is this close articulation that characterizes mental labour as separated from manual labour in the capitalist production process. Political relations are in fact always legitimized and encased by the dominant ideology, and it is this form of ideology (relation to 'knowledge') that prevails in the capitalist relations of the production process. This is more than ever the case today, in so far as the basis of legitimization of powers within the factory is shifting away from the 'natural knowledge' of the boss endowed with divine right and towards a technical one.

If the relation to a knowledge 'separate' from the direct producers thus includes tasks of management and supervision within the factory, these tasks are legitimized, for their part, by their relation to knowledge. Of course, there are still cases such as that of the ex-Foreign Legion men who control the Citroën assembly lines in military style. But these are not the most common today, and it is not by chance that the various categories of foremen who perform direct supervisory tasks also present themselves as bearers of a particular knowledge in relation to the workers whom they control. This is precisely how this work of management and control that is necessary to every 'cooperative process' falls to mental labour within the capitalist social division of labour.

The separation of the intellectual powers of production from the manual labour, and the conversion of those powers into the might of capital over labour, is, as we have already shown, finally completed by modern industry erected on the foundation of machinery. The special skill of each individual insignificant factory operative vanishes as an infinitesimal quantity before the science, the gigantic physical forces, and the mass of labour that are embodied in the factory mechanism and, together with that mechanism, constitute the power of the 'master' . . . The technical subordination of the workman . . . give(s) rise to a barrack discipline,

13. See on this subject, A. Gorz, 'Technique, techniciens et lutte des classes', in *Les Temps Modernes*, August–September 1971, as well as the essays selected and presented by Gorz, *Critique de la division du travail*, 1973.

which is elaborated into a complete system in the factory, and which fully develops the before mentioned labour of overlooking ...'[14]

V

What then is the structural class determination of the engineers and technicians? They do not belong to the working class, even though it is true that, as a result of the technological application of science to the production process in the present phase of monopoly capitalism (the dominance of relative surplus-value), they increasingly tend to form part of capitalist productive labour (the productive collective worker), as far as economic relations are concerned.

This is a real tendency, but, precisely because it is a tendency, it operates in a contradictory manner, even in relation to productive labour itself; the form of this contradiction is that of the limits of the tendency. There is hardly need to recall here that a portion of the technological applications of science under capitalism is intended not to increase capitalist productive forces but rather to destroy existing productive forces, particularly in the capitalist forms of 'replacement' and 'modernization' of the existing means of labour and equipment. This is a result of the bourgeoisie's struggle against current forms of the falling rate of profit tendency, a struggle which consists on the one hand, and principally, in increasing the rate of exploitation by the intensive exploitation of labour (productivity; role of scientific applications), and on the other hand, in devaluing, or even destroying, a portion of the existing constant capital (the parallel role of scientific applications). Yet if the engineers and technicians do not form part of the working class, this is not by virtue of the 'destructive' aspect of the application of science, since the tendency for them to form part of the capitalist productive worker is still at work, even in its contradictory form.

Furthermore, if these engineers and technicians do not form part of the working class, this is also not because these applications of science, as is often and justly said, serve the orientations and priorities of monopoly capitalism and not 'production' as such:

> To conclude, an appreciable portion of the productive forces developed by the capitalist mode of production, and even more so an appreciable portion of scientific and technical discoveries, inventions and research, are productive and functional only in relation to the specific orientations and priorities of the growth of monopoly capitalism. A good part of the scientific and technical

14. *Capital*, vol. I, pp. 423–4.

personnel, and a good part of this research, would have little use, if any, in a society in which priority was given to satisfying the social and cultural needs of the masses.[15]

To exclude engineers and technicians from the working class for this reason would mean falling into a false definition of productive labour based on utility (and the same thing could be said for workers in luxury or armaments industries).

Technicians and engineers do tend to form part of capitalist productive labour, because they directly valorize capital in the production of surplus-value. If they do not as a group belong to the working class, this is because in their place within the social division of labour they maintain political and ideological relations of subordination of the working class to capital (the division of mental and manual labour), and because this aspect of their class determination is the dominant one.

VI

Certain differentiations can of course be made among these engineers and technicians, in particular according to whether they are located in branches or industries in which they actually direct and command manual workers, or in branches in which they themselves form the main labour force and hence do not exercise tasks of direction and supervision over other workers. Serge Mallet's argument about this 'new working class' of engineers and technicians is based on Touraine's hypothesis of the 'three phases' of the capitalist labour process, which is itself located in a technicist perspective. Phase A supposedly corresponds to 'polyvalent skilled labour' (manufacture); phase B to machinery and large-scale industry as studied by Marx; phase C to the introduction of automation and to the massive dominance of engineers and technicians who control automated machines and have overall perspective on the labour process, and thus to the gradual disappearance of fragmented and unskilled labour ('manual labour'). In this phase C, engineers and technicians would thus themselves be the main labour force, if not the only one. Certain of Friedman's arguments according to which stage C of automation is supposedly abolishing the division between mental and manual labour in the production process also derive from this.[16]

15. Gorz, op. cit., p. 151.
16. These arguments of Touraine and Friedman, as well as others, can be found in their contributions to *La Sociologie du Travail* (two vols), ed. Friedman and Naville, 1967. As far as the PCF's position on the 'scientific and technical revolution' is concerned, I shall just quote here a few lines

It is clear that these arguments put forward in the fifties and sixties have proved false. They failed to take into account a *dual* process, one of qualification *and* disqualification of labour under monopoly capitalism, and they assumed an inherent and self-sufficient 'technological process' independent of capitalist relations of production. This does not mean that the present phase of monopoly capitalism does not display significant specific features. But these new transformations of the labour process, and the significant increase in the number of engineers and technicians, have not gone together with a decline in the proportion of unskilled workers; this has in fact increased, while there has been a stagnation and decline in the

	1954	*1952*	*1968*
Skilled workers	2,837,442	2,345,080	2,506,180
Semi-skilled workers	1,815,265	2,465,080	2,650,380
Unskilled workers	1,125,323	1,405,140	1,489,140
Technicians	192,220 (private sector)	343,986	533,940
Foremen	141,480 (private sector)	306,142	360,120
Engineers	81,140 (private sector)	138,061	190,440

Source: INSEE Census data.

proportion of skilled workers. This must of course be examined at the international level, but the situation in the United States, whose 'disqualified' labour processes have been exported, principally to the European countries, is in no way representative. If one looks at these European countries, and particularly at France, it is clear even from the purely descriptive statistics given by INSEE, that the celebrated industrial 'restructuring' and 'modernization' that has been taking

---

from the *Traité* (op. cit., vol. I, p. 189), which need no commentary: 'As a society of producers, socialism will inevitably give a new vigour and a new content to this deep change in the productive forces. The large-scale introduction of complex automation, combined with the development of information systems, and with new progress in the scope of possibilities for automated machine systems, will deepen the social division of labour and hence the variety of social needs satisfied, at the same time that the separation between mental and manual labour will finally come to an end, the latter disappearing in its fragmented form.'

place essentially from the sixties onwards, has not meant an increase in the proportion of skilled workers, but rather a decline, both in the French social formation as a whole, and even, save for a few exceptions, in the branches and industries where this 'restructuring' has taken place.

We shall discuss later the special case of the INSEE's category of 'engineers', the great majority of whom in fact belong to the bourgeoisie in so far as they occupy the place of directing agents of capital. Let us first concentrate on the relationship between the technicians and the working class. It should firstly be noted that the category of skilled workers is considerably exaggerated in these figures, since it includes more and more agents who in fact, as a result of the disqualification of labour, perform simple semi-skilled tasks. Further, the rapid decline in the number of unskilled workers since 1968 represents in part not a change in their functions but rather a shift in the classification, since great numbers of these unskilled workers obtained semi-skilled status after the May events. However, the following points should be made here.

(a) The proportion of semi-skilled workers is considerably greater in large-scale enterprises, rising from 17·6 per cent in enterprises with less than 10 employees to 40·6 per cent in those with more than 500. Given the former French backwardness in industrial concentration and the current massive tendency towards concentration in the form of 'restructuring', it would seem that it is the proportion of semi-skilled workers that will increase most considerably in the future.

(b) The introduction of 'automation' certainly does not necessarily lead to an increase in the number of technicians and a decline in semi-skilled workers. According to a CNRS investigation, automation has only brought about an increase in technicians and engineers in 36 per cent of the establishments affected.[17] Naville stresses that '80 per cent of personnel working with automatic equipment are semi- and un-skilled workers'. At Renault, for example, the number of technicians increased by around 60 per cent between 1965 and 1969, but the number of semi-skilled workers also increased by 60 per cent,[18] chiefly at the expense of the skilled workers. Even in certain exceptional and privileged branches, such as petrochemicals, which seems already to have attained a high degree of automation by the very nature of the labour process involved, engineers and technicians

17. 'L'automatisme, les travailleurs et les syndicats', in *La Documentation Française*.

18. P. Naville, *L'État entrepreneur*, 1971, pp. 182 ff. and 195 ff. It should be noted that Naville is one of the rare exponents of 'industrial sociology' not to have fallen into the various myths of the 'new working class'.

in 1968 only formed between a tenth (chemicals) and a quarter (petroleum) of the total number of employees.[19]

In a word, despite the imprecise character of statistics on this question, and their various confusions, it is clear that the transformations that mark the present phase of monopoly capitalism are being carried out not under the influence of some intrinsic and self-sufficient technical process, but under that of exploitation and a shift in dominance towards the intensive exploitation of labour (relative surplus-value). Although this is accompanied by an increase in the number of technicians, it is chiefly expressed, as far as its effects on the working class are concerned, in a massive *disqualification* of labour.

As a whole, therefore, engineers and technicians are still in a situation in which they command and control the work of the direct producers. It should be added to this that when Marx relates the division between mental and manual labour to the fragmentary work organization of machinery, he does not do so in a technicist way. I stress this because of the current debate and experience of the 're-organization of tasks' among semi-skilled workers. This 're-organization' within the context of capitalist relations of production cannot alter the division between mental and manual labour and the place that this gives engineers and technicians, since this division is here constantly reproduced in new forms.

VII

The existence of this class barrier between engineers and technicians on the one hand, and the working class on the other, is also verified by a whole series of particular points.

1. Let us re-examine the division between mental and manual labour. This basic division actually tends to reproduce itself in a specific manner on each side of the dividing line: within the 'camp' of mental labour, and within that of manual labour. Mental and manual labour both tend to internalize and reproduce within themselves the barrier which divides them. As far as manual labour is concerned, the labour of the working class, it is evident that its capitalist organization into different levels of 'skill' is not a mere technical division, but that the categories of skilled work, semi-skilled work

19. P. d'Hugues and M. Peslier, *Les Professions en France*, ed. INED, 1969, and G. Rerat and C. Vimont, 'L'incidence du progrès technique sur la qualification professionelle', in *Population*, January–February 1967. On this subject, see also C. Berger, 'Non au révisionnisme sénile', in *Cahiers du CERES*, January 1972, and G. Pottier, 'Électronique: quelle nouvelle classe ouvrière?', in *Politique Aujourd'hui*, October–November 1972.

and un-skilled work are themselves marked by a reproduction of the division between mental and manual labour (this touches obliquely on the question of the labour aristocracy). The induced reproduction of this division is, in this respect, simply the form of the effects of capitalist ideological and political relations within the working class itself, or even within the actual capitalist labour process.

Nevertheless, the class barrier still remains the same. The skilled workers do not exercise over the semi-skilled, nor the semi-skilled over the unskilled, the kind of management and supervision, coupled with the legitimation of the secrecy and monopoly of knowledge, that the engineers and technicians, for their part, exercise over the working class as a whole. This goes completely against the whole institutionalist/functionalist tendency which, in analysing the 'enterprise' (as a bureaucracy) sees in it an 'institution' characterized above all by relations of 'power' in an almost psycho-sociological sense of this term, a power and authority that circulates from the top to the bottom by a continuous ladder of 'hierarchical' delegation: managers, intermediate staff, technicians, foremen, skilled workers, semi-skilled workers, unskilled workers.

2. The existence of this class barrier is also verified by a series of significant indices, in the first place that of income. There are of course also wage differentials within the working class itself. But there is nevertheless a very significant jump, quite distinct from the gradations of wage scale within the working class, between the 'best paid' skilled workers on the one hand, and the 'worst paid' technicians on the other. The following figures are available on average net annual earnings, for full-time employees in the private sector and nationalized industries in France, for the year 1969: unskilled workers, 8,854 francs; semi-skilled workers, 10,467 francs; skilled workers, 13,116 francs; then, foremen, 20,667 francs; technicians, 22,272 francs; finally, engineers, 45, 756 francs.[20]

It is plain that, if wages correspond, in the abstract and taking the social labour as a whole, to the cost of the reproduction and maintenance of the labour-power involved, this does not mean that every specific differentiation in the wage hierarchy represents a real difference in these costs: the wage hierarchy always contains political components. This is even true of wage differentials among the working class itself, since the spread of wage categories her represents, at least to a considerable extent, the bourgeoisie's policy of seeking to divide the working class. Hence, the significant gap

20. These and the following figures on wages and salaries are taken from 'Les salaires dans l'industrie, le commerce et les services en 1969', by N. Chabanas and S. Volkoff, in *Les Collections de l'INSEE*, M.20, January 1973. See also P. Ranval, *Hierarchies des salaires et luttes des classes*, 1972.

between working-class wages and the salaries of engineers and technicians is only partly a function of real differences in the costs of training and reproducing their respective labour-powers; it also represents to a major degree certain '*faux frais*' that capital has to lay out in order to reproduce the ideological conditions for the extraction of surplus-value and for the tasks of direction and control of the labour process, and thus coincides here with the class barrier.

3. Finally, the existence of this barrier is verified by analysing the reproduction of the agents who occupy the places of the working class and those of the engineers and technicians respectively. This can be seen from the distribution and circulation of agents among these places. Although this aspect of reproduction is secondary in relation to the reproduction of the places themselves, it still has an important value here as an index.

As far as intra-generational movement is concerned, i.e. agents who change their place in the course of their working life, there is within the working class itself a certain movement of unskilled workers into the semi-skilled bracket, and of semi-skilled workers into the skilled bracket, although we should not lose sight of how rigid the distribution of agents is even within the working class. The proportion falls appreciably, however, and this is extremely significant, when we consider the movement of agents from the skilled worker position to that of technician, and this indicates the existence of a practically insuperable obstacle which is simply the effect on these agents of the class barrier. But while of those unskilled male workers who manage to move into a different category in the course of their working life, 48·5 per cent become semi-skilled workers and out of the semi-skilled men who move, 43·7 per cent become skilled workers, out of the skilled men who move categories, only between 10 and 14 per cent become technicians.[21] The great majority of those rare working-class agents who leave the working class in the course of their working life (an average of 4 to 5 workers out of 100 over a five-year period: once you are a worker, you remain one), move into wage-labour in distribution, services, and especially into the self-employed artisan sector. The proportion of those who remain in production and move upwards into positions of control, in the broad sense, is infinitesimal: approximately 1 skilled man out of 100 over a five-year period; and the number of semi-skilled or unskilled men doing so, let alone women, is nil. This is absolutely contrary to what is claimed by the bourgeois ideology of 'social mobility'. Things are

21. It must be stressed that these percentages are not based on the total of skilled and semi-skilled working, but only on those that change their place.

slightly different for inter-generational mobility (the children of these agents), but the basic tendency is the same.[22]

VIII

The class determination of engineers and technicians, however, also depends on their place in relation to capital. Since they increasingly form part of the capitalist productive worker, and increasingly contribute to the self-expansion of capital by the production of surplus-value, they are also exploited by capital. Their situation *vis-à-vis* capital also depends on the political and ideological relations in which they are involved. In fact, there is no more a continuous ladder for non-working-class agents within the enterprise than there is for the enterprise as a whole; contrary to the view put forward by the celebrated ideologies of the 'technostructure', non-working-class agents are not all located in the same position *vis-à-vis* capital. This is why it is necessary to be very careful in using the term hierarchy, which for a number of writers assumes the existence of a linear continuity between these agents and obscures the class barriers.[23]

Hence, within the political relations of management and supervision of the labour process, these agents belong to the the subordinate instances, while the various categories of manager who directly occupy the place of capital and directly exercise the powers that derive from it form the directing instances. In relation to the latter, the engineers and production technicians are in a situation of subordination (they are dominated by capital), and the purposes of monopoly capitalist production are imposed on them.

It is still more important, however, to note the situation of these agents in the articulation of political and ideological relations, i.e. in mental labour. Just as the division between mental and manual labour tends to reproduce itself in specific forms within the camp of manual labour, so it similarly reproduces itself in the camp of mental labour. It could even be said that, taking mental labour as a whole, this reproduction is considerably more intense than it is for manual labour, with the fantastic paths of the secrecy of knowledge

22. In re-working this information and the statistical data, I have based myself on the INSEE studies of industrial qualifications of 1964 and 1970, more precise references being given below. It is clear from their presentation that these studies were governed by the ideology of social mobility, which is why I had to go back to the 'crude figures' and reorganize them.

23. See the very correct remarks on this point in C. Gajdos, 'Culture et impasse de la technique: les cadres de l'industrie', in *Cahiers Internationales de Sociologie*, supplement for 1972, as well as my own remarks on pp. 275 ff, below.

finding here, as it were, their happy hunting ground. The technicians themselves are directly subjected to the secrecy and monopoly of knowledge maintained by the directing instances. Their mental work itself tends to exhibit the features of fragmentation that are characteristic of manual labour, sometimes even giving the appearance of a real assembly line. This is directly expressed in the differentiation of channels of training: firstly the Grandes Écoles (Polytechnique, Centrale, Mines, Ponts et Chaussées, etc.), then the various lesser specialist schools (Arts et Métiers). The first category prepare their students for what is considered 'polyvalent' work, requiring an overview of the economy; their agents, though they receive the title of engineer, are only to a limited extent employed in production, and most of them soon occupy managerial and administrative positions they then often belong to the directing instances of capital (to the bourgeoisie), while the other category generally remains directly oriented to production.

This leads us to some additional points.

(a) There is a lack of precision and even confusion in the official INSEE statistics which have a classification by 'profession', so that 'engineers' appear as a single 'socio-professional category' by virtue of their educational qualifications. This means that certain agents referred to in the statistics as 'engineers' actually form part of the managers and directing instances of capital as far as their real functions are concerned; and thus they belong to the bourgeoisie.

(b) The reproduction of the mental/manual labour division within the sphere of mental work also affects the properly petty-bourgeois grouping of 'engineers and technicians', and it leads to a division of this grouping into petty-bourgeois fractions. This is particularly the case with technicians and certain inferior categories of engineers (e.g. designers, chemical technicians, technical personnel in the building trades, or alternatively mechanical engineers and transport engineers), each of whose work is itself being constantly disqualified and fragmented in relation to that of the higher fraction. The effects of this fragmentation are visible in the salary differentials within this grouping.

We find here, in the official INSEE statistics, an error that is symmetrical with, and exactly opposite to, the former. Certain 'technicians' and 'lower-level engineers', classified as such by virtue of their professional training and formal qualifications, actually occupy working-class positions and must be considered as belonging to the working class, not by way of the celebrated productive collective worker, but because they simply do not occupy the place of an engineer or technician (a 'controlling' or 'white-collar' one).

* * *

To conclude: engineers and technicians do not belong to the working class, even though they tend more and more to form part of the productive collective worker, because the dominant aspect of these situation is the political and ideological relations that they support. These relations affect their structural class determination in the social division of labour (mental labour/manual labour) and cannot be identified with their class position in the conjuncture. In fact, as a result of the polarization of their determination in relation to the working class on the one hand and to capital on the other, specific fractions of this grouping sometimes adopt bourgeois class positions and sometimes those of the working class. In the latter case, however, the agents involved do not thereby become workers. Even their class positions continue to be marked by their divergence from the working class, and besides the several cases from May 1968 that could be adduced as evidence of this, there is the recent example of the struggles of the workers at Lip.

4

The Role of the Mental/Manual Labour Division for the New Petty Bourgeoisie as a Whole

I

So far, we have established certain common characteristics of the class determination of the new petty-bourgeois groupings: wage-earning employees who do not belong to the working class but are themselves exploited by capital, either because they sell their labour-power, or because of the dominant position of capital in the terms of exchange (services). This determination is chiefly a function of economic relations (unproductive labour). However, this common economic situation is obviously not a sufficient basis for us to consider these various groupings as belonging to a single class, the new petty bourgeoisie. We must also refer to their place in the political and ideological relations of the social division of labour, and this place will in fact reveal how far-reaching are the common determinations of these groupings.

We have already seen the importance of the mental/manual labour division for the supervisory staff, and for engineers and technicians. This played a decisive role in so far as, by way of the primacy of the social division of labour over the technical, it excluded these groupings from the working class despite the fact that they too performed 'capitalist productive labour'. The mental/manual labour division also plays a very important role for the other new petty-bourgeois groupings, which are excluded right from the start from the working class, simply by economic relations (unproductive labour in the sphere of capital circulation and realization, civil servants, etc.). I would in fact say that the mental/manual labour division characterises the new petty bourgeoisie as a whole, which in contrast to the working class is located on the 'side', or in the 'camp', of mental labour, either directly or indirectly. This new petty bourgeoisie, the product of the extended reproduction of monopoly capitalism itself, is located by the extended division between mental and manual labour that characterizes the capitalist mode of production in general. This means that it is located in a quite specific place in the reproduction of capitalist political and ideological relations.

II

Certain basic remarks are immediately necessary here, in order to avoid any misunderstanding that might arise as a result of the above thesis. What precisely is the 'mental' content of the work of those employed in accounting, banking advertising, marketing, insurance and the commercial sector in the broad sense, or in the work of the great majority of civil servants, 'service' workers of various kinds (health service, hospitals, articled clerks, etc.), office workers such as secretaries and typists, and clerical workers in general, in relation to the work of the working class? The following notes are intended to make the above arguments more systematic. I shall base myself here on certain arguments of the only western Marxist to have gone into this question in detail, i.e. Gramsci.[1]

1. To say that these various forms of work are located on the side of mental labour, in contrast to that of the working class, and partake of mental labour either directly or indirectly, does not mean that their agents are all 'intellectuals'.

The question of the 'intellectuals' is too vast for me to go into here. I would simply say that the term intellectual, that of a social category, should be reserved for a specific grouping of agents who fulfil particular social functions in relation to the elaboration of class ideologies. These agents, though they are 'ideological functionaries' (Gramsci's term), do not form a 'social group' above, alongside or marginal to social classes. They have a class membership that derives from their complex relationship to the various class ideologies (they are 'organic intellectuals' of social classes, to use Gramsci's term). Gramsci has two achievements to his credit here: (a) he based his analysis of the intellectuals on a historically determined division between mental and manual labour, which is how his analysis is distinguished from the writings of Kautsky on the subject; (b) he thus based the extension of the concept of 'intellectuals' on the social role that these agents play in the various social formations. Gramsci

1. The following references to Gramsci are taken from 'The Intellectuals', in *Prison Notebooks* [selection], London, 1971, pp. 5 ff.

was led in particular to extend the concept of intellectuals, under capitalism ('modern intellectuals'), to a series of agents whose social role in the functioning of class ideologies had not previously been recognized, for example, the case of the engineers and technicians.

It is clear, however, that this concept of the intellectuals, even as thus extended, cannot embrace the whole grouping of agents of the new petty bourgeoisie, although this does not mean that these agents are not located, if to varying extents, on the side of mental labour. It is not only the intellectuals as a social category who perform mental labour, or rather who are located on the side of mental labour; the intellectuals as a specific social category are only a product of a mental/manual labour division that goes much further.

2. The capitalist division between mental and manual labour, based on the specifically capitalist relations of production (the separation of the direct producers from their means of production), tends in fact to reproduce itself in all the relations of a capitalist social formation, and goes beyond the places where the actual relations of production are constructed (the factory), just as does the wage form.

(a) It must be stressed again that the content of this division and its terms can in no way be reduced to empirical criteria of the kind 'those who work with their hands' and 'those who work with their brains', those in direct contact with 'machines' and those who are not. The division is rather a function of the ideological and political relations that mark the places occupied by the agents. In fact, criteria of this kind would make it difficult to place on the side of mental labour a series of non-productive agents who themselves work with their 'hands', as for example agents who are subjected to the development of 'machinery' in unproductive labour, or shop assistants in the big stores. Besides the fact that Marx never reduced mental labour to 'non-material production', this would mean ignoring the considerable effects of the complex reproduction of this division in political and ideological relations.

We certainly need to extend the concept of mental labour. Gramsci already came up against this problem, in relation to the specific question of the 'intellectuals', when he wrote:

> This way of posing the problem has as a result a considerable extension of the concept of intellectual, but it is the only way which enables one to reach a concrete approximation of reality.[2]

I would say that as far as the question of mental labour is concerned, it is only by grasping the actual constitution of the concept of mental

2. ibid., p. 12.

labour in the reproduction of its complex division from manual labour, that we can come to grips with the real situation.

(b) This is equally true, if not more so, in regard to manual labour, i.e. to that of the working class. The political and ideological division between mental and manual labour should never give rise to the belief that the working class (manual labour) only works with its 'hands', that these 'unfortunate' workers, 'stupefied' by the fragmentation of labour, do not use their 'heads'. Thus Gramsci notes:

Can one find a unitary criterion to characterise equally all the diverse and disparate activities of intellectuals and to distinguish these at the same time and in an essential way from the activities of other social groupings? The most widespread error of method seems to me that of having looked for this criterion of distinction in the intrinsic nature of intellectual activities, rather than in the ensemble of the system of relations in which these activities (and therefore the intellectual groups who personify them) have their place within the general complex of social relations. Indeed the worker or proletarian, for example, is not specifically characterised by his manual or instrumental work, but by performing this work in specific conditions and in specific social relations . . . in any physical work, even the most degraded and mechanical, there exists a minimum of technical qualification, that it, a minimum of creative intellectual activity . . . There is no human activity from which every form of intellectual participation can be excluded: *homo faber* cannot be separated from *homo sapiens*.

As Gramsci sums up his position,

All men are intellectuals, one could therefore say: but not all men have in society the function of intellectuals.[3]

I would put it myself that every kind of work includes 'mental activity', but that not every kind of work is located on the mental labour side in the politico-ideological division between mental and manual labour.

3. The mental/manual labour division cannot be reduced to an identification between the bearers of mental labour and those who provide 'science'. Science as mental labour separate from the direct producer is only one effect of the capitalist division of mental and manual labour, the principal form that it assumes in the actual production process.

(a) This explains why many kinds of work that have nothing

3. ibid., pp. 8–9.

scientific about them can be considered as located on the mental labour side. It is not just the engineers and technicians who perform mental labour. But this in no way means that scientific work can be identified with other kinds of work located on the mental labour side, in so far as scientific work increasingly tends to form part of productive labour.

(b) To come back now to the working class, i.e. manual labour itself: the mental/manual labour division in no way means that manual labour does not contain elements of science. We have already seen in relation to the differentiation between engineers/technicians and the working class, firstly, that the effective subject of science is in the last instance manual labour itself, since science is ultimately based on the experience accumulated by manual labour; secondly, that this differentiation does not coincide with a real and intrinsic boundary between those who 'know' and those who do not (the working class). What is involved is rather an ideological encasement of science in a whole series of rituals of knowledge, or supposed knowledge, from which the working class is excluded, and it is in this way that the mental/manual labour division functions here.

(c) The last point can be taken further: the working class itself (manual labour), and not just those skilled or professional workers for whom this is evident, acts as the support of elements of 'science' to a much greater extent that do the great majority of employees that we are dealing with here. Their differentiation from the working class in the sense of the mental/manual labour division, is essentially based on political and ideological relations; their work is legitimized on the basis of the knowledge that it is intrinsically deemed to possess (mental labour), and is hence valued more highly than the work of the working class, whose actual knowledge shares in the general devaluation of manual labour.

4. These groupings of agents, while they are located on the side of mental labour in its separation from manual, do not all stand in the same relationship to mental labour. The mental/manual labour division tends in fact to be again reproduced, in specific forms, on both sides of the basic division, and particularly on the side of mental labour.

This is an essential point that is totally ignored by certain contemporary studies, chiefly originating from 'progressive' British sociologists such as Lockwood, Goldthorpe and Runciman.[4] These works are interesting for two reasons: (a) because these writers explicitly attacked the ideologies that identified and assimilated

4. Goldthorpe, Lockwood and others, *The Affluent Worker* [3 vols.], Cambridge, 1968 and 1969; J. Lockwood, *The Black-Coated Worker*, 1958; W. Runciman, *Relative Deprivation and Social Justice*, 1966.

non-productive workers to the working class (which were the rage in the fifties), either in the sense of an 'embourgeoisement' of the working class (as typified by Crozier in France),[5] or in the sense of an effective 'proletarianization' of these employees (C. Wright Mills); they stressed the class barrier that separated these groupings from the working class, and concretely demonstrated its existence; (b) because they were oriented in particular to the division between manual and 'non-manual' labour in what they called the 'work situation' of these agents. However, besides the fact that they ignored the problem of productive labour, they analysed this division in a technicist and empiricist fashion as a separation between 'clean' and 'dirty' jobs, between those who worked directly with machines in the factory, and 'the rest'; hence the term 'non-manual', which attempts to gloss over the incongruities of an empiricist definition of types of labour according to their intrinsic content. This makes it impossible to view the boundary between the working class and the new petty bourgeoisie in a rigorous manner, and thus leads to the inclusion of a series of agents who in fact belong to the working class; and at the same time it makes it impossible to grasp the cleavages and differences, from the standpoint of the mental/manual labour division, that exist within non-productive wage-labour itself.

I would now like to make my basic thesis more precise.

(a) The mental/manual labour division is reproduced as a tendency, in the sense that it does not provide a typological 'classification' into rigid compartments for this or that particular agent, and that what matters for us here is its social functioning in the existence and reproduction of social classes.

(b) The mental labour aspect does not affect the new petty bourgeoisie in an undifferentiated manner. Certain sections of it are affected directly; others, subjected to the reproduction of the mental/manual labour division within mental labour itself, are only affected indirectly, and while these sections are still affected by the effects of the basic division, they also experience a hierarchy within mental labour itself.

Gramsci himself stressed this point in relation to the question of the agents of the state apparatuses, the civil servants. Here is just one quotation about the theoretical problem that I have just raised:

The function of organising social hegemony and state domination certainly gives rise to a particular division of labour and therefore to a whole hierarchy of qualifications in some of which there is no apparent attribution of directive or organisational functions. For

5. *Les Employés du bureau*, op. cit., p. 42.

example, in the apparatus of social and state direction there exist a whole series of jobs of a manual and instrumental character (non-executive work, agents rather than officials or functionaries). It is obvious that such a distinction has to be made just as it is obvious that other distinctions have to be made as well. Indeed, intellectual activity must also be distinguished in terms of its intrinsic characteristics, according to levels which in moments of extreme opposition represent a real qualitative difference – at the highest level would be the creators of the various sciences, philosophy, art, etc., at the lowest the most humble 'administrators' and divulgators of pre-existing, traditional, accumulated intellectual wealth.[6]

This enables us to add:

(a) The differential place of the agents of the new petty bourgeoisie in the reproduction of the mental/manual labour division within mental labour itself (and therefore in ideological and political relations), thus appears as a major factor in the differentiation of the new petty bourgeoisie into class fractions. We shall see, however, that this differential place does not just coincide with different groupings of the new petty bourgeoisie in economic relations: certain agents in services, for example, may from this standpoint occupy a place similar to certain agents in the circulation and realization of surplus-value, while it is by no means necessary that the agents of the 'service' sector, or those of the circulation sphere, should all occupy the same place.

(b) As far as the current transformations of the non-productive wage-earning sector as a whole are concerned the chief effect of these transformations is to accentuate the fragmentation and polarization of the new petty bourgeoisie. But accentuating the reproduction of the mental/manual labour division within mental labour, these transformations bring certain fractions of the new petty bourgeoisie close to the barrier that separates them from manual labour and from the working class. But these transformations do not undermine the basic barrier between mental and manual labour, since they simultaneously reproduce it in a new form. This is why we will stress the role of these transformations in examining the fractions of the new petty bourgeoisie, while first of all locating their common place in the basic division between mental and manual labour.

6. op. cit., pp. 12–13.

III

These notes should enable us to grasp the 'mental labour' aspect in the kinds of work that are involved in accounting, banking, insurance, 'services' of various kinds, 'office work', and the greater part of the civil service.

This mental labour is in fact encased in a whole series of rituals, know-how, and 'cultural' elements that distinguish it from that of the working class, i.e. from productive labour within the material labour process. If these ideological symbols have little in comon with any real differentiation in the order of elements of science, they nevertheless legitimize this distinction as if it had such a basis. This cultural symbolism is well enough known for us not to have to dwell on it. It extends from the traditional esteem given to 'paper work' and 'clerical workers' in general (to know how to write and to present ideas), to a certain use of 'speech (one must know how to 'speak well' in order to sell products and make business deals – the 'art of salesmanship'), and finally includes ideological differentiations between general culture and *savoir-faire* on the one hand, and technical skills (manual labour) on the other. All these things, of course, require a certain training: learning to write in a certain way, to speak in a certain way, to dress in a certain way for work, to take part in certain customs and usages. This 'certain way' is always the *other way*, opposed to that of the working class, and moreover, it claims to be the sign of a particular '*savoir-faire*', which is evaluated positively in opposition to that of the working class. Everything that needs to be known in this respect is that which the others (the working class) do not know, or even cannot know (through original sin); this is the knowledge that matters, genuine knowledge. 'Brain workers' are defined in relation to others (the working class). The main thing in fact is to know how to 'intellectualize' oneself in relation to the working class; to know in these practices that one is more 'intelligent', that one has more 'personality' than the working class, which for its part, can at most be 'capable'.[7] And to have the monopoly and the secrecy of this 'knowledge'.

This division of mental and manual labour, and its ideological implications, affect the whole of the new petty bourgeoisie, though

7. This is of course precisely what is shown by the dismal psychological phenomenon of 'intelligence tests', these being today one of the main forms of educational selection. These tests are specially designed for the mental/manual labour division, and completely designed to legitimate it. In point of fact, statistics based on 'intelligence tests' show a constant decline in the IQ of higher-level staff in relation to manual workers. Of course!

to an unequal extent and in very complex forms, in its relations to the working class. It has direct and considerable ideological repercussions, which need no further demonstration, on the perceptions that the agents of the new petty bourgeoisie and those of the working class respectively have of their own work and that of the 'others'. Throughout the discourse of the agents of the new petty bourgeoisie (which is only an index, but an important one), the recurrent and principal feature that emerges whenever they have to define their relationship to the working class is that of a distinction between their work and 'simple manual work', work that is directly located in the material production process. This is not just considered as more laborious, but as requiring, in their judgement, less 'knowledge' or 'aptitude', work that lacks the indefinable quality that makes their own work intellectually superior, in short respectable, even though they can themselves in other contexts rebel against this very respectability. The working class also introduces the mental/manual labour distinction into its own perception of the world of salaried staff and civil servants, giving the latter a higher evaluation. Everything goes to show, in fact, that this division of mental and manual labour still has a role to play in the class barrier between the new petty bourgeoisie and the working class. While it is derived from capitalist ideological relations and from a particular policy pursued by the bourgeoisie, it has in its turn considerable effects on the formation of the class ideology of the new petty bourgeoisie.

IV

The particular place of this new petty bourgeoisie in the mental/ manual labour division is directly reflected in the 'training and qualification' of the labour-power of its agents within the educational apparatus, an apparatus that also plays a role of its own in the reproduction of this division and in the distribution of agents to the various places of social classes. The capitalist school is located in relation to, the mental/manual labour division; this division goes beyond it and assigns it its role (this involves the separation of the school from production, which is bound up with the separation and dispossession of the direct producers from their means of production). The school is also reproduced qua apparatus as a function of this. It plays a role of its own in the training of mental labour, a role that is particularly characteristic, and quite specific, in the case of the new petty bourgeoisie. In other words, this school, located in relation to mental labour, reproduces the mental/manual labour division within it in specific forms, and is itself divided.

This leads me to mention the book by Baudelot and Establet,

L'École capitaliste en France,[8] which marks a decisive step towards resolving this question. These writers have in particular stressed that education is divided into two essential systems, one located on the side of mental labour, the other on the side of manual labour. This seems to me to be basically correct, on condition that we make clear that the 'bipolar' division involved here is a tendential one, and takes specific forms for the various social classes affected.

This is where the argument of these writers seems to fall short. Their conclusion directly leads them to obscure the specific place of the new petty bourgeoisie in the educational apparatus. For Baudelot and Establet, this takes the form of asserting that there is no 'third system' in education that is specific to the new petty bourgeoisie,[9] and that the two systems comprise on the one hand a system specific to the bourgeoisie, and on the other hand a system specific to the working class and the popular masses. The new petty bourgeoisie is dissolved in an apparatus that produces within itself either agents of the 'upper classes' or agents of the 'lower classes'. This conclusion, which seems to me to be false, is based on certain debatable premises which govern the authors' treatment of the empirical material.

1. First, it is based in part on an institutionalist analysis of the educational apparatus, which identifies the two systems with a given number of educational branches and sub-branches (primary/vocational and secondary/higher). This, however, makes it impossible to grasp the forms in which the mental/manual labour division is actually reproduced within the various apparatuses which are located as such on one side or other of the basic dividing line in education. It is plain enough that this is not just a question of degree, but that my point bears on the reproduction of social classes, and particularly that of the petty bourgeoisie. Once we shift the terrain of debate from educational institutions to social classes, it is clear that, as far as the petty bourgeoisie is concerned:

(a) Although it is true that there is no specifically petty-bourgeois educational 'system', yet these systems should not be identified with institutional apparatuses, but should rather be understood as a bipolar tendency towards the reproduction of the mental/manual labour division within the school.

(b) The new petty bourgeoisie is educated to an overwhelming extent in forms that lean towards the 'mental labour' side of the educational division, or are strongly impregnated with it, and this is even, indeed especially so in those cases where it is educated in the so-called primary/vocational system. In other words, everything takes place as if, even when the petty-bourgeois agents are educated

8. Paris, 1971.
9. ibid., pp. 81–2.

in apparatuses that appear from formal considerations as over-whelmingly designed for the working class, their forms of education are still radically distinct from the forms of the latter.

(c) Taking all this into consideration, it is possible to speak of a specifically petty-bourgeois form of education.

2. The other reason why Baudelot and Establet obscure these problems is that they interpret the empirical material provided by official statistics in a questionable way. In particular, their dissolution of the specific place of the new petty bourgeoisie in the educational apparatus is largely a function of the way these authors regroup the various 'socio-professional categories' of French statistics into social classes, i.e. into 'upper classes' (bourgeoisie) and 'lower classes' (popular classes).

3. The empirical material on which these arguments are based deals exclusively with the social origin of students in the two 'systems' (based on the father's class membership). The lacuna here lies in the fact that the forms of education experienced by the agents are never once analysed in terms of the actual places that they themselves occupy in the relations of production, i.e. once they have left school (the relation between 'education' and 'qualification'). The underlying idea is that the educational apparatus is the principal apparatus, if not the only one, that distributes agents to the places of social classes; everything happens in the school. If, however, we take this latter element into consideration, then the differences between the working class and the new petty bourgeoisie appear perfectly clear.

The quite specific education of the new petty bourgeoisie, on the mental labour side of the educational division, can be seen from a whole series of indices.

Firstly, to take the criterion used by Baudelot and Establet themselves, the new petty bourgeoisie as a whole has a considerably greater chance of being educated in the secondary/higher system than the working class.

In fact, the authors themselves established[10] that a child from the working class has a 54 per cent chance of being educated in the primary/vocational system, and only a 14 per cent chance of being educated in the secondary/higher system, while a child from the 'bourgeoisie' (in their terms) has a 54 per cent chance of being educated in the higher/secondary system and only a 14 per cent chance of being educated in the primary/vocational.

In so far as the chances of working-class children are concerned, there is a clear distinction between them and children of non-manual

10. ibid., pp. 79 ff.

'employees', who have a 33 per cent chance of being educated in the secondary/higher system, and a 27 per cent chance of being educated in the primary/vocational. In other words, the children of these employees have a greater chance of being educated in the secondary/higher system than in the primary/vocational one, which is quite the opposite of what is true of the working class.

There is more to it, however. In establishing these figures, the authors include in the bourgeoisie (contradicting what they themselves stated at the beginning of their book), not only the various 'higher managerial' staff, as INSEE classifies them, but also the entire category of 'intermediate' staff.[11] How arbitrary this procedure is will be clear if we recall that, for the INSEE, all schoolteachers, qualified nurses, and social workers, are considered to be part of the 'intermediate staff', and in fact make up the bulk of this category. Thus these authors count the children of a simple schoolteacher or social worker as 'children of the bourgeoisie', and this clearly leads to obscuring the class criterion.

The difference is substantial. In fact, as we shall see, the great majority of 'intermediate staff' belong to the new petty bourgeoisie. If this is taken into consideration, then: (a) on the one hand, children of the bourgeoisie proper have a far greater chance of reaching the secondary/higher system than these authors maintain, since it is obvious that the children of the 'intermediate staff' whom they wrongly include in the bourgeoisie have a considerably lower chance of reaching the secondary/higher system than do the children of the higher managers; (b) on the other hand, however, the children of the petty bourgeoisie (now including 'intermediate staff') have a still greater chance of reaching the secondary/higher sytem, compared with children from the working class, than would appear from these authors' classification, which only includes in the petty bourgeoisie routine non-manual 'employees'; it is clear that children from the 'intermediate staff' have a greater chance than children of these

11. These authors state on p. 67, note 9, where they put forward their position on the higher managers: 'On the whole, the liberal professions, higher management, big industrialists and traders very closely correspond to the bourgeois class, i.e. to all those who, by their ideology and their style of life are objectively associated with the capitalist class.' This however does not prevent them, throughout the remainder of their book, from considering the 'intermediate managers' as also forming part of the bourgeoisie: 'The middle classes have no specific educational system of their own. For routine white-collar employees, the probability of their being educated in the secondary/higher system is midway between that of the liberal professions, of higher and middle management, and that of manual workers' (p. 81). This is also the position of Grignon (and the Bourdieu school in general): cf. Grignon, *L'Ordre des choses*, 1972.

'employees' (although there are also important differences in this respect among the employees themselves according to their class fraction). We could thus say, roughly, that although the chances of children from the working class reaching the secondary/higher system really are as Baudelot and Establet have it, yet the chances of children from the petty bourgeoisie are considerably higher than they indicate (around 40 per cent being educated in the secondary/ higher system and 20 per cent in the primary/vocational one).[12]

We can still go further. One index that is useful here as far as the education of the working class and of the new petty bourgeoisie is concerned is that of the difference between general education and technical (or 'vocational') education. Even though this distinction certainly does not refer to two distinct 'channels' of education, since part of technical education belongs to the higher system and part to the primary system, as is also the case with general education, it is still significant. General education, in fact, represents the complex reproduction, on both sides of the main dividing line in education, of mental labour (general culture) as opposed to manual labour ('technical skills').

From this standpoint, the differences between the new petty bourgeoisie and the working class are striking; if we just consider the non-manual 'employees', then only 18·5 per cent of their children follow technical and vocational courses, as against 48 per cent of working-class children.[13]

12. Baudelot and Establet's assertion of the existence of only two systems is based on the probabilities of access to the secondary/higher and primary/ vocational systems for routine non-manual employees alone: 'It can moreover be established that the probabilities of education chances of children from the so-called middle classes (white-collar employees, industrial and commercial employers) are fairly equally divided between the secondary/ higher and primary/vocational: 0·33 and 0·27 for employees, and 0·27 and 0·35 for small and large employers. This clearly shows that there is no education specific to the middle classes.' (p. 81). It should be noted here, in passing, that for the sake of their argument, Baudelot and Establet have included here among the 'middle classes', small and large industrial and commercial employers, i.e. a large selection of the bourgeoisie proper. The main aspect of the question here, however, is that these chances are not compared with those of the working class; on the other hand, with the corrections that I have made to them, these chances do not to my mind establish a third educational 'system' for the petty bourgeoisie, but rather, account being taken of what I have said on this subject, show the education of the new petty bourgeoisie to be on the side of mental labour, and the existence of a form of education specific to this.

13. M. Praderie, op. cit., p. 94.

Let us now return to what Baudelot and Establet call the primary/ vocational system, which they see as working in a unified way for the 'popular classes' as a whole. To take just the distinction between the BEPC, a general certificate of education that can be obtained as early as age 15, and the CAP, a technical certificate that cannot be obtained before age 17: in 1962, 70 per cent of CAPs were awarded to children of workers and peasants, as against only 30 per cent to children of the new petty bourgeoisie. On the other hand, 72 per cent of the BEPCs were awarded to children of the new petty bourgeoisie, and only 14 per cent to children of workers and peasants.

The same phenomenon is demonstrated by certain basic distinctions among establishments all belonging to the primary/vocational system. Grignon's[14] investigations show in fact that these establishments themselves display basic class differences. Just to look at the differences between the working class and the new petty bourgeoisie, out of students in the CETs (colleges of technical education), 48·5 were sons of workers and around 32 per cent sons of the new petty bourgeoisie, while in the CEGs (colleges of general education), around 60 per cent had parents belonging to the new petty bourgeoisie, and only 22 per cent to the working class.

In other words, the divisions within the primary/vocational system itself are not simply differences of degree, as Baudelot and Establet maintain, but are decisive class barriers. Moreover, these barriers appear far more clearly here, where there are key differences between the working class and the new petty bourgeoisie, than they do in the secondary/higher apparatus in the strict sense, where the main differentiation is between the new petty bourgeoisie and the bourgeoisie. This is also contrary to what Baudelot and Establet maintain, since they see these 'differences of degree' as being only in the secondary/higher system. The reason for this is simple. The job of the primary/vocational system is, among other things, to divide and separate the popular classes, while that of the secondary/higher system, although still distinguishing the new petty bourgeoisie and the bourgeoisie (for example the Grandes Écoles), is to seal their alliance, by permitting children from certain petty-bourgeois groupings (e.g. intermediate staff) a much greater penetration of the institutions designed for bourgeois personnel.

What is more, there are clear differentiations between the types of teaching followed within one and the same apparently technical apparatus, in particular the CETs, and among the certificates obtained particularly the CAPs, between the agents who are destined for the new petty bourgeoisie and those who are destined for the

14. *L'Ordre des choses*, op. cit., pp. 35, 45.

working class, differentiations that are in fact far more important than those that separate, for example, the classical and technical baccalauréats. The forms of education within the CETs themselves, and the CAPs to which they lead (the CETs are correctly seen by Baudelot and Establet as *par excellence* part of the primary/vocational system), differ radically according to whether this education is that of agents destined for the petty bourgeoisie, or of agents destined for the working class. The fact that the various courses that are provided for 'office work', or 'bookkeeping', for example (there are 'commercial' and 'bookkeeping' CETs, etc.), lean towards the mental labour side, while those provided for a lathe operator's CAP lean towards the manual labour side, is too obvious to need any emphasis. But this leads us still further, as Grignon notes:

> Both the trades that the majority of girls want to learn when they enter the CETs and the trades that are actually taught to them have in common the fact that they are not in the strict sense 'technical'; the arts of fashion and decoration (sales girl, hairdresser, beautician, pattern cutter, window-dresser . . .) . . . the clothing trades and commercial skills that are taught them invoke their 'taste', their 'sensitivity', their 'eye' for something . . . rather than specific technical knowledge; for trainee secretaries, 'technology' is little more than the acquisition of spelling, vocabulary and grammar. The same is true for social work, para-medical and para-educational vocations . . . which are neither really 'manual' nor really 'technical'. While a worker's successful application to his task depends on the strict application of technical rules and prescriptions . . . [these trades] may depend to a high degree on the 'manner' in which they are carried out . . . The professional practice [of these agents] provides them with an opportunity of acquiring certain urbane or even worldly proficiencies, one which is not available to the young worker confined to purely manual tasks.[15]

This situation becomes clearer when we take account of the relations between education and the actual tasks that these agents perform in their work, or even their class place. In this respect, the role of the educational apparatus in 'training' the labour-power of the new petty bourgeoisie is considerably different to the case of the working class. In fact, it could only be said in a very loose and approximate

15. ibid., p. 97. These remarks of Grignon's are certainly still only descriptive. What he does not see, in fact, is that these differences are not in the last analysis due to a different 'cultural capital' (technical prescriptions *versus* 'style'), but rather to differences between labour directly involved in the production process and other forms of labour.

way that the school 'trains' students for mental labour on the one hand, and for manual labour (technical training) on the other. Several studies have shown quite fully that the capitalist school, completely located as it is on the mental labour side, cannot train students in the essentials of manual labour. The worker does not acquire his basic professional training and his technical skills in the capitalist school (they cannot be 'taught' there), not even in the streams and apparatuses of technical education. What is chiefly taught to the working class is discipline, respect for authority, and the veneration of a mental labour that is always 'somewhere else' in the educational apparatus. One well-known aspect of this question is the discrepancy between the training that the agents of the working class are supposed to receive at school (formal training through vocational, i.e. educational courses), and the actual place and posts that they occupy in production; this is the gap between the 'school' and the 'factory', which today has reached considerable proportions.[16]

Things are quite different for the new petty bourgeoisie, and for mental labour, the labour-power of this class. As far as mental labour is concerned, it is in fact actually trained as such by the school.

The school reproduces the mental/manual labour division within itself through its training of mental labour: the 'training' of manual labour essentially consists, within the school, in excluding it from mental labour, the very condition of the training of mental labour by the school being this internalized exclusion of manual labour (keeping it in its proper place). The main role of the capitalist school is not to 'qualify' manual and mental labour in different ways, but far more to disqualify manual labour (to subjugate it), by only qualifying mental labour. From this standpoint, the role of the educational apparatus in training the new petty bourgeoisie is a considerable one, and even quite typical: we need only mention the role of the various certificates and diplomas on the petty-bougreois labour market. This tendency is very pronounced today, now that 'apprenticeship on the job' is replaced, for a large section of the new petty bourgeoisie, by training within the educational system.

This can even be seen at the lowest level of the educational apparatus. In 1964, for those born in or after 1918, the proportion of workers having no certificate at all (not even the CEP – certificate of primary education) stood at around 40 per cent, while this applied only to some 10 per cent of the new petty bourgeoisie (excluding intermediate staff, otherwise the difference would have been even greater). Furthermore: 27 per cent of skilled workers did not

16. See in particular the special number of *Les Temps Modernes*, August–September 1971, 'L'Usine et l'École'.

possess any kind of certificate, as against only 3 per cent of 'skilled' office workers (still excluding intermediate staff).[17]

Finally, the role of these educational levels is far more important for circulation within the new petty bourgeoisie (the 'promotion' of its agents, and their 'careers', etc.), than it is for the working class. I would just like to note that in 1968, among males aged 25 to 34 (i.e. brought up in a period supposedly marked by an advanced 'democratization' of education), only some 44·6 per cent of skilled workers (and 19 per cent of semi-skilled) possessed any certificate higher than the CEP, including those for examinations held at the end of the apprenticeship period, which are actually outside the educational apparatus and held 'on the job'. On the other hand, 53·3 per cent of routine white-collar employees and some 90 per cent of the various intermediate staff had such certificates, these disparities being still more pronounced for women.[18] If the situation is analysed in more detail, particularly by relating the various categories of agents, their respective shares of income (the relation between 'skill' and 'wage differential') and the types and levels of educational certificate, it becomes extremely clear that the educational apparatus plays a quite specific role in the circulation and internal relations of the petty-bourgeois agents.[19] It should finally be noted that the elements I have used here to support my thesis have not involved at all the much discussed question of length of study in the various social classes, a criterion which, as Baudelot and Establet have perfectly well shown, assumes a unified and uniform educational 'ladder', and is thus completely fallacious.

It could be objected, however, that the same discrepancy between educational training and the labour market, among other things the posts actually occupied by the agents of this petty bourgeoisie, is

17. cf. the INSEE inquiry of 1964 on the 'training and qualification of the French', results published in *Économie et Statistique*, no. 9, 1970. These results are corroborated by a new more recent similar inquiry of 1970, whose results are not yet published but are available to the public at the INSEE.

18. INSEE, 'Results of the 1968 Census', volume entitled *Formation*, 1971, pp. 52 ff. and 116 ff.

19. I would like to mention in passing the quite different role that the modern re-training schemes have for the new petty bourgeoisie and for the working class. These are fairly important for the new petty bourgeoisie, where they operate within the actual sites and apparatuses of education, directly relevant to promotion. For the working class, they are less important, and in the main the 'recycling' that they effect operates simply to redistribute labour-power for the needs of the current industrial 're-structuring' (the mass of workers do not rise any higher as a result of re-training, and they know it). See on this subject, INED, *Travaux et Documents*, cahier no. 50.

also found in the case of mental labour, current forms of this including the devaluing of certificates, and their lack of adaptation to the mental labour market. However, if there can be no doubt that the process of qualification and disqualification of labour-power is currently reproduced, and on a massive scale, within the ranks of mental labour (something which plays a part in the internal fractioning and class positions of the new petty bourgeoisie), this process here assumes specific forms. The same fragmentation of skills and tasks affects certain processes of mental labour, just as it does the working class, but it does not directly take the form of a discrepancy between the educational apparatus and the process of mental labour, parallel to that separating the school and material production.

Such a 'discrepancy', in fact, cannot exist in the strict sense, for the simple reason that the training of mental labour does not essentially correspond to genuine differentiations in the 'knowledge' required in order to occupy this or that 'specialist' post. The training of mental labour essentially consists, to a greater or lesser extent, in the inculcation of a series of rituals, secrets and symbolisms which are to a considerable extent those of 'general culture', and whose main purpose is to distinguish it from manual labour. Once distinguished in this way, mental labour is to a great extent universally employable. Proof of this is given by the attempts made to establish an objective 'code of qualification' (levels of mental labour in the civil service, offices and the service sector), which would correspond to the particular knowledge acquired in training for these types of work; the fantastic aspect of this is quite evident, since such a code would be directly based on the relationship to the secrecy of knowledge.[20] Thus to say today that a university degree in social science, literature, law, or a certain baccalauréat, etc., does not offer openings that correspond to the 'qualification' that it represents, is not strictly correct, on the sense that this degree, is not basically intended to guarantee this or that specialist knowledge, but rather to locate its bearer in the camp of mental labour in general and its specific hierarchy, i.e. to reproduce the mental/manual labour division.

If I stress this point, it is to emphasize that this reproduction is to a considerable extent successful, i.e. that the school is perfectly adequate for its purpose, and fulfils its formative role, despite the 'discrepancies' in the educational training of mental labour and the posts actually occupied by its bearers. Just to take one simple example: the fact that holders of elevated educational certificates are often confined to subordinate places in the new petty bourgeoisie

20. One aspect of this question is dealt with, among other places, by Benguigui and Monjardet, 'La mesure de qualification du travail des cadres', in *Sociologie du Travail*, no. 2, 1973.

(a widespread phenomenon today), may be evidence of the disqualification of mental labour and have certain effects on the class positions
of those involved, but at the same time it reproduces the division
of mental and manual labour between the places they occupy and the
place of the working class. These subordinate places themselves are
thus invested with a 'mental labour' quotient which distances them
even more, in a certain way, from the working class. If a secretary/
typist with a baccalauréat feels frustrated in her ambitions, it is not
clear why she should automatically thereby become aligned with the
working class; it is just as possible that her 'proximity' to the working class, combined with her educational qualification, reinforces in
her those practices that distinguish her from the working class.

The educational apparatus thus plays a quite specific role for the
new petty bourgeoisie, directly contributing to reproducing its place
in the social formation. This is directly reflected in the role that this
apparatus plays in distributing agents among the places of the social
classes, a role which is very important for the new petty bourgeoisie,
while it remains a secondary one for both the bourgeoisie and the
working class. The agents of these two basic social classes, or alternatively their children, are not themselves distributed by the educational system in any literal sense, or rather they are distributed
while remaining in the same place, everything happening as if they
were bound to these places, with the school simply sanctioning and
legitimizing this connection. The petty-bourgeois agents, on the other
hand, exhibit, as we shall see, a quite remarkable shift, directly bound
up with the educational apparatus. These are real processes, with
considerable repercussions on the ideology of the new petty bourgeoisie, an ideology directly bound up with its special relationship to
'knowledge', 'instruction', 'culture' and the educational apparatus.

These remarks thus lead me to formulate an additional theoretical
proposition. On the basis of their premises, and in the course of their
discussion, Baudelot and Establet were led to put forward the thesis
that the educational apparatus is the dominant ideological state
apparatus in the capitalist mode of production, as far as the reproduction, distribution and training of agents is concerned, supplanting
the role of the church in this respect in the feudal mode of production. This thesis seems to me to be over general and incorrect,
particularly because which apparatus (or apparatuses) is dominant
depends on the class struggle in specific social formations; also,
however, for an additional reason: the dominant apparatus in
this sense can vary, even within a particular social formation,
between the various social classes of that formation. The above discussion tends to show that, although the educational apparatus is
certainly the dominant apparatus in France for the petty bourgeoisie

(which is connected to the specific support that the petty bourgeoisie has long given the French bourgeoisie), it is not so for the working class, either in France or in the other capitalist countries. It would seem in fact that for the working class, this dominant role falls directly to the economic apparatus itself, to the 'enterprise'.

V

To sum up: the new petty bourgeoisie, by its place in ideological relations and in contrast to the working class, is characterized by mental labour. This place directly confirms the same mental/manual labour division that the working class experiences on the other side of the barrier, and forms part of the monopoly and secrecy of knowledge from which the working class is excluded.

In relation to capital, however, and to the agents who directly occupy its place, this petty bourgeoisie itself occupies a dominated and subordinate place in the order of mental labour. The secrecy and monopoly of knowledge, which become 'functions of capital', draw lines of domination and subordination within the very mental labour in which they are reproduced. These lines here coincide with the basic division of exploiters and exploited, with the non-productive wage-earners being themselves in their great majority exploited by capital. This class domination/subordination assumes the form of a differentiation between, on the one hand, functions of control and their supports (the bourgeois personnel: managers and directors in the public and private sectors), and on the other hand, the subaltern functions, and it is particularly sharp in the educational apparatus. The latter, while it reproduces as a whole the mental/manual labour division between the working class and everyone else, simultaneously reproduces, by way of specific channels such as the Grandes Écoles in France, the separate places of the bourgeoisie and the new petty bourgeoisie.

Finally, this mental/manual labour division, which is reproduced in a specific form within the ranks of mental labour itself, also marks lines of internal cleavage within the new petty bourgeoisie, which are in this sense hierarchical cleavages rather than cleavages of domination; these are the result of the fragmentation of knowledge and the standardization of the tasks of mental labour that affect certain sectors and levels subjected to capitalist 'rationalization', i.e. to the process of qualification and disqualification internal to mental labour. These cleavages are related to internal differentiations in the system of exploitation undergone; the agents of the new petty bourgeoisie are not all exploited to the same extent. This will emerge more clearly in the following discussions.

5

The New Petty Bourgeoisie and the Bureaucratization of Mental Labour

What we now have to examine, in the mental labour of the non-productive employees, is the articulation between these ideological relations and the political relations that also determine their place, mental labour being simply the form assumed by the close articulation of the two.

I

With the exception of certain employees directly connected with the capitalist production and labour process in the strict sense, such as the managers and supervisors of the labour process, the engineers and the production technicians, the new petty bourgeoisie does not exercise, or at least does not directly exercise, functions of political domination over the working class. The articulation of ideological and political relations that locates these employees within the social division of labour follows its own roundabout paths.

Before we go on to examine these, let us mention the case of those non-productive wage-earners who, while they neither belong to the supervisors of the labour process nor to the engineers and technicians (to control in the broad sense), are nevertheless located within the industrial enterprise; this is the case for 32 per cent of 'office workers' and 13 per cent of 'commercial workers'.[1] It is obvious that this phenomenon is currently becoming more important as a result of the concentration of capital, with the extension of the enterprise apparatus leading to the inclusion of agents performing activities that it annexes. (Upstream from production: research; downstream: marketing, etc.) If this in no way affects the non-productive character

1. M. Praderie, *Les Tertiaires*, 1968, p. 46.

of their work, it has its effects on the relationship between these employees and the working class. These agents, although they are thus increasingly dependent on and subordinated to capital and the enterprise management, often find themselves at the same time involved in legitimizing the power that this management exercises over the workers.

David Lockwood, after several investigations of this phenomenon, albeit in his own terms, describes this situation as follows:

> The work situation of clerical labour forms a social context in which office workers tend to be separated from each other on the one hand, and closely identified, as individuals, with the managerial and supervisory cadres of industry on the other . . . The converse of the working co-operation of clerks and management is the social isolation of the office worker from the manual workers. The completeness of the separation of these two groups of workers is perhaps the most outstanding feature of industrial organization. Because of the rigid division between the 'office' and the 'works' it is no exaggeration to say that 'management', from the point of view of the manual worker, ends with the lowest grade of routine clerk. The office worker is associated with managerial authority, although he does not usually stand in an authoritarian relationship to the manual worker, the orders governing the labour force being transmitted from management through the foreman rather than through the clerical staff . . . the administrative separation of the office worker from the operative . . . is based primarily on the conception of the secret and confidential nature of office work . . .[2]

The propensity of these agents to be particularly influenced by 'those in charge', in the broad sense, and to identify with the white-collared management in the struggles currently taking place in the factories, is well known. It can generally be said, without great risk of error, that a large part of blacklegs among the personnel of an enterprise on strike are accounted for by these employees.

If we now examine the political relations within the social formation as a whole, we can also see the particular place that the civil servants and agents of the state apparatus hold in this respect. There is no need to refer to the blatant case of the intermediate and subordinate personnel of the branches of the repressive state apparatus in order to understand the role of these agents in the realization and materialization of the relations of political domination/subordination that the dominant class exerts over the whole of the dominated classes

2. *The Blackcoated Worker*, op. cit., p. 81.

by way of the state. By certain aspects of their functions, a large part of the agents of the repressive and ideological state apparatuses (teachers, journalists, social workers, etc.) participate, even if in a simple executive capacity (which is what distinguishes them from the bourgeois heads of the apparatuses, to whom they are themselves subjected and subordinated), in the tasks of ideological inculcation and political repression of the dominated classes, and particularly of the chief victim, the working class itself. This is so even if these agents are not always directly in command of the working class: a tax collector, for example, does not have manual workers under his orders in his administrative department.

II

It is necessary to go further, however, in order to grasp the particular place of the non-productive wage-earners in the political relations of the social division of labour, in relation to mental labour 'separate' from manual labour, in cases where these agents do not exercise actual domination over the working class. The principal aspect of this question, in fact, relates to the internalization and induced reproduction, within this new petty bourgeoisie, of the dominant political relations of a capitalist social formation. The place of the new petty bourgeoisie is essentially characterized by this induced reproduction, with certain of its agents exercising over others political relations in the (deformed) image of the relations of domination that are preponderant in the social formation as a whole. From this point of view, the new petty bourgeoisie forms part of an 'intermediate' class, not because it is directly the effective intermediary (a 'link' or 'transmission belt') in the bourgeoisie's domination over the working class, but rather because it forms within itself an experimental crucible, and a living example, of the internalized (and therefore specific) functioning of this relation. Its place does not so much legitimize *either* domination *or* subordination, but rather the relation of capitalist dominaton/subordination, by concentrating it in a disfigured form.[3]

This is where we encounter the pronounced tendency, which several writers have stressed, towards a marked bureaucratization affecting the organization of the work of the great mass of non-productive wage-earners. This is·a very broad question, and I do not intend here to go into it from first principles. Neither will I attempt to refute a whole number of theories of 'bureaucracy' which, deriving from an institutionalist problematic of 'organization' in

3. See below, p. 275.

general, see in this the chief phenomenon of 'industrial societies', even affecting the organization of the production units themselves (the 'bureaucratization of the enterprise'). I would simply like to recall here[4] that this bureaucratization is in no way simply a technical organization of labour, corresponding to some kind of intrinsic 'rationality' or 'irrationality' of capitalism. In the only possible rigorous sense of the term, bureaucratization is the effect, in the social division of labour at the institutional level, of a combination of bourgeois ideology and the petty-bourgeois ideological sub-ensemble, and of an embellished and deformed reproduction of the bourgeois political relations of domination/subordination. Its characteristics, which have been studied by Max Weber as well as by Marx, Engels and Lenin, consist in an axiomatized system of rules and norms which distribute spheres of activity and competence; the impersonal character of its various functions; the payment of officials by fixed salaries; recruitment by appointment from above, either on the basis of competitive examination or of educational qualification; specific forms of obscuring knowledge within the organization by bureaucratic secrecy; specific forms in which the 'hierarchy' operates by way of successive stages of delegation of 'authority' (we shall come back to these terms); centralism, in so far as each level communicates with others by way of the higher level, which gives rise to a specific form of isolation of the agents, etc.

What we are concerned with here, however, is bureaucratization as a tendency that materializes certain ideologico-political effects on unproductive labour, rather than bureaucracy in the sense of a model of 'organization' with continuous and uniform relations from top to bottom, as it is understood by the overwhelming majority of sociologists who write about it.[5] We shall soon see the practical effects of this distinction between bureaucratization and bureaucracy.

Today, this bureaucratization is no longer confined to the public sector, the state apparatus proper, but also affects, if not always to the same extent, the 'private' situations of the great majority of

---

4. I have dealt fully with this question in the final chapter of *Political Power and Social Classes*.

5. Besides Talcott Parsons' well-known analyses, this is particularly the case with Dahrendorf; P. Blau, *Bureaucracy in Modern Society*, 1956; A. Gouldner, *Patterns of Industrial Bureaucracy*, 1964; A. Etzioni, *Modern Organization*, 1965; and finally M. Crozier, *Le Phénomène bureaucratique*, 1963. Claude Lefort has made some excellent critical comments on these tendencies, in the several discussions on the subject that have taken place in France from the 1950s onwards (now reproduced in *Critique de la bureaucratie*, 1972).

non-productive employees: in banking, insurance, advertising and marketing ('office workers'), trade, and the 'service' sector (hospitals, research institutes, etc.). The contemporary spread of bureaucratization is essentially due to the process of concentration and centralization of capital, the new forms of social division of labour that this imposes, and the generalization and expansion of wage-labour in the sector in which mental labour predominates. This bureaucratization has considerable, if contradictory, effects on the agents subjected to it.

If we look in particular at the essential features of the 'secrecy of knowledge' (bureaucratic secrecy) and the delegation of authority, it is plain that these agents, while they are all subjected and subordinated to the management above, also reproduce these features in their own internal relations. The various petty-bourgeois agents each possess, in relation to those subordinate to them, a fragment of the fantastic secret of knowledge that legitimizes the delegated authority that they exercise. This is the very meaning of the 'hierarchy'. Each bureaucratized instance both subordinates and is subordinated; everyone is at the same time both 'superior' and 'inferior' to someone else. But this bureaucratization should not be considered as a 'model of organization', thus identifying it with a certain ideal type of 'bureaucracy', such as that of the various state apparatuses, let alone the traditional one of the Napoleonic or Bismarckian state. The forms of bureaucratization are complex, and they are themselves subject to transformation. It might even be said that a certain form of bureaucratization, closely modelled on the military type of centralization, has had its day and now belongs to the past. Yet this does not mean that the essential features of bureaucratization are not still being reproduced today.

There is no need here to describe facts that are already well known. It can be said, however, that through the articulation of ideological relations (secrecy and the internalized monopoly of knowledge) and political relations, bureaucratization essentially appears as the specific materialization, in the social division of labour, of a mental labour 'separate', in the capitalist manner, from manual labour.

This bureaucratization is in fact something different from the factory despotism which is the specific feature of the social organization of manual labour, despite what is maintained by the majority of industrial sociologists (the bureaucratization of the 'firm'), who in this respect follow Max Weber himself. In this factory despotism based on the extraction of surplus-value, i.e. on the dominant relation of exploitation, the bourgeoisie dominates and oppresses the working class, but the working class in no way reproduces within itself these relations of domination/subordination. Even where there is a tendency towards the reproduction of the mental/ manual labour division within manual labour, this reproduction does not assume anything like the same forms that it does for mental labour. In their internal relations, the various strata of manual workers (skilled, semi-skilled, unskilled), and the various gradations within these categories, do not exercise over the strata below them authority relations and a monopolization of knowledge, certainly not in the same way as this takes place in the internal relations of the bureaucratized petty bourgeoisie. In this respect, i.e. in the actual organization of labour within the factory, those who exercise power are in fact the supervisory and managerial staff, i.e. foremen, technicians, etc. For the new bureaucratized petty bourgeoisie, on the other hand, in conformity with the specific internalization of ideologico-political relations that characterizes it in the actual organization of its labour, every agent tends to exercise induced relations of authority and of the secrecy of knowledge over subordinate agents.

Now the bourgeoisie's policy is precisely to internalize these types of relations within the working class itself, but here it comes up against the irreducible kernel of the socialization of the productive labour process, which constantly leads the working class to undermine these relations. This is the basis of the anti-hierarchical demands of the working class, which are generally quite distinct in content from the demands of the new petty bourgeoisie. It is not by chance that the bourgeoisie, in its attempt to introduce these ideologico-political relations within the working class, has to proceed via the 'labour aristocracy' and the 'trade-union bureaucracies of class collaboration' (Lenin). These factors certainly remain cosubstantial with the domination of the bourgeoisie over the working class, but they are also constantly undermined by the work relations within the working class ('class instinct'), whereas the internalization of these relations within the bureaucratized new petty bourgeoisie is a function of the reproduction of its very place in the social division of labour. In this sense, bureaucratic reproduction within the firm only works for the internal relations among white-collar employees.

We can thus see how those relations which are involved in the bureaucratic organization of labour are only the induced reproduction, and moreover the deformed reproduction, of the politico-ideological relations of class domination/subordination. The petty-bourgeois agents do not exercise over their subordinates the same domination (i.e. a class domination) that capital and the agents that occupy its place exercise over the petty bourgeoisie as a whole. The petty-bourgeois agents do not exercise actual *powers* over one another (power being a property of class relations), but rather *authority* (which refers precisely to the induced reproduction of these powers). Capital is still there, its existence in fact determines this particular social organization of labour, and class domination is in no way replaced by a uniform domination/subordination that is a function of the very 'nature' of 'organization'. Furthermore, this domination (the exercise of power) of the bourgeoisie over the bureaucratized section of the petty bourgeoisie assumes quite different forms in the labour process to those of the domination (exercise of power) that it exercises over the working class, through the factory despotism, in the extraction of surplus-value.

We can now answer certain questions pertaining to the apparatuses:

1. The various 'firms' in which the labour of these employees is organized are indeed apparatuses; they materialize and embody the ideologico-political relations that are articulated to the specific exploitation that these agents undergo. With the exception of the state apparatuses, these apparatuses are economic ones. We have in fact already seen that the concept of apparatus cannot be reserved just for the state apparatuses (repressive and ideological).

2. It is clear that, contrary to the view of the institutionalist arguments about 'organization theory', the various apparatuses are not defined by their intrinsic organizational structure, but rather by their social functions. In particular, the materialization of bourgeois politico-ideological relations ('capitalist apparatuses') does not always occur in the same manner; the internal structure of the apparatuses itself depends on the classes present there, and thus on the class struggle which takes place within them. An apparatus in which the working class is massively present and preponderant is always distinct from others. This is not just true for the economic apparatus (the production unit), but also for the ideological state apparatuses that are specifically designed for the working class. Even a social-democratic party or a class collaborationist trade union, despite the fact that they materialize the domination of bourgeois and petty-bourgeois ideology over the working class in quite specific ways, can never be compared with other apparatuses. The presence of the working class always gives rise to characteristic effects; this is in fact the nub of Lenin's analyses of the social-democratic type 'workers' parties'.

3. These assumptions make for a radical distinction between Marxist analyses and the various institutionalist conceptions of 'power', 'authority' and 'hierarchy' within the apparatuses. The only possible field of application for the concepts of domination and power is that of class relations, both within and outside of the apparatuses, e.g. the domination of the bourgeoisie over the petty

bourgeoisie or over the working class. What the terms 'authority' and 'hierarchy' properly refer to is the induced reproduction of these (dominant) relations actually within each class itself, which always takes a specific form, particularly in the case of the petty bourgeoisie located in the apparatuses. The apparatuses are the effect of class domination and class powers, but they also materialize and embody, at the same time, this induced reproduction.

4. It is apparent, therefore, that the apparatuses are themselves divided:

(a) First and foremost, according to the class barriers. Not only is each firm divided vertically by the places of bourgeois, petty bourgeois and workers, but it is also often partitioned horizontally; a complex firm or production unit is in fact divided into two apparatuses, the factory with its despotism (working class), and the administrative' apparatus with its offices, etc. (petty bourgeoisie).

(b) Secondly, according to the division into fractions of the various classes located there. This is above all the case for the petty bourgeoisie, and in a very particular manner. By seeing the authority and hierarchy in the ranks of the petty bourgeoisie as an induced reproduction of class powers, we can see how the very field of application of these powers, i.e. their induced reproduction within the petty bourgeoisie, also does not have a straightforward linear structure.

III

The internalization of the politico-ideological relations of domination/subordination, something which is particularly characteristic of the bureaucratized sectors of the new petty bourgeoisie, has also more distant effects on the agents who occupy this place. This is a specific function of the fact that these petty-bourgeois agents have a *career*. An agent of the new petty-bourgeoisie can often reasonably hope to climb up the 'ladder' during the course of his professional life, and by the time he reaches fifty he may have increased by 15, 20 or 50 per cent the salary that he had at twenty. This is of course not a universal phenomenon, and for a large section of the subaltern levels, the progress of such a career is relatively short; these are the levels affected by the fragmentation of tasks within mental labour itself. Statistics easily show, however, the difference that there is here as compared with the working-class situation. The overwhelming majority of manual workers reach their maximum earning capacity at between twenty and thirty years old, and their wages then begin to decline. Hence the difference in superannuation arrangements (and the basis of their calculation) between the agents of the new petty bourgeoisie and those of the working class, even if the latter have acquired the 'right' to this and have not already died of over-work. It is also a known fact that life expectation is greater for the petty bourgeoisie taken as a whole than for the working class. More-over, it is only a small stratum of the working class today that have graduated to receiving a monthly salary; for them this is the acknow-ledgement of a whole lifetime spent at work, while it is a matter of course for the great majority of white-collar employees.

The importance of the career and of promotion contrasts with the working-class situation, firstly, in the movement of these agents during their working life (intra-generational movement). Out of those male skilled workers who change their status, scarcely 14 per cent become technicians, this proportion falling almost to nothing in the case of the semi-skilled and unskilled workers. Moreover, what is more and more common here is the massive process of disqualification; thus around 34 per cent of the skilled workers who change their status become semi- or unskilled workers. On the other hand, out of the male clerical workers who change their status in the course of their working life, 48 per cent become intermediate or higher managerial staff (25 per cent become manual workers), while 57 per cent of such female clerical workers become intermediate and higher managers (only 6 per cent becoming manual workers). Out of male workers in commerce, 29 per cent of the movement is into executive positions (28 per cent to manual work). The upward mobility of the petty-bourgeois agents within the new petty bour-geoisie itself is also visible between generations. Just to take the case of clerical workers, around 23 per cent of their sons obtain inter-mediate managerial positions, while this is only the case for some 10 per cent of the sons of manual workers.[6]

Finally, in the case of petty-bourgeois agents affected by bureau-cratization (public or private), the salary spread is much wider and more open than for the working class and its various strata. Just to take the private and nationalized industries sector, net average earnings in 1969, which in the case of the working class were 8,854

6. INSEE, *Enquête sur la qualification professionnelle de 1964*, a study of those economically active between 1959 and 1964. The results of this study on intra-generational movement have been presented in *Études et Con-jonctures*, October 1966, and on inter-generational movement in *Études et Conjonctures*, February 1967. There are also, on inter-generation movement, the exemplary works of D. Bertaux, including 'L'hérédité sociale en France', in *Économie et Statistique*, February 1970, and 'Nouvelles perspectives sur la mobilite sociale en France', in *Quality and Quantity*, vol. V, June 1971. These conclusions are essentially confirmed by the subsequent study made in 1970, the results of which have not yet been published.

francs for unskilled, 10,467 for semi-skilled and 13,116 for skilled workers, were for the petty bourgeoisie as follows: commercial workers, 12,344 francs; office workers, 13,350 francs; intermediate managerial and administrative staff, 27,958. (We have left out here the higher managerial staff who most often belong in fact to the bourgeoisie.) It should be noted that the gap separating the basic salaries of routine white-collar employees from those of the intermediate staff is much greater than that separating the working class from the technicians. These figures are of course of limited significance. Things become clearer when we compare these figures with the wage distribution by type of economic activity and level of average net annual earnings. If we take on the one hand those economic activities that interest us here (various forms of commerce, services, banking, insurance, agencies, health, and administrative services), and on the other hand industrial activities, the differences are quite apparent. While the great majority of manual workers very soon reach a ceiling at a certain level, other employees exhibit, of course with certain inequalities that we shall go on to examine, a more balanced distribution over a wider spread of salary levels.[7] The case of civil servants is still more obvious.

In any case, what is important for us here is that the significance of differentials is very different in the working class from the petty bourgeoisie with its career structure. Even if a grade 1 semi-skilled worker moves up to grade 2, 3 or 4, or a skilled worker from grade 1 to grade 2, this does not mean anything like the same thing for him, within the ideologico-political relations of authority and the secrecy of knowledge, as does the promotion of a petty bourgeois who, even without rising all that high (for the greater part of these agents circulation is very limited, even within the petty bourgeoisie), exercises a certain authority over the agents immediately below him.

This has considerable effects on the specific ideology of social mobility that these agents have. These effects are connected with the competitive isolation of these agents from one another in the 'bureaucratized' ideologico-political relations, an isolation that contrasts with the class solidarity within the working class, has its repercussions on the class struggle, and is visible daily, particularly in the specific difficulties and problems faced by strike movements on the part of this new petty bourgeoisie.

IV

The bureaucratization of the work of non-productive employees, even though it is today a pronounced tendency, does not affect all

7. op. cit., in Collections de l'INSEE, p. 58.

of this grouping, as we shall see, nor does it always affect them in the same way. It should already be clear, however, that this bureaucratization, the materialization and embodiment of ideologico-political relations, as well as the differentiation that there is in this respect within the new petty bourgeoisie, is an important factor in dividing the new petty bourgeoisie into class fractions. These differentiations and fractions of the new petty bourgeoisie do not necessarily coincide with its differentiation at the level of economic relations (employees in circulation, in services, and in the state apparatuses), since bureaucratization stretches laterally across these different groupings.

The reason for this is that this bureaucratization itself has contradictory effects on the new petty bourgeoisie. Several writers, including C. Wright Mills, and David Lockwood, have maintained that bureaucratization brings the working conditions of these employees into line with those of the working class, in terms of the impersonality of functions, authoritarian and hierarchic relations, etc. These assertions applied as they are to the bureaucratized petty bourgeoisie as a whole, are false, in so far as they equate this bureaucratization with the factory despotism. The problem is a different one. Bureaucratization itself contributes, within the sectors of the new petty bourgeoisie that are subjected to it, to new internal cleavages between the mass of subaltern agents, progressively dispossessed of their 'knowledge' (by the internal functioning of bureaucratic 'secrecy') and the exercise of authority, and the intermediate agents. This is always articulated to the differentiation within the petty bourgeoisie in the order of the exploitation suffered, and has major effects which we shall return to later on the class positions of this subaltern fraction of the petty bourgeoisie.

6

The New Petty Bourgeoisie: Distribution of Agents

Finally, there is a further element affecting the distribution of these agents into the place of the new petty bourgeoisie and their reproduction in relation to this place. This time we are no longer dealing with the circulation of these agents within the petty bourgeoisie, but with the forms of their movement into other social classes. Even though the official INSEE statistics are, here again, considerably muddled, as a result of the classifications that they make (the famous 'socio-professional categories'), we can still draw certain indications from them.[1]

In the contemporary capitalist formations, the agents of the new petty bourgeoisie seem to display (though unevenly, depending on their various groupings) a particularly high level of movement into other social classes, both in the course of their own working lives and between generations; this movement also has its characteristic forms.

(a) The proportion of these employees who move into other 'socio-professional categories' in the course of their own working lives, something which indicates a change of class, is considerably higher than for the bourgeoisie or the working class.

(b) Between generations, the proportion of children of these petty-bourgeois agents who belong to the same class as their parents is considerably lower than for the bourgeoisie or the working class; more than 70 per cent of working-class children themselves become manual workers, and more than 43 per cent of the children of the bourgeoisie themselves become bourgeois, while only some 27 per cent of the children of the new petty bourgeoisie, taken as a whole, remain in their class of origin.[2]

1. Sources as cited above.

2. This percentage is obtained by considering those children (of both sexes) of the intermediate staff and various grades of white-collar employees who become either intermediate staff or routine white-collar employees

Moreover:

(1) While the actual place of this petty bourgeoisie has expanded in the present phase of monopoly capitalism, its agents display a characteristic instability in their occupation of this place. This also distinguishes these agents from those of the bourgeoisie and those of the working class, while also being different from the formally similar case of the poor peasant classes and the traditional petty bourgeoisie. In these last cases, the massive movement of agents has been due to the actual elimination of their place in the course of development of monopoly capitalism.[3]

(2) A large proportion of the agents who shift their place 'fall' into the working class, this being particularly the case for the routine white-collar 'employees'. Among the male employees in this category, 24 per cent of those who moved out of the commercial sector, and 25 per cent of office workers, fell into the working class. Between generations, 40 per cent of the sons of this category, and 17 per cent of their daughters became manual workers.

(3) On the other hand, however, the proportion of petty-bourgeois agents who move up into the place of the bourgeoisie is far and away greater than for the working class, even though this bourgeois elevation still only accounts for a minority of transfers out of the petty-bourgeoisie, and is very slight in absolute terms. There are almost no manual workers at all who move up into the bourgeoisie in the course of their working lives, while this does occur for some 10 per cent of the male white-collar 'employees' who change their position (becoming higher-level managers), and the proportion is still greater for the intermediate staff. Between generations, around 10·5 per cent of the sons of the new petty bourgeoisie lift themselves into the bourgeoisie, while this is only the case for some 1 per cent of the sons of manual workers.

We must pause for a moment on this last point. Firstly, to stress

---

themselves. I have based this re-working on the 'crude' figures of the INSEE inquiry already cited, a re-working which studies of this kind, governed as they are by the ideology of social 'mobility', never carry out. It should be noted that the figure of 43 per cent for children of the bourgeoisie who themselves become bourgeois is deceptive. In point of fact, the inquiry only dealt with agents aged 45 or under at the time (for the 1964 inquiry, those born in and after 1919). Now an appreciable number of children of bourgeois parents have not yet had the time, at this age, to come into their inheritance (not in Bourdieu's sense of cultural inheritance, but in hard cash), and thus become themselves directly bourgeois, i.e. to assume their actual place. This phenomenon of 'counter-mobility' has been investigated and explained by Girod in Switzerland.

3. See on this subject the articles cited by D. Bertaux.

the stupidity of the bourgeois problematic of social mobility: the basic aspect of the reproduction of social relations (social classes) is not that of the *agents*, but rather the reproduction of the *places* of these classes. If, on a totally absurd hypothesis, all children of the bourgeoisie were to become workers and vice versa, or any similar such wholesale movement between classes took place, the class structure of the capitalist formation would not change in any fundamental way. The places of capital, of the working class, and of the petty bourgeoisie would still be there.

This hypothesis is, however, quite absurd, since, although the social classes of a capitalist formation are not closed 'castes' or orders, the reproduction of both the places and the agents who occupy them are in fact only two interconnected aspects of the reproduction of social relations in general.

This connection is a quite specific one in the case of the new petty bourgeoisie. These agents have a much greater 'chance', if one can put it like that, of attaining the place of the bourgeoisie, than is the case for the agents of the working class. And the essential apparatus that effects this transition is again the educational apparatus, which in this respect, by the training and qualification of mental labour, also operates to distribute certain agents from the new petty bourgeoisie to the bourgeoisie.

It could also be said, if we cut short the complexity of the concrete phenomena, that we are dealing here with an actual policy on the part of the bourgeoisie, which is particularly clear in those formations where it has had to obtain the support of the petty bourgeoisie *vis-à-vis* the working class, notably in France. This support has long been maintained by the nature of the capitalist educational system in France, and the particularly important role it has played for the upward transfer of petty-bourgeois agents (e.g. the system of competitive examination). This state of affairs has in fact considerable ideological effects on the new petty bourgeoisie, i.e. the ideology of 'promotion' and of 'climbing' up into the bourgeoisie, coupled with the role ascribed to 'learning' in this respect. These ideological aspects have a real substratum, even if this is very far from how the new petty bourgeoisie imagine things in their own fantasies. In absolute terms, and for the class as a whole, this upward transfer is in fact very restrained, but it continues to feed the illusions and hopes that these agents have for themselves and especially for their children.

This last phenomenon also does not affect the whole of the new petty bourgeoisie in the same way or to the same extent. There are appreciable differentiations within this class, and these are also involved, as we shall see, in its internal division into class fractions.

7

The Class Determination of the Traditional Petty Bourgeoisie

Before coming onto the question of petty-bourgeois ideology, we have to examine the class determination of the traditional petty bourgeoisie. I can be very brief here, since the structural class determination of this grouping, which was what Marx, Engels and even Lenin had in mind above all in discussing the petty bourgeoisie, raises fewer problems than does that of the new petty bourgeoisie.

Confining ourselves to the place of the traditional petty bourgeoisie in the relations of production, we can say that it includes both small-scale production and small-scale ownership.

(a) Small-scale production essentially consists of forms of artisan production, or small family businesses, where the same agent is both owner and possessor of his means of production, as well as the direct producer. There is here no economic exploitation properly so-called, in so far as these forms of production do not employ wage-labour, or at least only do so very occasionally. Labour is chiefly provided by the actual owner or by the members of his family, who are not remunerated in the form of a wage. This small-scale production draws profit from the sale of its goods and through the overall redistribution of surplus-value, but it does not directly extort surplus-value.

(b) Small-scale ownership chiefly involves retail trade in the circulation sphere, where the owner of the trading stock, helped by his family, provides the labour, and again only occasionally employs wage-labour.

The common place of these two groupings of the traditional petty bourgeoisie in the relations of production lies in the fact that the direct producer is in each case himself the owner of the means of labour, i.e. in the combination of ownership with the absence of direct exploitation of wage-labour. This petty bourgeoisie does not belong to the capitalist mode of production, but to the simple commodity form which was historically the form of transition from the feudal to the capitalist mode. The contemporary existence of this petty bourgeoisie in the developed capitalist formations thus depends on the perpetuation of this form in the extended reproduction of capitalism, and on the political forms that this reproduction has assumed. Marx and Engels already stressed the tendency for this petty bourgeoisie to be undermined with the establishment of the dominance of the capitalist mode of production and its reproduction.

8

The Petty-Bourgeois Ideological Sub-Ensemble and the Political Position of the Petty Bourgeoisie

The structural determination of the new petty bourgeoisie in the social division of labour has certain effects on the ideology of its agents, which directly influences its class positions. We should say right away that these effects vary with the different fractions of the new petty bourgeoisie, fractions which the structural class determination enables us to define according to its current transformations. This does not prevent there from being a common stock of these ideological effects, which characterizes the new petty bourgeoisie as a whole. Finally, these ideological effects on the new petty bourgeoisie exhibit a remarkable affinity to those which the specific class determination of the traditional petty bourgeoisie has on the latter, thus justifying their attribution to one and the same class, the petty bourgeoisie.

I

We must firstly establish some guidelines for the examination of petty-bourgeois ideology. The petty bourgeoisie, in fact, given its place in the class determination of a capitalist formation, does not have in the long run any autonomous class position. The two basic classes are the bourgeoisie and the proletariat; the only real class ideologies, in the strong sense of this term, are those of these two basic classes, which are in fundamental political opposition. In other words, the only ideological ensembles that have a specific coherence and are relatively systematic are those of the dominant bourgeois ideology and of the ideology connected to the working class.

This is the reason why, as far as the petty bourgeoisie is concerned, we simply speak of a petty-bourgeois ideological sub-ensemble. In the context of the ideological class struggle (the various ideologies do not exist 'in themselves' in a closed field of 'ideology in general'), this sub-ensemble is formed by the effects of the (dominant) bourgeois ideology on the specific aspirations of the petty-bourgeois agents that are a function of their specific class determination. Bourgeois ideology, of course, also exerts its effects within the working class, otherwise it would not be the dominant ideology. There, however, coming up against the practices of the class which is as the heart of capitalist exploitation, it assumes other forms than in the case of the petty bourgeoisie. Even under the effects of bourgeois ideology, there still always breaks through in the working class what Lenin referred to as 'class instinct'. This is simply the constant resurgence, in its practices, of the class determination of that class which suffers, in the factory and in material production, the extraction of surplus-value.[1]

In this twisting and adaptation of bourgeois ideology to the petty bourgeoisie's own aspirations, the petty bourgeoisie itself inserts certain specific ideological 'elements' that derive from its own class determination, i.e. as a class itself exploited and dominated by capital, but in a form quite different from the exploitation and domination experienced by the working class.

Moreover, in a capitalist formation, there is at the same time an ideology bound up with the working class. As Lenin indicated, the dominant ideology itself (the 'culture' of a capitalist formation) includes, in its discourse, certain 'elements' deriving from this ideology. This can go so far as to take the forms indicated by Marx in the *Manifesto* of a 'bourgeois socialism', or even, in the early stages of capitalism, a 'feudal socialsm' of the great 'feudal' landed proprietors. In the case of the petty bourgeoisie, the situation is of course different. It is itself an exploited and dominated class, and this situation results in the fact that its ideology also includes, in close articulation with the elements deriving from its own particular exploitation and domination, elements specific to working-class ideology, this being actually present within the petty-bourgeois sub-ensemble in a far more direct and significant manner than in the case of the dominant ideolgy. This presence of working-class ideology in the petty-bourgeois ideological sub-ensemble fulfils certain particular functions, since it corresponds to the actual polarization of the petty bourgeoisie.

1. The specific role of bourgeois ideology in forming the petty-bourgeois ideological sub-ensemble makes it possible to understand a key fact that has today assumed its full importance. Every ideological crisis of the bourgeoisie is directly reflected within the petty bourgeoisie, and thus directly influences its class positions.

This points to two things:

1. On the one hand, this presence of working-class ideology in the petty-bourgeois ideological sub-ensemble always tends to be dominated both by specifically petty-bourgeois ideological elements and by the bourgeois ideology that is also constitutively present in the petty-bourgeois sub-ensemble. In other words, the petty-bourgeois ideological sub-ensemble is a terrain of struggle and a particular battlefield between bourgeois ideology and working-class ideology, though with the specific intervention of peculiarly petty-bourgeois elements. This terrain is in no way a vacant site, but is encircled right from the start by bourgeois ideology and by petty-bourgeois ideological elements. To continue the military analogy, the conquests and advances of working-class ideology on this terrain in a capitalist formation, even though they are of key importance, are none the less constantly surrounded by these petty-bourgeois ideological elements. More simply, even when petty-bourgeois sectors adopt working-class positions they often do so by investing them with their own ideological practices. This, however, is done unevenly, since the terrain of petty-bourgeois ideology is no more uniform than it is vacant, as a result of the fractioning and polarization that divide the petty bourgeoisie in its class determination. Hence, we can not rule out the possiblity of whole sections of the petty bourgeoisie not only adopting working-class positions, but even placing themselves on the actual terrain of working-class ideology. This is one of the specific tasks of the working class's revolutionary organizations.

2. On the other hand, however, this also means that certain ideological elements specific to the petty bourgeoisie may themselves have their effects on the working class's ideology, and because of the particular class determination of the petty bourgeoisie, this happens in a manner different to that in which bourgeois ideology acts. This is even the main danger that permanently threatens the working class. It may take the form of a convergence and amalgamation of these elements with working-class ideology, particularly the form of petty-bourgeois socialism, but also, as we have seen in the past, the forms of anarcho-syndicalism and revolutionary syndicalism, which can all affect the working class.

These points must be borne in mind in the following discussion. They are in fact based on certain important assumptions, in particular that the various ideologies and ideological sub-ensembles are only constituted in the course of an ideological class struggle, and must therefore be chiefly considered not as constituted conceptual ensembles, but rather as they are materialized in class practices.[2] These

2. L. Althusser, 'Ideology and Ideological State Apparatuses', in *Lenin*

are the principles on which we have to base our examination of the effects of the ideology on another. We are not dealing with already constituted ensembles which would 'then' act on 'others' by way of intermediaries, according to the simplist notion of a series of ideological links that 'convey' interactions, i.e. a chain of 'influences'. The very conception of the ideological field as being formed by this stage-by-stage conveyance (of 'reciprocal influence') is basically incorrect; ideological struggle is present as such in the actual formation of every class ideology, in its very midst. This is especially the case with the petty-bourgeois ideological sub-ensemble, which is neither a staging-post nor a transmission belt for the 'influence' of bourgeois ideology on the working class. If it is involved in this process, it is in so far as it is itself the site of a particular co-presence of bourgeois ideology, working-class ideology and petty-bourgeois ideological elements.

II

If we take into account the class determination of the new petty bourgeoisie, we can establish the following as its main ideological features:

(a) An ideological aspect that is anti-capitalist but leans strongly towards reformist illusions. This new petty bourgeoisie experiences its exploitation chiefly in the wage form, while the structure of the capitalist mode of production and the role of both ownership and possession of the means of production in this exploitation often remain hidden from it (unproductive wage-labour). Its demands are basically bound up with the question of incomes, often focusing on a redistribution of income by way of 'social justice' and an 'egalitarian' taxation policy, the constantly recurring basis of petty-bourgeois socialism. Although they are hostile to 'the rich', the petty-bourgeois agents are often still attached to wage differentials, while stressing the need for these to be more just and 'rational'. What we are faced with here is the permanent fear of proletarianization, (a fear which is expressed in resistance to a revolutionary transformation of society), as a result of the insecurity experienced at the level of earnings, and in the form of a monetary fetishism. This, together with the specific isolation of these agents in their

---

and Philosophy, NLB, 1971. This is of course the basic source of error of those abundant 'sociological investigations' that attempt to grasp the 'consciousness' of various social classes and fractions on the basis of their agents' answers to 'questions'. See on this subject the comments of D. Vidal, *Essai sur l'idéologie*, 1971.

competition on the capitalist labour market and in their actual conditions of work, since these agents are not affected by the socialization of the labour process (and thus class solidarity) in the way that the workers directly engaged in production are, gives rise to specifically corporatist forms of trade-union struggle; this competitive isolation is the basis of a complex ideological process that takes the form of petty-bourgeois individualism.

(b) An aspect that challenges the political and ideological relations to which these agents are subjected, but leans strongly towards rearranging these relations by way of 'participation', rather than undermining them. Demands are made on capital for a greater share of 'responsibility' in 'decision-making' powers and for a reclassification of their mental labour at its 'true value', but this does not generally lead to questioning the actual mental/manual labour division in their relations with the working class. Quite the contrary: it is often expressed in the form of demands for a 'rationalization' of society that would enable 'mental labour' to develop fully, without the shackles of the profit motive, i.e. in the form of a left-wing technocracy. The ambiguous form assumed by the demand for 'self-management' when raised by certain petty-bourgeois groupings (e.g. by technicians) is a familiar example of this, since this demand means in their eyes that they should take the place of the bourgeoisie in a new form, whereas for the working class it means workers' control. Their demands also take the form of a fixation on forms of 'organization', calls for 'decentralization' of the decision-making process, rearrangement of the 'authoritarian' structure of work, etc., but without questioning the basis of these. The anti-authoritarian struggle that develops here, in the form of a revolt against the bureaucratization and fragmentation of mental labour, is far from attaining the scope and content of the anti-hierarchical struggle of the working class. The petty-bourgeois agents are, moreover, strongly attached to a hierarchy, even though they want this 're-arranged' in respect to their relations both among themselves and with the working class.

There is no need to stress here that this is neither a constant nor a general aspect affecting the new petty bourgeoisie as a whole. The parallel aspect of submitting to and internalizing the moral values of 'order', 'discipline', 'authority' and the 'legitimate hierarchy' of management can often be present in the groupings subjected to the already-noted social division of labour and while they may challenge their conditions of existence and furnish an appreciable base of support for social-democratic governments, they can also provide just as significant a base for the celebrated silent majority.

(c) An ideological aspect that seeks to transform their condition, but which is bound up with the myth of social promotion, rather than with a revolutionary change in society. Afraid of proletarianization below, attracted to the bourgeoisie above, the new petty bourgeoisie often aspires to 'promotion', to a 'career', to 'upward social mobility', i.e. to becoming bourgeois (the ideological aspects of bourgeois imitation) by way of the 'indivdual' transfer of the 'best' and 'most capable'; this is again a case of petty-bourgeois individualism. For the new petty bourgeoisie, this is particularly focused on the educational apparatus, given the role that the latter plays in this respect. Hence the belief in the 'neutrality of culture', and in the educational apparatus as a corridor of circulation by the promotion and accession of the 'best' to the bourgeois state, or in any case to a higher state in the specific hierarchy of mental labour. This leads to the demands for a 'democratization' of the apparatuses, so that they offer 'equal opportunity' to those individuals best fitted to take part in the 'renewal of elites', without questioning the actual structure of political power. The elitist conception of society, in the form of meritocracy, is closely linked with the petty bourgeoisie's aspirations for social justice. This attitude is not confined to the educational apparatus; it can embrace, to a greater or lesser extent according to the social formation, all the state apparatuses (sometimes even the army itself), which are seen as ladders of promotion for their sub-altern and intermediate agents who often originate from the petty bourgeoisie. This attitude of the petty bourgeoisie can be summed up by saying that it does not want to break the ladders by which it imagines it can climb.

(d) An ideological aspect of 'power fetishism' that Lenin spoke of, and which concerns the attitude of the new petty bourgeoisie towards the political power of the state. As a result of the situation of this petty bourgeoisie as a intermediate class, polarized between the bourgeoisie and the working class, as a result also of the isolation of its agents (petty-bourgeois individualism), this class has a strong tendency to see the state as an inherently neutral force whose role is that of arbitrating between the various social classes. The class domination that the bourgeoisie exert over it by way of the state apparatus is often experienced as a 'technical' deformation of the state, which can be 're-arranged' through a democratization that would bring it into line with its own true nature. This involves demands related to the 'humanization' and 'rationalization' of the 'administration', against the state's technocratic centralism', and such demands do not comprehend the actual nature of political power.

Furthermore, we must take into consideration both this intermediate situation and petty-bourgeois individualism which make it impossible for the petty bourgeoisie to organize itself, at least in the long run, into a specific and autonomous political party, and also:

(a) The petty bourgeoisie's situation in relation to mental labour, and the fact that the state apparatus itself, sanctioning the mental/manual labour division, is located on the side of mental labour;

(b) the fact that the state organization sanctions the same hierarchy and bureaucratic authority to which a large part of the petty-bourgeois agents are subjected;

(c) the role of the state apparatuses in the distribution and training of the petty-bourgeois agents.

These facts all contribute to determining a complex attitude of identification that the petty bourgeoisie has towards a state which it sees as being by rights *its* state, and *its* rightful representative and political organizer. This was for a long time expressed in France by left-wing republican Jacobinism, and is far from having disappeared today. The role of the state as an apparatus of class domination is seen as a perversion of a state whose authority is to be restored by 'democratizing' it, i.e. by opening it up to the petty bourgeoisie, making it respect the 'general interest', it being understood that this general interest corresponds to that of the intermediate class, the mediator between the bourgeoisie and the proletariat. This is the origin of the conception of the 'corporate state', a debased form of state socialism. It should be added that this ideological aspect is particularly strong among petty-bourgeois civil servants, since these are themselves directly subjected to the internal ideology that characterizes the state as an apparatus. The ideological aspect of the neutral state that represents the general interest is particularly pronounced here, as an essential element of the internal ideology of the state apparatuses.

It is clear that these ideological aspects often take the form of demands for 'socialism' by way of the 'welfare state', the regulator and corrector of 'social inequalities'. They can, however, also be articulated to certain aspects of the 'strong state' in the form of 'social Caesarism'. This has been shown in the past by the specific relationship between fascism and bonapartism of various kinds and large sectors of this new petty bourgeoisie.

(e) These aspects are also combined with particular forms of revolt by these petty-bourgeois agents against their conditions, forms which are also bound up with their class determinations. This is a very broad question, and links up with the problem of class positions. I should just like to indicate here that violent outbreaks of revolt on the part of this class can often assume the forms of 'petty-bourgeois jacquerie', bound up with petty-bourgeois individualism: the cult of violence as such, associated with a contempt for the problem of organization; globally anti-state reactions which directly coincide with the forms of 'petty-bourgeois anarchism', etc. These revolts are characteristic of situations in which these agents, deprived of an autonomous long-run political expression but not having taken up the positions of the working class, act in a manner that is symmetrically opposed to the attitudes that previously determined them, i.e. a revolt still determined, in its opposition, by bourgeois ideology. This is the nub of 'petty-bourgeois ultra-leftism'.

III

To return now to the traditional petty bourgeoisie. The latter, although it occupies in economic relations a place different from that of the new petty bourgeoisie, is nevertheless characterized at the ideological level by certain analogous features, though there are also still some differences. The reason for this is that the economic relations that characterize the place of the traditional petty bourgeoisie are themselves located, by certain specific features, in the context of a polarization in respect to the bourgeoisie and the working class. These common ideological effects lead to analogies in the positions of the two petty-bourgeois groupings, both of which are affected by class polarization.

We can therefore maintain that these two groupings both form part of the same class, the petty bourgeoisie. But the basis for this is still that the petty bourgeoisie is not a class like the two basic classes of the capitalist social formation, the bourgeoisie and the proletariat; in particular it does not exhibit the same unity that marks both of these. The traditional petty bourgeoisie (small shopkeepers, artisans) is not related to the new petty bourgeoisie in the same way as are banking capital and industrial capital in the case of the bourgeoisie. There is still this heterogeneity in the economic relations of the petty-bourgeois groupings. If the traditional and the new petty bourgeoisies can be considered as belonging to the same class, this is because social classes are only determined in the class struggle, and because these groupings are precisely both polarized in relation to the bourgeoisie and the proletariat.[3]

3. I put forward and sought to prove this thesis in *Fascism and Dictatorship*, though probably in rather too abrupt a manner, since it was not the basic object of my analysis there. It still seems to me basically correct, however. I should mention here that the same position has since been argued by Baudelot and Establet: 'The petty bourgeoisie . . . is composed of heterogenous social strata left over from earlier modes of production . . . and of new strata produced by the development of the capitalist mode . . . These different strata acquire their unity at the economic level in a negative

In the case of the traditional petty bourgeoisie, these ideological effects, which are essentially a function of the petty commodity form, have been studied in detail by Marx, Engels and Lenin. They are based on the facts that, at the economic level, (1) small-scale production and small-scale ownership are distinguished both from the bourgeoisie (they do not belong to capital as such and are gradually ruined by it) and from the working class (their agents are owners of their means of production and trading stock, and although the artisans are direct producers, they do not perform capitalist productive labour – surplus-value); (2) they also have points in common both with the bourgeoisie (being fiercely attached to their property) and with the working class (being themselves direct producers).[4] This polarization often has the following effects at the ideological level:

(a) An ideological aspect that is anti-capitalist but in a '*status quo*' fashion. This is against 'the rich', but the traditional petty bourgeoisie are often afraid of a revolutionary transformation of society, since this grouping fiercely holds on to its (small) property and is afraid of being proletarianized. It makes sharp demands against the monopolies, since it is gradually itself being ruined and eliminated by monopoly capitalism, but these often aim at restoring 'equal opportunity' and 'fair competition', which is how the fantasies of the petty bourgeoisie picture the past stage of competitive capitalism. What this petty bourgeoisie often seeks is change without the system changing. It aspires to share in the 'distribution' of political power, in the form of a corporate state, and exhibits characteristic resistance towards the radical transformation of this power.

(b) An ideological aspect strongly tied not to the radical transformation of society but to the myth of social promotion. This myth is related to the economic isolation of these petty-bourgeois agents in the competitive market, which is also what gives rise to petty-

---

fashion (they are neither bourgeois, nor proletarians); this unity is not just that of a residue that theory has had difficulty in integrating, it rests rather on objective contradictions in the material conditions of life of every petty bourgeois. This unity is welded together at the ideological level, and is expressed in compromise arrangements that are constantly renewed, though identical in their structure, between bourgeois and proletarian ideology.' (*L'École capitaliste en France*, p. 169, note 28.)

4. We should note here, just in passing, that the role of the mental/manual labour division is secondary as far as the class determination of these agents is concerned, precisely because based as they are on the simple commodity form, they are not directly subjected, in their relations to the bourgeoisie and the working class, to this division in its specifically capitalist form (the obvious case here being that of the artisans).

bourgeois individualism. Afraid of proletarianization below, attracted towards the bourgeoisie above, these petty-bourgeois agents also aspire to become bourgeois by way of 'individual' upward transfer (becoming small businessmen) for the 'best' and 'most capable'. This aspect also often takes elitist forms, those calling for a renewal of elites, and a replacement of the bourgeoisie which is 'not fulfilling its role' by the petty bourgeoisie, by way of a 'democratization' of capitalist society.

(c) An ideological aspect of power fetishism. Its economic isolation (petty-bourgeois individualism) and its distinction from both the bourgeoisie and the working class give rise to the belief in a neutral state above classes; this petty bourgeoisie expects the state, duly 'democratized', to bring it rain and sunshine from above, although this does not rule out virulent pressure on the state. Moreover, this petty-bourgeois isolation, combined with the general inability of the petty bourgeoisie to orgainize itself into an autonomous party of its own, and the fact that this grouping, too, considers the state apparatuses (administration, army, police) as gangways leading upwards, often gives rise to a statolatry. In this case the traditional petty bourgeoisie also identifies itself with the state, whose neutrality coincides with its own, and conceives itself as a neutral class between the bourgeoisie and the proletariat, and thus as the pillar of a state that would be 'its' state. It always hopes for social 'arbitration'. This state then appears as the direct political organizer of this petty bourgeoisie, by way of its apparatuses and branches. The traditional petty bourgeoisie has often been a pillar of the 'democratic republican' order, an essential component of left-wing Jacobinism or even petty-bourgeois socialism, but it has equally provided a mass base for various forms of fascism and bonapartism.

(d) The complex attitude of the traditional petty bourgeoisie to the state is also related to the ideology inculcated in it by the ideological state apparatuses. The principal role here does not fall to the educational apparatus (mental labour), but rather to that very specific apparatus provided by the family, the family unit playing a particular role in the economic existence of these agents. This is one of the most tenacious sites of the inculcation of bourgeois ideology into this class, as a result of the decisive role in resisting a radical transformation of social relations that the family plays; it is particularly effective for these agents, who thus link up with the new petty bourgeoisie in the family-school couple.

(3) On last element which is well enough known not to need stressing here: since the traditional petty bourgeoisie is without an autonomous long-run political position, the forms of violent revolt which characterize it in specific conjunctures are often marked by

the specific 'anarchism' of petty-bourgeois individualism, if it has not already adopted working-class positions.

IV

This community of ideological effects that marks the petty bourgeoisie as a whole is reflected at the level of class positions.

The petty bourgeoisie actually has, in the long run, no autonomous class political position of its own. This simply means that, in a capitalist social formation, there is only the bourgeois way and the proletarian way (the socialist way): there is no such thing as the 'third way', which various theories of the 'middle class' insist on. The two basic classes are the bourgeoisie and the working class; there is no such thing as a 'petty-bourgeois mode of production'. This means, among other things, that the petty bourgeoisie has nowhere ever been the politically dominant class. What has occasionally happened is that:

(1) It has in certain conjunctures and specific regimes held the place of *governing class*, in the context of the political domination and hegemony of the bourgeoisie. This was particularly the case in the first period of fascist rule, but it is still the case today in certain military and bonapartist dictatorships in the dependent countries, either in a 'progressive' form, coinciding with the political domination of certain sectors of the bourgeoisie with 'nationalist' fancies (Peru, for example, or in the past, Peronist populism), or in a 're-actionary' form which then coincides with the political domination of a comprador bourgeoisie (Brazil for example). It has also occurred, however, in other forms, in the European countries: for example, the beginnings of the Third Republic in France, or certain social-democratic regimes today.

(2) It has succeeded, in certain regimes and certain political crises, in dislodging a large section of the old bourgeoisie, and taking its place by way of complex economic and political processes (the case of Nasser's Egypt, for example), even sometimes replacing a foreign colonial bourgeoisie in the form of a state bourgeoisie (as in certain African countries). In such cases, however, it is as a bourgeoisie, whose place it has occupied, that it is politically dominant class, and no longer as a petty bourgeoisie.

To return to our problem. The fact that the petty bourgeoisie has no long-run autonomous class political position means that the class positions taken by the petty bourgeoisie must necessarily be located in the balance of forces between the bourgeoisie and the working class, and thus link up (by acting for or against) either with the class positions of the bourgeoisie or with those of the working class.

This can certainly occur in a complex way; above all, because the petty bourgeoisie can still intervene on the political scene in certain short-term conjunctures as an authentic social force, with a weight of its own and in a relatively autonomous manner. This is an essential point which often escaped Marxist analysis and the practice of the Communist Parties in the period of the Third International. But even in these rare cases (rare because they involve the exceptional fact of the organization of the petty bourgeoisie into a specific petty-bourgeois political party), this relatively autonomous conjunctural position, when seen in a longer historic perspective, also works either for the bourgeoisie or for the working class. This complexity is also due to the fact that, when petty-bourgeois positions link up with those of one or the other of the basic classes, this often happens in an indirect way, particularly when these positions link up with those of the bourgeoisie. This process only rarely takes the form of a direct, explicit and declared alliance between bourgeoisie and petty bourgeoisie, since such an alliance is in fact extremely contradictory and explosive. It is generally achieved by way of a particular support provided by the petty bourgeoisie to the state, which it considers as 'its' state. Finally, this is also the case, in a different form, when these positions link up with the position of the proletariat; they do so even while they are still marked by petty-bourgeois ideological features.

This polarization of the petty bourgeoisie's class position, due to its polarization in the structural determination of the social divison of labour (intermediate class), is manifested in the well-known fact of its political instability, how it 'oscillates' or 'sways' between a bourgeois and a proletarian class position. These petty-bourgeois groupings can often 'swing' according to the conjuncture, sometimes in a very short space of time, from a proletarian to a bourgeois class position and vice versa (the development in France between May and July 1968 is a case in point). It should be understood here that this 'oscillation' should not be taken as a natural or essential feature of the petty bourgeoisie, but refers to its situation in the class struggle. The oscillation does not take place in a vacuum, but depends on the limits provided by the stages and phases of capitalism and by the conjunctures that mark these.

This polarization of class positions runs through the petty bourgeoisie as a whole, both traditional and new, while following complex lines. This is manifested in the fact that in the overwhelming majority of conjunctures experienced by a capitalist formation, in particular in the present phase, there are 'sections' of the traditional and new petty bourgeoisies that adopt bourgeois class positions, and 'sections' that adopt proletarian class positions.

This directly refers us to another series of questions relating in particular to the new petty bourgeoisie, given its contemporary importance:

(1) How far does a polarization of its class position towards the working class go together with current transformations affecting its conditions of existence?

(2) How far does the differential polarization of class positions actually within the new petty bourgeoisie ('sections' of it adopting bourgeois class positions, others proletarian ones) go together with its differentiation into class fractions? In this case, how are these fractions to be defined?

(3) What is the situation of the traditional petty bourgeoisie in this respect?

9

The Class Fractions of the New Petty Bourgeoisie in the Present Situation

I. CURRENT TRANSFORMATIONS

I

The main problem is how these transformations affect the new petty bourgeoisie, and so I shall not dwell on the much discussed question of the present increases of this petty bourgeoisie in the developed capitalist countries in relation to the working class, but confine myself here to a few very brief remarks on this point.

The various theories of a global all-embracing expansion of the 'tertiary' sector, which had already appeared between the two wars, and have multiplied since 1945, are chiefly based on: (a) a technicist conception of 'technological progress' (automation, etc.) which assumes a 'technical and scientific revolution' that, developing independently of the relations of production, would itself involve a radical decline of the working class; (b) a prodigious manipulation of statistics, the most blatant example of which is the distinction between 'primary', 'secondary' and 'tertiary' sectors itself; compared with these, even the INSEE's 'socio-professional categories' seem a model of rigour, and this is saying quite a lot; (c) taking the case of the United States as a model indicating the path that the other imperialist metropolises, Europe in particular, must inevitably follow, and ever the 'under-developed' countries.

The errors of the two former assumptions are too obvious for me to need to stress them here. I would like to take the opportunity offered by the last point, however, to say right away that, in the present phase of the internationalization of capitalist relations, there is in fact an absolute and relative increase of the working class, if this is considered, as it must be, in the context of the imperialist chain as a whole, and not just in the metropolitan zone alone, or in this or that metropolitan country. To go further, it is clear that the situation of the United States in this respect cannot be considered a model for Europe. The significant decline of the American working class, both absolutely and in relation to the increase of non-productive workers in the United States, which has been particularly evident since the Second World War, is essentially due to the scale of American capital exports and to the fact that the United States has become, as it were, the global administrative centre (a path that cannot foreshadow that of Europe). An argument *a contrario* is provided by Great Britain, where the number of non-productive workers, which had previously increased considerably, experienced a characteristic regression from the time that this country ceased to play the role of a first-order imperialist power.

It still remains that the rapid increase of non-productive workers is a real fact, and a major one, in the main developed capitalist countries. Without taking the risk of putting forward precise figures, which would require a considerable and rigorous work which I do not believe has yet been undertaken,[1] I would say that, in France, the working class, which is increasing both absolutely and relatively, grew between 1954 and 1968 by some 5 to 6 per cent (being today some 41 or 42 per cent of the active population), while non-productive workers displayed a greater rate of growth, amounting to around 10 per cent. However, it is necessary to keep in mind the absolute figures to which these proportions apply; the 5 to 6 per cent of the working class represents a considerably greater number of individuals than the 10 per cent of non-productive workers.

In any case, the main reasons for this phenomenon, abstracting from the particular features of each individual social formation, are due to the characteristics of monopoly capitalism, in particular its present phase:

(a) the shift in dominance, as far as the exploitation of the working class is concerned, towards the intensive exploitation of labour (which includes the productivity of labour and technological transformations), signifying a decline in the ratio of living labour to dead labour;

(b) the extension of wage-labour by the radical subjection (subsumption) of the labour-power of non-productive sectors to monopoly capital, combined with the present dissolution effects that monopoly capitalism has on other forms of production (decline of the various 'independent' producers);

1. I would like to mention here the very interesting articles (despite my reservations on the 'state monopoly capitalism' theory), by C. Quin and C. Lucas, in *Économie et Politique*, June 1973.

(c) the considerable, but subordinate increase in activities dealing with the marketing of goods and commodity circulation (diversification of finished products, and with the realization of capital (money-capital, banking, insurance, etc.);

(d) the increase, also considerable, in the number of civil servants (including public services), which accounts for a large section of the general increase in non-productive labour, and which is also related to the growth in the functions of state intervention that is specific to monopoly capitalism and to its present phase.

I would still say, however, that once the various ideologies of the 'tertiary' sector are jettisoned, this aspect of the problem is not the most important. Firstly, because the hegemonic role of the working class is not a function of any statistical data; secondly, because the fundamental question, today more than ever, is that of the working class's alliances.

II

We now come back to the question of the class fractions of the new petty bourgeoisie. The common coordinates of the class determination of the new petty bourgeoisie, and their ideological effects, show very simply (but this is already a very important point) that this class and the groupings of which it is composed are distinguished from the working class. They can thus still be polarized towards the bourgeoisie, and even when they are polarized towards the working class, they often remain marked in their positions by the ideological effects specific to their class.

We have already noted, however, that this class determination in the social division of labour, which lies in the order of exploitation itself, in the mental/manual labour division, in the bureaucratization of their labour process (ideologico-political relations) and in the reproduction of agents, although it defines a common place for the new petty bourgeoisie as a whole, does not mark out this place in exactly the same way for all its components, and at the same time introduces certain cleavages within the new petty bourgeoisie.

It is these cleavages that we now have to indicate, introducing here a few particular factors concerning the present situation. We should not lose sight, however, of the facts:

(a) That the stress on these factors as they are at this point in time, should in no way be taken to mean that they alter the class membership of the new petty-bourgeois groupings, which still remain petty-bourgeois (a point that is essential as far as alliances are concerned).

(b) That these factors are not just appearing for the first time in the present phase of monopoly capitalism, but are only the accentuated form of tendencies already at work in the inter-war period, the period of the consolidation phase of monopoly capitalism. This is an indirect rejoinder to those who maintain that the 'new' factors must inevitably lead automatically to transformations in the class positions of these agents in comparison with those that they 'previously' held.

It is still the case that these current transformations are very significant. They are related to the cleavages that the new petty bourgeoisie's class determination draws within the new petty bourgeoisie, and they sharpen these cleavages. These cleavages thus fall along the boundaries of the fractions of the new bourgeoisie, certain of which present objective preconditions, that are today very clear, for the adoption of proletarian class positions. The partial coincidence of these multiple cleavages even forms the particular objective preconditions for an alliance of these fractions with the working class. These transformations, particularly in the sense of a 'decline in living standards', are precisely focused, and not by chance, on certain fractions of this class, which are already indicated in its structural class determination. These multiple cleavages indicate that we are not faced here, in these current transformations, either with purely conjunctural elements, or with elements that, as has often been maintained, affect indifferently the new petty bourgeoisie as a whole. Thus although these transformations do not signify the objective polarization of the entire new petty bourgeoisie towards the working class, they nevertheless reinforce still more the polarization of certain of its fractions in this direction, by being massively focused on them.

These transformations are thus reflected in differential forms of the petty-bourgeois ideological sub-ensemble, which is basically shared by the petty bourgeoisie as a whole. In fact, the articulation of bourgeois and proletarian ideology with petty-bourgeois ideological elements does not always occur in the same manner for the new petty bourgeoisie as a whole; the current transformations reinforce the proletarian elements which are already stronger in these polarized fractions as a result of their structural class determination.

There are two particular reasons for stressing this fractioning. We only need mention the PCF's analysis, within the general framework of its theory of state monopoly capitalism.[2] This analysis, besides what has already been said about it, scarcely makes any differentiation, in this respect, among the celebrated 'wage-earning middle strata'. It bases its differentiation of these strata on empirical criteria

2. The *Traité* is very clear on this point (vol. I, pp. 226–51).

(trade, services, civil service, etc.), and the cleavages produced by the objective polarization within the new petty bourgeoisie are almost totally absent. These strata are seen as all equally affected, from the top down to their subaltern levels, by an objective polarization to the side of the working class, from the engineer to the saleswoman in the department store, from the university professor to the supply teacher, from the executive to the simple clerk (middle strata = anti-monopoly strata). This analysis has effects quite contrary to those that we have indicated up till now. By failing to locate the class difference between the new petty bourgeoisie and the working class, by giving out that the whole of these swaying 'middle strata' 'fall' on the side of the working class, one cannot avoid at the same time underestimating the cleavages that there are among these strata, and thus spoiling the real possibilities of a new alliance between the working class and certain particular fractions of this petty bourgeoisie by seeking the broadest alliance conceivable.

There is also a further reason for stressing the fractional division of the new petty bourgeoisie. It is plain that the working class itself does not form a 'homogenous' whole, and that there are often major differentiations between, say, the skilled French worker and the semi-skilled immigrant, to take a characteristic example. Now, certain petty-bourgeois fractions are affected by a decline in their living standards in comparison with those of certain strata of the working class. This, however, should not hide the fact that there is still a key difference between a saleswoman in a chain store and a skilled worker, even if the latter may in certain respects (particularly wages) be considered 'privileged' in relation to the former. This is a *class* difference, which has considerable effects on the possibility of actually adopting proletarian class positions. If I stress this, it is to point out the error contained in many conceptions current on the left which, by a completely idealist use of the terms 'people' and 'popular masses', obscure class divisions; they see certain 'proletarianized' petty-bourgeois agents as presenting more 'revolutionary' possibilities than do certain working-class agents, who are considered as belonging *en bloc* to the labour aristocracy. (This is particularly false in so far as the labour aristocracy is not simply determined by economic criteria such as the wage level. If that were the case, then the Lip workers would have had to be considered as part of the 'labour aristocracy' *par excellence*.)

III

The most important current transformations in the sector of non-productive wage-labour are as follows:

1. Its marked feminization, which is a function of several factors, including the considerable increase in the number of non-productive employees and the massive entry of women into the 'economic activity' which is subject to the capitalist exploitation of labour. In France the proportion of women in the working class remained more or less constant between 1946 and 1968, while it grew by around 40 per cent in the so-called 'tertiary' sector. Given the prodigious imprecision of this 'tertiary' sector, the proportion has to be more accurately established on the basis of the 'socio-professional categories', which show that in 1954, 486 women workers out of every 1000 fell into the category of non-productive employees, as against 563 in 1962. Making the necessary corrections, and considering economically active persons as a whole (men and women together), this phenomenon appears rather more modest, but the tendency is still very clear.[3]

But the tendency is still not a uniform one, nor in the process of becoming so. This movement of women into the labour market has occurred above all (and this is true to a greater or lesser extent for all the capitalist countries) in those branches of non-productive labour that are the least skilled (the retail trade, office work, services, whereas the proportion of women in managerial positions has remained more or less stable), that are located in relatively subaltern places in the hierarchy of authority (this applies to a greater or lesser extent in all branches of non-productive wage-labour), and finally that are the lowest paid. Although it is not directly the movement of women into these jobs that is the root cause of the social disqualification of mental labour (as the theorists of 'prestige' and 'social status' would have it), of a bureaucratization of this labour and of the current decline in wage differences between these workers and the working class, it still remains true that: (a) it is women who are the chief victims of this, and this is not by chance; (b) the massive penetration of women into these sectors has itself considerably sharpened these tendencies, by virtue of the specific exploitation, domination and oppression that characterize female labour as such, and which are simply the expression of a much broader sexual division of labour.

Not only are women the main victims of the reproduction of the social division of labour within non-productive wage-labour, but this is supplemented in their case by various forms of sexual oppression in their actual work itself, in the relations of exploitation and politico-ideological domination. This element plays a specific role of

3. cf. the INSEE Censuses of 1954, 1962 and 1968. See also R. Leparce, 'Capitalisme et patriarcat', in *Critiques de l'Économie Politique*, nos. 11–12, pp. 159–64.

its own, analogous to the phenomenon of racism which the immigrant workers have to suffer.

The question of this massive 'feminization' of non-productive wage-labour, however, can only be dealt with in the full complexity of its effects if it is related to the structure of the family apparatus, and in particular to the class and class fraction of the husbands of those women who belong to this or that fraction of the new petty bourgeoisie. It is well-known how detrimental a factor it can be for the struggles of women in these sectors that their wages may be thought of in the family apparatus as simply providing a little extra for the housekeeping.

In any case, this element, in the context of the rise of women's struggles, is sure to have considerable repercussions in the near future. Such examples as the recent strikes in France at Nouvelles Galeries in Thionville, and at the Giro and Social Security offices, are striking signs of this.

2. The relation that has now been established between the wages of productive workers (working-class wages) and the wages of non-productive workers: most writers have seen this as a tendency towards the reduction of the gap between 'average' working-class wages and 'average' wages in the tertiary sector, and as the loss of wage privileges for the whole of the tertiary sector in relation to the working class. It is relevant, however, that comparisons between so-called 'average earnings' do not mean very much.

There is certainly a general tendency towards the reduction of the gap between the wages of non-productive labour and those of productive labour in the extended reproduction of capitalism, something to which Marx already drew attention, in particular with respect to the circulation sector (though his remarks can be generalized):

> The commercial worker, in the strict sense of the term, belongs to the better-paid class of wage-workers – to those whose labour is classed as skilled and stands above average labour. Yet the wage tends to fall, even in relation to average labour, with the advance of the capitalist mode of production. This is due partly to the division of labour in the office . . . [also] because the necessary training, knowledge of commercial practices, languages, etc., is more and more rapidly, easily, universally and cheaply reproduced . . . Moreover, this increases supply, and hence competition. With few exceptions, the labour-power of these people is therefore devaluated with the progress of capitalist production.[4]

4. *Capital*, vol. III, pp. 294–5.

Other factors that intensify this tendency could be added; these are ones related to the present-day forms of expansion of monopoly capitalist exploitation, of the redistribution of surplus-value between the various capitalist fractions and the equalization of rates of profit.

But this general tendency, which is also modified by the political factors that enter into wage differentials, does not operate in anything like the same manner for all sections of the new petty bour-itself, thus indicating a relative reduction in the wage gap between 'average' working-class earnings and 'average' petty-bourgeois earnings was already present, with various ups and downs, after the First World War and during the inter-war period, and, after a period of regression in France between 1945 and 1950,[5] is it again asserting itself today. It operates in particular by effecting a major reduction of the gap between the agents who occupy certain dis-qualified and subaltern petty-bourgeois places (clerks, lower-level workers in commerce, services and offices, and minor civil servants) and certain strata of the working class.

This is the principal way in which this tendency operates, though the concrete paths it takes still depend on political factors that enter into wage differentials. It is the same even in those capitalist countries (Great Britain, Germany, etc.) where this tendency is also expressed in a small decline in differentials within the new petty bourgeoisie itself, thus indicating a relative reduction in the wage gap between this class as a whole and the working class[6] (which of course does not affect the forms of payment of the managers and controlling agents of capital). This is not the case in France, however, and this clearly shows the involvement of political factors. Here, in fact, the statistics for earned incomes show that between 1952 and 1968 it was the various intermediate managerial staff, within the new petty bour-geoisie, who enjoyed a relative increase, far more than other petty-bourgeois groupings (simple 'employees') or the working class.[7] This means that the working class in France is less well paid than in other European countries (particularly Germany and Great Britain), although the higher levels of the new petty bourgeoisie (various

5. H. Mercillon, *La Rémunération des employés*, 1954. See also the series of articles devoted to white-collar workers in no. 228 of *Économie et Politique*, July 1973.

6. D. Lockwood, op. cit., pp. 43 ff.; R. Hamilton, 'Einkommen und Klassenstruktur in BRD', in *Der 'neue' Arbeiter*, ed. K. Hörning, 1971.

7. INSEE, 'Données statistiques sur l'évolution des rémunérations salairiales de 1938 a 1964', *Études et Conjonctures*, August 1965; 'Salaires, prestations sociales et pouvoir d'achat depuis 1968', Collections de l'INSEE, M 9, April 1971; 'Les salaires dans l'industrie le commerce et les services en 1969', in Collections de l'INSEE, M 20, January 1973.

intermediate staff, as well as the engineers and technicians) are better paid.[8] In other words, the gap between working-class wages and the earnings of these strata has in fact increased in France during these years. This can be confirmed empirically from the very typical broadening of the overall spread of working-class and petty bourgeois earnings in France. This is due to this particular relative increase of the salaries of 'intermediate': the average money earnings of manual workers increased by 52 per cent between 1962 and 1968, while those of routine non-manual employees increased by only 49·6 per cent.

This must be seen as essentially a feature of the French bourgeoisie's general policy, which has in fact marked its whole history. This class has always sought a very specific 'support' from the petty bourgeoisie in the face of the militancy and class struggle of the workers. This was already the strategy of the French bourgeoisie towards the traditional petty bourgeoisie after the revolution of 1789, in the form of 'Jacobin radicalism';[9] it was long expressed in a considerably slower rate of elimination of this petty bourgeoisie than in the other countries mentioned. The same policy was then extended towards the new petty bourgeoisie; its original effect was on the rate of decline of the earnings differentials between the *subaltern* levels of the new petty bourgeoisie and the working class, a rate much slower than in other capitalist countries. In the last few years, however, this policy has taken on a different form, being now concentrated on the higher levels of this new petty bourgeoisie ('intermediate staff'). Given the need for monopoly capital to intensify the exploitation of the petty bourgeoisie, this policy assumes particularly selective forms, but in this very way it sharpens the cleavages within the new petty bourgeoisie, by increasing the spread of differentials. Investigations tend to show, on the other hand, that during the same period of time wage differentials within the working class declined, particularly after the increase in the SMIG [guaranteed minimum wage] at the time of the Grenelle agreement in 1968.

In any case, the significance of the decline in the income gap between certain fractions of the petty bourgeoisie and the working class is evident. A white-collar worker in commerce, in office work, in the service sector or the lower levels of the civil service, particularly a woman worker, often has a basic salary lower than that of many skilled manual workers, especially at the beginning of his or her working life (although the average working week of these employees is still 2·4 hours less than that of manual workers). The

8. *Le Monde*, Dossiers et documents: 'L'inégalité des revenus en France', May 1973.

9. *Political Power and Social Classes*, pp. 178–80.

most important aspect of this process is not simply the *relative pauperization* (ratio of wages to profits) that these fractions experience (for the working class is similarly affected by this), but rather what I shall refer to as the process of *relational pauperization* (in relation to the working class).

A further point, which links up with the 'feminization' of non-productive wage-labour, is that we can see the selective strategy of the bourgeoisie clearly at work even within those fractions of the new petty bourgeoisie that are being objectively polarized in a proletarian direction; particular attention must be paid to the effects of this. Although it is true that a woman employee in commerce, or office work, receives a salary lower than the earnings of many male manual workers (especially to start with), it is no less true that her earnings are generally considerably higher than those of a woman manual worker. While the gap between average earnings of male manual workers and male salaried employees is around 8 to 10 per cent, it is some 20 per cent in the case of female workers. In other words, this relational pauperization affects non-productive women employees far more than women manual workers, which of course has considerable effects on the former. To put it loosely, it may well be the case that, as far as the class positions of a woman white-collar worker are concerned, the fact of earning less than a male manual worker is less important than the fact of earning more than a woman manual worker.

3. The reproduction of the mental/manual worker division actually within mental labour: this point, which I already discussed above, produces certain cleavages within the ranks of the new petty bourgeoisie: the fragmentation of knowledge and standardization of tasks in certain of its sectors and levels, the divisions within the bureaucratized petty bourgeoisie between levels of decision and levels of execution, the process of qualification and disqualification within mental labour that is bound up with the 'rationalization' of their work, etc.

In point of fact, these cleavages are only in part due to the direct introduction of machinery in the labour of these employees, hence to a mechanization of their work (i.e. fragmentation). As early as the 1930s it was maintained that this mechanization was effecting a 'technical proletarianization' of the work of these people. But this mechanization assumes specific forms in the case of mental labour, while on the other hand it is far from displaying the wholesale expansion that is often attributed to it. Machines here generally serve auxiliary functions (calculators, typewriters, comptometers, etc.). It is only in rare cases that such a mechanization leads to the worker becoming the 'bodily appendage of the machine', as Marx put it (certain cases of the use of computers, for instance).

According to Lockwood,[10] office mechanization that leads to an assembly line form of work in the proper sense (tied to the 'autonomous' rhythms of the machine) only affected 3·5 per cent of the total number of white-collar workers in Britain in 1952. This phenomenon has certainly become more widespread in the intervening period, but it is apparent that it could in no way be compared with manual work; here, 'technical progress' and the constant 'revolutionization' of the means of production are closely bound up with the production and extraction of surplus-value (relative surplus-value). Even in the case of manual labour, however, technical progress comes up against social obstacles, i.e. capitalist relations, for it is always subjected to the social conditions of production. There is thus no reason to think that, in the present-day conditions of non-productive wage-labour (the social division of mental and manual labour, the reduction of the salaries of these employees facilitating their exploitation, the growing abundance of this form of man-power), this tendency will ever take on significant proportions. The principal aspect here too is the rate of exploitation and the rate of profit; productivity of labour does not have the same meaning here as in the production of surplus-value.

The phenomenon must still not be underestimated, for where it actually occurs it intensifies the fragmentation of tasks and of knowledge, especially in an indirect way, as well as the disqualification of mental labour.

Even in other cases, however, the same phenomenon occurs, though in different forms, particularly in the context of bureaucratization. Contrary to what is maintained by certain arguments which see bureaucratization and mechanization as opposites, and only admit the disqualification of mental labour in the latter case, it is important to note that this bureaucratization, which is here simply the effect of the 'separation' of mental and manual labour, reproduces this division within itself; this is where the current 'rationalization' of mental labour comes in, tending to increase its productivity.

This disqualification of manual labour is finally expressed, on a massive scale, in the employment of agents in positions that are un-qualified in relation to their training, making allowances for the points made above on the qualification of mental labour through the educational apparatus. This form is particularly important for us to note; it chiefly affects young people in certain groupings of the

10. *The Blackcoated Worker*, op. cit., pp. 87 ff.

new petty bourgeoisie (shop and office workers, and the subaltern levels of the new petty bourgeoisie in general), by way of agents who find themselves there having hoped to find a 'superior' employment as a result of their educational 'qualification'. To give some significant statistics on this point: the proportion of routine non-manual employees under 25 in France who held a baccalauréat certificate rose from 10·5 per cent in 1962 to 21·6 per cent in 1968 (and the proportion of manual workers from 3·5 per cent to 6·2 per cent), while the proportion of these employees who held a certificate higher than the baccalauréat rose from 4·8 to 8·1 per cent (for manual workers, from 2·5 to 4 per cent). Other figures show clearly that even a young university graduate had a far smaller chance of obtaining even an intermediate managerial position than in 1962.[11] This devaluation of educational certificates, bound up in fact with the general disqualification of mental labour, also contributes to restricting the possibilities of internal promotion open to these agents.

4. An additional point concerns the current situation of unemployment among mental workers. We still do not have enough information on this subject, but in the forms it takes, and its massive scale, this phenomenon is something relatively new, something which has appeared in the last few years.in the majority of capitalist countries. The phenomenon of unemployment among non-productive salaried employees actually began to assume significant proportions in the crisis of the 1930s and has since become part of the conditions of life that these agents face on the labour market.[12] In the past, however, this never assumed anything like the importance of the industrial reserve army among the working class.

It now seems, however, as if the last few years have seen the development, in the majority of capitalist countries, of an actual mental labour reserve army, over and above any cyclical phenomena. This should not in fact be surprising, given the massive investment of monopoly capital in the sector of non-productive labour. According to official figures, unemployment in France in 1971 was 2·1 per cent among manual workers, 2 per cent among routine non-manual, and 1·1 per cent among intermediate staff. Between 1971 and 1972, the figures were stable for manual workers, but rose to 2·3 per cent for routine non-manual and 1·4 per cent for managerial staff.[13]

11. C. Delcourt, 'Les jeunes dans la vie active', in *Économie et Statistique*, INSEE, no. 18, December 1970, pp. 10 ff.

12. R. Ledrut, *La Sociologie du chômage*, 1966.

13. Collections de l'INSEE, 'Demographie et Emploi', no. 19, pp. 76 and 87. Of course, given the tremendous official manipulation of unemployment figures, these can only be taken as simple indices of a tendency.

The recent increase in unemployment has meant that its new forms chiefly affect young people whose education has destined them for mental labour. We should certainly not lose sight of the fact that the phenomenon of youth unemployment (persons under 25, plus any others who have only recently become economically active), which is more significant than adult unemployment, also affects manual workers. However, even the crude unemployment figures already show significant differences. An INSEE investigation in 1972 brought to light the fact that the proportion of CAPs among the young unemployed was 17·6 per cent, the proportion of baccalauréats 3 per cent, and the proportion of university degrees 0·6 per cent. In 1968, the proportion of these categories among the economically active population as a whole (including unemployed) was: CAPs 19 per cent, baccalauréats 3·3 per cent and university degrees 0·8 per cent.[14] The difference in date between the data compared here must of course be taken into consideration, but it still emerges that there is a tendency for baccalauréats and university degrees to be over-represented among the young unemployed in comparison to holders of a mere CAP. This is a remarkable change in relation to even the recent past.

What is still more important are the several forms of concealed unemployment prevalent among the young: various forms of under-employment, illegal work, season and temporary work, etc. There is no need either to stress the now considerable phenomenon of young people escaping the statistical grid altogether; the number of these in France today is estimated at between three and five hundred thousand, living off various types of self-employment or petty services. Various ideologists happily present as 'drop-outs' those who have rejected 'alienated labour' out of conviction.

5. Finally, there are major transformations in the conditions of life of these employees, even outside of their work relations.[15] Today capital is directly invading all sectors 'outside' the economic relations of labour in the strict sense, both those involved in the reproduction of labour-power (town planning, housing, transport, etc.), or the sphere outside of work altogether (leisure, 'free time', etc.). What is more, given the present subordination of the sphere of capital circulation to finance capital in the process of capital concentration, it is finance capital that imposes the modes of collective consumption of the commodities produced. We have to allow here for the fact that, on the one hand, the direct subjection of these relations to capital is

14. *Économie et Statistiques*, no. 18, op. cit.

15. Among others, F. Godard, 'De la notion de besoin au concept de pratique de classe', in *La Pensée*, no. 166, December 1972; M. Castells, *Luttes urbaines*, 1973.

effected under the domination of ideologico-political relations, through which capital reproduces the divisions within the exploited and dominated classes (in town-planning, housing, leisure, etc., the political aim of capital is to separate this new petty bourgeoisie from the working class), while, on the other hand: (a) certain fractions of the new petty bourgeoisie are rapidly and massively losing their privileged position over the working class in the wage scale; (b) the new petty bourgeoisie is particularly sensitive to these conditions, in so far as it even lives its work relations outside of actual production: hence the importance that consumption models have for the new petty bourgeoisie; (c) women are particularly involved here, in so far as their exploitation at work is supplemented by the accumulation of 'household tasks' in the family apparatus.

There is thus every reason to believe, as more precise analysis tends to show, that the articulation of these elements is currently reinforcing the cleavages that there are within the new petty bourgeoisie in sectors outside their actual work relations, and that the objective polarization of certain of its fractions towards the working class; these fractions see their 'quality of life' constantly declining, at least in a relative or 'relational' sense. This is why class struggles in these sectors, and over issues that affect them (community struggles for example, the new petty bourgeoisie being like the working class massively concentrated in urban agglomerations), often take the form of class alliances between these fractions and the working class, something that is particularly clear-cut at the present time.

However important this certainly is, I shall not go into it here. Although it is clear that these elements exist together with the relations of production and the labour process as part of a unity, a unity that consists not just in the reproduction of labour power but in the process of the reproduction of social relations as a whole (class relations), it is still true that the determining role falls to the relations of production.[16]

16. I cannot start to examine here the elements of the conjuncture currently affecting the new petty bourgeoisie. However, the above analysis, which locates its class determination and the current transformations in the social division of labour as a whole, makes it possible to grasp the importance of the various elements of the conjuncture in this respect. A key element here, given the specific place of the new petty bourgeoisie in politico-ideological relations and the particular features of the petty-bourgeois sub-ensemble, consists in the ideological crisis that currently affects the bourgeoisie, since this crisis is directly reflected in the new petty bourgeoisie (which has specific effects on its class positions). However, this ideological crisis does not affect the whole of the new petty bourgeoisie in a uniform way: its effects follow the internal cleavages of its class determination.

2. THE CLASS FRACTIONS OF THE NEW PETTY BOURGEOISIE

By thus taking into account the cleavages induced within the new petty bourgeoisie as a result of its actual class determination, together with the current transformations (the two most often coinciding), it is possible to isolate the fractions of the new petty bourgeoisie.

Since the new petty bourgeoisie is polarized between the bourgeoisie and the working class in the class struggle, its division into fractions must be seen in relation to this polarization. I shall be concerned in this section therefore to isolate those fractions of the new petty bourgeoisie which are clearly polarized in the direction of the working class, both in their class determinations and in the current transformations affecting them, leaving the question of the other fractions to the discussion in the preceding sections. This does not mean that these other fractions form part of the bourgeoisie, any more than the fractions to be considered here have become part of the working class; these other fractions should not be seen as abandoned for all time to outer darkness.

The fractions which we shall be dealing with here are thus those that display the most favourable objective conditions for a quite specific alliance with the working class and under its leadership, an alliance which is of key importance at the present time. Their class determinations place them in the petty-bourgeois camp, but in such a way that they are clearly objectively polarized in the direction of the working class. This section of the petty bourgeoisie, however, is not thereby unified. It is itself divided into fractions, though the heterogeneity of the living and working conditions of the petty-bourgeois agents polarizes them in the direction of the working class, often by specific demands and particular aspects of their existence. This is the reason why we must speak of *fractions* (in the plural) of the new petty bourgeoisie with a proletarian polarization, fractions which are marked out by the sum total of their class determinations (and not simply, as is often done, of *the section* of the new petty bourgeoisie with a proletarian polarization), even if these fractions as a whole are divided from other petty-bourgeois fractions by a major cleavage, in so far as they are situated in the camp polarized towards the proletariat. This situation has its effects at the level of class positions in the conjuncture; this 'section' of the new petty bourgeoisie cannot attain a political unity of its own in the conjuncture, but can only be unified by uniting itself with the working class under the hegemony and leadership of the latter.

This is precisely the sense in which we should understand these fractions and cleavages in that camp of the new petty bourgeoisie that is polarized towards the proletariat; we should understand them in the sense of specific paths of polarization. There is also no question here of undertaking, as is sometimes done, a typological classification in which differences are examined by some 'measure' of the positions of these fractions cannot be reduced to these inequalities, among these fractions, but the issue here is decided directly by the class struggle in determinate conjunctures, and the actual class positions of these fractions can not be reduced to these inequalities, since the fractions concerned are already located in the camp with an objective proletarian polarization. In short, if it is true that a lower-level teacher and a saleswoman in a chain store, while they belong to the same camp, nevertheless belong to different fractions of it (which is important), and are polarized in the direction of the working class by specific paths, this does not mean that there is a greater chance of one rather than the other taking up proletarian positions as a result of inequalities in their objective polarization.

This leads me to recall that neither the main cleavage within the new petty bourgeoisie between the fractions polarized towards the proletariat and the others, nor the boundaries of the former fractions (the latter especially), purely and simply coincide with the economic relations in which their agents are located.[17] An intermediate manager in the circulation sphere, whose payment forms part of the *faux frais* of capital, is separated from the saleswoman in the chain store by the main cleavage, although she also belongs to the circulation sphere, she is dependent on the same (commercial) capital and she is paid out of the same *faux frais*. However this manager is not divided by the same cleavage from, say, an administrator in the service sector, who is paid out of revenue. Conversely, if the chain store saleswoman does not belong to the same fraction as the lower-level teacher, this is not because she is paid out of the *faux frais* and he is paid out of revenue in the form of taxation. A single fraction of the new petty bourgeoisie with an objective proletarian polarization can contain employees belonging to commerce (process of circulation), banking (process of realization), and the service sector.

In fact, it is the overall coordinates of the social division of labour that mark out these fractions. They certainly have in common at the economic level, as against the other fractions of the petty bourgeoisie, the fact that they undergo a particularly intense exploitation. But it would plainly be wrong:

(a) to try to determine their boundaries by the economic forms of exploitation alone (circulation of capital, services, state functions,

17. Contrary to the position maintained, for example, by P. Salama, in *Critiques de l'économic politique*, op. cit.

etc.). From this standpoint there is only one key difference, that which divides this exploitation from the exploitation experienced by the working class in the extraction of surplus-value, which brings us back to our discussion of productive and non-productive labour;

(b) to stick strictly to the degree of exploitation that they experience. A lower-level civil servant, a saleswoman and a secretary may be exploited to the same degree, without this meaning that there are no cleavages between them.

Finally, these petty-bourgeois fractions must be considered as defined by certain tendencies marked out by their class determination and the current transformations, and not by empirical and rigid boundaries according to some 'statistical' classification. It should particularly be noted here that the INSEE statistics with their various 'socio-professional categories', which are already deceptive enough as far as class boundaries are concerned, are even more inadequate in the cases that we are dealing with now; they often include in the 'petty-bourgeois' categories groupings of agents who actually belong to the most diverse fractions.

I

The first fraction of non-productive workers with an objectively proletarian polarization includes (i) the great majority of lower-level workers in the commercial sector (shop assistants, etc.), who are particularly subject to the current concentration in this commercial sector (increase in size of stores); (ii) employees who are affected by the introduction of machinery actually within the non-productive sector, and acutely so by the mechanization of labour (whether they belong to the sphere of circulation and realization of capital, to the service sector, or to the state apparatus); (iii) those employed in certain parts of the service sector – workers in restaurants, cafés, theatres, cinemas, as well as lower-level health workers (e.g. hospital orderlies), etc. In point of fact:

(a) In the social division of mental and manual labour, these are the non-productive workers who are nearest the barrier that separates the new petty bourgeoisie from the working class, in their relation to knowledge and to the symbolic and ideological ritual with which it is surrounded. As far as those employees who are directly subjected to the introduction of machinery in non-productive labour are concerned, they are particularly affected by the reproduction of the mental/manual labour division within the ranks of mental labour itself (fragmentation of tasks). The fact that these agents are all clearly polarized towards manual labour is directly reflected in the education process; although this differs from the kind of education that the working class undergo, the education of the mass of these agents is also relatively different from the other petty-bourgeois fractions. In the case of women this is particularly obvious. Out of women workers in commerce born in or after 1918, 21 per cent in 1964 did not even hold the CEP, as against only 8 per cent of office workers; around 20 per cent of commercial workers held a certificate higher than the CEP, as against more that 55 per cent of office staff, the CEPs of the latter being also distributed much more towards general education. For men, the situation is not quite so pronounced: around 39 per cent of commercial workers held a certificate higher than the CEP, as against 55 per cent of office staffs.[18] This is because managerial positions in the commercial sector are practically monopolized by men.

(b) In relation to the other petty-bourgeois fractions, these agents are the least affected by the tendency towards the bureaucratization of non-productive labour; this is because they are nearest the barrier of manual labour. In the case of the agents directly subjected to the introduction of machinery, the low level of bureaucratization that affects them is due to the reproduction of the mental/manual labour division within the camp of mental labour. It could loosely be said that even when these agents belong to sectors that are strongly bureaucratized, they are located rather on the margin of the bureaucratic hierarchy and its various levels, both in the public and private sectors; this is something that can only be understood by breaking with the institutionalist conception of bureaucratization and bureaucracy as a model of organization. Thus while a big store or hospital displays a real tendency towards bureaucratization, the saleswomen and nurses are more or less separate from the actual bureaucratic hierarchy which other agents belong to, although they are still affected by the effects of this bureaucratization and by the reproduction of the mental/manual labour division. The characteristic isolation of the salespeople in a big store has often been remarked on, this being affected, among other things, by the fantastic reproduction of isolating distinctions between the departments on the basis of the 'quality' of the products which they sell (those selling 'luxury' goods playing the part of 'mental workers'), the differentiation between different grades of assistants, etc. It is in this grouping, therefore, that the organization of the labour process assumes that most openly repressive forms.

(c) The factor of 'career' and 'promotion' takes on a rather different form here than it does for the other petty-bourgeois groupings, even though it still remains distinct from the case of the working

18. The INSEE study cited above, in *Économie et Statistique*, no. 9. February 1970, p. 55.

class. Genuine career opportunities are restricted, as a result not only of the organization of work and its fragmentation, but also of the instability of employment characteristic of this sector. The range of earnings and hierarchy is here fairly compressed, particularly in the case of commercial workers, i.e. it is marginal to the bureaucratic hierarchy.[19] The proportion of agents who move upwards, even within their own class (e.g. become 'middle managers') is much more restricted in the case of commercial workers than for those who are classed in the statistics as 'office workers', or for civil servants.

This can be seen from certain statistical findings on wage levels: (a) dividing these employees according to economic activity and net annual salary (in 1968), those working in various forms of commerce and in health display the smallest range of earnings, and the most pronounced ceiling at a certain salary level; (b) if the same employees are examined by age group, it is found that the salary ceiling is generally reached at around 45–50 years, whereas other fractions of the new petty bourgeoisie only reach their ceiling rather later (55–60 years). It also emerges that a considerably smaller proportion of commercial workers become 'middle managers' (28·7 per cent of those changing their status become managers, while 28 per cent become manual wokers) than is the case for 'office workers' (47·7 per cent of those changing their status become managers, 25 per cent manual workers). Finally, while average net earnings are on the whole lower for commercial workers than for office workers (12,344 francs as against 13,350), earnings classified by sex display the opposite picture: salaries of male commercial workers are higher than those of male office workers (16,071 francs as against 15,028). This difference is attributable to differences in female earnings, which are quite considerable: 9,283 francs for commercial workers as against 12,336 francs for office workers. This confirms the fact that managerial positions in commerce are practically a male monopoly.[20]

To come back to the question of the reproduction of agents in this fraction, we are faced here with a phenomenon somewhat analogous to that of the children of these agents in inter-generational movement. It should also be noted that the educational apparatus and education in general play a less important role here, both on the labour market and in the circulation of these agents within their class.

This is shown in the case of movement across class barriers, both during the working life of these agents and between generations.

19. This information was provided by the investigations of the CFDT Services division, in *Inform' action*. See also J. Chatain, 'L'évolution de l'appareil commercial', in *Économie et Politique*, July 1973.

20. In Collections de l'INSEE, op. cit., pp. 52, 54, 56 ff.

Movement upwards into the bourgeoisie is much more restricted here than in the case of other petty-bourgeois groupings with an objectively proletarian polarization.

There are in fact remarkable forms of distributive affinity between these agents and the working class in this respect, in a double sense:

(1) The proportion of these agents and their children who fall from the petty bourgeoisie into the working class is greater than for the other petty-bourgeois fractions.

(2) It is precisely towards this particular fraction that those female workers who move up into the new petty bourgeoisie from the working class in the course of their working life seem to direct themselves. In fact, it is particularly among women that this phenomenon is to be found: male workers who leave the working class go chiefly into the 'independent' sector, while female workers move above all into this fraction of the petty bourgeoisie (commerce, and also various services). Moreover, it is here that we find the majority of those wives of manual workers who themselves occupy places in the new petty bourgeoisie.

We should of course not lose sight here, either of the rigidity that marks the working class as a whole, or of the fact that the great majority of economically active married women belong to the same class as their husbands (around 80 per cent). In the case we are dealing with here, around 40 per cent of married women under 55 who were working in commerce in 1968 were married to a manual worker. In other words, it is chiefly female labour that forms this characteristic penumbra around the working class. This factor is already beginning to have its effects on the forms of class struggle of this grouping, and these effects can only intensify in the future.

(3) To these factors of polarized class determination should be added the reduction of differentials and the absolute decline in salaries in relation to the working class. It is often in this fraction that we find the lowest earnings among those groupings of the petty bourgeoisie with an objective proletarian polarization. But this is still not always the case; there is also a tendency towards a levelling down of the earnings of other similar fractions of the petty bourgeoisie, in particular the lower grades of civil servants, and this brings them into line with this fraction. What is more important in commerce are the forms linking earnings to output by way of various bonus schemes, even though the old system of a commission on sales is currently being replaced by bonuses directly included in salary. Even here, however, the situation is still different from that of the working class, of whom only a small section even today have salaried status. On the other hand, this commercial sector is probably the only place in the

developed capitalist formations where the actual length of labour-time is tending to increase (night work, Sunday opening, etc., all part of 'putting ourselves at the customer's disposal').

As far as the 'feminization' of this fraction is concerned, it is particularly strong among those agents subjected to the introduction of mechanization. The same figures that we used earlier show that, while the proportion of the new petty bourgeoisie as a whole that was directly subjected to this mechanization was around 3·5 per cent in Great Britain in 1952, it was already as high as 9·5 per cent for women in the same category.

It is also possible, in the way that we have done before, to isolate particular *strata* within this fraction. A distinction that is important here is that between the highly concentrated sectors (big stores) on the one hand, and those with a low level of concentration on the other. (The latter include workers in small shops, whose proportion of the total is still significant: around 40 per cent of commercial workers are in firms with under 5 employees.) These latter, even though they are subjected to an exploitation just as considerable as the rest, still display a tendency to identify with their bosses; they are also subjected to a personalized clientism specific to petty-bourgeois ideology in the form that characterized the old-style commercial workers. It is a well-known fact that the small shops are the sector in which struggle is least developed, and where trade unions are virtually absent.[21]

Sufficient attention has been paid elsewhere to this distinction, particularly in relation to the rise of struggle in the inter-war period in the big stores; this struggle culminated, in France, in the active participation of these agents in the great strikes of 1936.[22] But there is a further distinction, which has not up to now received enough attention, and which is still more important that the former, though it has recently been analysed by militants in the Services division of the CFDT.[23] We are now beginning to witness a differentiation within the concentrated commercial sector, between on the one hand, the traditional department stores, and on the other hand, the super-markets and hypermarkets (the various self-service stores, Euro-markets, the Carrefour chain, etc.). This new type of concentration is now the predominant tendency. In 1972, some 62 hypermarkets were opened (30 in 1971), as well as 265 supermarkets (253 in 1971); the number of department stores is increasing less rapidly, and

21. P. Delon, *Les Employés*, Editions Sociales.

22. F. Parent, *Les Demoiselles de magasin*, 1970.

23. See among others the *Inform' action* pamphlets and M. Appert, *Situation professionelle des vendeuses de grands magasins et magasins populaires*, 1967.

certain of them are even starting to convert themselves into super-markets.

These supermarkets and hypermarkets alter the working con-ditions of their employees in a significant way. In the self-service system, the majority of these employees are engaged in simple tasks of handling, packing and storage (here the distribution of a given mass of goods in a minimum time replaces the 'art of selling'). As we saw in our analysis of productive labour, these tasks belong to-gether with transport to labour that is productive of surplus-value in the strict sense, and this from the most rigorous Marxist stand-point. Their agents thus tend increasingly to form part of the working class. This is the only sector of the new petty bourgeoisie in which we find an actual proletarianization, in the rigorous sense of this term, of labour itself. The disqualification of tasks that is present here on a massive scale is a sign that these agents are in-volved in manual labour. They thus escape the direct contact with the clientele that gives the saleswoman of the traditional department stores their characteristic 'hostess' role (the 'art' of correct dress and speech, 'taste', etc.), and leads many of them into imitating the bourgeoisie, as well as to commodity fetishism. Even those actual salespeople who still remain in the new type of store are increasingly mere demonstrators, who have no guarantee of their earnings or job security. Finally, one should notice with repetitive and fragmented work of the cashiers, who are the spearhead of struggle in this sector.[24]

It is still too soon to make any predictions as to the future evolu-tion of this tendency. But although the commercial sector was relatively quiet, on the whole, during the 1968 strikes, these sectors of it have been very lively over the subsequent four years. This new type of store has expanded greatly, and their workers are for the most part very young.

II

The second fraction of the new petty bourgeoisie with an objectively proletarian polarization is that of the subaltern agents of the public and private bureaucratized sectors; this is where the various types of 'office workers' among others, are located. It is immaterial here whether these agents belong to the sphere of capital circulation and

24. It should none the less be noted that even this type of concentration induces considerable changes in the structure of employment of wage-labour in commerce; the number of jobs for workers who are proletarianized (handlers, etc.) undergoes a sharp decline, while the administrative personnel increase.

commercial capital (sales, advertising, marketing, etc.), to banking and finance capital (banking, insurance, etc.), to the service sector (various sectors dealing with research or information), or to the state apparatuses (public services, lower grade civil servants, etc.).

This fraction is quite different from the previous one. We find here a sharper emphasis on the 'mental' aspect of its agents' labour, in opposition to manual labour, as well as certain significant effects of bureaucratization in the relations to which they are subjected. This fraction is also more affected by 'promotion' and 'career', and educational qualifications play here a more important role, as well as promotion according to length of service. These agents also display a relatively more significant tendency to circulate and change their place, during their own working lives and between generations, and both within their own class and upwards into the bourgeoisie. Moreover, 'profit-sharing' and bonuses designed to give employees an 'interest' in the firm play a special role here.

It thus appears that, here too, the principal cleavage relevant to objective proletarian polarization cuts through the sectors in which these agents are situated. Nothing would be more false here than to make a distinction within the new petty bourgeoisie, (such as Dahrendorf does, for example), between all those, from top to bottom, who belong to the public and private 'bureaucracies' (and who according to Dahrendorf form part of the bourgeoisie), and all those who do not (and according to the same writer form part of the working class).

In actual fact, the objective proletarian polarization of this sector follows specific paths. It takes the form of distinctions within the new petty bourgeoisie, covering all the dimensions of class determination, between the subaltern levels and the agents belonging to these, and those levels that occupy a higher place in the hierarchy. The 'bureaucracy' does not form a continuous and uniform pyramid, descending from the bourgeois at the top down to the petty-bourgeois levels (since there is a direct and clearly visible class cleavage in between); nor does it take an analogous 'organizational' form for the petty-bourgeois levels themselves; there are rather divided by the line of objective polarization.

The fraction that is objectively polarized in the direction of the working class is affected, though in a specific way which is different to the previous case, by the reproduction of the mental/manual labour division within mental labour itself, a tendency which is in fact co-substantial with bureaucratization, and which is at work today in a very marked fashion: the fragmentation and standardization of tasks of the great mass of subaltern agents; a particular form of obscuring knowledge (the secrecy of knowledge) that affects these;

repetitive tasks of execution which disqualify their work (the classic example being the typing pool), with its corollary of an intensification of the authoritarian and hierarchical relations that these agents experience in the context of their labour process. In banking and insurance, for example, to say nothing of the giro sector which has recently received so much attention, the handling of records by subaltern agents consists more and more in simply filling in stereotyped boxes with a cross, and here we see clearly the indirect effect of the use of computer 'techniques'; it is not without reason that these agents have been described as semi-skilled red tape workers.

At the same time as wage-labour has been extended to these agents and their numbers have swollen, the opportunities of 'promotion' and a 'career' have been reduced. It is only above a certain threshold that it is possible to climb higher, but this threshold (the various categories of intermediate staff) is more and more rarely attained by the broad mass of these agents. The threshold of the circulation system is constantly moving upwards. An index of this is provided by the fact that in recent years the various managerial positions in the private sector have increased much more slowly than the lower-level positions. Although office workers are still distinguished from commercial workers as far as their circulation within the hierarchy of their class and their movement up into the bourgeoisie are concerned, both in their own working life and between generations, there is now a much more important cleavage dividing them from the various categories of intermediate staff.

This is also where the current devaluation of educational certificates and attainments is most important, given the significance that these have on the labour market and for the promotion chances of these agents. It can be seen in the currently massive occupation of subaltern posts by agents whose educational qualifications led them to have different aspirations. In actual fact, this is the fraction into which young people holding devalued university degrees gravitate on a massive scale. It leads to the various forms of disguised unemployment that ravage this fraction: various forms of illegal work, vacation work, temporary and auxiliary work. These affect all those fractions with an objectively proletarian polarization, but are particularly pronounced in this case. This is also the fraction that in the last few years displayed the most pronounced and accelerated tendency towards 'feminization' (banking, insurance, administration); we thus have the phenomenon of a considerable intensification of the hierarchical cleavages between the massively feminized subaltern levels and their management.

It is also apparent that the general decline in the situation of these employees in the advanced capitalist countries since the Second

World War has not always taken the same form, particularly for those already economically active at the beginning of this period. A large section of these moved up to managerial positions as a result of the expansion of this sector and its feminization, while this decline has chiefly affected women, intensifying the internal cleavages. These cleavages today chiefly affect young people and women in this sector, as a result of a combination of different factors.

We must still, however, stress the following points:

1. The particular cleavages that divide these sectors of the new petty bourgeoisie, distinguishing this fraction with an objectively proletarian polarization, depend on the actual social division of labour in each branch, sector, etc. It is this division that determines the precise boundary of the cleavage; thus a civil servant who, considered in the abstract, is 'formally' similar to a middle-level manager in a bank, and not to a mere clerk, may still belong like the latter to the fraction with an objectively proletarian polarization, as a result of the social division of labour in the state apparatus in which he operates; whereas the middle-level bank manager does not. It is necessary to remember here:

(a) how arbitrary, in a particularly characteristic way well known to trade-unionists, are the 'classifications' and 'grades' of mental labour, which can cover completely different situations from one sector to another, whereas the various grades of manual worker coincide with the capitalist logic of production;

(b) how arbitrary also is the INSEE classification by 'profession' and 'socio-professional category', since the fractions which we are here concerned with do not coincide with the INSEE classifications, which can only be used as a simple index. We only need recall for example that a simple schoolteacher is considered by the INSEE as belonging to the ranks of 'intermediate managerial' staff, just the same as a middle-level manager; but while the former is at the bottom of the teaching hierarchy, the latter occupies a privileged place in relation to the ordinary employees in the labour process which he supervises. In other words, the various categories of INSEE's 'intermediate staff' are far from all exercising a genuinely managerial function, and they certainly do not all do so to the same extent.

2. It is still possible, following the same guidelines, to isolate different strata. This is particularly the case in research and the teaching profession. In the case of research, where the agents are not directly involved in the labour process, we are confronted today not just with the characteristic expansion of this sector but also with its transformation into wage-labour and its marked bureaucratization, along with new forms of intensified unemployment (vacation

work for example). This situation in the research laboratories has been fully studied in recent years.[25] Here the subaltern agents of a sector that formerly enjoyed real caste privileges are affected by the disqualification and fragmentation of mental labour, which here takes particular forms, including the virtual pillage of their mental labour by the higher levels (the various 'bosses'), and their intensified subjection to the immediate objectives of monopoly capitalist production. This is combined with the considerable reduction in salaries that the subaltern levels have experienced, and the current restriction of their promotion opportunities, and it is in this real reserve army of mental labour that the challenging of capitalist mental labour is probably taking the most advanced forms. It is plain that there are analogous phenomena within the teaching profession, on the side of its subaltern levels (supply and auxiliary teachers), as a result of the disqualification and fragmentation of mental labour which sharpens the cleavages between them and the higher levels (the established secondary school *professeurs*). On top of these points, great importance must be given to the role that the current ideological crisis of the bourgeoisie plays for these agents, given their particular social function.

3. Special mention must be given here to the lower grade civil servants. These of course belong to the social category of agents of the state apparatuses; they belong together with the intermediate levels to the petty bourgeoisie, while the 'top' agents of these apparatuses belong to the bourgeoisie. As members of this social category, the subaltern agents of the civil service are particularly subject to the specific internal ideology of these apparatuses.

Nevertheless, the decline in the situation of the subaltern agents of this category is clear enough. Their salaries have been levelled down to those of the other petty-bourgeois groupings with an objectively proletarian polarization, as a result of the general squeeze on public sector salaries in relation to the private sector, and they have also been affected by the decline in the gap between themselves and the working class. The average yearly household income, according to the socio-professional category of the 'head of the household', was in 1962, 15,637 for intermediate administrative staff in the civil service (category B), as against 23,210 francs for intermediate managerial staff in the private sector; it was 10,588 francs for clerical staff in the public sector (categories C and D) as against 11,755 for their equivalents in the private sector.[26] Since 1968,

25. J.-M. Lévy-Leblond and A. Jaubert (*Auto*) *critique de la science*, 1973, which is one of a whole series of similar analyses of this question.

26. Table given by C. Seibel and J.-P. Ruault in Darras, *Le Partage des bénéfices*, 1966, p. 91.

salaries in the public sector have increasingly lagged behind in
relation to those in the public sector.[27] At the same time, the
traditional civil service privileges, which contributed towards the
caste character of the celebrated *Beamtentum*, are in decline, in two
ways: on the one hand, certain advantages of job security, retirement
pensions, etc., have been more generally extended to other petty-
bourgeois strata and fractions; on the other hand, while they still
remain particularly characteristic of the civil service, they have
largely been undermined as far as the subaltern levels are concerned.
We find here, too, the extension of auxiliary and temporary work
(lack of established positions), together with the considerable growth
in agents related to the expansion of the state's interventionist functions in all sectors of public life (from the subaltern agents of the
traditional public services through to the community organizers,
social workers, youth service and cultural personnel, social security
agents, etc.).

III

The third and last fraction of the new petty bourgeoisie with an
objectively proletarian polarization is that of the technicians and
subaltern engineers directly involved in productive labour, the production of surplus-value, whom we investigated above. This fraction
still belongs to the petty bourgeoisie, but the cleavages that mark
out its boundaries also cut through the statistical category of engineers, technicians and managers. This is, however, a different case to
that of the other petty-bourgeois fractions with an objectively proletarian polarization. Although these agents are directly involved in
the production of surplus-value, and thus display certain objective
preconditions for grasping the essential mechanisms of capitalist
exploitation, they still remain marked by their place in the politico-
ideological relations of the enterprise as an apparatus. In recent
years the forms of struggle of this fraction have distinguished it from
the various groupings of intermediate engineers and managers, but
have also shown the ambiguous character of its relations with the
working class (since they retain their sense of being 'those in charge').
I do not want to stress points that are already well known; I would
simply like to note that one of the reasons, besides those already
mentioned (verbiage on 'automation' and the 'disappearance of the
semi-skilled worker'), which contributed towards this fraction being
assigned a quite disproportionate role in the struggles of the 1960s
(the 'new working class'), lay in the particular opportunities that they

had, according to various technicist theories, of impeding production. It has since become clear that the capitalist organization of labour certainly does offer new possibilities of struggle (bottle-neck strikes, etc.), but that these possibilities are precisely those open to the semi-skilled workers.

10

The Present Position of the Traditional Petty Bourgeoisie

We must finally return to the gradual decline of the traditional petty bourgeoisie. This decline is a function of the dissolution effects that monopoly capitalism, in its present phase, imposes on the simple commodity form.

In France, we have seen between 1954 and 1968 a characteristic rate of decline of this petty bourgeoisie.[1]

	1954	1962	1968
'Artisans' [i.e. independent craftsmen]	734,280	637,897	619,808
(*% of the economically active population*)		(*3·3*)	(*3·0*)
Small shop-keepers	1,268,740	1,133,965	1,026,216
(*% of the economically active population*)		(*5·9*)	(*5·0*)

This requires a few points to be made:

1. This process, although it is currently marked by a particular acceleration, is in fact not at all new. It was already quite apparent in all the advanced capitalist countries, including France, in the inter-war period, i.e. during the phases of the transition to monopoly capitalism and its consolidation. In France, however, it used to be slower and more drawn out, as a result of the characteristic support that the French bourgeoisie sought in this petty bourgeoisie *vis-à-vis* the working class.

2. The current decline, while it certainly has assumed major dimensions, is still far from attaining the same proportions and forms of actual elimination that it has done for the poor peasantry (the share of the agricultural sector in the economically active population has fallen from around 19 per cent in 1954 to around 11 per cent today).

1. INSEE Census data.

3. One section of these agents expelled from the petty bourgeoisie, if a fairly small one, has not been proletarianized, but has advanced from this petty bourgeoisie up into non-monopoly capital, within the context of the constant resurgence of this class under monopoly capitalism. If the number of 'artisan' enterprises with fewer than 5 employees fell by 127,000 between 1954 and 1966, the number of those with from 6 to 9 employees increased by 73,000 part of this increase coming from the advance of certain petty bourgeois to the status of small capitalists.

4. These points must be considered together with one other: the transfer of a certain number of manual workers, mostly young ones, to this petty bourgeoisie. Between 1959 and 1964, 40,000 skilled workers and 20,000 semi-skilled workers managed to set up on their own account as artisans (a third of these being the sons of artisans), and a rather smaller number as small shopkeepers and in the service sector (this being also the case, though to a much smaller extent, for poor peasants leaving the land). If this is taken into account, then it is clear that the rate of expulsion of these petty-bourgeois agents is greater than the rate at which the place of this petty bourgeoisie is being restricted, at least to judge from the census figures. The number of new agents entering the traditional petty bourgeoisie hides the fact that the same number of former petty-bourgeois agents are leaving. The great majority enter the working class, while a small proportion become white-collar workers. Thus the life expectancy of traditional petty-bourgeois enterprises is much shorter than in the past, and this also has significant effects by way of the characteristic insecurity that affects these agents in their conditions of life.

However, more is involved than just the restriction of the traditional petty bourgeoisie. What must also be taken into consideration are its living standards, which steadily decline, in particular as a result of the growing transfer of profit from this sector to monopoly capital; this is particularly clear in the case of the relationship between small-scale retailers and the big stores of concentrated commercial capital. This decline must still be considered in relation to the conditions of the working class, and also to those of the new petty-bourgeois fractions that we were dealing with previously (clerical workers in particular). Given the poverty of French statistics particularly on the question of incomes not deriving from wages and salaries, it is not possible to give any precise figures here. We should bear in mind, however, the very clear-cut tax policy of the French bourgeoisie, which gives considerable privileges to the traditional petty bourgeoisie, and particularly small-scale retail trade, in relation to the working class and the above-mentioned fractions of the new petty bourgeoisie, this making the latter pay the price of its desperate attempts to maintain the allegiance of the traditional petty bourgeoisie. This is effected, among other ways, through the manner in which the flood-gates of tax evasion have recently been opened to the traditional petty bourgeoisie, by the abolition of correctives that previously existed in favour of wage and salary incomes, and could not be dissimulated. Nor should we forget the political mechanisms of inflation and price increases by which the bourgeoisie, while taking back the gains in wages struggled for by the popular masses, concedes crumbs to the small retailers at the masses' expense.

Here too, we can establish a differentiation of this petty bourgeoisie into class fractions. The artisans in particular, by the very nature of their work and the specific permeability that it presents to working-class agents, have always displayed an objectively proletarian polarization, far more than have the small retailers. Artisan production was the cradle of revolutionary syndicalism, and its traditions of struggle are still very much alive.

As far as the small retailers are concerned, it is plain that the precariousness of their situation has recently given rise to very lively struggles (such as the Nicoud movement). Probably for the first time since 1920 in the history of such movements in France, these seem to have broken with their traditional support for the bourgeoisie, which was generally expressed, among other things, by way of such 'inter-class' modes of bourgeois recuperation as organizations of 'small and medium enterprises'. Given the current changes in the situation of this sector, it would be completely wrong to identify these movements with traditional Poujadism, and look on them with the *a priori* suspicion that was justified in the past, as movements bearing within them the germs of fascism, as the cloud bears within it the storm. On the other hand, however, these contemporary changes are far from being automatically transposed into class positions which bring this sector into line with the working class. It is obvious that the typical difficulties of this shop-keeping petty bourgeoisie are not entirely new; they were already serious at the time of the fascist movements that this fraction supported, and were even one of its causes. This was still the case with the Poujadist movement in France. The objective basis for this petty bourgeoisie remaining loyal to the bourgeoisie is certainly becoming over more slender, despite such somersaults as the recent 'Royer law'; but even in the case of classic fascism, the support that the petty bourgeoisie brought the bourgeoisie did not correspond to any real concessions on the part of the latter. The petty bourgeoisie was rather, together with the poor peasantry, the chief economic victim of fascism; in this case, ideological and political factors are decisive.

Given the current importance of this question, we should remind ourselves that we are not dealing with non-monopoly capital and other 'small employers', but with agents who do not exploit wage-labour, or at least only do so incidentally, and that it is wrong to identify this petty bourgeoisie with capital by considering it as a bourgeoisie that is 'smaller' than the others (though this differentiation is often obscured by official statistics). This would be to commit a similar error to the PCF, though in reverse; the PCF in practice considers non-monopoly capital as forming part of the petty bourgeoisie. In an amalgamation of the 'small and medium enterprises' type, and under the label 'small-scale capital', the PCF is led to extend the allies of the working class to include non-monopoly capital (i.e. certain sections of the bourgeoisie), assimilating this capital to the petty bourgeoisie; in the reverse form, one can be led to an *a priori* restriction of alliances, by reducing this petty bourgeoisie to capital and ignoring the opportunities it presents, depending on the conjuncture, for alliance with the working class. It is still true, however, that, in the case of this petty bourgeoisie (small retailers in particular), the chances of this certainly appear more restricted than in the case of those fractions of the new petty bourgeoisie with an objective proletarian polarization. This is not only for economic reasons (small-scale ownership), but also for politico-ideological reasons that are the product, among other things, of the historical tradition of class struggle in France.

I I

Conclusion:
Political Perspectives

We can now attempt to draw a few conclusions. To begin with the most important point: it is necessary to state that, in Europe the objective polarization which, together with the current transformations, marks the class determination of these petty-bourgeois fractions, has not till now been accompanied by a polarization of their class positions. In other words, no alliance has yet materialized between the major sections of these fractions and the working class, based on the specific objectives of a socialist revolution. That much is clear, as soon as one ceases to confuse the process of revolution with social-democratic governments of one kind or another.

This is a key question, particularly in France, and it bears first and foremost on the new petty bourgeoisie. It is all very well to repeat the old dogmatic chants about a 'special' worker-peasant alliance, but the facts are there, and we must get used to them. On the one hand, we are dealing with sectors that are certain to increase still further, and considerably so, in the developed capitalist countries, to play a very major role in the reproduction of social relations, and thus also in their revolutionization; on the other hand, the popular classes in the countryside, and the smallholding peasantry in particular, are inevitably condemned in all the European countries, if to a varying degree, to a rapid decline in their social weight and the number of their agents – France in the last few years has provided a very typical example of a tremendously accelerated rate of this decline.

I would even go so far as to say, at the risk of being accused of heresy, that what we are dealing with here is a historic possibility of socialist revolution, particularly in France. We should remember an important phenomenon that has marked the history of class struggles in France. The French peasantry, including the smallholders, has been one of the chief bulwarks of the bourgeois order, and one of the chief obstacles to socialist revolution in a country marked by the exceptional and exemplary militancy of the working class. The historic achievement of the French bourgeoisie (in its terms) has been to have known how to obtain the allegiance of the small peasant proprietors, by way of a series of significant compromises. Their support has hardly ever been lacking at key turning-points in the class struggle: from the two Bonapartes and the Paris Commune, to the post-First World War crisis, the Popular Front and Gaullism – the list is long enough. On the other hand, the historical failure of the leaderships of the working class has been not to have been able, or not to have known how, to forge and cement a worker-peasant alliance in France, with the probable exception of a section of the small peasants during the Second World War and the Resistance. It is not a question of attributing blame, but of establishing the facts. The French peasant smallholders have paid dearly, and they have not finished paying, for their support for the bourgeoisie against the working class, but the working class has also had to pay. There is certainly good reason to believe that the remaining sections of this small-holding peasantry will manage to become aware of their real class interests, although their attitude, even during the process of their rapid elimination over the last few years, shows with a few exceptions that the weight of the past, still weighs heavily upon them. But even though this alliance still remains very important, it could be said that in any case, the game is, as it were, already up. What we have to look towards is not so much the smallholding peasantry itself as a rural class, but rather the children of these peasants who, have been driven from the land, and are working in the factories and towns, as well as to the 'labouring peasants'.

Thus the massive development of wage-labour in the towns, including the new petty bourgeoisie, combined with the objective proletarian polarization of those fractions of the new petty bourgeoisie that comprise its great majority, is what provides the new historic possibility for the socialist revolution in France. It is not that the French bourgeoisie has not for a long time sought, to obtain support from the urban petty bourgeoisie as well, and even succeeded in doing so: the phenomenon of Jacobin radicalism, among other things, is evidence of this. But these attempts have been most success-ful, in so far as the traditional petty bourgeoisie is concerned, as part of the general support that the French bourgeoisie has managed to obtain from small-scale production and small-scale ownership. What support it has managed to obtain from the new petty bourgeoisie, which has always been relatively restricted, has taken a specific form – republican radicalism; and the new petty bourgeoisie in France has scarcely been affected by fascist mass movements, as has been the case in certain other advanced capitalist countries.

In the present phase of monopoly capitalism, the objective bases of this support are precisely being undermined, and radically so as far as the above-mentioned fractions of the new petty bourgeoisie are concerned. This is one of the basic reasons for the developing crisis of hegemony that is currently affecting the French bourgeoisie (and not just the French) and which may well have decisive effects.

It can lead to an alliance between the working class and these fractions of the new petty bourgeoisie in the protracted development of social revolution, a development that is uninterrupted and proceeds by stages. This of course does not mean that it will necessarily have this effect. We must rid ourselves once and for all of the illusions that have often affected the revolutionary movement, throughout its history, to the effect that an objective proletarian polarization of class determination must necessarily lead in time to a polarization of class positions.

We thus come to the second aspect of the question. This polarization of the new petty bourgeoisie towards proletarian class positions depends in a sense on the balance of forces between the bourgeoisie and the working class. One of the features of the petty bourgeoisie's characteristic 'oscillation' is that it is polarized towards both the bourgeoisie and the working class in the context of the strategic relationship of the two main forces in capitalist formations, and that its tendency to adopt proletarian class positions depends on the strength of the working class itself in relation to the bourgeoisie. The nub of the problem, however, is precisely that the balance of forces between the bourgeoisie and the working class can only be radically changed by the working class establishing alliances with other popular classes and class fractions, and thus welding the 'people' together against the bourgeoisie.

This leads us to a second assertion. This polarization of the new petty bourgeoisie towards proletarian class positions essentially depends on the strategy of the working class and its organizations of class struggle. The petty bourgeoisie for its part has no autonomous long-run class position, and as history has shown, it cannot in general have its own political organizations. Petty-bourgeois political parties in the strict sense of the term, i.e. parties actually and predominantly representing the specific long-run interests of the petty bourgeoisie, have rarely existed. What we find most often, rather, are bourgeois parties with a petty-bourgeois (and also working-class) clientele, that is parties that predominantly represent bourgeois interests, but manage to obtain the support of the petty bourgeoisie.

These points are very important. The polarization of the petty bourgeoisie towards proletarian class positions depends on the petty bourgeoisie being *represented* by the class-struggle organizations of the working class themselves; these organizations cannot just take hold of the petty bourgeoisie and drag it along like a ball and chain. This polarization thus depends essentially on the strategy of these organizations, unifying the people in the process of class struggle and the formation of alliances, under the hegemony of the working class; it depends, therefore, on the leadership of the working class in the popular alliance.

This is in fact a process that is uninterrupted and takes place by stages. The working class cannot simply hope that on the day of reckoning that it has brought about by its own efforts, the petty bourgeoisie will leap to its side, or at worst be neutralized. These petty-bourgeois fractions must not be seen as by nature and essence immutable, so that they could only be won to the cause of the working class by simple 'compromises' and 'concessions' towards them.

This means, firstly, that popular unity under the hegemony of the working class can only be based on the class difference between the classes and fractions that form part of the alliance; unification goes hand in hand with the gradual resolution of the 'contradictions among the people'. On the other hand, however, this unification and the establishment of working-class hegemony over these classes and fractions is a process of development, and they have themselves to be transformed in the struggles which will mark the stages of this process; they will thereby adopt the class positions of the working class. These positions themselves are only established in so far as this alliance and hegemony are established; not by way of concessions, in the strict sense, by the working class to its allies taken as they are, but rather by the establishment of objectives which can transform these allies in the course of the uninterrupted struggle and its stages, account being taken of their specific class determination and the specific polarization that affects them.

I am well aware of the indicative and summary character of these remarks. They are simply intended to locate the problem, and cannot claim to provide a solution to the question: 'what is to be done, and how?'. Besides the fact that it is not up to me to provide such a solution to a question which is at the centre of the current debate on revolutionary strategy, this was not in fact the aim of this essay. For this, it would have been necessary, among other things, to undertake a study of the history and experiences of the workers' and international revolutionary movement in this respect – of its organizations, of its theories, and the changes in them, on the questions of the revolutionary process, of organization (party and trade unions), and of alliances, and finally to understand in more detail the significance of social-democratic ideology and social-democratic tendencies, and their real basis. My aim in the present essay was to contribute towards a more precise knowledge of these allies, of their objective determinations and of the struggles that are going on today, while trying in the course of this to draw certain lessons and to warn against certain current theoretical and political misconceptions. The reason for this is that I am convinced that it is high time to undertake precise investigations of this kind, however difficult they may be. Without precise knowledge, the various strategies that may be elaborated run the risk of, at best, remaining a dead letter. At worst, they can lead to serious defeats.

Index